DISCARD

CQ Researcher on
Saving the Environment

CQ Researcher on
Saving the Environment

CQ PRESS

A Division of Congressional Quarterly Inc.
Washington, D.C.

CQ Press
A Division of Congressional Quarterly Inc.
1414 22nd Street, N.W.
Washington, D.C. 20037

(202) 822-1475; (800) 638-1710

www.cqpress.com

Printed and bound in the United States of America

04 03 02 01 00   5 4 3 2 1

♾ The paper used in this publication meets the minimum requirements of the American National Standard for Information Sciences—Permanence of Paper for Printed Library Materials, ANSI Z39.48-1992.

Library of Congress Cataloging-in-Publication Data

CQ researcher on saving the environment.
      p. cm.
Includes bibliographical references and index.
ISBN 1-56802-627-7
  1. Environmental protection—United States. 2. Environmental policy—United States. I. CQ researcher.
TD171.C69 2000
333.7'2'0973—dc21

00-045485

Photo credits: 1, 10, 65, AP; 5, AP/National Environmental Trust; 13, 99, 103, 109, 111, 112, PhotoDisc; 16, 63, 128, 135, Reuters; 21, 22, 23, 26, 28, 31, 32, 34, Environmental Justice Resource Center; 33, Environmental Proctection Agency; 39, 41, 46, The Nature Conservancy/Harold E. Malde; 44, Colorado Open Lands; 48, Gathering Waters; 52, Vermont Land Trust; 59, AFP Photo; 64, Chevron Corp; 68, Congressional Quarterly; 74, TreePeople/Becky Villasenor; 79, 82, 85, 92, U.S. Department of Agriculture; 117, 127, 156, 158, 161, Corbis; 155, UPI Photo; 162, National Park Service; 163, KRT Photo; 167, Newsmakers; 173, 186, World Wildlife Fund; 177, Greg Miller/The Nature Conservancy; 180, Lamb Studios/Conservation International.

Text credits: 2, Congressional Research Service; 6, International Energy Agency; 43, 48, Land Trust Alliance; 60, 64, Energy Information Administration; 61, Worldwatch Institute; 80, Consumers Union of the United States; 81, American Crop Protection Association; 102, 113, Environmental Defense Fund; 104, Environmental Protection Agency; 105, R.W. Beck; 113, Cato Institute; 118, 121, Texas Transportation Institute; 136, 140, Population Reference Sheet; 138, U.S. Census Bureau; 149, James P. Pinkerton; 149, John F. Rohe; 150, Natural Resources Defense Council; 156, 160, National Park Service; 169, Political Economy Research Center; 175, 178, World Resources Institute.

Appendix: The publisher wishes to thank Kathryn L. Schwartz for permission to use *A+ Research and Writing for High School and College Students,* copyright 1997 by Kathryn L. Schwartz. Published by the Internet Public Library: http://www.ipl.org.

Contents

Introduction   vii

1   Setting Environmental Priorities   1
    Should the United States do more to slow
        global warming?   3
    Should the federal government cede to
        the states some of its power to set
        environmental policy?   5
    Are Americans willing to pay for the next
        round of environmental-protection
        measures?   7
    Background   8
        Status Report   8
    Current Situation   14
        Global Warming   14
        Combating Sprawl   16
    Outlook   17
        Cost-Benefit Approach   17
    Notes   17
    Bibliography   19

2   Environmental Justice   21
    Do poor and minority populations suffer
        disproportionately from exposure to toxic
        materials?   23
    Does President Clinton's 1994 executive
        order provide sufficient guarantees of
        environmental justice?   24
    Does the focus on environmental justice
        distract attention from bigger health
        problems in poor and minority
        communities?   26
    Background   27
        Plight of the Poor   27
        Birth of a Movement   27
        Clinton's Policies   28
    Current Situation   28
        Recent Cases   28
        Pressure on EPA   32
        Aid for "Brownfields"   34
    Outlook   34
        Impact on Business   34
    Notes   37
    Bibliography   38

3   Saving Open Spaces   39
    Should the federal government spend more
        money to conserve open space?   41
    Should tax breaks for conservation easements
        be expanded?   42
    Are private acquisitions of land for
        conservation in the public interest?   45
    Background   45
        Patterns of Development   45
        Buying Public Land   46
    Current Situation   48
        Clinton's Initiatives   48
        Action in Congress   50
        State, Local Initiatives   52
        Land Trusts   54
    Outlook   55
        Action Stalled?   55
    Notes   55
    Bibliography   57

4   Energy and the Environment   59
    Has the threat of global warming restored
        nuclear power's potential as an alternative
        to fossil fuels?   61
    Should states be required to curb the
        emission of air pollutants that contribute
        to smog beyond their borders?   62
    Does electric-utility deregulation pose an
        additional threat to the environment?   65
    Background   66
        Clean Air Act   66
        Greenhouse Gases   68
    Current Situation   70
        Transportation Trends   70
        Alternative Fuels   72
    Outlook   72
        Nuclear Waste   72
        Candidates' Views   75
    Notes   75
    Bibliography   77

5   Regulating Pesticides   79
    Is food treated with chemical pesticides
        safe to eat?   82
    Is the government doing enough to regulate
        pesticide use?   83

Can farmers feed the country without using
    chemical pesticides?   85
  Background   86
    DDT Paves the Way   86
    Action by Congress   88
    Political Stalemate   90
  Current Situation   92
    Big Job for EPA   92
    Will Congress Act?   94
  Outlook   95
    Consumer Education   95
  Notes   96
  Bibliography   97

6   The Economics of Recycling   99
  Do the environmental benefits of recycling
    outweigh the costs?   102
  Do government recycling mandates impede
    the creation of efficient markets for
    recyclables?   103
  Is a "pay-as-you-throw" system a more
    rational approach to waste management
    than other programs?   105
  Background   106
    Birth of a Movement   106
    Federal Role   109
    Landfill "Crisis"   109
  Current Situation   110
    An Uncertain Market   110
    Communities Pitch In   112
  Outlook   114
    No End of Trash   114
  Notes   115
  Bibliography   116

7   Traffic Congestion   117
  Does building new roads ease congestion?   119
  Is congestion inevitable with urban sprawl?   120
  Can mass transit relieve traffic congestion?   121
  Background   122
    Rise of the Car Culture   122
    Mounting Congestion   124
    A Shift in Policy   124
  Current Situation   126
    Battle in Atlanta   126
    Life in the Fast Lane   130
  Outlook   132
    High-Tech Solutions   132
  Notes   133
  Bibliography   134

8   Population and the Environment   135
  Can agricultural productivity increase
    without causing irreversible damage to
    the environment?   138

Should the U.S. government support
    international efforts to curb population
    growth?   139
Should immigration be limited to protect
    the U.S. environment from overpopulation?   141
  Background   142
    A Radical Idea   142
    20th-Century Concerns   142
    Green Revolution   145
  Current Situation   147
    Population Explosion   147
    Environmental Impact   148
  Outlook   151
    Grain Crunch?   151
    Consumption to Blame?   151
  Notes   152
  Bibliography   153

9   Protecting the National Parks   155
  Does America need more national park land?   157
  Will additional federal funding solve the
    National Park Service's problems?   159
  Can the Park Service protect both natural
    resources and cultural monuments?   162
  Background   164
    A New Concept   164
    An Expanding Mandate   164
    Postwar Expansion   166
    Wilderness Act of 1964   164
  Current Situation   168
    Legislative Initiatives   168
  Outlook   170
    Resources First   170
  Notes   171
  Bibliography   172

10   Saving the Rain Forests   173
  Are the rain forests doomed?   175
  Can people profit from rain forests without
    destroying them?   176
  Are wealthy nations contributing to tropical
    deforestation?   178
  Background   182
    A Profusion of Life   182
    Disastrous Schemes   184
  Current Situation   185
    Government Initiatives   185
    Market-Based Solutions   186
  Outlook   189
    A Question of Money   189
  Notes   190
  Bibliography   191

Appendix: How to Write a Research Paper   193

Index   203

Introduction

Since the first Earth Day in 1970, the environment has occupied a central place in public policy. Government officials in Washington and across the country regularly debate issues such as regulating pesticides and conserving open space. But reaching a consensus is no easy matter. Although virtually everyone agrees that clean water and clean air are desirable, policy-makers and interest groups repeatedly engage in battles over how much to pay for environmental cleanup and how to assess the health effects of pollutants. Moreover, as difficult as it is to solve domestic environmental issues, tackling worldwide issues such as global climate change is even more daunting because of the competing agendas of scores of nations.

This book aims to add context to the environmental debate by reprinting 10 recent articles from *The CQ Researcher,* a weekly magazine that focuses on issues of public concern. Each *Researcher* examines a single topic, such as environmental justice or traffic congestion. It gives the reader a broad overview of the subject, including the historical background and a discussion of the current controversies and initiatives.

The *Researcher,* which began life in 1923 under the name of *Editorial Research Reports,* is distributed primarily to libraries and media offices. Each article is as long as 11,000 words, which could be the length of a term paper. Articles are based on intensive research, drawing on information from interest groups, universities and the government. Each piece generally uses at least 15 interviews.

An Overview of the Chapters

The 10 *CQ Researcher* articles in this book have been reproduced essentially as they appeared when first published. In some cases, important developments have taken place since the original publication. The capsule summaries at the end of this introduction mention a few of those developments.

Each chapter follows a similar format. It begins with an introductory overview of the topic, then seeks to answer several important "issue questions." These could include, for example, "Can technology provide the solution to water shortages?" and "Do the environmental effects of recycling outweigh the costs?" The answers to these questions are never conclusive because the issues are controversial. Instead, they highlight the range of opinions among experts.

Next comes the "Background" section, which provides a history of the issue, including important government actions and court decisions. Then an examination of existing policy (under the heading "Current Situation") is followed by an "Outlook" section, which gives a sense of what might happen in the near future.

All the chapters contain an "At Issue" section in which two experts provide opposing answers to a relevant question. Finally, each chapter has sidebars on matters related to the main issue, a chronology of key events and a bibliography that explains the usefulness of each source.

Here are summaries of the 10 chapters:

Setting Environmental Priorities

The environmental movement is facing increasingly difficult challenges, ranging from domestic issues, such as preventing multiple causes of water pollution, to international issues, such as global warming. The business community favors cost-effective, voluntary efforts to curb pollution. In early 2000, businesses won a major court decision to defer proposed clean air regulations, possibly foreshadowing more legal challenges to environmental regulations.

Environmental Justice

Since the 1980s, a number of studies have demonstrated that hazardous-waste facilities, incinerators and other types of waste plants are found disproportionately in or near poor or minority neighborhoods across the country. The federal government has taken steps to address this problem. The issues are complex because waste facilities, although undesirable in many respects, can produce jobs in low-income areas.

Saving Open Spaces

The preservation of open space is a popular environmental cause. In 1998 voters expressed their frustration over urban sprawl by approving more than 120 ballot initiatives to conserve undeveloped land. Lawmakers in 2000 debated a proposal to permanently fund a federal land acquisition program, although property-rights activists say the government already owns too much land.

Energy and the Environment

Despite decades of energy conservation efforts, the nation remains heavily dependent on fossil fuels, such as oil and coal. Combustion of the fuels causes serious air pollution problems and produces carbon dioxide, a greenhouse gas blamed for global warming. Some officials say it may be time to reassess nuclear energy; others want to put a greater emphasis on alternative fuel sources.

Regulating Pesticides

Farmers rely on pesticides to grow crops, just as city and suburban dwellers rely on the chemicals to keep bugs and other pests in check in homes, offices and gardens. However, scientists are concerned about the potentially severe impacts of pesticides on public health. The Environmental Protection Agency has struggled to regulate the chemicals, drawing fire through such actions as its 2000 decision to bar the pesticide Dursban for most household uses.

The Economics of Recycling

Setting aside old newspapers, bottles and other items for recycling is a popular way of helping the environment. However, recycling efforts are doing little to reduce consumption in the United States, and critics say markets for recycled materials are so volatile that it often costs more to recycle than to bury the waste in a landfill. Environmentalists believe that the market situation will eventually improve.

Traffic Congestion

Whether to build new highways has become a major environmental issue because increased traffic can aggravate air pollution and lead to sprawling development. With Americans driving more and more every year, many officials say new roads are needed to prevent permanent gridlock. The issue has spilled over into the courts and could embroil Congress.

Population and the Environment

With more than 6 billion people on Earth, environmentalists worry about food shortages, as well as the effects of population growth on water supplies and the global climate. In the United States, new census figures estimate that the population will reach about 570 million people by 2100, stirring concerns about overpopulation.

Protecting the National Parks

Crowds are such a problem that many national parks charge admission and maintain long waiting lists for campgrounds and cabins. Development pressure on adjacent lands creates air and noise pollution, and maintenance funds are inadequate. Meanwhile friction is intensifying between commercial interests eager to profit from the parks and environmental purists who want to protect them from all human intrusion. Some park supporters want to use federal budget surpluses to aid the parks and purchase new parklands. Critics say the nation can't afford any new parks.

Saving the Rain Forests

Tropical rain forests, which may contain half of the planet's plant and animal species, are a top environmental priority. Industrialized nations and the World Bank are urging Brazil and other developing nations to step up restrictions on destructive activities such as logging. Environmentalists warn that the forests may be nearly gone by 2050 because of the needs of a growing population.

CQ Researcher on
Saving the Environment

1 Setting Environmental Priorities

MARY H. COOPER

First the good news: "We've really made tremendous progress in the United States since the birth of the environmental movement 29 years ago," says environmentalist Paul Portney, president of Resources for the Future. "The air is dramatically cleaner, big strides have been made in reversing water pollution and there is much more careful treatment of hazardous waste and toxic substances."

Now the bad news: According to many scientists and environmental advocates, the successes of the past few decades represent just the first, easy steps in the battle to restore planet Earth to health. The next phase of environmental action, they say, will have to address much tougher threats — among them global warming linked to fossil-fuel combustion, water pollution from multiple sources and air pollution that crosses state and even national borders.

"Over the last 30 years, America has made great progress," says Carol M. Browner, administrator of the U.S. Environmental Protection Agency (EPA). "But the job is not done. Today we face a new, and somewhat more difficult, generation of pollution problems.

"To cite a major example, polluted runoff from our city streets, suburban lawns and rural areas today accounts for more than half of all water pollution nationally. We have taken unprecedented steps to reduce polluted runoff, but it will take all of us — the federal government, states, communities and businesses — to solve the problem."

Business representatives, however, say the improvements in the nation's environmental quality demonstrate that the need for massive federal

From *The CQ Researcher*, May 21, 1999.

intervention to reverse environmental damage is now obsolete. They believe that further progress should rely more heavily on state and local government initiatives and on voluntary efforts by businesses, consumers and other potential polluters.

"We still have the best environment in the world," says William L. Kovacs, vice president for environmental and regulatory affairs at the U.S. Chamber of Commerce. "You have to ask what it is we're trying to do today and whether there are real health and safety issues at stake. If there are, the business community will go along with it. But if there aren't, we won't."

High on the Chamber's list of priorities is opposing recent efforts by the EPA's Office of Environmental Justice and others to bar factory construction in poor neighborhoods because, environmentalists argue, the added pollution violates residents' civil rights. [1]

"The administration's position that too much business in any one area is a violation of civil rights is one of the dumbest ideas that anyone could have ever come up with," says Kovacs. "If you want to have real environmental protection for people in the center cities, whether they be minorities or the poor, you need to help them get good-paying jobs. Because at the end of the day, the only way you're going to have real

environmental protection is when you have the wealth to make sure you have a good house, good food, a safe neighborhood and decent health care."

Other critics of current policy agree that economic development — not government regulation — is the key to improving environmental quality. "A healthy environment and a healthy economy are directly linked," writes H. Sterling Burnett, environmental policy analyst at the National Center for Policy Analysis, a conservative think tank. The significant reductions in air and water pollution in the United States over the past three decades, he notes, occurred at a time of rapid economic growth. "Pollution wastes resources. In market economies, as companies become more efficient they pollute less." [2]

Environmentalists generally give the Clinton administration high marks for championing environmental protection in the 1990s. "They've done a tremendous job in raising the visibility of the threat of global warming and in taking this issue to the American public," says Greg Wetstone, program director for the New York-based Natural Resources Defense Council. "Overall, they have a very strong record on issues like clean air, protection of our national parks and right down the list of environmental priorities."

In his bid for the Democratic presidential nomination next year, Vice President Al Gore continues to place environmental quality near the top of his political agenda. In January, for example, he unveiled a sweeping $10 billion administration proposal to promote "smart growth" by curbing suburban sprawl and preserving open space. Environmental policy has not yet emerged as a prominent theme in the evolving campaign debate. But that may change as Texas Gov. George W.

Attacking Wind-Blown Pollution

To combat the production of pollutants that are blown across state lines, the Environmental Protection Agency wants 22 states and the District of Columbia to reduce their emissions of nitrogen oxides — which cause acid rain and smog — by up to 48 percent beginning in 2007.

States	Estimated Emissions in 2007 (tons of nitrogen oxides)	Proposed Reductions in 2007 (tons of nitrogen oxides)	Percent Reduction
Alabama	241,564	155,617	36%
Connecticut	52,014	39,909	23
Delaware	30,568	21,010	31
District of Columbia	7,978	7,000	12
Georgia	246,243	159,013	35
Illinois	350,154	218,679	38
Indiana	340,084	200,345	41
Kentucky	263,855	158,360	40
Maryland	118,065	73,628	38
Massachusetts	103,445	73,575	29
Michigan	283,821	199,238	30
Missouri	185,104	116,246	37
New Jersey	132,032	93,464	29
New York	230,310	185,537	19
North Carolina	234,300	153,106	35
Ohio	391,012	236,443	40
Pennsylvania	328,433	207,250	37
Rhode Island	12,175	10,132	17
South Carolina	169,572	109,267	36
Tennessee	291,225	187,250	36
Virginia	219,835	162,375	26
West Virginia	158,240	81,701	48
Wisconsin	142,759	95,902	33
TOTAL	**4,532,790**	**2,945,046**	**35%**

Source: "Air Quality: EPA's Proposed Ozone Transport Rule, OTAG, and Section 126 Petitions — A Hazy Situation?" Congressional Research Service, May 14, 1998

Bush, the current front-runner among Republican presidential hopefuls, comes under closer scrutiny for his position that industrial emissions in his state can be cut solely through voluntary efforts.[3]

Gore has clearly tapped into an issue that concerns Americans across the country. Last fall, voters approved a number of initiatives aimed at curbing development. Indeed, opinion polls suggest that voters continue to place environmental protection high on their list of priorities. More than two-thirds of Americans surveyed in a recent Gallup Poll said they worried "a great deal" about drinking-water pollution. Other big concerns to more than half the respondents included toxic waste contamination, pollution of rivers, lakes and reservoirs and air pollution.[4]

Despite public support for environmental protection, the prospects for major legislative initiatives in this area are uncertain. Since Republicans took control of both houses of Congress in 1995, few new environmental proposals have become law. Congressional opposition to targeted cuts in emissions of carbon dioxide and other gases linked to global warming runs so high that President Clinton has not even submitted the 1997 Kyoto Protocol on global warming for Senate consideration and ratification (*see below*). Indeed, conservative lawmakers have tried repeatedly to roll back existing environmental laws by attaching anti-environmental riders to appropriations bills.

"It's really one of the tragedies of the past few years that the environmental community has had to devote tremendous time and resources to beat back a variety of efforts to move in the wrong direction on environmental protection," says Wetstone. "The evidence abounds that we need to be making progress just to keep up with our problems, much less gain on them."

Some lawmakers defend the practice of adding riders to appropriations bills as a last-ditch effort to protect taxpayers. As chairman of the Senate Interior Appropriations Subcommittee, Sen. Slade Gorton, R-Wash., has authored many of the controversial clauses, which he defends as "an important way for Congress to save taxpayers from wasteful agency spending."[5]

Partisan politics, some experts say, has prevented both sides in the ongoing policy debate from undertaking the kind of sweeping review of environmental priorities necessary to address today's threats to the environment and public health. "There's a noticeable absence of long-

range thinking and commitment both in Congress and the executive branch," says Terry Davies, director of the Center for Risk Management at Resources for the Future. "Everyone in authority is thinking 10 days ahead instead of taking the big picture and thinking 10 years ahead. That's not

"The administration has made it clear that all nations must play a role in reducing the pollution that causes global warming, and that it will not submit the Kyoto Protocol for ratification unless developing nations fairly participate in this effort."

— *Carol M. Browner,*
administrator,
Environmental Protection Agency

good because the process does need some major, long-range thinking, and it's not getting it."

High on Davies' environmental wish list is a better way to collect, analyze and disseminate data on the environment. "We don't have enough

information to tell us where we are or where the trends are going," he says. "We don't really know whether air quality, and especially water quality, are really improving or not under current law. As for solid waste, the situation is hopeless. We don't even know where it is, much less whether it's getting better or worse."

As environmentalists, industry representatives and policy-makers consider the current state of the environment, these are some of the questions they are asking:

Should the United States do more to slow global warming?

In December 1997, representatives of the United States and 175 other countries met in Kyoto, Japan, and agreed to take steps to reduce emissions of carbon dioxide and other "greenhouse" gases believed to be causing a dangerous rise in global temperatures.

For decades, the scientific evidence had mounted suggesting that combustion of coal, oil and — to a lesser extent — natural gas was increasing the level of greenhouse gases, which trap solar heat within the atmosphere. If the emissions continued to mount, scientists warned, the polar ice caps would begin to melt, causing water levels to rise around the globe and flood coastal regions. In addition, infectious diseases would spread and food supplies would be threatened by widespread drought.[6]

The Kyoto Protocol, which the Clinton administration formally signed on Nov. 12, 1998, sought to avert this global environmental disaster by setting targets and timetables for countries to reduce their carbon emissions. The treaty required the United States and other industrial countries, which account for the vast majority of emissions, to make the biggest reductions, while developing countries were given more time to meet the treaty's conditions. The target set for the United States was a 7 percent reduction in carbon emissions below 1990 levels by 2012.[7]

Opposition to the Kyoto Protocol runs high in the U.S. business community, which fears that meeting the treaty's emissions targets will raise energy prices, thereby reducing consumption and cutting into corporate profits. Critics also attack the treaty's mild demands on developing countries. Although historically they have contributed only marginally to the buildup of greenhouse gases, some rapidly developing nations — such as India and China — now have some of the fastest rates of growth in carbon emissions.

"What Kyoto gets you is the United States and the rest of the developed world undertaking a huge reduction of energy use while the rest of the world doesn't," says Kovacs. "If we're going to be serious about reducing emissions, then everyone should be using the best available technology, not just the United States and the other developed countries."

Administration officials say the cost of complying with Kyoto could be kept down to about $7-12 billion a year if Congress passes the administration's Comprehensive Electricity Competition Act to deregulate the electric utility industry and if the United States is allowed to engage in international emissions trading.[8]

Emissions trading would allow big polluters like the United States to "buy" carbon emission "credits" earned by countries with low emissions and use them to offset excessive U.S. emissions. That would enable American industries to delay the

costlier approaches to reducing emissions, such as switching to less polluting fuels. Similarly, the protocol's Clean Development Mechanism allows industrialized countries to earn credits by investing in clean-technology projects in developing countries. Electric-utility deregulation also would reduce the cost of complying with Kyoto if, as expected, it makes electric power cheaper.

"Assuming that effective mechanisms for international [credit] trading, joint implementation and the Clean Development Mechanism are established, and assuming also that the United States achieves meaningful participation by key developing countries, the . . . economic cost of attaining the targets and timetables specified in the Kyoto Protocol will be modest for the United States in aggregate and for typical households," Janet Yellen, chair of the president's Council of Economic Advisers, told a Senate committee in March.[9]

Some environmental experts are uncertain about the best way to deal with global warming. "With apologies to Saddam Hussein, climate change is the mother of all environmental problems today," says Portney. "I think there's no question that it would cost a lot of money to do something dramatic here, but it's the kind of problem you have to take seriously because of the potential environmental risks involved."

In his view, however, the scientific evidence pointing to an imminent threat from global warming is not yet convincing enough to justify requiring U.S. businesses and consumers to shoulder the enormous cost of meeting the treaty's targets, which he estimates at a minimum of $50 billion a year. "It may be that five or 10 years from now we will become convinced that this is a problem that we would really be willing to spend a lot of money on," he says.[10]

The high pricetag also gives many Republicans pause. "The cost of complying with Kyoto is estimated to be up to $338 billion in lost gross domestic product by the year 2010," said Senate Energy and Natural Resources Committee Chairman Frank H. Murkowski, R-Alaska. "That equates to $3,068 per household by that year. So it is a substantial investment and deserves our attention now." Murkowski introduced legislation in April that calls for voluntary cuts in carbon emissions as an alternative to the targets outlined by the Kyoto Protocol. "Our emphasis remains on encouraging voluntary action and not creating new regulatory burdens," he told his Senate colleagues on April 27.[11]

Browner acknowledges the progress made by American industry in dealing with global warming but says it isn't enough. "Global warming is one of the greatest global environmental challenges," she says. "American industry has been a leader in developing and introducing new, more energy-efficient technologies and products that both reduce pollution and cut energy costs for consumers and businesses.

"But science tells us we need to do more. The president has put forth a comprehensive, cost-effective plan that will reduce pollution while allowing our economy to continue to grow. And the administration has made it clear that all nations must play a role in reducing the pollution that causes global warming, and that it will not submit the Kyoto Protocol for ratification unless developing nations fairly participate in this effort."

But waiting to act on pollution will only make things worse, many environmentalists say. "We've got to move forward on reducing the greenhouse pollution that comes from our transportation and electricity-producing sectors," says Wetstone. "This is an issue we're going to have to grapple with, and the sooner we do it the less expensive it's going to be and the easier it's going to be to deal with successfully."

The most effective ways to reduce carbon emissions, Wetstone says, would be to tighten fuel-efficiency standards for vehicles and close the legal loophole that exempts old, coal-fired utilities from the 1970 Clean Air Act's pollution standards. "We could dramatically reduce our pollution just by moving to these common-sense measures in these two big sectors," he says. "The technology is already there to have better fuel economy for motor vehicles across the board. And we need to eliminate this outrageous loophole for coal-fired plants and move to cleaner power production."

Short of amending the Clean Air Act, Congress could help reduce carbon emissions by providing tax incentives for coal-powered utilities to switch to less-polluting plants fueled by natural gas.

"Whether Congress passes utility deregulation or not, the states are moving in this direction, and we will end up eventually with a deregulated utility industry," says Philip E. Clapp, executive director of the National Environmental Trust, which monitors environmental legislation and regulations. "That's going to mean high competition, and there are significant economic incentives for converting old, coal-fired plants, with their high maintenance and operation costs, to natural gas. If lawmakers don't want to accelerate the natural turnover process through regulations, they can always do it through tax incentives."

Clapp and eight other leaders of

major environmental organizations recently criticized the Clinton administration for not pressing more aggressively for reductions in carbon emissions. In a letter to the president, they expressed "deep disappointment with the lack of an administration proposal

Aerial view of Martha's Vineyard

Computer-enhanced view

Sea levels would rise about three feet in 100 years and much of today's Martha's Vineyard (above) would be flooded (computer-enhanced photo below) if global warming isn't reduced, according to the National Environmental Trust.

to require significant reductions in global warming pollution. We are particularly frustrated that the administration has not sought meaningful emission reductions from either power plants or passenger vehicles." [12]

Should the federal government cede to the states some of its power to set environmental policy?

The federal government has traditionally taken the lead in setting environmental policy. When the EPA was created in 1970, it was given the authority to establish and administer regulations to satisfy the provisions of environmental laws. It was left to the states to draw up detailed plans to implement these regulations. Only in cases where states fail to fulfill their role is the federal EPA authorized to step in and implement environmental policy as well.

But over the past three decades of expanding environmental legislation, states have taken on more prominent roles. "Now that state environmental protection agencies have gotten stronger, better funded and more sophisticated," says Portney, "they're saying, 'Look, we shouldn't be just the monitoring and enforcement arm of the federal government; we actually can set some standards for ourselves now.' For the big issues like air and water pollution, you have to have at least a regional, and probably a federal, approach. But if California wants a tight drinking-water standard and Nevada doesn't, I don't see why EPA should say everybody everywhere has to meet the same standard."

"I certainly have no problem with environmental issues being dealt with at the local or state level as long as adequate programs are actually being put in place at that level," says

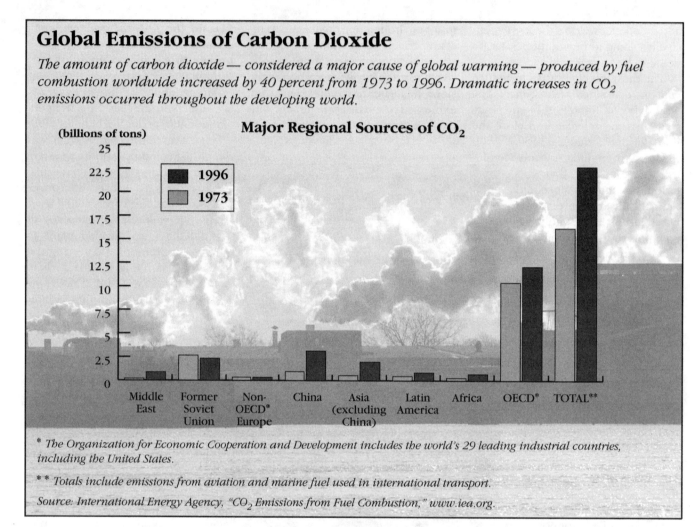

Global Emissions of Carbon Dioxide

The amount of carbon dioxide — considered a major cause of global warming — produced by fuel combustion worldwide increased by 40 percent from 1973 to 1996. Dramatic increases in CO_2 emissions occurred throughout the developing world.

Major Regional Sources of CO_2

(billions of tons)

Legend: ■ 1996 ▨ 1973

Categories: Middle East, Former Soviet Union, Non-OECD* Europe, China, Asia (excluding China), Latin America, Africa, OECD*, TOTAL**

* *The Organization for Economic Cooperation and Development includes the world's 29 leading industrial countries, including the United States.*

** *Totals include emissions from aviation and marine fuel used in international transport.*

Source: International Energy Agency, "CO_2 Emissions from Fuel Combustion," www.iea.org.

Hilary French, vice president for research at the Worldwatch Institute. "Ideally, we feel that as a general matter problems should be dealt with at the most appropriate level, ideally as close to the ground as you can get."

French cautions that decentralization of policy-setting authority has its limits. "If the problems are truly contained within state borders, it's perfectly appropriate for them to be dealt with at that level," she says. "But many problems cross state borders, and for those there is an obvious federal interest."

Kovacs at the Chamber of Commerce and other critics of the Clinton administration say the EPA has usurped the states' rightful authority in implementing national environmental policy. "The EPA has expanded its authority from being a standard-setting body to being a national zoning board," he says. "The authority to plan and implement policy has always been with the states. But since Browner took over as administrator, the delegation of authority has not been acceptable to EPA, and they go in and tinker with the details of state environmental plans."

As an example of "EPA interference," Kovacs cites the agency's involvement in local environmental-justice cases, where communities have tried to keep out polluting factories. "This is the most egregious instance of the feds simply deciding that

they don't like the permit that was issued by a state," he says. "So they go in and overfile at the local level," imposing new permit conditions.

In arguing for looser federal control, industry spokesmen point to the steps U.S. businesses have taken voluntarily to reduce pollution. According to the Chamber, American industry has spent more than $1 trillion to improve environmental quality. Bethlehem Steel has reduced its discharge of toxic materials by 85 percent since 1994, for example, and brewer Anheuser-Busch has reduced its production of solid waste by half since 1991. [13]

But many environmentalists say that businesses would never have undertaken such efforts without federal mandates. They also say that history clearly shows that the states can't always be trusted to set effective environmental policy, even for problems that fall neatly within their jurisdiction.

"The reason the Safe Drinking Water Act was passed in 1974 and the EPA was given enforcement authority in that area was precisely because the states had refused over a significant period of time to do anything about setting and enforcing strong standards on drinking water," says Clapp of the National Environmental Trust. "The fact is that state legislatures continue to be extremely cozy with local industries, which often use the heavy-handed threat that they will just go somewhere else if they're required to live up to environmental laws. That's a very powerful argument, and it shows that there continues to be an appropriate role for the federal government in environmental protection."

For its part, the Clinton administration appears to support greater power-sharing with the states on environmental issues. In his budget request for fiscal 2000, submitted on Feb. 1, the president included funds to help states exercise greater leeway in addressing environmental problems within their borders, such as buying ecologically sensitive land and making payments to cities for curbing carbon emissions. [14]

"Protecting the nation's health and environment requires all of us — the federal government, states, industry and local communities — to work together," says Browner. "There are some environmental challenges best addressed

through partnerships with local communities, such as cleaning up and redeveloping lightly polluted industrial areas known as "brownfields." And there are other challenges that require federal-state partnerships, such as protecting the nation's watersheds.

"But there are other problems that

"Many Americans today are reaching for a new prosperity defined not just by the quantity of their bank accounts but also by the quality of their lives. They want smart growth that produces prosperity while protecting a high quality of life."

— *Vice President Al Gore*

require a strong federal role, such as setting tough public health standards for our air and our drinking water. By working together with all of our partners, we are providing the strongest protection of our health and environment."

Are Americans willing to pay for the next round of environmental-protection measures?

In a highly industrialized country like the United States, maintaining a healthy environment does not come cheap. The Clinton administration is asking Congress for $34 billion to fund environmental programs in fiscal 2000, a 5 percent increase over the previous year.

Government expenditures are only part of the picture, however. Industry spends billions more to install chimney scrubbers, waste-water treatment facilities and other technologies to limit pollution in accordance with government mandates. Those costs are passed along to consumers, who pay for a clean environment through higher prices for goods and services.

The Chamber of Commerce calculates that the annual cost of complying with environmental laws has risen from $80 billion in 1985 to $170 billion, or about $1,800 per household. "Business has spent a trillion dollars cleaning the environment," the group says. "Additional progress requires regulations based on common sense and sound science. Unfortunately, federal regulations often fall far short." [15]

To environmental advocates, such statements are a familiar refrain. "Any industry that has to do something to cut its pollution immediately turns around and says that it will make Americans lose jobs, bankrupt America and force consumers to give up essential products," says Clapp. "Americans don't have to drive less in order to cut pollution; Detroit has to produce more fuel-efficient cars, which are actually an advantage to the consumer."

But some environmentalists warn that the costs of environmental progress will rise with the next round of programs. "We've picked off all of the cheap fixes," says Portney of Resources for the Future. He cites programs to reduce urban air pollution and water pollution caused by clearly identifiable sources, such as factories or sewage-treatment plants. "After 30 years of environmental legislation, the marginal cost — the cost of additional improvements — is much bigger than it has ever been."

The next phase of air pollution efforts, for example, is likely to deal with more complex, and costly, matters, such as regional, rather than local, pollution. Nitrogen oxides emitted by Midwestern and Eastern coal-fired electric utilities is blown across state boundaries and contributes to dirty air in the Northeast. Pollutants from Los Angeles are largely responsible for the haze over the Grand Canyon, hundreds of miles away. Solving such problems will require far more sweeping steps than installing catalytic converters on cars and "scrubbers" on factory smokestacks.

Portney, perhaps surprisingly, questions the need for immediate action in some cases. "Environmental advocates get jerked out of shape when I say this," Portney says, "but I don't think there are very many serious environmental problems left in the United States. That doesn't mean that we shouldn't do more to clean up the environment. But it does mean that we've got to look a lot more carefully than we did back in 1970, when you could throw a dart at a list of environmental problems and feel confident that whatever you hit was a good candidate for regulation. That means that we need better research to make sure that we're not

spending our money on problems that aren't worth the money."

Some environmental advocates say Americans don't want to wait for further scientific proof. "Americans feel very, very strongly about cleaning up air and water," Clapp says. "Those are the two strongest issues, and they are willing to pay for them. The arguments of industry, that environmental protection threatens job security, resonate at times of economic hardship. But we've had nine years of extremely healthy economic conditions, and people just don't believe that we can't have good environmental protection and economic growth at the same time."

Recent opinion polls suggest Clapp is right: 67 percent of Americans surveyed on the eve of Earth Day agreed that "protection of the environment should be given priority, even at the risk of curbing economic growth." Only 28 percent of those responding to the April Gallup Poll thought that "economic growth should be given priority, even if the environment suffers to some extent." A survey conducted for the Sierra Club the same month had similar findings. When asked whether they would rather see $2 billion of the federal budget surplus used to buy and protect open space or for military spending, respondents chose environmental protection over defense spending by a margin of 50 percent to 34 percent. [16] ∎

BACKGROUND

Status Report

O ver the past three decades, the federal government has attacked an array of environmental prob-

lems. [17] Here is a status report on key environmental issues:

Air quality — The landmark 1970 Clean Air Act set standards for emissions of 189 pollutants that cause smog. Industries were required to install smokestack scrubbers to prevent the release of particulate matter and cut their emissions of sulfur dioxide, a product of fossil-fuel combustion that causes acid rain. Oil companies had to remove lead from gasoline, and automakers were required to install catalytic converters in cars to reduce tailpipe emissions.

Congress strengthened the law in 1990 with amendments that required heavily polluted cities to use oxygenated gasoline in the winter to reduce carbon monoxide emissions and reformulated gasoline to cut ozone pollution in the summer.

The 1990 amendments also permitted the EPA to establish regional boards to address air pollution that crosses state boundaries. In August 1997, eight Northeastern states petitioned the agency to force Midwestern states to reduce emissions of nitrogen oxides, which contribute to urban smog in Northeastern cities. Midwestern states have filed suit to block the action. [18]

In 1997, the EPA announced a tightening of standards on ground-level ozone and particulate matter, microscopic particles that contribute to haze. In announcing the new guidelines, due to go into effect beginning in 2003, the agency promised they would help reduce the incidence of respiratory illness, especially asthma among children. A broad coalition of industries challenged the new regulations, saying they were too costly and of unproved scientific benefit. On May 14, an appeals court panel sided with industry and reversed the regulations. [19]

In April, the Clinton administration announced requirements for cleaner

Chronology

1970s Grass-roots activism produces landmark environmental protection legislation.

April 22, 1970
On the first Earth Day, millions of Americans exhort policy-makers to restore the country to environmental health.

1970
The Environmental Protection Agency (EPA) is created. Congress passes the Clean Air Act.

1972
The Clean Water Act requires factories, utilities and sewage-treatment plants to reduce the discharge of toxic wastes into rivers and streams.

1973
The Endangered Species Act authorizes the EPA to list plant and animal species threatened with extinction because of environmental degradation.

1974
The Safe Drinking Water Act authorizes the EPA to set national standards for water purity. The law, amended in 1996, also requires states to monitor their supplies of groundwater.

1980s Controversies erupt over the economic impact of environmental laws.

1980
Congress passes the Comprehensive Environmental Response, Compensation and Liability Act — the "superfund" law — requiring polluters to clean up toxic-waste sites.

1990s A backlash against environmental regulations slows new legislation.

1990
Congress amends the Clean Air Act, requiring heavily polluted cities to use oxygenated gasoline in the winter to reduce carbon monoxide emissions and refor-mulated gasoline to cut ozone pollution in the summer. The amendments also permit the EPA to establish regional boards to address air pollution that crosses state boundaries.

1994
The U.S. Fish and Wildlife Service begins a controversial program to reintroduce wolves into Yellowstone National Park and other remote areas.

August 1997
Eight Northeastern states petition the EPA to force Midwestern states to reduce emissions of nitrogen oxides, which contribute to urban smog in Northeastern cities.

December 1997
Representatives of the United States and 175 other countries meet in Kyoto, Japan, and agree to take steps to reduce emis-sions of carbon dioxide and other gases believed to cause global warming.

January 1998
The Energy Department misses its deadline to begin storing the radioactive waste from commer-cial nuclear power plants. Construction of a federally run, permanent repository under Yucca Mountain in the Nevada desert is not expected to be completed before 2010.

Nov. 12, 1998
The Clinton administration formally signs the Kyoto Proto-col, which sets targets and timetables for countries to reduce their carbon emissions. The United States is to reduce its carbon emissions by 7 per-cent below 1990 levels by 2012.

February 1999
The administration announces an 18-month moratorium on new logging-road construction in national forests.

April 1999
The administration announces requirements, starting in 2004, for cleaner gasoline and stricter pollution standards for automo-biles, which would also apply to sport utility vehicles and light trucks for the first time. The rules would also require oil companies to remove most pollution-causing sulfur from gasoline. On April 27, the administration imposes sweeping limits on fishing for shark, tuna, marlin and other sport and commercial species.

May 14, 1999
A U.S. Court of Appeals panel blocks the EPA's 1997 standards on ozone and particulate matter. A broad coalition of industries had challenged the regulations, saying they were too costly and of unproved scientific benefit.

July 1999
The Clinton administration's $8 billion plan to restore the Ever-glades is scheduled to be sub-mitted to Congress.

gasoline and stricter pollution standards for automobiles, which would also apply to sport utility vehicles and light trucks for the first time. The rules would also require oil companies to remove most pollution-causing sulfur from gasoline. Both requirements would take effect in 2004. Congressional critics of the new rules, including Sen. James M. Inhofe, R-Okla., chairman of the Senate Environmental and Public Works Subcommittee on Clean Air, have promised to introduce legislation to cancel the standard on sulfur in gasoline.

"In their rush to issue new environmental regulations, I fear the administration is short-changing important considerations which need to be addressed in the proposed sulfur rule," Inhofe said in a statement issued April 30. Specifically, he charged that the EPA had failed to provide sufficient data to justify the new regulations. "The Clean Air Act requires that these standards be cost-effective, and my subcommittee will ensure that this is the case," he said.

At the same time, automakers are voluntarily developing innovative vehicles designed to run on hydrogen-powered fuel cells. That effort has intensified as a result of a California decree that "zero-emission" vehicles must account for 10 percent of a carmaker's total vehicle sales in the state by 2003.

On Earth Day this year, Gore announced a new federal regulation that calls for clearing the air pollution that shrouds the country's national parks and forests by 2064. Because no funds were set aside to comply with the "regional haze rule," states will have to pay for the cleanup, which will require

coal-fired utilities, in particular, to reduce their particulate emissions.

Water quality — The quest to clean up America's waterways has focused on two fronts: eliminating toxic waste and ensuring the safety of drinking water. The 1972 Clean Water Act required factories, utilities and sewage-treatment plants to reduce the discharge of toxic wastes into rivers and streams. As a result, the most egregious and easily identifiable sources of water pollution have been removed or greatly reduced, and fish and wildlife have

AP Photo/Terry Renna

Newly constructed filter marshes designed to reduce pollutants in the water are the centerpiece of the 1994 Everglades Restoration Act.

returned to many lifeless waterways.

But water pollution remains a serious problem. According to the EPA, more than a third of the country's waterways still fall short of existing standards. Outbreaks of the bacterium *Phiesteria piscicida* in and around the Chesapeake Bay in recent years have caused massive fish kills and disease in humans, as have poisonings linked to infected shellfish in coastal areas. These problems are believed to result from runoff of fertilizers, pesticides and other toxic materials from a multitude of sources, such as farms, city storm sewers and

suburban lawns. But curbing pollution from these "non-point" sources will be much harder, and costlier, to achieve than simply fixing toxic releases from large, distinct sources. EPA estimates that it would cost $9.4 billion a year to control non-point source pollution. [20]

Some environmentalists say legislators are using concerns about high costs as an excuse to avoid taking on powerful constituents in the quest to clean up water supplies. "I don't think that Congress or EPA have the guts to tell farmers they're polluters, even though in many areas runoff is now the overwhelmingly largest contributor to impaired water quality," says Portney at Resources for the Future. "Also, the biggest violators every year are sewage treatment plants, but the EPA doesn't want to beat up on [local governments like] Arlington, Va., or Seat Pleasant, Md. Politically, it's much easier to target industry as the bad guys."

The Clean Water Act also provides some protection for marshes, estuaries and other wetlands. These areas, vital as wildlife habitats and for flood control and water purification, are fast disappearing as development intensifies in coastal areas. More than half of U.S. wetlands have been destroyed. Last October, the administration strengthened federal rules protecting wetlands by requiring builders to go through a more rigorous application process before filling a wetland.

The biggest wetland in the United States, the Everglades, has been greatly reduced in size and polluted from runoff from surrounding Florida cities and farms. But a proposed administration plan to restore the Ever-

What *You* Can Do to Make a Difference

Lawmakers, scientists and industry aren't the only ones to make crucial decisions about the environment. Consumers also make choices — about the products they buy and way they use energy — that have a significant effect on the environment.

Americans have enthusiastically embraced voluntary efforts to help protect the environment. Curbside recycling services have been a big hit across the country, many grocery shoppers routinely ask for paper bags instead of plastic and backyard gardeners compost yard waste instead of sending it to the landfill.

But not all of these efforts are of equal ecological value, according to a recent study by the Union of Concerned Scientists (UCS).[1] Some are worth pursuing; others are a waste of time, says the UCS. Here's what it found:

Worth Pursuing

❏ **Transportation** — Not surprisingly, transportation tops the UCS list of environmentally harmful activities. Cars and light trucks cause the most damage, contributing almost half the toxic air pollution and more than a quarter of greenhouse gas emissions produced by household consumption. Choosing a popular sport-utility vehicle instead of a subcompact car, for example, will increase fuel consumption and emissions of air pollutants, including carbon dioxide, the leading cause of global warming. So will driving to work instead of taking public transportation.

❏ **Food** — The UCS' second biggest consumer-related threat to the environment is food. Red meat is the most harmful food product of all because cattle-raising pollutes water and contributes to deforestation as ranchers cut down trees to make way for pasture. According to the study, cutting meat and poultry consumption by half would reduce food-related land use by nearly a third and water pollution by a quarter. Consumers should replace beef with grains, fresh fruits and vegetables, the authors advise.

Not Worth the Trouble

❏ **Cloth vs. disposable diapers** — During the 1980s, cloth diapers made a big comeback on evidence that plastic-covered, non-biodegradable disposable diapers were taking up precious landfill space. It now seems apparent that laundering cloth diapers uses more energy than making disposables. UCS's recommendation: "Choose whichever type of diaper makes the most sense in terms of cost, convenience and the comfort of the child."

❏ **Paper vs. plastic bags** — In the 1980s retail stores started offering plastic bags, which were cheaper than traditional paper sacks. Many environmentalists decried the change for the same reasons that they opposed the use of disposable diapers. But paper sacks, even if they contain recycled material, contribute to deforestation. UCS concludes, "No matter what you do, it's not all that big a deal."

❏ **Disposable cups, paper plates, plastic utensils and paper napkins** — Using ceramic dishes, metal utensils and cloth napkins helps reduce consumption of paper or plastic. But the use of electricity to run the dishwasher or washing machine may ultimately do as much harm to the environment.

❏ **Spray cans and Styrofoam cups** — Propellants for spray cans and the ingredients in Styrofoam utensils once contained ozone-depleting chemicals. These have since been replaced, however. "You should not feel embarrassed or guilty to spray away," advises UCS. The same goes for using Styrofoam "in moderation."

❏ **Cotton vs. synthetic clothes** — Although cotton is more "natural" than manmade fibers, buying cotton clothing may cause more harm to the environment because of the heavy use of pesticides and other chemicals required for cotton cultivation. "If you want to limit the environmental impact associated with the manufacture of clothing," UCS suggests, "you can purchase vintage clothes and avoid unnecessary clothing purchases rather than worry about whether you are dressing in cotton, rayon, wool, polyester, silk or something else."

[1] Michael Brower and Warren Leon, *The Consumer's Guide to Effective Environmental Choices* (1999).

glades to ecological health has run into trouble amid criticism that the ambitious, $8 billion project will fall short of its goal of restoring water flow. The plan, the most comprehensive such restoration effort ever attempted in the United States, is to be submitted to Congress in July.

Together with overfishing, pollu-tion also has contributed to the rapid decline of many coastal fisheries. On April 22, the House passed a bill (HR 999) that would require all coastal states to adopt new federal water-quality standards and notify the public when levels of pathogens and microorganisms exceed acceptable levels.[21]

The Clean Beach and Coastal Protection Act was referred to the Senate, where Environment and Public Works Committee Chairman John H. Chafee, R-R.I., has expressed support for the measure.

The 1974 Safe Drinking Water Act, the other main focus of water regulation, authorized the EPA to set national standards for water purity. The law, amended in 1996, also requires states to monitor their groundwater, the source of more than half the country's drinking water. But recent findings suggest that the standards are inadequate. The National Research Council, an arm of the National Academy of Sciences, reported in March that high levels of arsenic in drinking water put many Americans at risk for cancer and urged the EPA to strengthen guidelines for this dangerous pollutant. [22]

Water projects — American rivers are dotted with hydroelectric dams, flood-prevention levees and canals. Although the states help build and maintain these facilities, the federal government provides most of the maintenance funds. As development continues to spread, so does competition for freshwater supplies, especially in the arid Southwest. The $4.3 billion Water Resources Development Act, for example, was held up for more than a year by a dispute over water allocations in California. Finally, in April, both the House and Senate versions of the bill omitted a request from Rep. John T. Doolittle, R-Calif., for additional water from the Sacramento and American rivers to feed his fast-growing Northern California district. [23] The House and Senate versions now go to conference.

In recent years the negative environmental impact of hydroelectric dams has become increasingly apparent in the Northeast and Pacific Northwest, where several species of salmon are threatened with extinction because dams block their yearly migration to upstream spawning areas. In April 1999, American Rivers, a conservation group, blamed the U.S. Army Corps of Engineers, which builds and maintains flood-control projects along more than 30,000 miles of rivers and streams, for placing hundreds of species at risk of extinction. [24]

Interior Secretary Bruce Babbitt has sparked intense controversy with his plan to dismantle small dams in an effort to save the fish. "There are more than 75,000 dams in the nation, most built long ago, many clearly obsolete," Babbitt said in a statement last October. "The role of many of these structures needs to be reassessed, especially those that have an obvious and adverse effect on our rivers and threatened and endangered species." [25] Among the dams removed thus far are the Edwards Dam on the Kennebec River in Maine and the Roy's Dam on a Lagunitas Creek tributary in Marin County, Calif.

Opponents of dam removal say there are less drastic alternatives. "Even under current circumstances, the difference between removing dams to save fish or barging them around dams is too close to call," said Sen. Gorton, who has long argued against the removal of dams as a means of restoring salmon runs to the Columbia River basin. "And when all the costs of dam removal are factored into this equation, it is hard to imagine why anyone would want to take this dubious course of action." [26]

Endangered species — The Interior Department in March added nine species of Pacific salmon and trout to the list of species to be protected under the 1973 Endangered Species Act. During the 1980s, the controversial act triggered violence between environmentalists and loggers in the Pacific Northwest when it was invoked to force timber companies to stop cutting down forest tracts that were home to the endangered northern spotted owl.

But the law has been effective. Last year, the administration removed the bald eagle, peregrine falcon and 27 other plant and animal species from the endangered list. Recent efforts to save species from extinction include programs

to breed animals in captivity and reintroduce them into the wild. The California condor and black-footed ferret have been successfully reintroduced, but remain threatened by pollution and overdevelopment. A controversial project begun in 1994 to reintroduce wolves into Yellowstone National Park and other remote areas also had some success. But a federal judge recently ruled in favor of ranchers and ordered the U.S. Fish and Wildlife Service to end the program.

Stocks of many ocean-dwelling fish have been seriously depleted in recent years by overfishing, including tuna, shark and cod. In 1996 Congress limited the catch in offshore U.S. fisheries. On April 27, the Clinton administration also imposed sweeping limits on fishing for shark, tuna, marlin and other prized sport- and commercial-fishing species.

Toxic waste — The 1980 Comprehensive Environmental Response, Compensation and Liability Act — better known as the "superfund" law — required the creators of toxic-waste sites, usually industries, to clean them up. Superfund's critics cite the program's huge costs — an average of $30 million per cleanup — and call on Congress to water down the law. Over the last several years, lawmakers have provided the EPA with about $1.5 billion a year on average to run the program. Criticism has blocked efforts to reauthorize superfund, including a measure to provide $7.5 billion for the program over five years that stalled in the 105th Congress.

Radioactive waste from nuclear power plants is treated outside the superfund program. The Energy Department was scheduled to begin storing the deadly byproducts from commercial plants in January 1998. But construction of a federally run, permanent repository under Yucca

Treaties on Everything From Timber to Polar Bears

In addition to the Kyoto Protocol to reduce greenhouse gases, there are dozens of other international environmental treaties. Some have been in force for decades, such as the International Convention for the Regulation of Whaling (1946). Many, including the Convention on Nature Protection and Wildlife Preservation in the Western Hemisphere (1940), are regional. Others aim to protect specific plants or animals, such as the International Tropical Timber Agreement (1983) and the Agreement on Conservation of Polar Bears (1973).

Recognition of the global nature of some environmental threats in recent years has paved the way for increasingly ambitious treaties. Before the Kyoto Protocol, the most sweeping agreement was the Montreal Protocol to eliminate the production of chlorofluorocarbons (CFCs), chemicals used in refrigerators and air conditioners the world over. CFCs, it was found, float into the stratosphere high above Earth where they destroy the layer of ozone that shields the planet from the sun's harmful ultraviolet rays

The United States played a leading role in garnering global support for the protocol. As the world's main producer of CFCs, the United States had to make the biggest changes, including phasing out CFC production and redesigning air-conditioning systems to accommodate alternative refrigerants. Evidence that the ozone hole in the Earth's atmosphere was growing dispelled early opposition to the treaty from the chemicals industry, and the agreement was adopted in 1987. Indeed, the treaty's provisions have been subsequently toughened as the scientific evidence pointed to even greater threats posed by ozone depletion.

The Montreal Protocol remains the chief model for future global environmental treaties. But the United States is generally far less supportive of environmental treaties today than it once was. Both the Kyoto Protocol and the Convention on Biological Diversity, the two main accords that came out of the United Nations-sponsored Earth Summit in Rio de Janeiro in 1992, are stalled in the ratification process.

"We are particularly concerned with our government's failure to ratify these treaties, as well as the 1982 Law of the Sea convention and the 1994 Convention to Combat Desertification," says Hilary French, vice president for research at the Worldwatch Institute. "That sends a very bad signal to the international community, which finds it very difficult to take U.S. positions all that seriously."

Critics often cite sovereignty concerns to explain their opposition to environmental treaties. In the case of the Kyoto Protocol, said Sen. John Ashcroft, R-Mo., "The concessions made to other nations would cause severe damage to the American economy, and would deprive our people of good jobs, income they need to meet the needs of their families and economic opportunity for the next generation. In our nation, a president is not empowered to make treaties that unilaterally bind American sovereignty." [1]

Global environmental treaties include the 1994 Convention to Combat Desertification, not yet ratified by the Senate.

PhotoDisc

But some, such as the desertification treaty, would have little impact on the United States, where land degradation is not critical. "Ratifying a treaty like that, which doesn't really require the United States to change its policies, would send a very important signal to developing countries that we care about the problems that they face," French says. "That would also make them more eager to deal with problems that we see as priorities, such as climate change. By not ratifying these treaties, we are leaving people with the view that the United States is just trying to throw its weight around in the world and is not willing to work in a cooperative way with other countries."

U.S. reticence about global environmental treaties like the Kyoto Protocol stems from several factors. For one thing, the burdens imposed on the United States are often far greater than on other nations. The CFC phaseout was burdensome to only a few industries, such as producers of chemicals and autos. Reducing carbon emissions will impact virtually all industries, as well as consumers, who may pay more for gasoline and myriad other products. In addition, political opposition to international treaties in general — and environmental agreements in particular — has grown since 1994, when the Republican Party gained a majority of seats in the Senate.

"It's basically an ideological, ultraconservative position that has developed," says French. "It doesn't reflect the full tradition of the Republican Party at all, which has quite an internationalist tradition."

[1] From a statement, April 30, 1998.

Mountain in the Nevada desert is not expected to open before 2010.

Meanwhile, utilities are fast running out of space to store their waste on site, and both the Chamber of Commerce and House Commerce Committee Chairman Thomas J. Bliley Jr., R-Va., are pushing the 106th Congress to pass a temporary-storage measure. But Nevada legislators are fighting the proposal, and President Clinton has threatened to veto the measure, as he did a similar one in 1997.

Another priority for the Chamber is reversing rules that are slowing development of some 500,000 brownfield sites. Although EPA runs a program to develop these sites with new industries, business representatives say they are moving too slowly. "Most of these sites are prime real estate," says Kovacs. "Before superfund, they would have just been cleaned up under state law, but the federal government has now crippled center cities across the country with its regulations."

Public land — Ranchers, mining companies and timber companies pay below-market fees to use public lands. Efforts to reduce these subsidies have had mixed success. Measures to increase grazing fees were blocked in the 105th Congress by lawmakers from Western states. Efforts to revise the 1872 Mining Law, which allows mining companies to drill for hard-rock minerals on federal land for $5 an acre, also have failed to overcome industry opposition.

The main focus of the administration's efforts to curb commercial activities on public land is a moratorium on new logging-road construction in national forests. Announced in February, the 18-month moratorium is intended to give Congress and the Forest Service time to review a longstanding policy that has enabled timber companies to harvest trees on public lands that have not been set aside as official wilderness areas.[27]

"Congress should encourage the administration to put an end to all logging" in national forests, says Clapp of the National Environmental Trust. "We have very little of our original forest left, and we don't need to allow the timber industry to go in at taxpayer expense and cut down the remaining virgin forests in the United States."

But Republican lawmakers, notably Sen. Murkowski, oppose any legislative bar to continued logging on public land. He has called the administration's moratorium on road-building in national forests "a top-down, inside-the-Beltway initiative that undermines the ability of local forest managers and scientists to properly manage forests based upon local environmental conditions in cooperation with local communities. As such, it is unwise in concept, ambiguous in execution and most likely unlawful in intent."[28]

Murkowski and other conservative lawmakers assailed another administration ruling issued in April, which reduced by a third the maximum allowable timber harvest in the 17-million-acre Tongass National Forest, one of the world's last remaining temperate rain forests.

One of the few land-policy issues that appears to have garnered bipartisan agreement is restoration of the Land and Water Conservation Fund. Created in 1964 to finance the purchase of new parkland and forests, the fund was supposed to be financed by revenues from federal offshore oil and gas leases, which total about $900 million a year. But Congress has rarely appropriated the full amount, using most of the money to reduce the federal budget deficit.

Now that the federal budget is finally in balance, lawmakers from both sides of the aisle have introduced proposals to replenish the fund. A bill introduced by Sen. Dianne Feinstein, D-Calif., would ensure that all offshore lease revenues go to the fund as intended. A less sweeping proposal has been introduced by Murkowski and Sen. Mary L. Landrieu, D-La. ■

CURRENT SITUATION

Global Warming

Congressional opposition to U.S. participation in the Kyoto Protocol has escalated to the point that lawmakers tried last fall to prohibit the administration from even conducting public seminars on global warming. The language, attached to a fiscal 1999 spending bill, was subsequently weakened somewhat, and the EPA was barred from using funds to "propose or issue rules, regulations, decrees or orders for the purpose of [implementing] the Kyoto Protocol."[29]

Congress did approve $1 billion for climate-change initiatives, mostly earmarked for research into alternative fuels and renewable energy, as part of the fiscal 1999 omnibus appropriations bill. But the funding came with a restriction on the administration's ability to promote U.S. participation in the protocol.

Treaty opponents continue to support voluntary efforts to curb greenhouse gas emissions. On May 3, Sens. Murkowski, Chuck Hagel, R-Neb., and Larry E. Craig, R-Idaho, introduced legislation that would provide $2 billion in incentives for industry to

At Issue:

Can the United States afford to ratify the Kyoto Protocol to curb global warming?

JAY HAKES

Administrator, Energy Information Administration,
Department of Energy

FROM TESTIMONY BEFORE THE SENATE ENERGY AND NATURAL RESOURCES COMMITTEE, MARCH 25, 1999.

*t*he Kyoto Protocol calls for the United States to reduce its total net emissions of six greenhouse gases, weighted for their global warming potential, by 7 percent relative to 1990 emissions levels. This reduction is to be achieved on average during the years 2008 to 2012. Much of the focus on emissions reduction is on the energy sector because energy use is the primary source of greenhouse gas emissions. In 1997, carbon dioxide emissions from the combustion of energy totaled 83 percent of all U.S. greenhouse gas emissions. . . .

Carbon emissions from energy can be reduced in several ways. First, there can be a shift from fossil to non-fossil fuels, such as nuclear power or renewable sources of energy. Second, energy use can shift from highly carbon-intensive fossil fuels to those with lower carbon intensity. For example, natural gas produces only about half the carbon emissions per unit of thermal output as coal. Also, energy consumers can use more energy-efficient technologies, thereby using less energy to achieve the same level of energy service. Finally, consumers can reduce the level of energy services, for example, by traveling less or lowering their demand for heating and cooling. . . .

It is estimated that the loss in potential GDP will range from $13 billion to $72 billion (1992 dollars) in 2010. In an economy today of more than $7 trillion, which is expected to grow to more than $9.4 trillion in 2010, the percentage loss in output ranges from 0.1 percent to 0.8 percent in 2010. . . . When viewed from the perspective of growth rates, the economy continues to grow, but at a slower rate. . . .

The finding that economic growth slows only moderately in the transition period and slows only slightly when averaged to 2020 results from two factors. First, energy costs have become a smaller part of the overall economy than in the past, muting broader impacts of energy price increases. Second, some revenues from the higher costs of energy can be recycled back into the American economy, as opposed to, for instance, going to foreign oil producers. The continued growth of the economy and of personal disposable income during the period of carbon reductions is one of the reasons that energy prices reach the high levels in our projections. With growing personal income, energy consumers will be more willing to pay higher energy costs to maintain desired lifestyles.

CECIL E. ROBERTS

President, United Mine Workers of America

FROM TESTIMONY BEFORE THE SENATE ENERGY AND NATURAL RESOURCES COMMITTEE, MARCH 25, 1999.

*t*he Kyoto Protocol is a fatally flawed treaty that promises no meaningful environmental benefit, but threatens serious economic harm to American working families. . . .

All forms of fossil energy will experience price increases. Gasoline prices are projected to increase $.21-$2.70 per gallon over the base case in the 2008-2012 period. Residential natural gas prices are projected to be $1.47-$1.89 per million Btu higher in 2008-2012, and electricity prices are projected to be $1.82-$2.41 per kilowatt-hour higher than the base case.

For the average household, this means about $1,000 more each year in energy expenditures. At the same time, the average family will have about $1,000 less in household income with which to pay such increased costs. In addition, this only reflects the increase in direct energy costs. As energy prices rise, so too will the cost of all goods and services. Increases in energy prices as a result of Kyoto will be felt in everyday necessities such as food, clothing and medicine.

Achieving the required reductions in carbon emissions will require substantial investments by both businesses and consumers to improve energy efficiency and to substitute lower-carbon sources of fuels for higher-carbon fuels. These investments will result in the diversion of funds from savings or investment in other things, such as housing, education or health care.

Numerous economic analyses, including some by the Clinton administration, indicate that efforts to meet the obligations arising out of the Kyoto Protocol may be quite costly. Over a million American jobs could be lost, and the losses will occur in every region of the country. . . .

Nearly every sector of the economy, including service industries and state and local governments, could be affected. The loss of high-paying mining and manufacturing jobs, along with the general decline in other jobs, will lead to a severe reduction in wage growth, further exacerbating the widening disparity of wealth in America. And greenhouse gas reduction efforts are likely to increase the U.S. trade deficit as exports of U.S. goods decline and imports increase.

The loss of real GDP would be significant under the proposed Kyoto Protocol. Based on the trading assumptions outlined above, the decline in GDP would be about 1.2 percent on average in the 2008-2012 compliance period. This represents economic losses in excess of $100 billion per year. Clearly, the costs of Kyoto are large and significant.

reduce emissions as part of a market-based approach to slowing global warming. The bill would fund research and development of new technologies to curb carbon emissions that the United States could then apply at home and sell to developing countries.

"Our bill would improve the provisions in existing law that promote voluntary reductions in greenhouse gas emissions," Murkowski said. "Our emphasis remains on encouraging voluntary action and not creating new regulatory burdens." [30]

Environmental advocates say that voluntary efforts alone will do little to reduce the threat of global warming. "We've had voluntary programs on climate change since George Bush, and none of them has done anything to stem the growth in pollution levels," says Wetstone of the NRDC. "Not only are we not reducing them, the growth has continued to accelerate. The record is quite clear that we need to do more than just a voluntary program to reduce pollution, particularly from the electric utility and transportation sectors."

Recognizing that congressional support for the Kyoto Protocol is unlikely anytime soon, some Democrats and moderate Republicans support another alternative approach to combating global warming. Sens. Chafee, chairman of the Environment and Public Works Committee, Joseph I. Lieberman, D-Conn., and Connie Mack, R-Fla., last fall introduced a bill that would encourage companies to voluntarily reduce carbon emissions in return for credit against any future

reduction requirements levied on U.S. industries. "I believe that climate change presents a serious threat," Chafee said. "I believe it makes sense to curb greenhouse gas emissions now. And, as many leading American companies do, I believe that there are sensible, fair and voluntary methods to get on the right track." [31]

Wetstone says tougher steps are needed. "This bill is not the solution to the global warming problem," he says. "It's another voluntary program.

Secretary of State Madeleine K. Albright pledged an all-out diplomatic effort to persuade developing countries to join the international global-warming treaty in an Earth Day speech last year at the Smithsonian Institution.

Reuters/Larry Downing

It doesn't hurt, but it is not going to get us started in dealing with the problem."

Combating Sprawl

Since the late 1940s, suburban housing developments and strip malls have eaten up more than 40 million acres of rural land. But last November's elections indicated that Americans want government to stop urban sprawl. Voters approved about

170 of the 240 initiatives on state and local ballots to preserve open space. [32]

Vice President Gore is trying to tap into voters' apparent frustration with the traffic congestion and visual pollution that have accompanied urban sprawl. In January, he announced a $10 billion administration plan to protect open space, improve water quality and clean up brownfields and other polluted sites.

Gore's "livability agenda" figures prominently in his speeches as he gears up for the coming presidential election campaign. "Many Americans today are reaching for a new prosperity defined not just by the quantity of their bank accounts, but also by the quality of their lives," he said. "They want smart growth that produces prosperity while protecting a high quality of life." [33]

Federal policies, chiefly spending for highway construction, have contributed to urban sprawl, but most land-use decisions are typically made at the state and local levels. In the past few years, governors in Maryland, New Jersey and other states have advanced "smart growth" programs that encourage more high-density development in existing communities and bar new construction in many rural areas.

"For 50 years, Americans have acted as if moving out is moving up," said Gov. Parris N. Glendening, D-Md., whose land-use initiative became law in 1997 and has become a model for similar smart-growth measures in a number of other states. "In the process, we have taken our natural resources for granted. We have paid too little attention to what happens to agricultural communities when farms are fragmented by development. Or what happens to forests, and the wildlife that lives in them, when they're destroyed by roads or malls.

"Across this nation, we have let too many of our great and historic cities and towns collapse. This has been done, in part, through an indifference to urban needs that has fueled the great flight to the suburbs." [34]

Gore has taken up the call for "smart growth" and on March 8 proposed a number of initiatives to help commuters cope with traffic congestion. These include a tax break of up to $240 a month for carpooling, biking or taking mass transit to work and the creation of a universal telephone number commuters could call to get current traffic information. [35]

Gore is betting that voters will support a more prominent federal role limiting sprawl. But critics say he is heading in the wrong direction. "If we want to create incentives for cities to move in a certain direction, that's one thing," says Clapp. "But I have some hesitancy about any sort of federal regulatory involvement. The federal government can assist cities much more by providing funds for mass transit and protection of open space. But fundamentally, the movement to reverse sprawl is going to have to come from the local level because there will never be a uniform solution to the problem." ∎

OUTLOOK

Cost-Benefit Approach

For the past three decades, environmental policy-making has been neatly compartmentalized, for the most part. Congress set broad goals, the EPA wrote regulations to achieve those goals and states developed specific plans to bring them to fruition. Now, at the same time that ecological problems are becoming more complex, the various governmental roles are changing.

At no time has this trend been more apparent than in the May 14 decision by the U.S. Court of Appeals panel in Washington to reverse the EPA's new rules on ozone and particulate matter. The 2-1 ruling appeared also to challenge the agency's authority to write environmental regulations, which has been upheld by legal decisions over the past three decades. [36]

Whether the Senate decides eventually to ratify the Kyoto Protocol or not, efforts to curb global warming are forcing congressional lawmakers to consider the international implications of environmental policy. At the same time, growing public dissatisfaction with urban sprawl is drawing their attention to an area that has traditionally been the purview of state and local governments.

Some experts say the approach to environmental protection embodied in existing law must change to effectively address the changing nature of environmental threats. "The current system was designed to deal with large, obvious, point-source problems, and it's been effective, though at a very high cost," says Davies of the Center for Risk Management. "A lot of the current approaches are based on impacts on the immediate vicinity of a source and are almost entirely based on a medium-by-medium approach — that is, air, water or land. We need to adopt a more integrated approach that addresses threats to all three."

The business community and its allies on Capitol Hill would like to see a more voluntary, less regulatory approach to dealing with evolving environmental issues. Sens. Carl Levin, D-Mich., and Fred Thompson, R-Tenn., have introduced legislation that would require agencies to perform a cost-benefit analysis when issuing rules that cost $100 million or more to implement. "We all want an effective government that protects public health, well-being and the environment," Thompson told the Senate on March 25. "We want our government to achieve those goals in the most sensible and efficient way possible. We want to do the best we can with what we have and to do more good at less cost if possible. The Regulatory Improvement Act will help us do just that."

Some environmental experts predict that this view will prevent a significant expansion of environmental legislation in the 106th Congress. "I think the legislative outlook is going to be pretty barren," says Portney of Resources for the Future. "Particularly as we move into an election year, I really don't see very much at all." ∎

Notes

[1] For background, see Mary H. Cooper, "Environmental Justice," *The CQ Researcher*, June 19, 1998, pp. 529-552.

[2] H. Sterling Burnett, "Green Growth: Five Principles for a Better Environment," National Center for Policy Analysis, www.ncpa.org.

[3] See Mary Alice Davis, "What Bush Is Saying — and Not Saying," *The Austin American-Statesman*, April 30, 1999.

[4] The Gallup Poll was conducted April 13-14, 1999.

[5] Quoted in Rob Taylor, "Gorton in the Saddle for Debate on Contentious Environment Riders," *Seattle Post-Intelligencer*, Sept. 8, 1998. See also Art Pine, "Environmental Riders Survive Spending Battle in Washington," *Los Angeles Times* [Washington Edition], Oct. 20, 1998.

[6] For background, see Mary H. Cooper, "Global Warming Update," *The CQ Researcher*, Nov. 1, 1996, pp. 961-984.

[7] For background, see U.S. Department of Energy, *Impacts of the Kyoto Protocol on*

U.S. Energy Markets and Economic Activity (1998).

[8] For background, see Mary H. Cooper, "The Politics of Energy," *The CQ Researcher*, March 5, 1999, pp. 185-208.

[9] Yellen testified March 25, 1999, before the Senate Energy and Natural Resources Committee.

[10] A minority of scientists continue to challenge the existence of global warming linked to fossil-fuel use. A prominent dissident is Patrick J. Michaels, a professor at the University of Virginia and editor of *World Climate Report*, a newsletter.

[11] Murkowski addressed the Senate on April 27, 1999.

[12] Quoted in Charles Babington, "Environmentalists Criticize Gore," *The Washington Post*, April 14, 1999.

[13] Statistics provided on the Chamber's Web site, www.uschamber.org.

[14] See John H. Cushman Jr., "Clinton Pushes Environmental Power-Sharing," *The New York Times*, Jan. 31, 1999.

[15] Posted at www.uschamber.org.

[16] Sierra Club survey conducted by Lake Snell Perry & Associates, April 8-11, 1999.

[17] For background, see Mary H. Cooper, "Environmental Movement at 25," *The CQ Researcher*, March 31, 1995, pp. 273-296.

[18] See Larry Parker and John Blodgett, "Air Quality: EPA's Proposed Ozone Transport Rule, OTAG, and Section 126 Petitions — A Hazy Situation?" CRS Report for Congress, May 14, 1998.

[19] Joby Warrick and Bill McAllister, "New Air Pollution Limits Blocked," *The Washington Post*, May 15, 1999.

[20] U.S. General Accounting Office, "Water Quality: Federal Role in Addressing — and Contributing to — Nonpoint Source Pollution," February 1999.

[21] "House Votes to Set Standards for Quality of Coastal Waters," *CQ Weekly*, April 24, 1999, p. 968.

[22] See Joby Warrick, "New Arsenic Limits Proposed for Water," *The Washington Post*, March 24, 1999.

[23] See Charles Pope, "House Breaks Logjam on Flood Control Measure, Drops Doolittle's Diversion Plan," *CQ Weekly*, May 1, 1999, p. 1034.

[24] American Rivers released its most recent list, "America's Most Endangered Rivers," on April 12, 1999.

[25] From a statement, Oct. 7, 1998.

[26] From a statement dated April 26, 1999.

[27] For background, see Mary H. Cooper, "National Forests," *The CQ Researcher*, Oct. 16, 1998, pp. 905-928.

[28] From a Senate Energy and Natural Resources Committee press release, Jan. 22, 1998.

[29] See Carroll J. Doherty, "Congress Compiles a Modest Record in a Session Sidetracked by Scandal," *CQ Weekly*, Nov. 14, 1998, pp. 3090-3091.

[30] Murkowski addressed the Senate May 3, 1999.

[31] Chafee addressed the National Association of Manufacturers (NAM) in Washington on Dec. 3, 1998.

[32] *National Geographic* "Earth Almanac," May 1999.

[33] Gore spoke on May 4, 1999, in Detroit. See Terry M. Neal, "Gore Seeks to Tap Voter Concern on 'Livability' Issues," *The Washington Post*, May 5, 1999.

[34] Glendening spoke on Dec. 1, 1998, before a meeting of the American Association of State Highway and Transportation Officials and the Environmental Council of the States Conference on Smart Growth.

[35] See Charles Pope, "Suburban Sprawl and Government Turf," *CQ Weekly*, March 13, 1999, pp. 586-590.

[36] Warrick and McAllister, *op. cit.*

FOR MORE INFORMATION

Environmental Protection Agency, 1200 Pennsylvania Ave. N.W., Washington, D.C. 20460; (202) 260-2090; www.epa.gov. The EPA administers federal environmental policies, researches environmental issues and sets regulations .

Natural Resources Defense Council, 1200 New York Ave. N.W., #400, Washington, D.C. 20005-4709; (202) 289-6868; www.nrdc.org. The non-profit NRDC, staffed by lawyers and scientists, conducts research and undertakes litigation on a broad range of environmental issues and supports a strong federal role in environmental policy-making.

Resources for the Future, 1616 P St. N.W., Washington, D.C. 20036; (202) 328-5000; www.rff.org. This environmental research organization examines the benefits and costs of all aspects of environmental policy and provides information to the public.

U.S. Chamber of Commerce, 1615 H St. N.W., Washington, D.C. 20062-2000; (202) 659-6000; www.uschamber.org. The federation of businesses, trade and professional associations is a leading critic of federal regulatory policies, including those involving environmental protection.

Bibliography

Selected Sources Used

Books

Brower, Michael, and Warren Leon, *The Consumer's Guide to Effective Environmental Choices: Practical Advice from the Union of Concerned Scientists,* **Three Rivers Press, 1999.**

The authors advise ecologically concerned consumers to concentrate on driving less and eating less red meat and stop worrying about choosing paper bags over plastic at the grocery store, shunning disposable dishes and diapers or wearing only natural fibers.

Easterbrook, Gregg, *A Moment on the Earth: The Coming of Age of Environmental Optimism,* **Penguin Books, 1995.**

This highly controversial book, published 25 years into the environmental movement, argues that nature is far more resilient than activists and lawmakers thought when they passed the landmark environmental protection legislation of the 1970s.

Gelbspan, Ross, *The Heat Is On: The High Stakes Battle over Earth's Threatened Climate,* **Addison-Wesley, 1997.**

Global warming is becoming so evident, the author writes, that further delay in curbing greenhouse gas emissions poses a major threat to life on Earth.

Hertsgaard, Mark, *Earth Odyssey: Around the World in Search of Our Environmental Future,* **Broadway, 1999.**

The author says that rapid industrialization in developing countries like China poses a threat to the environment. But technological advances are also producing keys to future improvements to environmental quality.

Articles

Avery, Dennis T., "Global Warming — Boon for Mankind?" *American Outlook,* **spring 1998, pp. 12-16.**

The author presents the contrarian view that global warming may actually improve the environment by opening vast regions, now too cold or arid to cultivate, to large-scale agriculture.

Flavin, Christopher, "Last Tango in Buenos Aires," *World Watch,* **November/December 1998, pp. 10-18.**

Hopes that the world was ready to reduce carbon emissions held responsible for global warming have stalled as key provisions of the 1997 Kyoto Protocol have provided loopholes for governments to evade the treaty's targets and timetables, Flavin writes.

Graham, Mary, "Environmental Protection & the States: 'Race to the Bottom' or 'Race to the Bottom Line'?" *The Brookings Review,* **winter 1998, pp. 22-25.**

After 30 years of environmental regulation, states no longer routinely minimize environmental protection to attract businesses, as voters tend to support state or local efforts to clean up or conserve land, Graham writes.

Portney, Paul R., "Counting the Cost: The Growing Role of Economics in Environmental Decisionmaking," *Environment Magazine,* **March 1998.**

Legislative proposals to subject environmental and health regulations to cost-benefit analysis have yet to become law, but they stand a better chance of enactment today as further improvements to environmental quality are growing in cost, Portney writes.

Rifkin, Jeremy, "The Biotech Century: Playing Ecological Roulette with Mother Nature's Design," *E Magazine,* **May/June 1998, pp. 36-41.**

Alteration of food sources with recombinant DNA and other biotechnology innovations poses an uncertain but potentially dangerous threat to the environment and to public health, Rifkin writes.

Reports and Studies

Holt, Mark, "Transportation of Spent Nuclear Fuel," *CRS Report for Congress,* **Congressional Research Service, May 29, 1998.**

A key issue in the debate over proposals for storing nuclear waste from commercial power plants involves the public-health risk posed by transporting this lethal material over great distances.

U.S. General Accounting Office, "Water Quality: Federal Role in Addressing — and Contributing to — Nonpoint Source Pollution," February 1999.

Water pollution from factories and sewage treatment plants has been effectively reduced as a result of controls imposed under the 1972 Clean Water Act. Further improvements will require new efforts to control "nonpoint" runoff from farms, city storm sewers and suburban lawns.

2 Environmental Justice

MARY H. COOPER

An impoverished area of southern Louisiana has become the latest battleground in the struggle for civil rights. Only this time the goal is not desegregation or affirmative action but the right to a clean environment.

The controversy in rural St. James Parish focuses on 3,000 acres of sugar cane and a $700 million plastics plant planned by a Japanese manufacturer. The fight pits Shintech Inc. and a cadre of local supporters against environmental activists and other residents who want no part of it.

"This is our *Brown v. Board of Education*, our line in the dirt," says Robert D. Bullard, executive director of the Environmental Justice Resource Center at Clark Atlanta University. "This community is already overburdened with toxic plants."

Indeed, the parish lies along a stretch of the Mississippi River between Baton Rouge and New Orleans that is so heavily industrialized it's known as "cancer alley." More than 120 chemical plants line the 120-mile river corridor, many of which have spewed thousands of tons of dioxin and other carcinogens into the air, water and soil for decades. The parish itself is already home to 11 fertilizer and chemical plants.

Bullard and other activists argue that it is no accident that so many toxic polluters have zeroed in on the region. Throughout the country, they say, poor and minority communities are disproportionately exposed to noxious industry byproducts. Siting the Shintech plant in St. James Parish, they contend, would amount to yet another instance of environmental racism, another ex-

ample of a poor community not benefiting from the nationwide improvements in environmental quality over the past three decades.

Since Bullard helped lead the call for environmental justice in the early 1980s, the movement has won high-level support. In 1994, President Clinton issued an executive order directing all federal agencies with a public health or environmental mission to make environmental justice an integral part of their policies and activities. "All communities and persons across this nation should live in a safe and healthful environment," the president's order declared. [1]

Since then, 19 federal departments, agencies and executive branch offices, from the Environmental Protection Agency (EPA) to the Federal Highway Administration, have been required to ensure that their policies do not have a disparate impact on poor and minority communities.

In February, EPA Administrator Carol M. Browner lent an even stronger endorsement to the environmental justice argument by issuing "interim guidance," or guidelines, for processing a rash of claims of environmental injustice, based on the 1964 Civil Rights Act. Title VI of the act, the country's basic civil rights law, prohibits discrimination based on race, color or national origin in

programs or activities that are supported by federal funds.

Among the agencies covered by the law are state environmental commissions, which issue permits to factories and other potential polluters. According to regulations issued under Title VI, an agency violates the law if its policies or activities have a discriminatory effect, even if there was no intent to discriminate. An agency found guilty of such civil rights violations would face the loss of federal funds and be required to implement costly mitigation programs.

When Shintech proposed building the plant in St. James Parish, residents opposed to the move, together with Bullard, the Tulane University Environmental Law Clinic, Greenpeace and other environmental justice advocates lodged a formal complaint against the project. Although the state Department of Environmental Quality had already cleared Shintech to begin construction, last September Browner ordered the agency to rescind one of the project's permits and launched an investigation into charges that the choice of the site amounted to environmental racism.

Shintech joins a growing list of companies whose expansion plans have run afoul of the environmental justice movement in recent years. Since the first lawsuit of this type was filed in 1979 against a waste-dump operator in Houston, activists have turned increasingly to the courts on behalf of poor and minority communities seeking protection from pollution. [2]

Although environmental justice advocates have successfully lobbied companies to change their siting plans in a number of U.S. communities, they finally won their first legal victory in April. A Nuclear Regulatory Commission (NRC) hearing board rejected

From *The CQ Researcher*, June 19, 1998.

plans to build a uranium-enrichment plant in a poor, minority community in northwestern Louisiana (*see p. 30*).

Residents of Sierra Blanca, Texas, are fighting a plan, recently approved by Congress, that would allow Vermont, Maine and Texas to dump their low-level nuclear waste at a facility to be built near their largely Hispanic community. And the EPA has agreed to study a claim of environmental racism brought by the Coeur d'Alene Indians in Idaho, who have asked the agency to designate a 1,500-square-mile area polluted by decades-old mine tailings as a vast Superfund site.

Another case has made it to the U.S. Supreme Court. Residents of Chester, Pa., a majority-black town in overwhelmingly white Delaware County, went to court to block construction of a waste facility in their community. Because there are already five such facilities in the town, and only two in the rest of the county, residents charged the decision to build yet another dump in their midst amounted to environmental racism. The court announced June 8 that it would decide whether activists can bring suits in federal court alleging environmental racism. The state claims such charges can only be filed with the EPA.

But Shintech has become what the company's controller, Richard Mason, calls the "poster child" of the environmental justice movement. He rejects the claims of environmental racism made against his company. "We did not choose that site because there were African-Americans there,"

he says. "We chose it because there was nobody there."

Not only is the planned location a mile and a half from the nearest residential areas, Mason says, but the company's other U.S. plant, in Freeport, Texas, has a good environmental record. "In the 24 years we have produced polyvinyl chloride (PVC) resin at the Texas plant, we have had three or four incidents, in

Residents of Chester, Pa., went to court to block construction of a waste facility in their community. The Supreme Court agreed on June 8 to decide whether the activists can bring suit in federal court alleging environmental racism.

which no one was injured and no remediation was required."

Shintech has promised to provide jobs and training, including opportunities for management positions, to local residents. "We've worked very hard to get to know the people there and understand their concerns," he says. "And a lot of those concerns are economic in nature."

Indeed, not all local residents are opposed to Shintech's plan. The St. James and Louisiana chapters of the National Association for the Advancement of Colored People (NAACP) are vocal supporters of the new plant, which they hope will bring jobs and

economic development to a region that suffers 12 percent unemployment and where 44 percent of residents live in poverty. [3] "Poverty has been the No. 1 crippler of poor people, not chemical plants," Ernest L. Johnson, president of the Louisiana State Conference NAACP, said in a statement. "Also, the present mortality rate for African-Americans in St. James is less than the Louisiana state rate, despite the 11 previously existing petrochemical plants in the area." Johnson says an NAACP survey shows broad local support for the new plant. "Unequivocally, the residents of the 'affected community' want Shintech!"

But environmental justice advocates say jobs and other investments are inadequate tradeoffs for the health risks, noxious odors and sheer ugliness that many industrial and waste facilities impose on poor communities. "Citizens want control of their environment rather than money," says Robert Knox, acting director of EPA's Office of Environmental Justice. "The time is past when companies could come in and pay for new school buses or other amenities in exchange for locating in poor, minority communities. Everyone understands about environmental pollution now, and they are not going to accept that any more."

The Shintech case and the shift in policy that gave rise to it have created a growing backlash against the environmental justice movement. In March the Environmental Council of the States (ECOS), made up of the top appointed environmental regulators from the states, denounced the EPA's interim guidelines, claiming they were vague, detrimental to economic development and poorly devised because the state commissioners, who are EPA's partners in administering federal environmental laws, had no say in the guidelines. Furthermore, the state commissioners say the policy undermines the democratic process.

"Most decisions to locate industrial facilities are not made by bureaucrats but by locally elected officials," says ECOS member Russell J. Harding, director of the Michigan Department of Environmental Quality. "That is absolutely the way these decisions should be made in an elected democracy. The EPA guidance turns the process upside down by calling for us — the regulators who are unaccountable to local voters — to make those decisions. This is not right."

As this latest chapter in the struggle for civil rights unfolds, these are some of the questions being asked:

Do poor and minority populations suffer disproportionately from exposure to toxic materials?

"Poor and minority communities are where you find children with lead poisoning living near polluting industries, garbage dumps, incinerators, petrochemical plants, freeways and highways — all the stuff that other communities reject," says Bullard of the Environmental Justice Resource Center. "And the fact that the problem has existed for so many years seems to be still a matter of denial for a lot of people."

Statistics seem to confirm Bullard's view. A widely cited study of U.S. Census data by the NAACP and the United Church of Christ Commission for Racial Justice found that people of color were 47 percent more likely than whites to live near a commercial hazardous-waste facility. The study also found that the percentage of minorities was three times higher in areas with high concentrations of

Children play in a park across from a Shell Oil refinery in Norco, La.

such facilities than in areas without them. Moreover, the study suggested that minorities' exposure to environmental toxins was getting worse. [4]

The EPA found similar disparities in exposure to toxins depending on income and race. Ninety percent of the nation's 2 million farmworkers, the agency estimates, are people of color, including Chicanos, Puerto Ricans, Caribbean blacks and African-Americans. Of these, more than 300,000 are thought to suffer from pesticide-related illnesses each year. Even air pollution affects minorities disproportionately, according to EPA. The 437 counties and independent cities that failed to meet air-quality standards in

1990, for example, are home to 80 percent of the nation's Hispanics and 65 percent of African-Americans but just 57 percent of all whites. [5]

Some critics of the environmental justice movement say the stunning improvements in environmental quality brought by 30 years of anti-pollution legislation benefit everyone in the United States. They also claim that the remaining environmental threats do not necessarily impact poor or non-white Americans more than anyone else.

"Since toxic air emissions, pesticide runoffs and groundwater contamination cannot neatly select their victims by race or income, the inequities visited upon minorities afflict a great many others as well," writes Christopher H. Foreman Jr., a senior fellow at the Brookings Institution. "Indeed, the range of arguably significant environmental-equity comparisons is so broad that some doubtless cut the other way: Many Native Americans, for example, breathe cleaner air than urban Yuppies and live further from hazardous waste than New Jersey's white ethnics." [6]

Activists reject this reasoning out of hand. "Sure, everyone is exposed to some level of toxins," says the EPA's Knox, "but exposure is disproportionate in poor and minority communities. He points to a black neighborhood in Gainesville, Ga., that accounts for just 20 percent of the town's population but handles 80 percent of its waste. The predominantly black town of Chester, Pa.,

An Indian Leader Speaks Out for the Land . . .

Most instances of environmental racism that come to public attention involve black or Hispanic communities trying to keep polluting factories, sewage plants or toxic-waste dumps out of their communities. But an older and much less visible struggle is being fought by remote Indian tribes that are trying to clean up water supplies contaminated by mine tailings. Since the mid-19th century, miners and mining company executives have scoured the West for gold, silver and other minerals. They have left behind vast deposits of waste rock, or tailings, containing toxic materials. Cyanide and other chemicals used to separate some ores from rock also are left behind, usually in holding ponds. Over the years, rainwater carries these pollutants into streams and rivers, where they can be carried for miles, killing fish and contaminating drinking water.

Native Americans' pleas for environmental protection were ignored for decades, but now Indians are gaining a voice in the environmental justice movement. In what could turn out to be the most sweeping federal cleanup of pollution from mining activities ever undertaken, the Environmental Protection Agency (EPA) in February agreed to study the feasibility of designating the entire Coeur d'Alene River basin in Idaho as a Superfund site. The decision came largely as a result of the efforts of Henry SiJohn, environmental leader of the 1,600-member Coeur d'Alene tribe, whose reservation lies along the southern banks of Lake Coeur d'Alene. Staff writer Mary Cooper interviewed SiJohn by phone from his home in Plummer, Idaho.

How long has pollution in the Coeur d'Alene River basin been a problem?

In the 1920s and '30s, we noticed that the water potatoes, which grow along the lake, began to have a strange, metallic taste. We used to drink water from the lake, but we haven't since then.

How did government authorities react to your complaints about the water pollution?

The situation was different then because we were Indians, and everything was done by the superintendents of the Bureau of Indian Affairs. They had charge of us on our reservation. They said we didn't have any voice, that we couldn't buck the state or the federal government. They wouldn't do anything for us.

Do you think minority communities like yours are exposed to more pollution than white Americans?

I'm afraid that's true. It seems we have embedded an undercurrent of racism here in America. The Indian people have been for the longest time put into a situation whereby they were considered people who were unfamiliar with things. They couldn't participate in politics until 1924, when Congress allowed American Indians to have the vote. But even that didn't help for a long time because we

accounts for 11 percent of Delaware County's population but has 70 percent of the county's waste facilities. "That's clearly disproportionate," Knox says. "And it's not atypical for the country as a whole."

Some business representatives reject the notion that factory owners even look for communities of any kind to site their facilities. They say that when petrochemical companies flocked to southern Louisiana early in the century, for example, they were drawn primarily by the fact that such a long segment of the Mississippi River was deep enough to enable oceangoing barges to transport large shipments of raw materials and finished products.

"No one lived near the Baton Rouge Exxon refinery, the oldest in Louisiana, when it was built in the early 1900s," says Dan S. Borné, president of the Louisiana Chemical Association in Baton Rouge. "It and other chemical plants were built in agricultural areas, and communities literally grew toward them because that's where the jobs were. What's inferred in this debate — that people of color are targeted for chemical plants simply because they're people of color — is repugnant and ridiculous."

Does President Clinton's 1994 executive order provide sufficient guarantees of environmental justice?

When President Clinton issued his 1994 environmental justice executive order, more than 10 years had passed since the first complaints of environ-

mental racism gained public attention. In November 1992, in response to growing pressure to address the concerns of communities exposed to toxins, President George Bush created the Office of Environmental Equity within EPA to study the problem.

But it was not until Clinton's 1994 policy statement that the goal of environmental justice gained formal recognition at the federal level. "[E]ach federal agency shall make achieving environmental justice part of its mission by identifying and addressing, as appropriate, disproportionately high and adverse human health or environmental effects of its programs, policies and activities on minority populations and low-income populations," Clinton declared.

The agencies were not only re-

... An Interview with Idaho's Henry SiJohn

had to establish our tribal government as an entity in itself and prove to people we knew what we were doing. Then we had to do assessment screenings to determine the pollution in the river basin.

Is the government responding adequately to your requests now?

I wish the EPA would protect the environment, especially of Indian people, through the enforcement arm of their agency. I feel they have been neglectful of punishing people that are the perpetrators of this pollution. If the Indians were the polluters, the public would have gotten up in arms and demanded that the Indians pay. However, this isn't the case. And the federal government has not protected the Indian people or the environment to the point where they enforce the law.

Has President Clinton's support of environmental justice affected your dealings with EPA?

By good fortune, I feel optimistic, in that someone is getting to the president of the United States with this issue. I have a lot of faith in Vice President Al Gore and his staff. I feel they truly have the interests of the environment at heart. But they can't move without the Congress of the United States. Congress is for corporate America, and corporate America is the segment of society that has dug this hole for us, and I don't know if we can escape.

Has the environmental justice movement helped your cause?

Environmental justice advocates are trying to help, but they don't have any idea how to go about it. I feel they and the Clinton administration could do more if they would only take a stand and tell the perpetrators they're the guilty ones.

Industry is polluting the rivers of America. People need to understand the Indian philosophy of the cycle of life. Fish have to spawn, and the spawning beds have to be protected, so they can complete the cycle of life. Because people don't understand this, they jeopardize the species to the point where they're endangered, and then we have this big to-do with the Endangered Species Act. So we have a political response rather than a natural response. Things would be different if people let animals complete the cycle of life.

Do you think EPA will accept your request to clean up the Coeur d'Alene River basin?

I'm very optimistic. If America doesn't wake up and take hold of things, it's going to put us all in jeopardy. People need to realize they can't survive without the environment. That's where the Indian philosophical view comes in. It perpetuates the purity of the environment. Without the natural resources of fish, animals, birds and the like we can't live. We will starve.

quired to correct existing problems but also had to take steps to prevent environmental injustice from occurring in the first place. Clinton gave each federal agency a year to develop and submit its strategy for achieving environmental justice and another year to report on progress in implementing the strategy.

Even though the new policy directive does not change laws currently in force, environmental justice advocates say it strengthens both the 1964 Civil Rights Act and the 1969 National Environmental Policy Act, which calls for environmental information to be made available to citizens. "We have two important pieces of legislation on the books which, if used in tandem, can be very potent weapons against environmental racism," says

Bullard, pointing to several instances in which plans to build polluting facilities in communities of color were rejected after Clinton issued his executive order.

"These decisions make a lot of states nervous because they haven't really enforced equal protection when it comes to permitting," he says. "They could even lose transportation dollars because environmental justice is not just incinerators and landfills. It's also construction of highways, which have definite impacts on low-income communities and communities of color."

According to Knox of the EPA, the president's executive order has already changed the way states are dealing with the issue. At least three states — Louisiana, Maryland and Oregon

— have passed executive orders on environmental justice that mirror the president's policy in order to pre-empt possible complaints of environmental racism and the loss of federal funds for highway building and other state operations. "They did this as a result of the executive order," Knox says. "They want to look at problem areas in the states so they can get ahead of the problem and make recommendations to their governors."

But some civil rights activists fear the policy may tip the scales in favor of those who want to keep industry out of poor areas at all costs, even when vital job opportunities are at stake. "In light of the executive order, environmental justice requires balancing economic benefit with environmental risks," writes Johnson of the Louisiana NAACP. "It is critical that we not succumb to outside pressure by those who have otherwise failed to promote their ideologies and now use the 'environmental race card' for their own agendas."

Does the focus on environmental justice distract attention from bigger health problems in poor and minority communities?

Some observers suggest that by single-mindedly opposing industrial development in poor communities, environmental justice activists may be hurting the very people they purport to represent. "It's very common to meet people in St. James, both black and white, who say their great-great-grandfather lived here," says Mason of Shintech. "They also say they want to continue living here with their families but that there are no job opportunities that will allow them to stay. Because the base of employment there now is the parish government and the existing chemical plants, the only way to find a job is if someone quits, retires or dies."

Not only are poverty and joblessness more serious problems for most minority communities than pollution, critics say, but so are a whole range of health and social ills. "Hypertension, obesity, low birthweights, inadequate prenatal care, substance abuse and violence are only some of the forces that arguably deserve pride of place in the struggle to improve the lives

and health of communities of color," writes Foreman of Brookings. "That such forces are more intractable and harder to mobilize around than a Superfund site or a proposed landfill must not deter communities from asking . . . hard questions about overall health priorities." [7]

Activists say it's false logic to draw distinctions between their quest for environmental equity and these other goals of poor, minority communities.

Riverbank State Park was built on top of the North River Sewage Treatment Plant in West Harlem, N.Y.

"Environmental justice is also about health," Bullard says. "The No. 1 reason why children in these communities are hospitalized is not because of drive-by shootings. It's because of asthma." The incidence of respiratory diseases has increased, especially among children and the elderly, in areas of high concentrations of ozone and particulate matter, notably urban neighborhoods close to major roadways. [8]

Bullard also points to lead poisoning as an environmental threat to health in minority communities. "The No. 1 threat to kids is lead poisoning,

and this, too, is an environmental justice issue because African-American children are three to five times more likely to be poisoned by lead than are low-income white children," he says. "That's the direct result of residential segregation, so housing is another environmental justice issue."

Even crime and illiteracy can be traced to environmental racism, in Bullard's view. "There is a direct correlation between lead poisoning and learning disabilities, aggressive behavior and kids dropping out of school," he says. "So if you look at the root of many of the problems facing minority communities, both physical and environmental, you'll see they are all about health. It's no longer just a matter of a chemical plant."

Knox of the EPA agrees that environmental pollution has far-reaching effects on the quality of life in poor and minority neighborhoods. "Some people say the fight against crime should take precedence over other issues in these neighborhoods," he says. "But environmental problems only exacerbate such problems as crime and asthma in minority communities. Just because a community is poor doesn't mean the people there should not breathe clean air, drink clean water and be able to eat fruit from their gardens. You would not expect to find the same environmental quality in South Central Los Angeles that you find in Beverly Hills, but that doesn't mean that the people in South Central L.A. should not have clean air, clean water and clean soil." ∎

BACKGROUND

Plight of the Poor

The poor have always suffered the health effects of inferior living conditions. Even before the Industrial Revolution unleashed the toxic byproducts of the manufacturing process in Europe and North America, serfs, slaves and farm laborers often lived amid farm animals in crowded, drafty hovels under unsanitary conditions that took a disproportionately heavy toll in the form of infant mortality and premature death among adults.

Industrialization added numerous new environmental threats to health and well-being that were borne overwhelmingly by the poor. As factories sprang up along the railroads and rivers in the center of towns and cities, wealthy families moved out of range of the smoke and foul odors they emitted. Lacking transportation or the money to move away from the industrial centers, poor factory workers had little choice but to live close to their places of work. Where factories sprang up in rural areas along rivers and other transportation corridors, new communities of workers and job-seekers grew up around them.

In the United States, race compounded poverty as a factor in determining exposure to industrial toxins. Beginning in the 1950s, when many black farmworkers moved to cities in the East and Midwest in search of better-paying jobs, they were drawn to downtown neighborhoods where housing was affordable and close to work. Hispanic immigrants also gravitated to low-cost, inner-city neighborhoods where manufacturing jobs could be found, or to farming communities in remote agricultural areas of the West — frequent sites of toxic-waste dumps and pesticide contamination.

Native Americans were exposed to inordinate levels of toxic waste by virtue of another historical phenomenon — the relegation of Indians to remote reservations, many of which were later found to harbor vast deposits of uranium, gold, silver and other minerals. Mine tailings exposed many tribes to toxic runoff that contaminated their water supplies.

Birth of a Movement

The environmental plight of poor and minority communities was not an immediate priority of the modern environmental movement, which took shape in the late 1960s. [9] The first Earth Day, held April 22, 1970, marked the start of a national campaign whose main legislative victories were the 1970 Clean Air Act, the 1972 Clean Water Act, the 1973 Endangered Species Act and the 1980 Superfund legislation (the Comprehensive Environmental Response, Compensation and Liability Act).

These basic environmental laws focused on reducing the sources of pollution but basically ignored the varying impact of pollution on different income or racial groups. The first official acknowledgement that poor, non-white Americans were disproportionately impacted by environmental degradation was a statement in the Council on Environmental Quality's 1971 annual report that racial discrimination adversely affects the urban poor and the quality of their environment. [10]

That discrete communities could be disparately affected by environmental degradation became clear in 1978, when 900 families living in the Love Canal neighborhood of Niagara Falls, N.Y., discovered that their homes had been built near 20,000 tons of toxic waste. Initially rebuffed in their calls for reparations, residents demanded, and eventually won, relocation benefits. Their struggle also helped galvanize public support for federal legislation to clean up hazardous waste — the 1980 Superfund law.

Race and income were not the main issues at Love Canal. Working-class and mostly white, the neighborhood nonetheless served as a model for communities trying to ward off environmental threats. The first largely minority community to take up the challenge was in Warren County, N.C., where residents in 1982 demonstrated against a state plan to dump 6,000 truckloads of soil laden with polychlorinated biphenyls (PCBs), a highly toxic compound similar to dioxin. More than 500 protesters were arrested, calling national attention to the issue. Although the landfill was completed as planned, the protesters won agreement from the state that no more landfills would be put in their county, the state's poorest. [11]

A series of reports on environmental threats to poor and minority communities followed the Warren County protest, helping galvanize the nascent movement for environmental justice. The General Accounting Office found in a 1983 study that three of four hazardous-waste facilities in the Southeast were in African-American communities. In 1987, the United Church of Christ issued a widely cited study showing that landfills, incinerators and other waste facilities were found disproportionately in or near poor or minority communities across the country. [12]

In 1990, Bullard published the first of his four books on the subject. Like most other early works on environmental justice, *Dumping In Dixie* focused on toxic wastes and their close association with black communities in the Southeast. Bullard also called attention to the fact that black Americans are far more likely to be exposed to lead than whites, and that Hispanics are more likely to live in areas with high soot pollution. In his efforts to help impacted communities, Bullard was joined by Benjamin Chavis Jr., former executive director of the NAACP, other civil rights groups as well as mainstream environmental organizations such as Greenpeace and the Sierra Club, whose Earthjustice Legal Defense Fund works with poor communities.

The Bush administration recognized the environmental justice movement's growing clout in 1990, when then-EPA Administrator William K. Reilly established the Environmental Equity Workgroup to study the issue. Two years later, the movement gained permanent federal status with the creation of EPA's Office of Environmental Equity.

Office of Environmental Justice.

"Many people of color, low-income and Native-American communities have raised concerns that they suffer a disproportionate burden of health consequences due to the siting of industrial plants and waste dumps, and from exposure to pesticides or other toxic chemicals at home and on the job, and that environmental programs do not ad-

Residents claim that Fort Lauderdale's Wingate Incinerator, now contaminated and a Superfund cleanup site, spewed ash and soot for over 25 years on the mostly African-American Bass Dillard neighborhood.

equately address these disproportionate exposures," she said shortly after taking office.

"EPA is committed to addressing these concerns and is assuming a leadership role in environmental justice to enhance environmental quality for all residents of the United States. Incorporating environmental justice into everyday agency activities and decisions will be a major undertaking. Fundamental reform will be needed in agency operations." [13]

On Sept. 30, 1993, Browner established the National Environmental Justice Advisory Council (NEJAC), a 23-member group of representatives of environmental organizations, state and local agencies, communities,

tribes, businesses and other interested parties to increase public awareness of the issue and help EPA develop strategies to ensure environmental equity. By rotating membership in NEJAC (pronounced "knee-jack," or "knee-jerk" by its critics) every three years, the agency is trying to involve as many interested parties as possible in the ongoing policy debate.

President Clinton elevated environmental justice to yet a higher plane with Executive Order 12898, which required each federal agency involved in public health or environmental matters to "make achieving environmental justice part of its mission," particularly as minority and low-income populations were affected. The order also directed Browner to create and chair an interagency working group on environmental justice to coordinate federal policies aimed at furthering environmental equity. ∎

CURRENT SITUATION

Recent Cases

The cause of environmental justice has been advanced on several fronts since President Clinton's 1994 executive order. Activists cite three cases that they say set legal prece-

Clinton's Policies

President Clinton took office in January 1993 promising to restore federal environmental protections that he said had eroded during the previous 12 years of Republican administrations. His newly appointed EPA administrator, Browner, declared that environmental justice would be a priority for the agency and renamed the Office of Environmental Equity the

Chronology

1960s Job opportunities draw black workers to cities in the industrial East and Midwest and Hispanic farmworkers to agricultural areas of the West.

1964
Congress enacts the Civil Rights Act, establishing the country's basic law to protect the rights of minority groups. Title VI of the law prohibits discrimination based on race, color or national origin under programs or activities supported by federal funds.

1969
The National Environmental Policy Act calls for information on pollutants to be made public.

— • —

1970s The environmental movement produces major laws to curb pollution.

April 22, 1970
The first Earth Day marks the start of a national campaign to improve environmental protection, starting with the Clean Air Act, passed the same year.

1971
The Council on Environmental Quality acknowledges that racial discrimination adversely affects the urban poor and the quality of their environment.

1972
Congress passes the Clean Water Act, requiring reductions in polluting runoff into the nation's waterways.

1978
Residents of the Love Canal neighborhood of Niagara Falls, N.Y., discover that their homes sit atop a toxic-waste dump. They demand, and eventually win, relocation benefits, establishing a model for later action by poor, minority communities.

1979
The first lawsuit claiming environmental racism is filed against a waste-dump operator on behalf of a poor community in Houston.

— • —

1980s Environmental justice movement takes off.

1980
The Comprehensive Environmental Response, Compensation and Liability Act creates the Superfund to pay for the identification and cleanup of severely polluted sites.

October 1982
More than 500 protesters are arrested after trying to block a landfill being created for soil laced with polychlorinated biphenyls (PCBs) in Warren County, N.C., the poorest county in the state. The landfill project goes ahead, but the state agrees to build no more landfills there.

1983
The General Accounting Office finds that three of four hazardous-waste facilities in the Southeast are in black communities.

1987
The United Church of Christ issues a study showing that landfills, incinerators and other waste facilities are sited disproportionately in or near poor or minority communities.

— • —

1990s Environmental justice gains federal support.

November 1992
President George Bush creates the Office of Environmental Equity within the Environmental Protection Agency (EPA).

1993
Newly appointed EPA Administrator Carol M. Browner renames the Office of Environmental Equity the Office of Environmental Justice and promises to promote environmental protection for all Americans.

Feb. 11, 1994
President Clinton issues Executive Order 12898 directing all federal agencies with a public health or environmental mission to make environmental justice an integral part of their policies.

Sept. 10, 1997
The EPA delays permission for Shintech Inc. to build a new plastics plant in St. James Parish, La., a highly industrialized, largely African-American area.

Feb. 5, 1998
Browner issues "interim guidance" to provide a framework for processing claims of environmental injustice, based on Title VI of the Civil Rights Act.

June 8, 1998
The U.S. Supreme Court agrees to decide whether lawsuits alleging environmental racism can be brought in federal court.

Fighting for Environmental Justice . . .

The ongoing controversy over plans by Shintech Inc. to open a new plastics plant in St. James Parish, La., is among the most visible environmental justice cases. The following are some of the other notable battles being waged around of the country:

Sierra Blanca, Texas — Residents of this West Texas community, located in the 10th poorest county in the nation, fought construction of a low-level nuclear-waste facility outside the town. The facility would be the final repository for radioactive wastes from hospitals and research facilities in Texas, Maine and Vermont. Opponents complained that Sierra Blanca already is home to a large sewage sludge dump and said its selection as a dumping ground for nuclear waste amounted to environmental racism against the area's predominantly Hispanic population. Residents called on Congress to reject the three-state compact authorizing the facility. (See "At Issue," p. 35.) They lost their battle April 1, when the Senate approved the House-passed plan after adding amendments requiring an environmental review of the proposed site and barring other states from dumping radioactive wastes there as well.

Brunswick, Ga. — Contamination from lead, mercury, polychlorinated biphenyls (PCBs) and other toxins around an inactive LCP Chemicals-Georgia Inc. plant led to a $40-million, EPA-directed cleanup of this industrial area several years ago. Afterwards, the agency led a detailed area study, called the Brunswick Initiative, which failed to turn up other pollution threats to neighboring communities. But an environmental justice group called Save the People rejected the study's findings. The group and many residents of a mostly black community adjacent to another chemical plant, owned by Hercules Inc., claim that their yards are contaminated by toxaphene, an insecticide that Hercules manufactured until it was banned two decades ago.

Oak Ridge, Tenn. — Residents of the predominantly black neighborhood of Scarboro attribute a range of diseases in their community to the nearby Department of Energy (DOE) Y-12 nuclear weapons plant. The federal Centers for Disease Control and Prevention is investigating a possible link between the plant and respiratory illnesses in Scarboro. The DOE has offered to pay for health assessments but has not yet taken responsibility for any illnesses reported, some of which are the subject of pending litigation.

Houston, Texas — Three decades ago, the Kennedy Heights neighborhood was built over abandoned oil pits once owned by Gulf Oil. Today residents of this African-American community claim that leakage of oil sludge into their water supply is responsible for at least 60 cases of serious diseases found there, such as cancer and lupus, as well as hundreds of other lesser health complaints. In a lawsuit brought against Chevron, which bought out Gulf Oil, plaintiffs claim a corporate document slating the contaminated site for "Negro residential and commercial development" proves that environmental racism is at the root of their medical problems. Chevron denies that the incidence of disease in Kennedy Heights is high enough to prove a link with oil contamination. [1]

Huntington Park, Calif. — After four years of community opposition, the operator of a concrete recycling plant was forced to close it. Similarly, black and Hispanic residents of South East Los Angeles are organizing to get rid of the growing number of recycling facilities in their part of the city. Glass-recycling ventures spew ground glass into the air, residents say, aggravating asthma and other respiratory diseases and killing trees. Metal crushers at car- and appliance-recycling plants cause walls of neighboring houses to crack and release tiny fragments of oil and metal that contaminate the soil. [2]

Pensacola, Fla. — The Escambia Treating Co. ran a wood-treating facility here for 40 years, depositing highly toxic dioxin into the soil and prompting a $4 million Superfund cleanup of the site. Residents of the primarily low-income, black neighborhood adjacent to the site objected to the cleanup, saying it exposed them to an even greater health threat by bringing toxins to the surface. A local activist group, Citizens Against Toxic Exposure,

dents that will help reduce the incidence of environmental racism.

In northwest Louisiana in May 1997, a citizens' group blocked plans by a German-owned firm, Louisiana Energy Services, to build the first private uranium-enrichment plant in the United States. After nearly seven years of opposition, Citizens Against Nuclear Trash persuaded the Nuclear Regulatory Commission (NRC) to deny the company the required license based on evidence that race had played a part in site selection.

"The communities around that site are 97 percent black," says Bullard, who drafted a social and economic analysis of the area for the NRC. "The company didn't consider the fact that these people live off the land as subsistence hunters, fishermen and farmers whose water comes from wells.

... From New Jersey to California

convinced the Environmental Protection Agency (EPA) to test the soil and, as the results proved compelling, pay for the relocation of all 358 households around the site, which is expected to cost $18 million. [3]

Newark, N.J. — A section of the city's East End, known as Ironbound, lies in one of the most polluted areas of the country. It is home to a garbage incinerator that serves all of Essex County and a sewage-treatment plant serving 33 municipalities and 1.5 million people. The area also contains the now-closed Diamond Alkali plant, which once produced Agent Orange, the defoliant used in the Vietnam War. The area is thought to have among the highest concentrations of dioxin in the world. When Wheelabrator Technologies tried to build a $63 million sewage sludge treatment facility there, Ironbound's residents claimed that the placement of yet another waste plant in their community, home to many poor Portuguese immigrants, blacks and Hispanics, would constitute environmental racism. The Ironbound Committee Against Toxic Waste persuaded the state Department of Environmental Protection to deny the plant's final permits. [4]

Anniston, Ala. — In the low-lying industrial and residential neighborhood of Sweet Water, production of toxic PCBs had been going on since the 1930s. In 1996, the Alabama Department of Public Health declared Sweet Water and the adjacent community of Cobb Town a public health hazard. Monsanto stopped producing PCBs at the facility in 1971, eight years before EPA banned the chemical, a known carcinogen in laboratory animals. The company also began buying out residents and relocating them, even before agreeing with the state to do so and clean up the polluted areas. But

Responding to public health concerns in a black neighborhood in Anniston, Ala., Monsanto has begun buying out residents and relocating them.

the Sweet Valley-Cobb Town Environmental Justice Task Force charges Monsanto with environmental racism against the black communities by knowingly releasing PCBs from the plant after the environmental threat became apparent in the late 1960s. About 1,000 residents have sued the company.

Coeur d'Alene, Idaho — Silver mining came to the pristine area around Lake Coeur d'Alene in the 1880s. By the 1920s, members of the Coeur d'Alene Indian tribe began noticing that the water and root vegetables had taken on a metallic taste. Ignored by the mining companies and governmental officials for decades, the 1,600-member tribe finally convinced the EPA in February to consider declaring the entire Coeur d'Alene River basin a Superfund site. If the agency adds the site to its list — which is strongly opposed by local businesses in this recreational area — it will become the largest federal cleanup ever undertaken, covering an area of 1,500 square miles including the Idaho Panhandle and part of western Washington, where mine tailings have also polluted the Spokane River. [5] *(See story, p. 24.)*

[1] See Sam Howe Verhovek, "Racial Tensions in Suit Slowing Drive for 'Environmental Justice,'" *The New York Times,* Sept. 7, 1997.

[2] See David Bacon, "Recycling — Not So Green to Its Neighbors," posted on EcoJustice's Web page, www.igc.org, July 28, 1997.

[3] See Joel S. Hirschhorn, "Two Superfund Environmental Justice Case Studies," posted on Ecojustice's Web page, *op. cit.*

[4] See Ronald Smothers, "Ironbound Draws Its Line at the Dump," *The New York Times,* March 29, 1997.

[5] See Michael Satchell, "Taking Back the Land That Once Was So Pure," *U.S. News & World Report,* May 4, 1998, pp. 61-63.

(vertical caption at right of image) Environmental Justice Resource Center

That plant would have been slam-dunk, in-your-face racism."

The company appealed the ruling, but a three-judge NRC panel rejected the appeal. Not only was there evidence that racial discrimination had played a role in the siting process, the judges ruled, but also that the

NRC staff had failed to consider the plant's environmental and social impact on the surrounding community, as required by the executive order as well as by the 1969 National Environmental Policy Act.

"This was the first environmental justice case that we actually won

in court outright," Bullard says. It was also the first time a federal agency had used President Clinton's executive order to deny a license or permit.

In Flint, Mich., last year, environmental justice activists succeeded in delaying the issuance of a permit for a power plant sited in a mostly black neighborhood. The case began after the Michigan Department of Environmental Quality issued a permit to Genesee County to build a cogeneration electric power plant fueled in part by wood scraps from building construction and demolition, which might have been contaminated with lead-based paint. The permit allowed lead emissions from the plant of 2.4 tons a year. The Flint chapter of the NAACP and other plaintiffs sued the department, charging that the surrounding community was already overburdened by lead contamination and that by issuing the permit the state had violated its mandate to protect the health of all citizens.

In response, the department reduced the allowable level of lead emissions, but the plaintiffs proceeded with the suit, charging the department with practicing racial discrimination in issuing the permit in the first place. According to Director Harding, the department agreed to comply with additional demands but refused to settle the case because the plaintiffs would not drop their charges of racial discrimination.

Both sides claimed a victory of sorts from the judgment, handed down on May 29, 1997, by Circuit Judge Archie Hayman. Plaintiffs won an injunction against future permits, pending the state's performance of risk assessments to be paid for by applicants and the holding of broader public hearings when applications for toxic facilities are made. They also won recognition that compliance with

air-quality standards under the Clean Air Act does not necessarily mean that a community is not adversely affected by air pollution.

For its part, the state claimed vindication on the racial discrimination charges. "The judge said there was no racial discrimination," Harding says. "In fact, he complimented my agency, saying our overall environmental regulatory system

The Southwest Network for Environmental and Economic Justice staged a protest in Phoenix, Ariz., in 1995.

was sufficiently protective, though he directed the agency to do more initial determinations of environmental impact."

In Chester, Pa., residents complained that their predominantly African-American city had become the main waste dump for all of largely white Delaware County. In 1996, after the Pennsylvania Department of Environmental Protection issued a permit to Soil Remediation Services Inc. to build yet another waste facility in the city, Chester Residents Concerned for Quality Living sued the agency for racial discrimination in its permitting process.

Their suit, *Chester Residents Concerned for Quality Living v. Seif,* was the first filed against a state agency

under Title VI of the 1964 Civil Rights Act, which prohibits agencies that receive federal funds from practicing racial discrimination, either deliberately or by effecting "policies or practices [that] cause a discriminatory effect."

On Nov. 6, 1996, U.S. District Judge Stewart Dalzell dismissed the suit for technical reasons. On Dec. 30, 1997, however, the 3rd Circuit Court overturned the lower court, allowing the citizens' group's suit to proceed. The ruling also set an important legal precedent by enabling a low-income and minority community to pursue a charge of environmental racism regardless of whether the discrimination was deliberate. The Supreme Court has agreed to hear the case, addressing the question of whether lawsuits alleging environmental racism can be brought in federal court.

Pressure on EPA

The Circuit Court's ruling in the Chester case did not, however, elaborate on the question of evidence needed to mount a successful environmental justice suit against a state agency. [14] With the proliferation of charges of environmental racism in the 1990s, the EPA has come under increasing pressure to clarify the procedures for dealing with such cases. According to Knox of EPA's Office of Environmental Justice, the agency has received 49 complaints based on Title VI alone, about 20 of which are now under investigation. "EPA had to respond to a backlog of complaints," he says. "The agency had to do something to respond to this, so we issued guidelines to help identify who could bring claims and what constitutes a disparate impact on a community."

The backlogged complaints include the one in Louisiana brought against Shintech, which proposed in September 1997 to build a state-of-the-art plant to produce PVC, used to make a range of consumer products, such as plumbing pipes and shrink-wrap food wrapping. On May 23, 1997, the Louisiana Department of Environmental Quality issued three air permits for the facility. But on Sept. 10, in response to a citizens' petition, EPA Administrator Browner took the agency's first formal action on the environmental justice issue.

She canceled one of the firm's permits and directed the state agency to take environmental justice into greater consideration when reissuing the permit. In addition, she ordered further investigation of charges that the choice of St. James Parish for the plant site amounted to environmental racism. "It is essential the minority and low-income communities not be disproportionately subjected to environmental hazards," Browner wrote in her decision. [15]

The Shintech case is also the test case for the EPA's interim guidance, or guidelines. Browner issued the guidance on Feb. 5, 1998, in the wake of the Chester ruling, seeking to clarify the conditions under which a decision to issue a permit violates

Title VI. The guidance describes a five-step process by which EPA must identify the affected population, primarily on the basis of proximity to the site in question, determine the race or ethnicity of the affected population and decide whether the permitted activity will impose an "undue burden" on the community. The agency will then identify any other

Residents of Wagner's Point, a working-class enclave in South Baltimore, link the abnormally high cancer rates in their neighborhood to emissions from a nearby wastewater treatment plant, an oil refinery and other industrial sites.

S.C. Delaney/Environmental Protection Agency

permitted facilities in the vicinity that may compound the community's environmental threat.

If EPA determines that the community is impacted at a "disparate rate," the permit recipient may mitigate the environmental impact by offering other benefits to the community. Shintech, for example, has promised to spend about $500,000 for job training and small-business development in St. James Parish.

State environmental officials quickly identified what they saw as numerous flaws in the EPA's guidance, however, and asked the agency to rescind the guidance and draft a new policy together with the states. Fourteen state attorneys general and the U.S. Chamber of Commerce endorsed the environmental officials' request. "We believe the guidance is vague," says Robert E. Roberts, executive director of ECOS. "It speaks of mitigating or justifying 'disparate impacts' but doesn't make clear what such an impact is. So for those of us who have to carry out the policy, it's very difficult to know what the policy is."

Knox defends the guidance language and suggests that the state environmental officials are mainly concerned because they were left out of the drafting process. "The states are upset because they thought they should be sitting at the table," he says. "We think the guidance should work out pretty well."

Roberts says the state officials' exclusion is more than a matter of pique. "The fact that the states weren't included is important," he says, "because the state environmental departments will be making decisions that will be the basis for any environmental justice complaints that arise. Because we weren't involved in helping to craft the approach to this issue, chances are we won't do it the way EPA wants it done. At some point, we're bound to make decisions improperly because we don't know what their perspective is."

Since ECOS voiced its objections to

the new guidance, EPA has set up a special committee responsible for implementing Title VI, which also includes several state environmental officials.

Aid for 'Brownfields'

The EPA's latest attempt to promote environmental justice may prove to be a double-edged sword. For while the interim guidance is intended to make it easier for minority and low-income communities to protect themselves from environmental threats to their health, it may also weaken economic development in these communities by discouraging companies from building new, non-polluting facilities in their midst that could provide needed employment. EPA has led an effort to convert abandoned commercial and industrial sites into productive use.

Many of these so-called "brownfield" sites scare off investors, fearful of being held liable for potential lawsuits by users of the site. While the sites are polluted, they are not polluted enough to qualify for federally funded cleanup under the Superfund program. On Jan. 25, 1995, EPA launched a program to encourage investors to build non-polluting businesses on brownfield sites, which tend to be in urban areas in or near poor or minority communities. By the end of fiscal 1997, EPA had awarded $200,000 seed-money grants to 121 brownfield restoration projects. [16]

"A lot of brownfields are in environmental justice communities," says Knox of EPA. "These communities see brownfields as providing an opportunity to get involved in the siting process and address problems in the city, an opportunity for jobs and a chance to reverse the fiscal deterioration that has drained resources from their neighborhoods. Most of all, brownfields allow communities to get their vision involved in development because they have a seat at the table."

In Knox's view, furthering environmental justice goes hand in hand with brownfield development. "The interim guidance actually helps," he

Residents of this African-American neighborhood built on top of the Agriculture Street Landfill in New Orleans are petitioning the EPA to relocate them from the area, now a Superfund site. Activists call this the "black Love Canal."

Environmental Justice Resource Center

says. "By ensuring that environmental justice has to be considered in the permitting process and bringing affected communities to the table, we are educating residents so they can take over their own communities and bring in clean industries."

But state environmental officials predict the new guidance will be a killer for brownfield development. "The guidance enables anyone with a typewriter to stop a permit from being issued," says Harding, Michigan's environmental commissioner. "We're not opposed to environmental justice, but the guidance goes against getting brownfields going, especially in places like Detroit." Hit by widespread plant closings in the 1970s and '80s, Detroit and other Midwestern cities have many lightly polluted sites that qualify for brownfield development.

"Under the interim guidance, anybody who files an objection in an urban area can show a disparate impact," he says. "It makes it easy to make that showing and turns permitting into a nebulous process that can drag on for years."

Business representatives agree. "We're not saying there aren't concerns that need to be dealt with," says Borné of the Louisiana Chemical Association. "We are saying that with this interim guidance EPA is forever changing the landscape of development in this country. And you can forget about brownfield development because most brown-field sites are in minority communities."

OUTLOOK

Impact on Business

Industry representatives predict that EPA's policy to promote environmental justice will harm more than just brownfield development. Mason says that charging Shintech with environmental racism sends a message to industry that may not be what the activists intended.

At Issue:

Would constructing a low-level radioactive nuclear-waste dump near Sierra Blanca, Texas, constitute "environmental injustice"?

BILL ADDINGTON

Rancher, farmer and merchant, Hudspeth County, Texas

FROM TESTIMONY BEFORE THE HOUSE COMMERCE SUBCOMMITTEE ON ENERGY AND POWER, MAY 13, 1997.

i speak today on behalf of Save Sierra Blanca, our citizens group, and many people in West Texas who feel run over by the state and federal governments. These people are opposed to the forced placement of this risky radioactive-waste cemetery at Sierra Blanca near the Rio Grande River. . . .

Most of the people in Hudspeth County and Sierra Blanca are poor — the median annual income is $8,000. Seventy percent of the people are of Hispanic origin, like myself. This is the reason Texas "leaders" have focused on our county for the dump site since 1983. This appeared to be the political path of least resistance. But there is strong resistance locally, regionally and internationally. There are about 3,000 people and 1,300 registered voters in the county, and every one of them who was asked signed the petition against the dump. . . .

The siting of the Sierra Blanca dump by the state legislature was a violation of environmental justice and our civil rights. . . .

If the radioactive-waste dump is approved in Sierra Blanca, it is likely that additional radioactive and hazardous facilities will follow. Westinghouse Scientific Ecology Group has entered into an option agreement to lease 1,280 acres of land adjoining the proposed Sierra Blanca site for radioactive waste processing and storage, possibly including incineration. There is also a proposal for an additional sludge dump in the community. This concentrating of hazardous facilities in communities is a characteristic of environmental injustice.

The proposed radioactive dump site is geologically fatally flawed. It is in an earthquake zone, and there is a buried fault underneath the proposed trenches. . . .

The real reason for the compact is economic — to make it cheaper for nuclear power generators to bury their waste and shift their liability. It does not "protect Texas," as has been touted. . . .

Texas began negotiations with . . . Maine in 1988, and in 1992 passed the compact. Maine's and Vermont's legislatures have approved the compact. They failed to develop their own waste sites because of heavy opposition. Maine voters approved the compact by referendum, yet people in my home are not even heard or considered. We do not get to vote on the measure or placement of the dump like Mainers, who chose to dump on us, did.

SEN. OLYMPIA J. SNOWE, R-MAINE

FROM A SENATE FLOOR SPEECH, APRIL 1, 1998.

a s the law requires, Texas, Vermont and Maine have negotiated an agreement that was approved by each state. . . . So, we have before us a compact that has been carefully crafted and thoroughly examined by the state governments and people of all three states involved. Now all that is required is the approval of Congress, so that the state of Texas and the other Texas Compact members will be able to exercise appropriate control over the waste that will come into the Texas facility. . . .

Opponents of the Texas Compact would have you believe that should we ratify this compact it will open the doors for other states to dump nuclear waste at a site, in the desert, located five miles from the town of Sierra Blanca, exposing a predominantly low-income, minority community to health and environmental threats.

The truth is that Texas has been planning to build a facility for its own waste since 1981, long before Maine first proposed a compact with Texas. That is because whether or not this compact passes, Texas still must somehow take care of the waste it produces. . . .

The opponents of the compact would have you believe this issue is about politics. It is not about politics, it is about science: sound science. It is very dry in the Southwest Texas area, where the small amount of rainfall it receives mostly evaporates before it hits the ground. The aquifer that supplies water to the area and to nearby Mexico is over 600 feet below the desert floor and is encased in rock.

The proposed site has been designed to withstand any earthquake equaling the most severe that has ever occurred in Texas history. Strong seismic activity in the area is non-existent. All these factors mean that the siting of this facility is on strong scientific grounds.

Our opponents say we will be bad neighbors if we pass this compact because the proposed site is near the Mexican border. In fact, the U.S. and Mexico have an agreement, the La Paz Agreement, to cooperate in the environmental protection of the border region. The La Paz Agreement simply encourages cooperative efforts to protect the environment of the region.

Any proposed facility will be protective of the environment because it will be constructed in accordance with the strictest U.S. environmental safeguards.

FOR MORE INFORMATION

Center for Health, Environment and Justice, P.O. Box 6806, Falls Church, Va. 22040; (703) 237-2249, www.chej.org. The center helps community-based groups fend off environmental hazards. It was founded by a former resident of Love Canal, N.Y., the community built near a toxic-waste dump.

Earthjustice Legal Defense Fund, 180 Montgomery St., Suite 1400, San Francisco, Calif. 94014; (800) 584-6460; www.earthjustice.org. Formerly known as the Sierra Club Legal Defense Fund, this nonprofit law firm is active in cases involving environmental justice.

Environmental Justice Resource Center, Clark Atlanta University, 223 James P. Brawley Dr. S.W., Atlanta, Ga. 30314; (404) 880-6911. www.ejrc.cau.edu. Directed by Robert D. Bullard, a longtime environmental justice leader, the center helps communities protect themselves from pollution sources.

Environmental Council of the States, 444 N. Capitol St. N.W., Suite 445, Washington, D.C. 20001; (202) 624-3660; www.sso.org/ecos/. A membership group representing environmental officials of the states and the District of Columbia, ECOS opposes the EPA's new rules for handling environmental justice complaints.

Greenpeace, 702 H. St. N.W., Washington, D.C. 20001; (800) 326-0959; www.greenpeace.org. This research and activist group has recently become involved in several cases involving complaints of environmental racism.

Office of Environmental Justice, U.S. Environmental Protection Agency, 401 M St. S.W., Washington, D.C. 20460; (202) 564-2515 or (800) 962-6215; es.epa.gov/environsense/oeca/oej.html. The OEJ coordinates EPA activities and provides technical assistance to communities threatened by environmental hazards.

"The message is, 'You're stupid if you try to move into a community with a significant number of African-Americans, or any other racial minority,' " Mason says. "We don't want to be in a community that doesn't want us there. But this policy will deprive many people of economic opportunity, and it's bad news for economic development in general."

Some critics predict that the EPA's policy is such a deterrent to industrial development and job creation that many companies will shift production overseas.

"In the long run, this is the best economic-development program for Mexico that's ever come down the pike," Borné says. "If EPA really wants to chase our industry over the border, then this is a first-class ticket. I already see how detrimental this policy is to economic development in my state."

EPA is still investigating the Shintech case. However it is resolved, supporters of the environmental justice movement are optimistic that more aggressive steps to combat environmental racism will pay off, not only for poor and non-white Americans but also in the development of cleaner manufacturing and waste technologies.

"The movement has moved beyond the siting of facilities," Bullard says. "It's bigger than that. It embraces the full question of prevention, health and employment. We're now asking if we really need more chemicals entering the waste stream, as opposed to changing production processes to protect health and the environment. A company that produces waste is a wasteful company. So it makes sense to reduce waste so we won't need as many facilities to dispose of this stuff."

Knox agrees with Bullard's assessment and argues that the struggle for environmental justice need not be adversarial because it will benefit everyone. "If this is to be the greatest industrial society of all time, industry has to be clean," he says. "But we all have to work together to make that happen. There's a role for everybody, including business and communities. We all have to sit at the table."

Bullard says pressure from low-income and minority communities that have lodged environmental racism complaints has already spurred manufacturers to develop and adopt cleaner production processes and products, including soy-based ink for newspapers, recycled paper for packaging and pesticide-free fruits and vegetables.

"But I think the biggest impact of the environmental justice movement has not come yet," Bullard says. "That is consumers who are selective and educated about what they will buy and what they won't buy. Creating educated consumers who will start punishing companies that hurt the environment and rewarding those that adopt environmentally sound business practices will be the last civil rights battle." ∎

Notes

[1] Executive Order 12898, "Federal Actions to Address Environmental Justice in Minority Populations and Low-Income Populations," Feb. 11, 1994. For background, see "Cleaning Up Hazardous Wastes," *The CQ Researcher*, Aug. 23, 1996, pp. 752-776.

[2] In *Bean v. Southwestern Waste Management*, residents of a predominantly black subdivision in Houston charged that Browning-Ferris Industries had practiced environmental discrimination by choosing their community to site a municipal solid-waste landfill. They lost the case.

[3] For background, see "Jobs vs. Environment," *The CQ Researcher*, May 15, 1992, pp. 409-432.

[4] Benjamin A. Goldman and Laura Fitton, *Toxic Wastes and Race Revisited,* Center for Policy Alternatives, National Association for the Advancement of Colored People and United Church of Christ Commission for Racial Justice, 1994.

[5] U.S. Environmental Protection Agency, Office of Environmental Justice, *Serving a Diverse Society,* November 1997. For background, see "New Air Quality Standards," *The CQ Researcher*, March 7, 1997, pp. 193-217.

[6] Christopher H. Foreman Jr., "A Winning Hand? The Uncertain Future of Environmental Justice," *The Brookings Review*, spring 1996, p. 24. Foreman's new book, *The Promise and Peril of Environmental Justice,* is due to be published by the Brookings Institution in the fall.

[7] *Ibid.*, p. 25.

[8] See American Lung Association, "Health Effects of Outdoor Air Pollution," 1996.

[9] For background, see "Environmental Movement at 25," *The CQ Researcher*, March 31, 1995, pp. 283-307.

[10] See Environmental Protection Agency, Office of Environmental Justice, *Environmental Justice 1994 Annual Report: Focusing on Environmental Protection for All People,* April 1995.

[11] See Robert D. Bullard, *Unequal Protection* (1994), pp. 43-52.

[12] General Accounting Office, *Siting of Hazardous Waste Landfills and Their Correlation with Racial and Economic Status of Surrounding Communities* (1983); United Church of Christ Commission for Racial Justice, *Toxic Wastes and Race in the United States* (1987).

[13] Quoted in EPA, *Environmental Justice 1994 Annual Report, op. cit.,* p. 3.

[14] See Andrew S. Levine, Jonathan E. Rinde and Kenneth J. Warren, "In Response to Chester Residents, EPA Releases Environmental Justice Rules," *The Legal Intelligencer*, Feb. 18, 1998.

[15] See Paul Hoverten, "EPA Puts Plant on Hold in Racism Case," *USA Today*, Sept. 11, 1998.

[16] See "New EPA Report Lists Positive Effects of Agency Superfund Reform Efforts," *Hazardous Waste News*, Feb. 16, 1998.

Bibliography

Selected Sources Used

Books

Bullard, Robert D., *Dumping in Dixie: Race, Class and Environmental Quality,* Harper Collins, 1996.

A leading activist in the environmental justice movement examines the enforcement of environmental-protection laws in the Southern United States, where poor, mostly black communities are commonly chosen as sites for waste dumps and incinerators.

Bullard, Robert D., ed., *Unequal Protection: Environmental Justice and Communities of Color,* Sierra Club Books, 1994.

This collection of essays describes how communities of poor and non-white Americans are disproportionately exposed to toxic wastes and other environmental hazards.

Szasz, Andrew, *EcoPopulism: Toxic Waste and the Movement for Environmental Justice,* University of Minnesota Press, 1994.

The author describes the environmental justice movement's evolution from grass-roots activism to federal policy. By focusing on pollution prevention rather than cleaning up polluted sites, the movement is changing the focus of environmental policy.

Articles

Arrandale, Tom, "Regulation and Racism," *Governing,* March 1998, p. 63.

The Environmental Protection Agency's decision to overturn a state-issued permit to build a plastics plant near a poor, minority community in Louisiana last fall does not further the goal of environmental justice, the author writes, because it will discourage industry from bringing jobs to the very communities that are hardest hit by unemployment.

Hampson, Fen Osler, and Judith Reppy, "Environmental Change and Social Justice," *Environment,* April 1997, pp. 12-20.

The authors apply the tenets of environmental justice to global environmental issues, including global warming. Developed nations, which have contributed the most to this problem, should help devise solutions that reduce economic inequality between rich and developing nations, the authors contend.

Northridge, Mary E., and Peggy M. Shepard, "Comment: Environmental Racism and Public Health," *American Journal of Public Health,* May 1997, pp. 730-732.

The authors call for further study of the disparate impact of environmental hazards on poor, non-white communities and a broad public health initiative, similar in scope to the anti-smoking campaign, to prevent and remove toxins from these communities.

Parris, Thomas M., "Spinning the Web of Environmental Justice," *Environment,* May 1997, pp. 44-45.

This collection of Internet addresses provides a wealth of sources, including Environmental Protection Agency (EPA) reports and non-governmental studies, on efforts to combat pollution that affects poor and minority communities.

Sachs, Aaron, "Upholding Human Rights and Environmental Justice," *The Humanist,* March-April 1996, pp. 5-8.

The author reviews the international movement for environmental justice that took off after the 1988 murder of Chico Mendes, a Brazilian rubber tapper who fought for the rights of rain forest inhabitants against cattle barons who were clearing the forests for grazing land.

Schoeplfle, Mark, "Due Process and Dialogue: Consulting with Native Americans under the National Environmental Policy Act," *Common Ground,* summer/fall 1997, pp. 40-45.

The 1969 National Environmental Policy Act provides standards for informing Indian tribes of environmental hazards and taking steps to protect themselves from pollutants.

Reports and Studies

Goldman, Benjamin A., and Laura Fitton, *Toxic Wastes and Race Revisited,* Center for Policy Alternatives, 1994.

This update of a 1987 report on the racial and socioeconomic characteristics of communities with hazardous-waste sites finds that poor and minority communities are even more disproportionately exposed to toxins than before, despite the growth of the environmental justice movement.

National Environmental Justice Advisory Council, *Environmental Justice, Urban Revitalization and Brownfields: The Search for Authentic Signs of Hope,* December 1996.

An EPA advisory committee finds that the development of brownfields — abandoned industrial sites that are not polluted enough to warrant federal cleanup under the Superfund program — is an important contribution to the goal of environmental justice.

U.S. Environmental Protection Agency, Office of Environmental Justice, *Serving a Diverse Society,* November 1997.

This pamphlet summarizes the adverse impact of air pollution, pesticides, agricultural runoff and other environmental hazards on communities of color and suggests steps communities can take to minimize exposure.

3 Saving Open Spaces

MARY H. COOPER

First, a "For Sale" sign crops up in a field or woodland just beyond the new mall outside town. Soon the bulldozers arrive to level the landscape, including most of the trees, and to slash a road through the property. Then new houses erupt from the bare ground, and another sign pops up. "Welcome to Woodland Acres," it announces.

To developers and new residents, new suburban subdivisions embody nothing less than the American Dream, a chance to trade cramped apartments in chaotic, noisy cities for the good life of clean air, quiet surroundings and home ownership.

"Americans want open space in their back yards and beyond," says Neil Gaffney, director of environmental communications for the National Association of Home Builders. "And the best place for that is the suburbs."

But to others, so-called suburban sprawl and its tidy subdivisions are rapidly chewing up one of America's most cherished assets — open space.

"You see residential subdivisions spreading like inkblots, obliterating forests and farms in their relentless march across the landscape," noted Richard Moe, president of the National Trust for Historic Preservation. "You see a lot of activity, but not much life. You see the graveyard of livability." [1]

However the scene is viewed — nightmare or American Dream — it is familiar to communities across the United States. In the East, the megalopolis stretching from Boston to Washington continues to spread, consuming the few remaining tracts of open land. Rapid growth around Phoenix, Ariz., and other cities of the desert Southwest is threatening the region's water supplies. Even picturesque, rural communities in the Rocky

From *The CQ Researcher,* November 5, 1999.

The Nature Conservancy/Harold E. Malde

Mountains are mourning the loss of the open spaces that drew many residents there in the first place. [2]

"Open space is disappearing at an alarming rate," says Russ Shay, director of public policy for the Land Trust Alliance, a Washington-based organization of individuals and groups working to conserve land. "People are concerned about the lands right around their communities, where rapid development is not only destroying landscapes but also contributing to traffic congestion, leaving them hours instead of minutes away from their destinations."

Many Americans seem to agree. Last year, voters approved 168 of the 240 state and local ballot initiatives that provided more than $7.5 billion in new funding for open space preservation. [3] Some of the measures created boundaries that halted development beyond already-developed areas; others raised local taxes to buy land and keep it out of developers' hands.

Concern over disappearing open space is also reflected by the proliferation of land trusts in communities across the country. Typically, these private

conservation groups buy land outright or pay a landowner to refrain from developing it. The best-known trust is the million-member Nature Conservancy, based in Arlington, Va., an international organization that has helped protect more than 58 million acres around the world.

Most land trusts, however, are small, community groups. In the past decade, the number of local and regional trusts has grown more than 150 percent, to some 1,200. During that period, local trusts have permanently protected 2.7 million acres from development. [4]

Although support for environmental-protection laws often pits Democrats against Republicans, land conservation is one of the few issues that defy partisanship. In fact, the Democratic governor of Maryland and New Jersey's Republican chief executive backed two of the most sweeping state open-space initiatives ever proposed. In Maryland, Gov. Parris N. Glendening's "smart growth" initiative has barred much new development outside urban areas. Gov. Christine Todd Whitman of New Jersey has launched an ambitious plan to set aside 1 million acres in her densely developed state. Voters last year approved her plan to spend $1.9 billion on the project.

Although land-use policy has traditionally fallen under state and local government jurisdiction, the Clinton administration is calling for new federal initiatives to bolster the inventory of federally owned open land and to encourage land conservation at the state and local levels as well. In January, President Clinton announced a Lands Legacy initiative, which called for almost $1 billion in federal money to protect open lands as well as battlefields, archaeological sites and historic structures. In late October, however, lawmakers gutted the initiative by providing far less

Most States 'Not Effective' in Protecting Open Spaces

Only 22 states are effective in preventing the loss of open space, according to a recent survey by the Sierra Club. In the most effective states, parks and open space are purchased outright. Moderately effective states generally have passed initiatives to hold lands in trust.

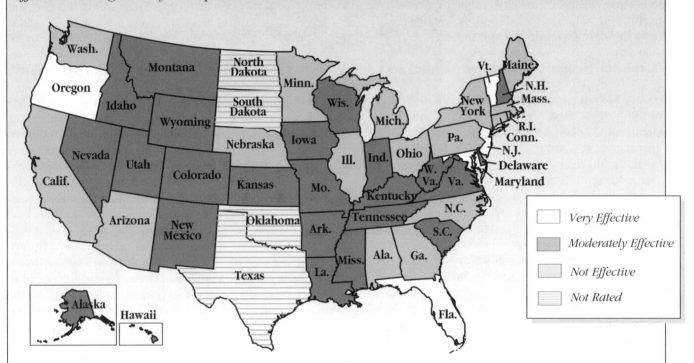

Legend:
- Very Effective
- Moderately Effective
- Not Effective
- Not Rated

Source: "1999 Sierra Club Sprawl Report." The rankings were based on information from the National Governors' Asssociation, private land trusts and Sierra Club grass-roots activists.

funding for land acquisition than the president had requested (*see p. 55*).

Undaunted by congressional reluctance to endorse his open-space initiative, Clinton announced on Oct. 14 one of the most sweeping land conservation proposals in U.S. history, calling for up to 40 million acres of national forest to be protected from development.[5] In addition to direct federal intervention to save open space, the administration would provide greater federal support for local land-conservation efforts. In January, Vice President Al Gore called for $700 million in tax credits to help state and local governments build more "livable" communities.

"Many of the green places and open spaces that need protecting most today are in our own neighborhoods," said Gore in announcing the administration's Livability Agenda. "In too many places, the beauty of local vistas has been degraded by decades of ill-planned and ill-coordinated development. In too many places, people move out to the suburbs to make their lives, only to find they are playing leapfrog with bulldozers."[6]

Critics of federal and state efforts to curb sprawl say they are not only redundant but may backfire as Americans discover that government regulations inhibit their freedom to move where they want.

"We have worked under land-use regulations for decades, so I'm be-

fuddled, to say the least, to hear that Gore or Glendening invented the concept of bettering communities through planning," says John T. "Til" Hazel, a lawyer and leading land developer in fast-growing Fairfax County, Va. "In any case, who is going to decide what land is to be set aside; who has the right to decide what the habits of our society are going to be?"

A number of initiatives to preserve open space are now before Congress. Every year since 1964, Congress has had the authority under the Land and Water Conservation Fund Act to spend up to $900 million a year on open space preservation. But for most of that time there was a deficit in the federal budget, prompting lawmakers to use most of the money for other programs. Now that there is a budget surplus, lawmakers are more willing to use the Land and Water Conservation Fund for its original purpose, and bipartisan proposals requiring full funding of the authorized amount are now before Congress.

"Lawmakers are listening to people's complaints about how long their commutes are and how they don't like to see the spaces they loved as children destroyed," says Helen Hooper, director of congressional affairs at The Nature Conservancy. "They have seen how people are raising their own taxes to save places in their communities and understand they can now get away with spending money on saving land."

Property-rights advocates oppose permanent and full funding of the Land and Water Conservation Fund because they fear it would escalate what they see as a massive land grab by the federal government in which landowners are coerced into selling their property. [7]

"We're not opposed to some acquisition of private land," says Chuck Cushman, executive director of the American Land Rights Association in Battle Ground, Wash. "But these proposals would really mean massive land acquisition, enormous abuses and nothing but trouble for landowners."

Critics of the property-rights argument against expanding public lands respond that taxpayers also have rights — rights to uncluttered landscapes, undisturbed wetlands and intact forests where they can escape the chaos of modern life. "It's easy to focus on property-rights issues," says

Ralph Grossi, president of the American Farmland Trust. "But the flip side of property rights is public rights."

Preserving open space promises to be a leading issue in the upcoming presidential election campaign. Alone among the major contenders, Gore has placed land conservation near the top of his policy agenda. His chief rival for the Democratic nomination, former Sen. Bill Bradley of New Jersey, has limited his comments on the issue to saying the vice president has failed to live up to his promise to protect the environment. For his part, Texas Gov. George W. Bush, the leading Republican contender

The Nature Conservancy's San Pedro River Preserve in Arizona features cottonwood-willow forests, the rarest forest type in North America. The property and surrounding lands support 350 species of migratory and resident birds.

for the presidency, strongly advocates property rights and opposes federal intervention in state and local land-use issues.

As the debate over open space and property rights heats up, these are some of the questions being asked:

Should the federal government spend more money to conserve open space?

Thanks to efforts pioneered by President Theodore Roosevelt and others, the federal government today

owns about 563 million acres, or about a quarter of the 2.3 billion acres that comprise the 50 states. Although almost a third of the federally owned land is in Alaska, the government also owns more than half the land in Idaho, Nevada, Oregon and Utah. [8] Although much of this property is open to cattle grazing, timber cutting and mining, about 104 million acres are designated as wilderness areas, where development and access by motorized vehicles are banned. [9]

As public concern over the loss of open space has mounted in recent years, the Clinton administration has undertaken some of the most sweeping land acquisitions in decades. In September 1996 the president designated 1.9 million acres of public land in southern Utah as the Grand Staircase-Escalante National Monument. In August of this year, the government agreed, pending congressional approval, to buy the 95,000-acre Baca Ranch in New Mexico's Jemez Mountains for $101 million and turn it into a park. The property is home to one of the country's largest elk herds as well as bears, mountain lions and eagles. In September, federal officials completed a $13 million purchase of 12,000 acres of ranchland abutting Yellowstone National Park, also to be preserved as permanent open space. [10]

For fiscal 2000, which began Oct. 1, the president intensified his land-acquisition efforts. He proposed to spend $440 million for land purchases — up from $328 million in fiscal 1999 — as part of his $1 billion Lands Legacy initiative, which lawmakers recently slashed. He also asked Congress to pass a law to ensure that the Land and Water Conservation Fund receive its full annual funding of $900 million, which would be used to protect open space.

Conservationists strongly support increasing spending to augment the federal government's landholdings. "The promise of the Land and Water Conservation Fund has never been fully kept," Interior Secretary Bruce Babbitt said in September. "It was set up to provide almost $1 billion a year through direct federal purchase and through grants to states that could then be used to protect land and open space. But rather than have these funds flow automatically, Congress has required that it appropriate the money every year. Unfortunately, Congress has usually approved less than one-third of the money available." [11]

According to a recent opinion poll, the public supports federal purchase of open space. When asked how the Land and Water Conservation Fund should be used, more than 80 percent of the respondents said the money should go toward expanding existing national parks, forests and recreation areas or creating new ones, rather than reducing the deficit. [12] The concern appears to extend beyond the suburban landscape to include remote areas as well.

Another survey asked, "How would you rather see $2 billion of the surplus spent — to buy and protect wildlands and other natural places or increase military defense spending? Half the respondents picked spending on the environment; 34 percent chose defense spending. [13]

"The best way to ensure that these special places remain special for our children and grandchildren," states a Sierra Club report, "is to acquire the land and hold it in public ownership for public purposes." [14]

Property-rights advocates say that federal acquisition of private land often violates the rights of landowners, who come under pressure to sell their property from heavy-handed government bureaucrats. "Experience has demonstrated that even the most reluctant landowner can be converted into a 'willing seller' by a persistent and determined agency," wrote Stan Leaphart, executive director of the Citizens' Advisory Commission on Federal Areas in Alaska, a state agency in Fairbanks. "We would submit that for each property owner who freely offers their property for sale to a federal land-management agency, there are dozens who are eventually manipulated into a situation where they are left with no real choice but to sell." [15]

Property-rights advocates also predict that federal acquisition of additional land will hurt landowners everywhere. "It's a billion-dollar boondoggle, the ultimate land grab that keeps on grabbing," said Cushman of the American Land Rights Association in a recent e-mail alert. "Do we really want the federal government buying up even more private land and taking it off the tax rolls? The federal government already owns nearly a third of the entire country. The purchase of more land will cause your property taxes to increase on the remaining private lands." [16]

Critics of federal land policy also say the government cannot properly maintain the land it already owns. [17] Rep. Ralph Regula, R-Ohio, chairman of the Interior Appropriations Subcommittee, for example, opposes Clinton's proposal to spend $747 million for new land purchases.

"The president's Lands Legacy initiative flies in the face of my panel's No. 1 priority for the past four years — focusing limited resources on addressing the critical backlog of maintenance problems and operational shortfalls in the national parks, wildlife refuges, national forests and other public lands, which now exceed $12 billion," Regula said. "It is simply irresponsible to take on new land responsibilities and give grants to cities, states and private institutions when we cannot afford to adequately take care of our primary federal responsibilities — the public lands." [18]

Some conservationists agree that more funding should go toward maintenance. "We need to address the crisis in our national park system, which is the real patrimony of our nation," says Paul C. Pritchard, president of the National Park Trust, which raises money to buy private property within or next to federal lands to keep them from being developed. "You can't just say we need more land; we also need more people to manage it. We aren't managing properly the land we have now, but the government doesn't want to address this, and the public is losing out."

But Pritchard also advocates more funding to purchase private land, especially "inholdings" — private property that lies within federally owned land. His organization has identified 200,000 acres of national park inholdings that are in "imminent" danger of being developed or resold and asks Congress to come up with the $70 million the trust estimates it would cost to buy them for the public good. [19]

"We can't save all the valuable parkland," says Pritchard. "The boat will go; we're just trying to keep the lifeboats from sinking by plugging the holes."

Should tax breaks for conservation easements be expanded?

Many advocates of land conservation are wary of federal involvement in conservation efforts that go beyond outright acquisition of land for parks, monuments and other federal holdings. Land-use decisions and zoning issues traditionally have fallen to state and local governments, and

Land Trusts Boomed in Rockies and South

The number of nonprofit state, local and regional trusts more than doubled from 1988 to 1998 in four regions, led by the Rocky Mountain states. New England, which gave birth to the land-conservation movement, still has the largest number of land trusts. Five states with no trusts in 1988 — Arkansas, Hawaii, Mississippi, Nevada and Utah — today each have at least one.

U.S. LAND TRUSTS	1988	1998
Rocky Mountains (Colo., Idaho, Mont., Utah, Wyo.)	20	52
Southwest (Ariz., N.M., Okla., Texas)	15	37
South (Ala., Ark., Fla., Ga., Ky., La., Miss., N.C., S.C., Tenn., Va., W.Va.)	65	142
West (Alaska, Calif., Hawaii, Nev., Ore., Wash.)	83	173
Mid-Atlantic (Del., D.C., Md., N.J., N.Y., Pa.)	117	222
Great Lakes (Ill., Ind., Mich., Ohio, Wis.)	84	145
New England (Conn., Mass., Maine, N.H., R.I., Vt.)	336	417
Plains (Iowa, Kan., Minn., Mo., N.D., S.D., Neb.)	21	23
Total	741	1,211

Photo: Lower Day Mountain, Acadia National Park (Maine Coast Heritage Trust)

Source: Land Trust Alliance, Oct. 1, 1998

some observers fear that federal funding of open-space initiatives opens the door to federal intrusion into local decision-making.

"I believe that fighting sprawl, planning or growth and preserving open space are primarily issues for state and local governments," Rep. Joseph M. Hoeffel, D-Pa., told a congressional committee. "States and municipalities must deal with these issues, develop their own plans and make local decisions about what should be saved." [20]

Federal incentives are another matter, however, especially when they take the form of income tax breaks to encourage conservation. "We need national vision with local control to fight urban and suburban sprawl," Hoeffel said. "I believe it is important for the Congress to establish programs that provide incentives for preservation and conservation goals to be achieved. It is appropriate for the federal tax system to reward those who choose to preserve our natural resources and protect our environment."

The tax code already offers landowners an incentive to conserve land by allowing them to deduct a percentage of the value of their property from their income taxes. Some conservation advocates say the tax code should offer bigger rewards for saving open space.

"There are obviously a variety of causes for this move away from our cities," said Rep. Nancy L. Johnson, R.-Conn. "But I do not believe that our tax code should be one of those causes." [21] Earlier this year, she introduced a measure that would increase the current income tax deduction for land donations from 30 percent to 50 percent of the value of the land and extend the time for taking the deduction from six years to 20 years.

The 1997 Taxpayer Relief Act, the first new tax incentive for land conservation in more than a decade, also allows executors to reduce a landowner's estate tax liability by donating a conservation easement on a property. The easement allows the land to be farmed or logged, but it can never be subdivided for development purposes, even after it changes hands.

In order to qualify for such a tax break, however, the property must be near an urban area or existing parkland.* That provision excludes much of the country, including most of the Midwest. Johnson's bill, as well as a proposal by Sen. Max Baucus, D-Mont., would eliminate the geographic requirements.

"Through some very simple tax measures," Johnson said, "we can give back a little in the form of a tax deduction to those who sacrifice high profits that come from selling their land to those who instead donate for the good of us all."

Some critics say tax incentives to conserve land amount to nothing more than tax breaks for the wealthy,

Colorado Open Lands, a Colorado land trust, purchased the 3,200-acre Evans Ranch, near Denver, to block a 1,100-home residential development. The property now supports five working ranches.

who already benefit from numerous loopholes in the tax code.

"In short, the conservation easement gizmo uniquely satisfies not one but two compelling needs of premillennial Homo Liberalus Americanus," says an editorial in *The*

_____

* The 1997 American Farm and Ranch Protection Act allows the exclusion from taxable estates of 40 percent of the value of open land subject to a qualified conservation easement. The exclusion is capped at $200,000 and applies only to lands within 25 miles of a Metropolitan Statistical Area or a national park or federal wilderness area, or within 10 miles of a National Urban Forest.

Wall Street Journal: "The need to reduce his tax burden and the need to make a show of doing something for the environment."

The editorial cites the extensive use of easements by celebrity landowners on Martha's Vineyard, Mass., and in wealthy enclaves of the West, such as Jackson Hole, Wyo., and Big Sur, Calif. Instead of reducing estate taxes for individuals who donate easements, the editorial proposes, "far better would be simply to repeal the whole tax, which would allow regular families the tax benefits now effectively confined to those with, say, a beachfront mansion or mountain." [22]

Conservation supporters reject the editorial's argument as totally distorted. "We don't deal with a lot of wealthy people, just farmers and ranchers," says Chris Montague, president of Montana Land Reliance, a statewide, private land trust. It has used donated conservation easements to protect some 322,000 acres of private land in Montana — about a fifth of all the land protected by private state and local land trusts in the United States. "These people really are giving up something huge when they donate a conservation easement — the right to subdivide their land — and they should be rewarded for it," he says. "It's a very cost-effective way to achieve land conservation."

Some developers are of two minds about tax incentives to save open space. "When we first looked at tax incentives for conservation easements, they looked like just another land grab," says Gaffney of the Home Builders Association. "But then we realized that parkland is a positive addition to a community."

The association estimates that up to 1.5 million new housing units will have to be built each year over the coming decade to accommodate an expected 30 million increase in the U.S. population.

"The crucial point in our view is that open space conservation must be decided at the local level and be part of a comprehensive plan that allows for new housing," Gaffney says.

Are private acquisitions of land for conservation in the public interest?

Mounting concern over sprawl in recent years has prompted the creation of more than 1,200 regional, state and local land trusts across the country. "The reason why land trusts have enjoyed fantastic growth," says Pritchard of the National Park Trust, "is that preservation of open space is one of the great American values."

Some property-rights advocates have no problem with local land trusts, which they say reflect the desires of the communities where they operate. "A lot of the local land trusts are really admirable because the locals get together and decide they want to save some land," says Myron Ebell, a property-rights lobbyist and environmental policy analyst at the Competitive Enterprise Institute. "They are an example of the voluntary associations of people accomplishing things through private and local means that [Alexis] de Tocqueville described as the genius of America. But the big national trusts are truly evil." [23]

Ebell targets his heaviest criticism at The Nature Conservancy, by far the largest land trust. This million-member organization has helped protect 11.3 million acres nationwide since it was founded in 1951 to protect habitat for plants and animals.

Despite the conservancy's status as a private, nonprofit organization, Ebell says that it often buys private property only to turn around and sell it at a profit to the government. "Like the other big trusts, The Nature Conservancy is just a halfway house to federal ownership of private land," he says. "It's a profit-making enterprise; it keeps getting bigger and bigger because it makes more and more money off these deals."

Not so, Hooper says. "We have a policy that we do not make a profit when we step in as a middleman. In fact, as a matter of practice, we lose money every year on these deals."

Property-rights supporters also maintain that land conservation efforts often spell disaster for local economies. "When they buy a ranch and shut it down, they disrupt whole communities in rural America," Cushman says. "A ranch isn't just some guy with a pickup truck; it may be all that's holding a small town together. Taking that ranch out of production takes taxes out of the system. Damn few of these deals are good for the government, and they certainly aren't good for the country."

But land trust advocates say opposition to their goals is waning fast. "Support for land acquisition for the pubic good is now just as strong in the West, even the Intermountain West, as it is in the Northeast, where every acre counts," says Shay of the Land Trust Alliance. "The Nature Conservancy is the biggest land trust in America, and it's fun to pick on winners," he says. "But the conservancy would not be successful if it violated the will of local communities. Indeed, the conservancy's success is due to the fact that it has extensive local roots and maintains chapters in every state."

Whatever the merits of national or local land trusts, conservationists point out that objections to protecting open space are inconsistent with the critics' overall property-rights agenda.

"The property-rights folks can't have it both ways," says Grossi of the American Farmland Trust. "If they want to protect the rights of land-owners, they have to include among those rights the right to sell, the right to develop or subdivide their own property." ∎

BACKGROUND

Patterns of Development

For much of the 20th century, population growth in the United States targeted urban areas, where the promise of industrial jobs in cities lured millions from small towns and farms. Beginning with the economic boom that followed World War II, however, housing development spread outside city centers in response to growing demand for larger houses, cleaner air and more open space. Suburban development continued to spread over the next 50 years, eventually producing the "sprawl" that has given rise to today's land conservation movement. [24]

Since the early 1970s, when the declining industrial centers of the Midwest's Rust Belt and other congested cities began losing population to the suburbs, concern over the loss of open space has also emerged in many towns and rural areas. After a lull in the 1980s, when a protracted recession hit farmers and rural industries and halted the trend, the exodus from cities resumed.

Today, many non-urban areas are experiencing a "rural rebound," as retirees, disenchanted city-dwellers and computer-equipped "telecommuters" come in search of a better life. [25] In many cases, the growing demand for housing inflates land values, prompting farmers and ranchers to subdivide vast tracts and raising concerns among residents that the open space that is part of their rural heritage is fast disappearing. (*See story, p. 49.*)

Sprawl has become an especially sensitive issue in both urban and rural areas of the South and West, where more than three-quarters of older Americans are settling in retirement. In part because of retirement trends, Las Vegas and Atlanta are among the fastest-growing cities in the country, while smaller cities and rural communities in the Rocky Mountain states are experiencing similar rates of growth. [26]

At the same time that privately owned open space has been consumed for housing and industry, public land also has come under pressure from development. According to the National Park Trust, many state and national parks and forests are threatened by the increasing number of "inholdings," or private property within public land. The organization reports that inholdings have grown by 1.6 million acres, or 35 percent, over the past decade, bringing the total to 84 million acres.

"The danger that this land could be sold for development, bulldozing, clear-cutting or for other destructive purposes constitutes the single greatest threat to the system of national and state parks," Pritchard said. [27] New inholdings typically are created when public land expansions envelop private property.

As support for land conservation mounts, some critics say public reaction to sprawl is overblown. The San

Francisco-based Pacific Research Institute for Public Policy, which promotes a limited role for government, estimates that development consumes only .0006 percent of the land in the continental United States each year and that the rate of sprawl is lower today than in the 1950s or '60s. [28]

Buying Public Land

The federal government has been buying land since the nation's origins. During the period of frontier expansion that ended in the

Recreationists enjoy Long Pond in the 6,000-acre Pocono Preserve in Pennsylvania. The Nature Conservancy property supports one of the most significant moth and butterfly habitats in the state.

late 1800s, the government spent $85 million to buy 1.8 billion acres — almost 80 percent of the country today. Thomas Jefferson made the biggest land deal when he paid France $23 million for the Louisiana Purchase in 1803, thus adding 530 million acres to U.S. territory, almost a quarter of total U.S. land today. Later acquisitions included the 1867 purchase of Alaska — 378 million acres — from Russia for $7 million and the 339-million acre Mexican Cession of 1848 for $16

million.

Most of the federally acquired public land was later granted to states as they joined the Union, granted or sold to homesteaders under the 1862 Homestead Act [29] or sold to railroad companies, timber companies and other private interests.

During the 20th century, the federal government has resumed land acquisitions, though on a far less sweeping scale than in the nation's early years. Beginning with the 2.2-million-acre Yellowstone National Park, created by Congress in 1872, the federal government began setting aside public land and buying or exchanging private property as parks, national forests and wildlife preserves. [30] States followed suit with purchases and set-asides for state parks, forests and recreation areas.

Congress has created several mechanisms for adding to the inventory of public lands. The 1949 Federal Lands to Parks program, for example, allows for the no-cost transfer of federal lands to state, regional and local governments for use in perpetuity as parks and conservation areas. Recent military base closings have enabled communities across the country to open to the general public open land that was formerly reserved for the military.

Arguably the most valuable land-acquisition tool at the federal government's disposal is the 1964 Land and Water Conservation Fund Act. Created specifically to protect outdoor recreational resources, the fund provides money for federal acquisition of land and easements and matching funds for states to be used

Chronology

1800s
Federal land acquisitions set the stage for later government purchases of land for parks, national forests and wildlife preserves.

1803
Thomas Jefferson completes the biggest land deal in U.S. history when he pays France $23 million for the Louisiana Purchase, adding 530 million acres to U.S. territory.

March 1, 1872
Congress approves the creation of the nation's first national park, Yellowstone, a 2.2-million acre tract in northwestern Wyoming.

— • —

1940s-1960s
Postwar economic prosperity sets the stage for suburban development.

1949
The Federal Lands to Parks program is created to allow federal land to be transferred at no cost to state, regional and local governments for use in perpetuity as parks and conservation areas.

1951
The Nature Conservancy is founded to preserve threatened plant and animal habitat. It eventually becomes the nation's largest private land trust, with 1 million members.

Sept. 3, 1964
Congress establishes the Land and Water Conservation Fund and authorizes spending of up to $900 million a year on open space preservation. The fund is to be used for federal government land purchases and to provide matching grants to states for outdoor recreational projects.

— • —

1970s-1980s
State and local land planners begin taking steps to slow suburban "sprawl."

1973
Oregon's legislature requires all cities to contain most development within clearly defined urban-growth boundaries, providing a model for state and local land-conservation efforts.

— • —

1990s
The Clinton administration calls for new federal efforts to relieve traffic congestion and preserve open space.

September 1996
President Clinton designates 1.9 million acres of public land in southern Utah as the Grand Staircase-Escalante National Monument.

1997
Congress passes the Taxpayer Relief Act, which allows executors to reduce a landowner's estate-tax liability by donating a conservation easement on undeveloped property, which allows the land to be farmed or logged but never developed, even after changing hands.

Nov. 3, 1998
Voters approve more than 120 state and local ballot initiatives that provide about $5.3 billion in new funding for land conservation. Some measures create urban-growth boundaries to halt development beyond already-developed areas, while others raise taxes to buy land.

January 1999
President Clinton introduces his Lands Legacy initiative and asks Congress to give the Land and Water Conservation Fund its full annual funding of $900 million. Vice President Al Gore presents an administration proposal to provide $700 million in tax credits for states and local governments to build more "livable" communities.

August 1999
The Clinton administration agrees, pending congressional approval, to buy the Baca Ranch, a 95,000-acre tract in New Mexico's Jemez Mountains, for $101 million and turn it into a park.

September 1999
Federal officials complete the $13 million purchase of 12,000 acres of ranchland abutting Yellowstone National Park to be preserved as open space.

Oct. 14, 1999
President Clinton announces a plan to protect as much as 40 million acres of national forest land from development.

Oct. 21, 1999
Congress approves a fiscal 2000 Interior spending bill that slashes funding for the Lands Legacy initiative and other administration requests related to land conservation. The president threatens to veto the measure.

Gathering Waters

Local Land Trusts Doubled Their Efforts

Nonprofit local and regional land trusts had nearly 5 million acres under protection in 1998, more than twice as many as in 1988. The protected land — covering more area than Connecticut and Rhode Island — includes family farms and ranches, trails and scenic views, wetlands and forests. Three-quarters of the land is used for public recreation.

METHOD OF PROTECTION	1988 ACRES PROTECTED	1998
Conservation easements	0.3 million	1.4 million
Owned by land trusts	0.3 million	0.8 million
Transfer of land to government agency or other means*	1.4 million	2.5 million
TOTAL	**2.0 million**	**4.7 million**

* Includes lands protected by trusts holding deed restrictions or negotiating for acquisition by other organizations or agencies.

Source: Land Trust Alliance, Oct. 1, 1998

to buy and develop outdoor recreation facilities. Since it went into effect on Jan. 1, 1965, the fund has been used to create almost 7 million acres of parkland, water resources and open space as well as more than 37,000 state and local park and recreational projects.

The law authorizes Congress to appropriate up to $900 million annually for acquisitions and state grants. The money comes primarily from royalties paid by oil and gas companies for the right to drill on the outer continental shelf, which is federal property. In this way, money derived

from exploiting non-renewable energy resources would be used to purchase another non-renewable resource — undeveloped land — for the public good.

But Congress has rarely appropriated the full amount that is authorized under the law. Instead it has used the bulk of the money intended to protect open space to reduce the federal budget deficit. Since fiscal 1995, the state matching fund portion of the Land and Water Conservation Fund has received no funding for new grants. ■

CURRENT SITUATION

Clinton's Initiatives

Two recent developments have refocused attention on the long-neglected fund. First, voters last November approved more than 120 ballot initiatives aimed at preserving open space and curtailing sprawl, sending a clear message to lawmakers facing re-election next year that land conservation is a high priority. Second, the federal budget surplus has freed lawmakers from the need to siphon off money from the fund to reduce the deficit. As a result, a new, largely bipartisan consensus has emerged this year between the Clinton administration and members of Congress to utilize the full Land and Water Conservation Fund as the linchpin of renewed land conservation efforts.

The administration has proposed the most ambitious set of federal initiatives to promote land conservation in decades, including a pro-

How Crested Butte, Colo., Tries to Manage Growth

In the Rocky Mountain states, many 19th-century mining towns now rely heavily for survival on the booming tourist trade. Each year millions of visitors flock to the region to admire its towering mountains, aspen-studded valleys and vast alpine forests.

But the same natural resources also draw new residents, many of whom have the same idea: Buy a big hunk of land — say 35 acres — outside of town and build their dream house. As houses spring up on previously undeveloped land, they mar the pristine landscape and detract from the beauty of what draws people there in the first place.

Many popular mountain resorts in Colorado, such as Aspen, Vail and Telluride, were dramatically altered by rapid residential development in the 1980s and '90s. Housing has spread up mountainsides and for miles down valleys where cattle once grazed. The demand for housing has driven property values so high that it has created a shortage of affordable housing for local workers, who are forced to commute long distances.

To avoid a similar fate, or at least slow the inevitable growth, residents of Crested Butte, another Colorado ski town, have taken steps to preserve the community's open space. "Aspen never made any pretense about being about anything but a highly ostentatious display of wealth, and Vail basically sold itself out," says Norm Bardeen, a Crested Butte builder. "Telluride once had a lot of charm, but you couldn't pay me to live there now. They started a day late and a dollar short by doing nothing to curb growth until after the most serious damage had been done."

Crested Butte residents became alarmed that their community was headed in the same direction in the early 1990s, when the Colorado Fuel and Iron Co. sold a forested, 2,200-acre parcel just outside of town to developers. The developers carved the land into homesites of about 35 acres each.

"The town wanted to purchase the property, but a private individual beat us in making the deal," says Jim Starr, a Gunnison County commissioner. To save the remaining open space around the town and near the Mt. Crested Butte ski resort, Starr, Bardeen and two other residents created the Crested Butte Land Trust in 1991.

To preserve mountain vistas, the land trust in Crested Butte, Colo., tries to consolidate new construction in developed areas.

The 500-member group raises money from residents and visitors alike to buy and receive donations of open space and conservation easements, which allow owners to keep the land but sell or donate their rights to develop it. The land trust also receives around $200,000 a year from a local real estate transfer tax, a 1.5 percent levy on each property sale. For the past several years, local businesses have helped support the effort by asking for a voluntary, 1 percent "sales tax" on goods and services, with proceeds earmarked for the land trust.

Cattle ranchers, traditionally the biggest landholders in the surrounding Gunnison Valley, initially resisted the trust's efforts. "The ranching community was very, very reluctant to be involved with the land trust," Bardeen says. "They thought it was just a tool to take their land away." But when they realized that donating conservation easements could help their families stay on their land — which was rapidly appreciating in value — by reducing estate taxes, many ranchers lent their support to the trust.

Since 1992, when the trust completed its first purchase of 11 acres along the Slate River, it has saved or helped to save more than 1,000 acres from development. In 1997, for example, the trust bought the Robinson parcel, 154 acres of highly visible open space between town and the ski mountain, for $1.2 million. More recently, the trust spent $1.9 million to preserve some 200 acres, including a trail linking the town to an outlying wilderness area.

"I really don't know of any opposition to the work we're doing with the land trust today," says Starr, a member of the land trust board. "Support for our work continues to grow."

For all its effort, the land trust can't buy out the whole valley, and today even Crested Butte is showing the signs of its success as a tourist mecca. New houses are springing up outside town, many of them huge structures built along ridgelines with no effort to hide them from view. "Unfortunately, many of the new houses are highly visible from town," Bardeen says. "But you can't stop growth. What the land trust is trying to do is consolidate development near areas that are already developed."

posal to fully appropriate money for the fund. The Lands Legacy initiative, a $1.2 billion measure included in the fiscal 2000 budget request, included $440 million for the fund to be used for federal land acquisitions and $150 million for state matching grants for conservation uses.

The initiative also included $200 million for coastal protection; $80 million for habitat conservation; $50 million in competitive grants for smart growth planning; $50 million for the Forest Legacy program, begun in 1997 to purchase development rights from owners of timberland; and $50 million for farmland protection.

In January, Vice President Gore unveiled the administration's $1 billion Livable Communities initiative, which would enable states and localities to raise a total of $9.5 billion through bond sales aimed at helping communities preserve green space and improve the local environment. It would be among the largest federal programs ever undertaken to curb sprawl.

The proposal includes $700 million in tax credits for state and local governments, with the rest of the money to be invested in public transit and other measures to ease traffic congestion as well as steps to promote regional planning among neighboring communities.

In March, the administration and the state of California agreed to pay Pacific Lumber Co. $480 million for 10,000 acres in Northern California that includes a rare grove of ancient redwoods known as the Headwaters Forest. The tract has been set aside as a nature preserve with public access. On Oct. 14, Clinton announced plans to ban road building and logging on 40 million acres of national forest wilderness. Scheduled to take effect late next year after a period of public comment, the plan would effectively

preserve a fifth of the 192-million-acre national forest system and constitutes the most sweeping land-conservation initiative since Theodore Roosevelt's administration. [31]

The administration's record on land conservation is a matter of some debate among environmental advocates. "We applaud the renewed attention the administration is giving to the issue, and we support the full funding of the Land and Water Conservation Fund as originally intended," says the American Farmland Trust's Grossi. "But we feel that the administration's proposals are heavily weighted in favor of federal acquisition of land, and not enough for the states."

Grossi would like to see more incentives for farmers to use conservation easements to protect farmland. "The federal government could play a major role without meddling in local affairs by providing the funding while leaving the decision about which land to protect to the local communities," he says.

But some environmentalists are disappointed in the administration's level of commitment to land conservation. "The Clinton administration has talked a lot, but done very little," says Pritchard, who argues that the Lands Legacy initiative does little to solve the problems of low funding for national parks. "The reason we're seeing a lot of people disenchanted with the federal government is its lack of commitment to protecting open space."

Action in Congress

Several land-conservation proposals are under consideration in Congress. In February, House Resources Committee Chairman Don Young, R-Alaska, and Rep. John D. Dingell, D-Mich., ranking member of the House Energy and Commerce

Committee, introduced the Conservation and Reinvestment Act, which would permanently fund the Land and Water Conservation Fund.

The Young-Dingell bill would place some restrictions on the fund's federal program, however. It would:

• Limit the fund to buying inholdings within existing federal property;

• Require that two-thirds of the money be spent east of the Rockies, where federal property is relatively scarce;

• Require congressional approval for purchases of more than $1 million; and

• Ban the use of condemnation, the process by which the government can force landowners to cede their property.

The bill also allocates $1.24 billion to coastal states for coastal restoration and mitigation based on a formula that ties funding to the proximity of offshore oil and gas wells, a feature that environmentalists charge would encourage new drilling.

The Senate version of the Conservation and Reinvestment Act, introduced by Energy and Natural Resources Committee Chairman Frank H. Murkowski, R-Alaska, and Sen. Mary L. Landrieu, D-La., is similar to the Young-Dingell proposal. It would dedicate half the offshore drilling revenues to support a permanently funded Land and Water Conservation Fund and allocate $340 million to each of the fund's two components. It contains the same restrictions, except for a more generous ($5 million) limit on the maximum value of acquisitions that could be made without congressional approval. It also includes a similar formula for allocating coastal impact aid.

A Democratic alternative to the two bipartisan bills is the Permanent Protection for America's Resources 2000, introduced in February by California Rep. George Miller, rank-

Efforts to Save Evans Farm Came Too Late

Evans Farm has been a local landmark for decades in McLean, Va., an affluent Washington suburb. In fact, it was seen by many area residents as an oasis amid the surrounding suburban sprawl that included Tyson's Corner, a booming residential and business center. Open to the public for 40 years, the property included a Colonial-style restaurant, a replica of an old mill, a duck pond and meadows where horses and other farm animals grazed.

When Ralph Evans, owner of the 24-acre site, decided last year to sell the property to a local developer for a reported $20 million, area residents rallied to block the transaction. [1]

"This was a beautiful piece of land, with gently rolling hills, a lovely pond and many old trees," says Diane D'Arcy, an officer of the McLean Citizens Association. "It was a favorite site for rehearsal dinners, wedding receptions and anniversary parties. People from all over Northern Virginia came to the farm."

Dismayed at the prospect that a 144-unit housing development would replace the bucolic site, D'Arcy helped form the Coalition to Save Evans Farm. The group offered to raise enough money to buy the property outright. But Evans, whose family had owned the property since 1938, turned down the coalition's offer and accused its members of trying to force his hand.

"They never got serious about taking ownership of the property and instead used despicable tactics to try to block the deal, including lies and personal attacks," he says. "They acted as though my wife and I had awakened one morning and out of the blue decided to sell the farm out of greed and with no thought to the community. They knew nothing about the anguish involved in deciding to close down the business we'd run for 40 years."

In Evans' view, the coalition's goals had more to do with political interests than land conservation. "The motive was not to save open space but to promote the so-called smart-growth agenda, which in my view amounts to no growth," he says. "Planning development is the way to go, not just stopping development. In any case, the last I heard, we have a Constitution in this country that protects property rights."

Unable to convince Evans to change his mind, the coalition proposed creating a special tax district in McLean to raise money to buy the property and turn it into a public park, but the Fairfax County Board of Supervisors rejected the proposal. Coalition members then tried to

block the rezoning permit required to develop Evans Farm, but county planners rejected their plea, saying the new development would comply with longstanding plans for the area. [2] When the developer, West Group, refused to scale back the project, coalition members organized a number of rush-hour protests in front of the developer's headquarters. In a final effort on July 28, residents pled their case before the Board of Supervisors. The board voted unanimously to let the development proceed.

West Group plans a mix of condominiums, townhouses and single-family houses on the site. The pond, the mill and some old trees will be saved, and the structures will be clustered to provide for open space within the development. But no recreational facilities are planned, and public access will be limited to sidewalks passing through the property.

From D'Arcy's point of view, the effort to save Evans Farm was crushed by a politically powerful developer. "Right from the get-go this was a political decision," she says. "All we were trying to do was buy the farm from Evans, and he called us communists and creeps who were trying to destroy his life. It was as nasty as can be."

For his part, Evans expresses relief but also bitterness about the experience. "I'll enjoy seeing the property developed the way West Group has planned," he says. "But I wouldn't want my worst enemy to go through what we did. For 40 years, we let the public use the property, maintained it at our expense and paid all the taxes. It just goes to show that no good deed goes unpunished."

Could Evans Farm have been preserved if a land trust had been involved in the negotiations? "It's impossible to say," says Russ Shay, public policy director of the Washington-based Land Trust Alliance, a national group representing groups and individuals involved in saving land. "But the most valuable lesson here is that people should recognize that if they're interested in preserving some aspect of open space in their community, they need to act early. Once a development agreement is made, it's very difficult to come in and undo that. They just got there too late."

---

[1] See Michael D. Shear and Peter Pae, "Evans Farm Loyalists Lose Out to Development," *The Washington Post*, July 28, 1999.

[2] See Michael D. Shear, "Evans Farm Vote Goes to Developer," *The Washington Post*, June 25, 1999.

ing Democrat on the House Resources Committee. The $2.3-billion bill would provide full and permanent funding of the Land and Water Conservation Fund from offshore drilling revenues and other conserva-

tion programs. The fund's federal and state-matching components would each receive $450 million. The bill contains no new restrictions on federal land purchases and limits coastal impact funding to current leases, thus

eliminating the incentives for new drilling present in the other two bills. In addition, the bill would create conservation easement programs for ranch, farm and timberland protection. The proposal has won the support of House Minority Leader Richard A. Gephardt, D-Mo., who last year introduced his own bill to permanently fund the Land and Water Conservation Fund.

Sen. Dianne Feinstein, D-Calif., introduced the Public Land and Recreation Investment Act, a more limited bill that would ensure permanent funding of the Land and Water Conservation Fund with no restrictions on federal acquisitions.

State, Local Initiatives

States typically set aside land for public parks, forests and recreation areas, while localities control land use primarily through zoning regulations. But in recent years, some state governments have decided to exercise greater authority over zoning issues by creating statewide development plans aimed at combating sprawl. According to a recent report by the Sierra Club, half the states have taken steps to protect farmland, mostly by compensating landowners for giving up development rights by placing conservation easements on their land. Eleven states also have passed growth-management laws barring development outside established boundaries around existing urban areas. [32]

Oregon set the stage for state land conservation efforts in 1973 when the state legislature required all cities to contain most development within clearly defined urban-growth boundaries. The requirement has attracted nationwide attention to Portland's efforts to curb sprawl. More recently,

Maryland and New Jersey have taken the lead in open-space conservation. Maryland's smart-growth plan, adopted in 1997, emulates Oregon's plan. On Oct. 8, Gov. Glendening approved an additional $25 million to buy more land around the state. Gov. Whitman of New Jersey has promised to follow through on her proposal to preserve a million acres of open space and push several smart-growth restrictions before term limits force her to step down on Jan. 1, 2002. [33] In August, Gov. Roy Barnes, D-Ga., announced plans to require fast-growing counties, such as those around Atlanta, to set aside at least 20 percent

By donating conservation easements on their property, ranchers and farmers can continue to use the land while protecting it from development in perpetuity.

of their undeveloped land for open space.

Local governments also are assuming a larger role in saving open space. Several cities in California's sprawling Central Valley are considering imposing impact fees on developers of new subdivisions to slow growth and help pay for the infrastructure and schools needed to serve new communities. [34] Planners in Montgomery County, Md., a fast-growing Washington suburb, recently proposed spending $100 million over the next decade to preserve undevel-

oped land and historic sites. The funding, to be financed by a special bond issue, would be in addition to the $3.5 million the county receives each year for land conservation from state coffers. [35] Voters in a number of localities, including Adams County, Colo., next to Denver, Springfield, N.J., and Phoenix, Ariz., the country's fastest-growing city, are being asked to approve new growth reforms and open-space proposals in this fall's elections.

In some areas of the country, local conservation efforts are highly controversial. When King County, Wash., bought a 12-mile stretch of railroad right-of-way to build a pedestrian and bike trail, nearby homeowners protested that it would encourage trespassing and threaten their privacy. [36] Similar concerns have been raised in many communities that have converted unused rail rights-of-way to recreational trails.

Land-use restrictions based on aesthetic considerations such as bans on ridge-line construction also generate intense debate. In a highly publicized case in Washington state, environmentalists went to court to force the builders of a new house overlooking the scenic Columbia River Gorge to move the house back because it violated regional building standards aimed at preserving the view for the public good. A state court upheld the regulation, but the owners said they would appeal. [37]

Some conservationists say state initiatives offer models for a shift in federal efforts to save open space. In Florida, for example, revenues raised

At Issue:

Should the federal government buy more land to help conserve open space?

PRESIDENT CLINTON

FROM HIS ANNOUNCEMENT OF THE LANDS LEGACY INITIATIVE, JAN. 14, 1999.

*t*oday I am proud to announce a Lands Legacy Initiative — $1 billion to meet the conservation challenges of a new century; . . . more than doubling our already considerable commitment to protect America's land. It represents the single largest annual investment in protecting our green and open spaces since [President] Theodore Roosevelt set our nation on the path of conservation nearly a century ago. And to keep on that path, we will be working with Congress to create a permanent funding stream for this purpose, beginning in 2001.

The first part of the plan builds directly on Theodore Roosevelt's conservation legacy by adding new crown jewels to our endowment of natural resources. Next year alone, we will dedicate $440 million, largely from the sale of oil from existing offshore oil leases, to acquiring and protecting precious lands and coastal waters. . . .

The second part of our plan, which works in tandem with the Livable Communities Initiative the vice president announced yesterday, represents a new vision of environmental stewardship for the new century. Today it's no longer enough to preserve our grandest natural wonders. As communities keep growing and expanding, it's become every bit as important to preserve the small but sacred green and open spaces closer to home — woods and meadows and seashores where children can still play; streams where sportsmen and women can fish; agricultural lands where family farmers can produce the fresh harvest we often take for granted.

In too many communities, farmland and open spaces are disappearing at a truly alarming rate. In fact, across this country, we lose about 7,000 acres every single day. And as the lands become more scarce, it becomes harder and harder for communities to then afford the price of protecting the ones that are left. That is why we have to act now.

So we will also dedicate nearly $600 million to helping communities across our country save the open spaces that greatly enhance our families' quality of life. With flexible grants, loans and easements, we will help communities to save parks from being paved over. We'll help to save farms from being turned into strip malls. We'll help them to acquire new lands for urban and suburban forests and recreation sites. We'll help them set aside new wetlands, coastal and wildlife preserves. There will be no green mandates and no red tape. Instead, the idea is to give communities all over our country the tools they need to make the most of their own possibilities.

MALCOLM WALLOP

Chairman, Frontiers of Freedom; former Republican senator from Wyoming

FROM TESTIMONY BEFORE THE SENATE ENERGY AND NATURAL RESOURCES COMMITTEE, MAY 4, 1999.

*g*overnment doesn't need to own any more land. It already owns far too much land and far more than it can take care of properly. The four federal land agencies, according to the [Bureau of Land Management], control about 676 million acres, or [more than] 29 percent of the country. Other federal agencies, such as the Department of Defense, own more millions of acres. State and local governments also own a lot of land, although no one knows exactly how much. . . .

I don't think a plausible case can be made that government needs to own even more land for the purpose of environmental protection. A much stronger case can be made that private owners provide, on average, a much higher level of environmental stewardship than does public ownership and, therefore, that the environment would be healthier if we had less public land rather than more. . . .

Before the Congress embarks on a land-buying spree, it would seem to me prudent to consider how all this new property is going to be maintained. There are only two alternatives. Either taxpayers are going to have to pay more to maintain these new acquisitions, or the current appropriation must be stretched ever thinner to maintain more and more land. The budget for Yellowstone National Park and many of our other great national treasures is not adequate now. Adding more land within the current budget constraints means even less money for Yellowstone. . . .

Removing hundreds of millions of dollars of private land from productive uses every year would significantly reduce economic activity in many areas and consequently reduce the tax base. After that is accomplished, these state and local governments would then be burdened with the cost of maintaining their public lands. . . .

The American system of constitutionally limited government was instituted in order to secure the blessings of life, liberty and property to all citizens. The revolutionaries of 1776 and the delegates to the Constitutional Convention of 1787 were very familiar with the old political maxim that "power follows property." The more property government owns or controls, the less power the people retain. As the balance of power shifts towards government, the more difficult it becomes for the people to maintain the blessings of life, liberty, and property. For this reason, the founders would have opposed our vast federal estate just as surely as they would have opposed our confiscatory levels of taxation.

by a land transfer tax imposed on real estate sales are used to purchase land for future use as parks and other public spaces. "We should be buying more land, even if we mothball it for later designation, as Florida does," Pritchard says. "Making public lands our first priority would require our federal agencies to adopt a totally different orientation toward land conservation."

Property-rights advocates, however, say that Washington should look to recent state land-conservation efforts as an example of what to avoid in fashioning federal land policy.

"Smart-growth supporters suggest to people that their livability will go up if land-use controls are imposed around urban areas," Cushman says. "But forcing people into urban corridors will mean much higher population densities and much worse living conditions."

At the same time, Cushman warns, the value of rural property outside the urban growth boundary will plummet, depriving landowners of the true market value of their land. "There's always some good in any of these smart-growth proposals," he says, "but the overall effect will be negative for both rural and urban populations."

Land Trusts

The growth of private land trusts has paralleled the increased efforts of governments at all levels to save open space. Most of the nation's more than 1,200 trusts were organized in the past 15 years. Operating in all 50 states, trusts are especially active on the East and West coasts, where urban development has been especially intense.

Land trusts trace their roots to the "village improvement societies" that emerged in New England in the mid-1800s." [38] They spawned the Society for the Protection of New Hampshire Forests and other early trusts, many still in operation. Around the turn of the century, trusts were also created to save redwood forests in California and historical and archaeological sites in the Midwest.

Today's land trusts vary in size and scope, including local groups concerned with one or two critical properties, to regional trusts that coordinate open-space initiatives across state lines, to national groups like the Nature Conservancy, which has chapters in every state and has also collaborated with foreign groups to save more than 55 million acres overseas. Collectively, U.S. land trusts have helped protect 2.7 million acres from development, about half through outright land purchases and half through conservation easements.

Private land trusts are responsible for conserving open space in and around some of the most popular vistas in the United States, such as Big Sur on the California coast, the San Juan Islands in Washington's Puget Sound and lands abutting Acadia National Park in Maine and the Appalachian Trail.

More than half of all land trusts are true grass-roots organizations, with no paid officers; most of the remainder have only a director or a few staff members on the payroll. Nationwide, 70 percent of all funds used to purchase land come from contributions from members and individual donors. Some trusts receive money from foundations and corporations, while a number of states allocate funds to local land trusts for specific projects.

For example, Great Outdoors Colorado, a state agency, has funneled more than $35 million in state lottery funds to land trusts to protect some 60,000 acres of open space in the state. Land trusts also borrow money from banks, individuals and foundations to buy land; they repay the loans by selling the land to conservationists and through fund-raising drives.

Although most land trusts work independently and focus on local projects, a number of groups have begun pooling their efforts on regional initiatives. Land trusts are collaborating with local trail enthusiasts, for example, in the nonprofit East Coast Greenway Alliance, formed in 1991 to create a 2,500-mile bike and walking trail from Maine to Florida. [39]

The alliance's effort is only one of a number of ambitious conservation efforts by private land trusts. Last December the Wildlands Conservancy, a California trust, coordinated the biggest private land purchase in the state's history, a $52 million deal to buy more than 400,000 acres of privately owned land around Joshua Tree National Monument in Southern California.

In March, the New England Forestry Foundation announced the largest private forest conservation deal in U.S. history, a $30 million purchase of development rights to 750,000 acres in Maine's North Woods. [40] In September, the Conservation Fund brokered the purchase of 76,000 environmentally sensitive acres on the Delmarva Peninsula of Delaware, Maryland and Virginia, the largest conservation deal in the history of the Chesapeake Bay watershed.

Among the reasons land trusts have grown so rapidly, supporters say, is that they offer property owners a more efficient way to protect their land from development than trying to persuade local, state or federal agencies to buy the property itself or the rights to develop it.

"Of course, governments have far more resources to buy land, but land trusts are better to deal with than public agencies because they're generally more skilled in working out deals," says Shay of the Land Trust Alliance. "Because their mandate is to protect the public dollar, government agencies usually buy land for its assessed value, rarely for its full market value, whereas a charity will look for the best possible net return to the landowner."

Land trusts can save property owners time as well as money. "Once a government agency agrees to buy the land, it has to go to Congress to get the money to buy it," Shay says, "and that can take years." ■

OUTLOOK

Action Stalled?

Congress appears unlikely to approve any major proposal affecting federal land conservation policy this year. Lawmakers already have gutted the president's Lands Legacy initiative, which was proposed as part of the $14.5 billion spending bill for the Interior Department. The conference agreement approved on Oct. 21 provided only $246 million of the $442 million Clinton had requested for the Land and Water Conservation Fund, a key item in the initiative. The approved funding level was down $82 million from last year's appropriation. Clinton is all but certain to veto the bill.

"This is a good bill," said John E. Peterson, R-Pa., during an Oct. 21 floor debate. "It is thoughtful; it has been a well-worked out compromise; it is the best we are going to get; and I think we should support it and the president should sign it." He added, "The agencies that are important to our environment have been thoughtfully funded."

But Rep. David R. Obey, D-Wis., ranking Democrat on the House Appropriations Committee, said the final version was not acceptable.

"We feel that the conference report does not sufficiently take account of the opportunities available to us to save precious natural resources by meeting the president's request, or something close to it, for his Lands Legacy program," Obey said. "We have no choice but to stick by our convictions and oppose the bill at this point." [41]

The Interior appropriations bill also contains many anti-environmental riders, mostly benefiting resource industries. The riders include a delay in increasing the royalty payments that oil and gas drillers pay to extract resources from public property and a relaxation of limits on livestock grazing, logging and mining on federal land. Before the vote, Clinton warned he would veto the measure. "If the Interior bill lands on my desk looking like it does now," he said, "I will give it a good environmental response — I will send it straight back to the recycling bin." [42]

Conservation advocates are pinning their hopes on the bills still before Congress to fully and permanently fund the Land and Water Conservation Fund or expand tax incentives for landowners who voluntarily conserve their land. But they are frustrated at the apparent reluctance of lawmakers to approve any of the bills, especially those that offer tax incentives for saving open space.

"Under current law, a third of the country doesn't even qualify for the break in estate taxes, so expanding estate tax benefits would have a big impact on conservation," says Shay of the Land Trust Alliance. "It's a no-brainer." Although several bills aimed at promoting land conservation enjoy bipartisan support, no major bill has moved out of committee for full House or Senate consideration.

Critics say land-conservation proposals may backfire if governments become overzealous in imposing land-use regulations. "Open space

and smart growth are slogans that politicians have coined for political benefit, but they have little foundation in reality," says Virginia developer Hazel, who adds that such efforts are ultimately doomed if they fail to respect suburban residents' needs and desires. "The people who need new roads and schools are already here, and they need to be provided for now, not by some future plan. The theory that you can just put them somewhere else is absurd, a fact that will resonate [among voters] sooner or later."

Despite congressional inaction thus far on land conservation bills, environmental advocates are confident that open-space efforts will continue to spread across the country, especially through support of local land trusts.

Fortunately, Shay says, no matter what governments do — or do not do — about land conservation, "a lot of people are pooling their resources to save open space. They are the ones who are looking to the future of their communities." ■

Notes

[1] Quoted by Steve Twomey, "Lots Not to Like," *The Washington Post*, July 5, 1999.

[2] For background, see Mary H. Cooper, "Setting Environmental Priorities," *The CQ Researcher*, May 21, 1999, pp. 425-448; Mary H. Cooper, "Urban Sprawl in the West," *The CQ Researcher*, Oct. 3, 1997, pp. 865-888; Tom Arrandale, "Public Land Policy," *The CQ Researcher*, June 17, 1994, pp. 529-552; and David Hosansky, "Traffic Congestion," *The CQ Researcher*, Aug. 27, 1999, pp. 729-752.

[3] See Sierra Club, "Solving Sprawl: The Sierra Club Rates the States," Oct. 4, 1999. See also Land Trust Alliance, "November 1998 Open Space Acquisition Ballot Measures," Feb. 12, 1999, which reports that voters approved 124 out of 148 initiatives for land acquisition only, raising a total of $5.3 billion.

[4] Land Trust Alliance, www.lta.org.

[5] For background, see Mary H. Cooper,

"National Forests," *The CQ Researcher*, Oct. 16, 1998, pp. 905-928.

[6] From remarks on the Livability Agenda on Jan. 12, 1999.

[7] For background, see Kenneth Jost, "Property Rights," *The CQ Researcher*, June 16, 1995, pp. 513-536.

[8] Bureau of Land Management, "Public Land Statistics 1998," March 1999. In addition to the bureau, the Forest Service, the Fish and Wildlife Service and the National Park Service administer federal land.

[9] See The Wilderness Society Web site, www.wilderness.org.

[10] For background, see Richard L. Worsnop, "National Parks," *The CQ Researcher*, May 28, 1993, pp. 457-480.

[11] Babbitt spoke on Sept. 30, 1999, during a visit to the Chattahoochee National Recreation Area in Atlanta.

[12] Luntz Research Companies conducted the survey for The Nature Conservancy. See "American Views on Land & Water Conservation," summer 1999.

[13] Sierra Club survey conducted April 8-11, 1999.

[14] Sierra Club, "SPARE America's Wildlands," April 1999, p. 6.

[15] From a letter to Rep. Don Young, R-Alaska, and Sen. Frank Murkowski, R-Alaska, dated May 24, 1999.

[16] E-mail dated Aug. 21, 1999.

[17] See Michael Janofsky, "National Parks, Strained by Record Crowds, Face a Crisis," *The New York Times*, July 25, 1999.

[18] From a statement on Feb. 8, 1999.

[19] National Park Trust, "Saving the Legacy of the National System of Parks," Aug. 25, 1999.

[20] Hoeffel testified on Sept. 30, 1999, before a House Ways and Means Committee hearing on the impact of tax law on land use, conservation and preservation.

[21] Johnson testified on Sept. 30, 1999, before the House Ways and Means Committee.

[22] "Vineyard Loophole," *The Wall Street Journal*, Aug. 24, 1999.

[23] Alexis de Tocqueville's classic, *Democracy in America*, was published in 1835-40.

[24] For background, see Mary H. Cooper, "Environmental Movement at 25," *The CQ Researcher*, March 31, 1995, pp. 283-306.

[25] See Kenneth M. Johnson, "The Rural Rebound," in *Reports on America*, Population Reference Bureau, August 1999.

[26] See William H. Frey, "New Sun Belt Metros

FOR MORE INFORMATION

American Farmland Trust, 1200 18th St. N.W., Suite 800, Washington, D.C. 20036; (202) 331-7300; www.farmland.org. This private, nonprofit organization works to stop the loss of productive farmland and to promote farming practices that lead to a healthy environment.

Competitive Enterprise Institute, 1001 Connecticut Ave. N.W., Suite 1250, Washington, D.C. 20036; (202) 331-1010; www.cei.org. This public policy organization advocates free enterprise and limited government, and opposes federal land-conservation policies that include new purchases of private property.

Land Trust Alliance, 1331 H. St. N.W., Suite 400, Washington, D.C. 20005-4711; (202) 638-4725; www.lta.org. The alliance represents more than 1,200 private land trusts around the country.

National Park Trust, 415 2nd St. N.E., Suite 210, Washington, D.C. 20002; (202) 548-0500; www.parktrust.org. This nonprofit group works to preserve America's parklands. It buys inholdings, or privately owned land inside national parks, from willing buyers to slow development.

The Nature Conservancy, 4245 N. Fairfax Dr., Suite 100, Arlington, Va. 22203-1606; (703) 841-5300; www.tnc.org. A nationwide land trust with a million members, the conservancy operates the largest private system of nature sanctuaries in the world. Its sole focus is on land that provides habitat for imperiled species of plants and animals.

---

and Suburbs Are Magnets for Retirees," *Population Today*, October 1999, pp. 1-3.

[27] From a statement of Aug. 25, 1999.

[28] Lloyd Billingsley, "Facts Versus Fantasy on Urban Sprawl," *Pacific Research Institute for Public Policy*, March 29, 1999.

[29] The act, which became law on Jan. 1, 1863, allowed anyone to file for a quarter-section (160 acres) of free land. Filers who built a house, dug a well, plowed 10 acres, fenced a specified amount and actually lived there gained title to the land after five years.

[30] In addition to buying private property, federal agencies often exchange low-priority public holdings for private property that is adjacent to parks, forests or other high-priority holdings.

[31] See Charles Babington, "Forest Protection Plan Is Unveiled," *The Washington Post*, Oct. 14, 1999.

[32] Sierra Club, "Solving Sprawl: The Sierra Club Rates the States," released Oct. 4, 1999.

[33] See David Kocieniewski, "Having Left Senate Race, Whitman Revels in the Job She Has," *The New York Times*, Sept. 12, 1999.

[34] See Mark Arax, "Putting the Brakes on Growth," *Los Angeles Times*, Oct. 6, 1999.

[35] See Scott Wilson and Susan DeFord, "Montgomery Bids for Open Space," *The Washington Post*, Oct. 14, 1999.

[36] See Patrick McMahon, "Residents Push to Derail Trails," *USA Today*, Oct. 7, 1999.

[37] See Stephanie Thomson, "Beas Appeal to High Court," *The Columbian* (Vancouver, Wash.), Oct. 8, 1999.

[38] Background information on land trusts from www.possibility.com/Land Trust.

[39] See Dieter Bradbury, "Greenway Fans Think Big: Maine to Florida," *Portland (Maine) Press Herald*, Sept. 26, 1999.

[40] See Pamela Ferdinand, "Private Deal to Preserve 750,000 Acres in Maine," *The Washington Post*, March 4, 1999.

[41] Charles Pope, "Senate Clears Interior Bill, Setting Stage for Post-Veto Talks on Policy Riders, Funding Levels," *CQ Weekly*, Oct. 23, 1999, p. 2527.

[42] From remarks during the Oct. 14 announcement of Clinton's new forest land policy.

Bibliography

Selected Sources Used

Articles

"Urban Sprawl: Not Quite the Monster They Call It," *The Economist*, **Aug. 21, 1999, pp. 24-25.**

Federal policies, such as generous spending for highway construction and tax breaks to encourage home ownership, have encouraged suburban development. Sprawl also is the result of an express desire on the part of middle-class Americans to leave congested cities for better living conditions.

Allen, Jodie T., "Sprawl, from Here to Eternity: It's Maddening as Hell. But What Can Washington Really Do about It?" *U.S. News & World Report*, **Sept. 6, 1999, pp. 22-23.**

Vice President Al Gore's Livable Communities initiative is criticized as "green pork" because it would preserve coastal regions in Alaska and other areas with powerful representatives in Congress.

Davis, Tony, "Tucson Paves Its Way across a Fragile Landscape," *High Country News*, **Jan. 18, 1999, p. 1.**

Like other Arizona communities, Tucson is growing fast to accommodate retirees and other new residents. Although growth continues, efforts are now under way to contain sprawl through land purchases and stricter zoning.

Gurwitt, Rob, "The State vs. Sprawl," *Governing*, **January 1999, pp. 18-23.**

Maryland Gov. Parris N. Glendening's "smart-growth" policy limiting most development to existing communities is being closely watched by other state officials to determine whether it can serve as a model for their own efforts to alleviate traffic congestion.

McChesney, Jim, "Portland: Urban Eden or Sprawling Hell?" *Oregon Quarterly*, **summer 1999, pp. 18-23.**

State urban-growth mandates introduced in 1973 have forced Oregon's biggest city to contain growth close to existing development. While many residents and planners praise the result of these policies, critics say they have merely raised real estate values, pricing many lower-income people out of the city.

Reports and Studies

"Building Livable Communities: A Report from the Clinton-Gore Administration," June 1999.

The report describes how open-space loss results from suburban development and how administration proposals would save undeveloped land.

General Accounting Office, "Community Development: Extent of Federal Influence on 'Urban Sprawl' Is Unclear," April 1999.

The independent investigative agency for Congress concludes that efforts to regulate land use to combat sprawl traditionally have come under the jurisdiction of state and local governments and that the eventual impact of closer federal involvement in this area is uncertain.

Johnson, Kenneth M., "The Rural Rebound," Population Reference Bureau, August 1999.

For most of the nation's history, people have migrated from the countryside to cities in search of employment. Computer technology and economic prosperity have recently fueled a reversal of the trend, posing new policy issues for land-use planners.

Riggs, David, and Daniel Simmons, "Anti-Sprawl Policy: Congested Thinking and Dense Logic," policy brief, Competitive Enterprise Institute, Aug. 9, 1999.

Growth-management policies are ineffective and little more than nostalgic attempts to recreate outmoded communities, according to this brief for CEI, a public policy group that advocates free markets and a limited role for government.

Sierra Club, "1999 Sierra Club Sprawl Report," Oct. 4, 1999.

The San Francisco-based environmental group rates the states in terms of their efforts to protect open space and emphasis on land-use planning. Maryland and Oregon receive the group's highest ratings.

Staley, Samuel R., "The Sprawling of America: In Defense of the Dynamic City," Reason Public Policy Institute, undated.

Less than 5 percent of the nation's land is developed, Staley writes. He argues that concern about suburban sprawl is overblown and that, in any case, development is a matter for local officials, not the federal government, to regulate.

United States Geological Service, "Perspectives on the Land Use History of North America: A Context for Understanding Our Changing Environment," 1998.

The Interior Department agency presents an exhaustive study of trends in land development across the country, including urban growth and agricultural production.

4 Energy and the Environment

MARY H. COOPER

Commuters in Washington, D.C., ran into heavier traffic than usual recently, thanks to Douglas Sorantino and his colleagues. The New Jersey truck driver wrestled his big tractor trailer onto the already crowded streets of the nation's capital along with more than 200 fellow truckers.

"We're dying," complained Sorantino, who helped organize a one-day protest against soaring fuel prices. "We need help now." [1]

Since the beginning of the year, diesel fuel has spiked 75 cents per gallon — just one of the consequences of a yearlong rise in world oil prices. The increases were sparked by the 11-member Organization of Petroleum Exporting Countries (OPEC), which curtailed oil-production quotas last March in an effort to inflate prices.

The ploy succeeded, driving the recent price of a barrel of oil past the $30 mark, the highest level since the 1991 Persian Gulf War. To the financial frustration of American motorists, the price of a gallon of unleaded gas increased to more than $1.50 in some areas, and the price of home heating fuel tripled.

Truckers and other heavy users of petroleum products have demanded a suspension of energy taxes or the release of some of the 600 million barrels of U.S. oil held in the Strategic Petroleum Reserve. "Truckers need immediate financial relief," said Sen. Robert G. Torricelli, D-N.J., who has asked the White House to tap into the reserve. "These higher costs will soon be felt by consumers if we don't take immediate action."

To environmentalists, the clamor for oil-price relief is just another indication that federal energy poli-

cies have done little to reduce America's insatiable thirst for oil and other fossil fuels — even in the wake of gas shortages and growing concern about global warming and other environmental problems.

"Certainly one of the reasons why an oil-price spike of this magnitude could happen is the fact that fuel-economy levels in the United States — the world's biggest oil consumer — have not increased for the past 15 years," says Dan Lashof, a senior scientist at the Natural Resources Defense Council. "We need to focus more on our ongoing vulnerability, which is a result of the U.S. transportation system being 97 percent dependent on petroleum."

In the 1970s and early '80s, a series of oil crises drove up energy prices, produced gasoline shortages that forced millions of motorists to line up at the pump and drove automakers to redesign cars with fuel efficiency, rather than power, in mind. But energy worries dissipated. Today, although the United States is more dependent than ever on foreign oil, gas-guzzling sport-utility vehicles (SUVs) now dominate the auto market. [2]

Nearly 90 percent of the energy consumed in the United States is produced by burning petroleum products, coal and natural gas. All three fossil fuels, but especially coal and gasoline, emit pollutants when

burned, including nitrogen oxides, sulfur oxides and volatile organic compounds, causing smog in areas of heavy industrialization and vehicle traffic. Coal, the main fuel burned by electric utilities and other industrial facilities, causes acid rain and also contributes to urban smog. Though slightly less polluting than coal, gasoline contributes heavily to smog because of the sheer number of cars on the road.

Air-quality standards set by the 1970 Clean Air Act and subsequent legislation have greatly improved air quality for much of the country. Because vehicles were found to contribute most air pollutants, automakers were required to fit new vehicles with catalytic converters, which trap smog-causing pollutants before they can escape into the atmosphere. States adopted stricter auto-inspection standards, and oil refiners were required to sell cleaner-burning gasoline in regions with the worst air pollution. Coal-burning industries, especially electric-power utilities, were required to install so-called scrubbers in their smokestacks to trap sulfur and other pollutants.

Such measures have greatly reduced some forms of air pollution. After the phaseout of leaded gasoline beginning in the early 1970s, lead poisoning in children fell dramatically. Requirements to reduce sulfur-dioxide emissions from coal-burning industries have helped reduce the killing effects of acid rain on Eastern forests and waterways. And caps on emissions of particulate matter have slowed the buildup of haze that enveloped many parts of the country.

Nonetheless, many cities continue to be covered in a thick blanket of smog. The problem is usually most acute in the summer, when pollutants emitted by gasoline-driven vehicles and coal-burning industries are heated by the sun, producing ozone,

From *The CQ Researcher*,
March 3, 2000.

Traditional Energy Sources Still Power the U.S.

Nearly 90 percent of the energy consumed in the United States in 1998 came from traditional sources: petroleum, natural gas and coal. Renewable sources — mainly hydroelectricity and geothermal energy — provided 4 percent of U.S. energy.

U.S. Energy Consumption by Source
(Total energy used: 90.9 quadrillion BTUs)

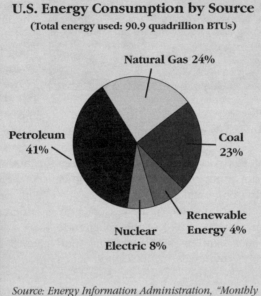

Natural Gas 24%

Coal 23%

Renewable Energy 4%

Nuclear Electric 8%

Petroleum 41%

Source: Energy Information Administration, "Monthly Energy Review, January 2000"

a lung irritant. Particulate matter, a dustlike byproduct of fuel combustion, adds to the mix, reducing visibility and posing further health risks.

The problem has prompted the governors of some Eastern states to look beyond their own borders — and pocketbooks — for solutions. They blame wind-borne pollutants emitted by coal-burning utilities in the Ohio River Valley for much of their pollution. Last November, the Environmental Protection Agency (EPA) sued seven Midwestern utility companies for violating the Clean Air Act by failing to install pollution-control devices in about 30 aging, coal-fired plants.

Midwestern industries say the Eastern states are merely dodging the politically unpopular steps of properly enforcing auto-emission standards at home — steps that could cost

incumbent governors at the polls. "All you have to do, if you want to cause a furor among the voting populace, is make them do something with their cars," says attorney David M. Flannery, who represents the Midwest Ozone Group, whose members include firms named in the suits. "It's pretty easy for the political leadership of Northeastern states to point their fingers upwind and call for regulating people in other states rather than take the political heat of regulating their own sources of pollution."

When it comes to the Earth's long-term health, however, a far more serious threat than ground-level air pollution is the buildup of carbon dioxide in the atmosphere caused by burning fossil fuels. Under normal conditions, tasteless, odorless carbon dioxide is essential to the life cycle of plants and animals. Together with

other naturally occurring gases, CO_2 also helps shield the planet's surface from the damaging effects of solar radiation and prevent drastic temperature swings, protecting life on Earth much as a greenhouse protects plants in winter.

Mounting scientific evidence suggests, however, that excessive emissions of carbon dioxide and other so-called greenhouse gases by fossil-fuel-burning industries and vehicles are causing a potentially devastating warming of Earth's atmosphere. These concerns prompted 84 countries, including the United States, to sign the Kyoto Protocol in November 1998. It committed the United States and 37 other developed countries to reduce their 1990 greenhouse gas emission levels by 5-8 percent by 2008.

"If we fail to reduce emissions of greenhouse gases, deadly heat waves and droughts will become more frequent, coastal areas will be flooded, economies will be disrupted," President Clinton told Congress, reiterating his support for Kyoto in his State of the Union address on Jan. 25.

Thus far, only 13 nations have ratified Kyoto. Opposition to the treaty runs so high in the United States that Clinton has not even sent it to the Senate, where a two-thirds majority must approve its ratification before it can go into effect in this country. Opponents of Kyoto — led by industries that produce or use fossil fuels — say the scientific data are too uncertain to justify the enormous expense required to comply with its mandates.

"There hasn't been, and there probably will never be, complete knowledge about climate change," says Urvan Sternfels, president of the National Petroleum Refiners Association. "Reasonable, justified steps that can be taken should be taken to deal with the concerns that there might be a problem, even though the science isn't perfect. But we clearly are very concerned about mandates that would put our nation and our industry — which has a lot to do with the nation's economy — at a disadvantage."

But environmentalists say that a new report by the National Research Council provides further evidence that the science is reliable and that global warming is, in fact, already under way. [3] They warn that continued inaction on climate change poses the greatest single threat to the environment today.

Indeed, 30 years after the first Earth Day launched the environmental movement, the central theme of the upcoming Earth Day 2000 is global warming. Organizers are calling for additional federal support for research aimed at moving from fossil fuels to renewable energy sources, such as solar and wind power. They also are seeking tightened air-quality standards to speed the development of cars that run on fuel cells and other less-polluting technologies.

As the debate continues over the link between energy use and environmental health, these are some of the issues that will be addressed:

Has the threat of global warming restored nuclear power's potential as an alternative to fossil fuels?

In the wake of the energy crises of the 1970s, nuclear power appeared to offer a solution to many of the country's energy problems. Because the United States had ample domestic reserves of uranium and the technology to harness it for civilian purposes, nuclear energy could not be held hostage to the whims of foreign suppliers, unlike petroleum. It also was much cleaner than fossil fuels; nuclear power plants emitted virtually none of the pollutants that contributed to urban smog.

Beginning with President Dwight D. Eisenhower's Atoms for Peace program in 1954, the government has supported the development of the civilian nuclear power industry. But the United States' fascination with nuclear power came to an abrupt halt on March 28, 1979, when a reactor at the Three Mile Island plant outside Harrisburg, Pa., developed a leak that sparked the country's only nuclear emergency to date.

Although the accident was quickly contained and caused little detectable harm to the environment, public reaction was swift. Orders for future plant construction dried up. After peaking at 112 in 1990, the number of nuclear power reactors now stands at 103 in 31 states, accounting for about 8 percent of total energy consumption in the United States. Nuclear power's fate appeared to be sealed after a devastating explosion at the Chernobyl nuclear power plant in Russia in 1986.

With the emergence of global warming as perhaps the most pressing environmental threat today, some experts say the time has come to reassess the role nuclear power should play in the country's energy mix.

"The Department of Energy reports that to reduce our carbon emissions below 1990 levels by only 5 percent — and not even by the 7 percent required under the Kyoto Protocol — we'd have to extend the license lifetime of all the nuclear plants we have now and build about 68 new nuclear plants in the United States by 2020," says Joe Colvin, president of the Nuclear Energy Institute, an industry group. "So, as they consider the security of the energy supply, the reliability of the system and our need to have a diverse fuel mix, people are going to look at nuclear in a whole different way."

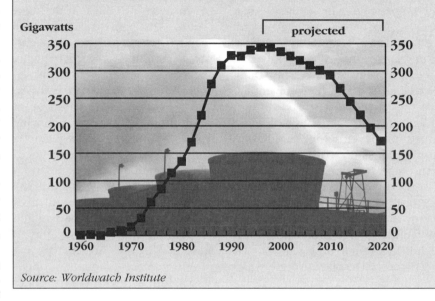

Nuclear Energy's Power Dive

After rising steadily in the 1970s and '80s, the generating capacity of the world's nuclear power plants peaked in the '90s and began what many experts think will be a steady decline. Nuclear plants now provide about 17 percent of the world's electricity. There are 103 U.S. nuclear plants, down from a high of 112 in 1990.

Global Nuclear Electrical-Generating Capacity

Source: Worldwatch Institute

Proponents of greater reliance on nuclear power say much of the public concern about its safety is unfounded. "Despite its outstanding record, [nuclear power] has been relegated by its opponents to the same twilight zone of contentious ideological conflict as abortion and evolution," write Pulitzer Prize-winner Richard Rhodes, author of *The Making of the Atomic Bomb*, and Denis Beller, a nuclear engineer at the Los Alamos National Laboratory. "It deserves better. Nuclear power is environmentally safe, practical and affordable. It is not the problem — it is one of the best solutions." [4]

Indeed, some countries have continued to develop nuclear power despite the safety concerns. Today, France and Belgium rely on nuclear energy for more than half of their electricity consumption, and nuclear energy accounts for 6.3 percent of the world's energy production, only slightly less than hydroelectric power (6.9 percent). Despite the decrease in the number of civilian reactors, nuclear power still accounts for one-fifth of U.S. electricity, and concerns about global warming have prompted some companies to increase their use of nuclear energy. According to an Energy Department survey, voluntary reductions in greenhouse gas emissions from nuclear energy usage increased by 43 percent in 1998. [5]

Industry representatives see this increase as evidence that nuclear power is on its way back in the United States. "The numbers are compelling evidence of nuclear energy's clean-air value," Colvin said. "They show irrefutably that nuclear energy, above and beyond the value it provides as a reliable source of one-fifth of our electricity, is doing double-duty in helping keep our air clean." [6]

But critics say nuclear energy is on its way out. "Nuclear power is basically dead," says Amy Shollenberger, senior policy analyst at Public Citizen's Critical Mass Energy Project, a watchdog group. "There's just no way that it's going to revive itself." For one thing, she says, nuclear power is not as clean as its supporters claim. "It's not emission-free when you consider the complete fuel cycle," she says. "A lot of the fuel is made in plants that use coal for the energy they need to make the fuel rods."

Even more damning, in the view of critics, is the high toxicity of wastes generated by nuclear power plants. Utilities currently store their highly radioactive, spent fuel rods on site under water in large pools or in cement casks. The Department of Energy promised to begin removing the waste and transporting it to a permanent repository under Yucca Mountain in the Nevada desert in January 1998. But concerns that the site may be vulnerable to earthquakes and may leak radioactive waste into the groundwater have delayed completion of the project.

Even if Yucca Mountain opens without further interruptions, critics say the transportation of nuclear waste to the site in trucks or on trains poses an unacceptable risk to the environment and to public health. An accident involving a truck rollover or train derailment, especially in a highly populated area, could be disastrous. "We're talking about 100,000 shipments of highly radioactive materials over 25 years," Shollenberger says. "Another problem is that current regulations allow a certain amount of radiation to escape from nuclear-waste containers at a constant rate, equal to one chest X-ray an hour. People who would be exposed repeatedly to this low level, such as truck drivers or policemen directing traffic, could end up with a high level of radiation exposure."

Proponents of nuclear power dismiss such fears. "Nuclear waste disposal is a political problem in the United States because of widespread fear disproportionate to the reality of the risk," according to Rhodes and Beller. "Substituting small, properly contained volumes of nuclear waste for vast, dispersed amounts of toxic wastes from fossil fuels would produce so obvious an improvement in public health that it is astonishing that physicians have not already demanded such a conversion." [7]

Some experts caution that ongoing operations of nuclear plants are not the only source of environmental threats. At some point, those plants are going to wear out and must be decommissioned, they say, and a number are already approaching the end of their useful lives.

The National Academy of Sciences is currently reviewing radiation-exposure standards that will help determine how to dispose of the contaminated concrete, steel and other materials when nuclear plants are dismantled. Its findings are expected by 2003.

Meanwhile, critics caution against weakening the standards to make it easier to dispose of the waste.

"Public fears of radiation are not irrational," writes Arjun Makhijani, president of the Institute for Energy and the Environment. "Rather, they are a reasonable response of people who, in the face of notoriously inexact science, have chosen not to trust those who have egregiously and frequently betrayed them. Before considering a relaxation of radiation-protection standards, policy-makers should discuss how they might restore public trust." [8]

Should states be required to curb the emission of air pollutants that contribute to smog beyond their borders?

Ground-level ozone, a central focus of the Clean Air Act, remains a serious problem in much of the United States east of the Rocky Mountains, causing respiratory distress during the summer months. In

1997, as smog continued to worsen in some urban areas, EPA Administrator Carol M. Browner tightened the ozone limit from 0.12 parts per million (ppm), measured over one hour, to 0.08 ppm over eight hours. To comply with the new standard, state and local governments were forced to adopt costly measures to further reduce industrial and tailpipe emissions. [9]

But many localities have been unable to meet even the old standard, and increasingly they say they will never be able to do so unless upwind polluters outside their boundaries take steps to curb emissions that contribute to the problem.

In 1995, environmental commissioners in the 37 states east of the Rockies, the EPA and industry representatives established the Ozone Transport Assessment Group to address the problem of "transboundary" air pollution. Two years later, the group proposed nitrogen-oxide emission caps for each state at an estimated total cost of $1.7 billion. The EPA subsequently issued a uniform standard requiring all upwind states to achieve an 85 percent reduction in nitrogen-oxide emissions. Since then, disagreement has flared among the states over how to apportion the responsibility for reducing smog.

"Clearly, we recognize that transportation of air pollutants doesn't stop at state borders," says Flannery of the Midwest Ozone Group. "And clearly, there are responsibilities that upwind states have to downwind states. The issue is how much impact must upwind states have on downwind states in order to be significant and therefore trigger some kind of responsive action."

Eastern politicians say there is no doubt where the responsibility lies for smog in their region. "Congress has long recognized the need to control transported air pollution," Sen. Joseph I. Lieberman, D-Conn., told the Senate on Nov. 10. "Provisions to study and address the issue have been included by major amendments to the Clean Air Act. Yet the problem still remains, and the statistics are staggering. They demonstrate just how much old, Midwestern power plants contribute to air pollu-

Support for nuclear energy plummeted after a radiation leak at the Three Mile Island plant in Pennsylvania in 1979. Today, nuclear energy generates about 20 percent of U.S. electricity.

tion in the Northeast. For example, one utility in Michigan emits six times more nitrogen oxides than all the utilities in the entire state of Connecticut. And one plant in Ohio produces as much nitrogen oxide as all of the plants in the state of New York." [10]

The plants in question include some older, coal-fired facilities that were exempted from the Clean Air Act's emissions caps in the expectation that they soon would be retired from service. Some of them are still running, however, because utilities

have modernized them over the years, but often without adding the pollution-control equipment required of other plants.

"The nation's dirtiest power plants have abused loopholes in federal law to dirty our air, pollute our lungs and kill our most vulnerable citizens," said Sen. James M. Jeffords, R-Vt. "These power plants have exploited the law for nearly 30 years. Now, EPA is exposing their effort for what it is: a blatant violation of the public trust." [11]

To strengthen their position, 12 Eastern states and the District of Columbia created the regional Ozone Transport Commission to coordinate air-quality policy along the heavily urban coastal corridor from Maine to Northern Virginia. The commission established nitrogen-oxide caps aimed at reducing emissions to half of 1990 levels by 2003. But coal-fired utilities and other industrial facilities to the west and south continue to emit pollutants that are borne by prevailing winds to East Coast cities. New York and other Eastern states have asked the EPA to force Midwestern states to cut their emissions.

Last May, the D.C. Circuit Court of Appeals overturned EPA rulings designed to reduce ozone transport from Midwestern states. The agency has since shifted its focus from state regulators to the offending companies. In December, Browner ordered 400 plants in 12 states to halve their emissions by 2003.

"Our commitment is to solve the long-distance ozone transport problem," Browner declared on Dec. 18. "We're going to get there one way or

Billions of Tons of Greenhouse Gases

Chevron Corp.

Nearly 2 billion metric tons of greenhouse gases — blamed for causing global warming — were emitted in the United States in 1998. More than 80 percent was produced by burning fossil fuels. About 15 percent was methane and nitrous oxide, which largely come from the decomposition of various waste sources and fertilizers.

U.S. greenhouse gas emissions, 1998
In millions of metric tons (mmt)

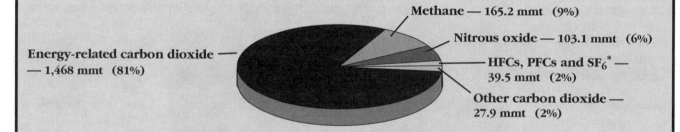

Methane — 165.2 mmt (9%)

Nitrous oxide — 103.1 mmt (6%)

Energy-related carbon dioxide — 1,468 mmt (81%)

HFCs, PFCs and SF$_6$* — 39.5 mmt (2%)

Other carbon dioxide — 27.9 mmt (2%)

* HFCs (hydrofluorocarbons) are used primarily as refrigerants; PFCs (perfluorocarbons) are gases released in aluminum smelting; and SF$_6$ (sulfur hexafluoride) is used as an electrical insulator.

Source: Energy Information Administration, "Emissions of Greenhouse Gases in the United States, 1998"

the other."

Midwestern states and industries say the EPA is targeting them unfairly. For example, the EPA has required utilities in 22 states to reduce their nitrogen-oxide emissions by 85 percent. Critics say that the "one-size-fits-all" approach is unfair.

"We know plants in different locations have very different impacts on air quality," Flannery says, "and yet a power plant in Alabama gets the same level of control as a power plant in New York or Connecticut, where the non-attainment is occurring. You can get virtually all the benefits of regulating pollution sources by regulating the sources that

are located along the Amtrak corridor itself. You could shut down all the power plants in the Ohio River Valley and not improve air quality in those parts of the country at all. In other words, we're regulating the wrong sources."

Eastern states insist that they are doing everything they can to reduce smog. New York's Republican governor, George E. Pataki, recently tightened emissions caps for utilities in his state that exceed federal requirements by 50 percent for sulfur dioxide and by 25 percent for nitrogen oxides. But in some cases, political leaders in downwind states are buckling under a popular backlash against stricter

environmental policies. In January, for example, Gov. Christine Todd Whitman, R-N.J., reverted to the traditional auto-emissions testing system in response to widespread complaints that the state's stringent new testing system caused unacceptable delays for motorists. [12]

Critics say such action merely demonstrates the Northeast's unwillingness to take responsibility for its own air quality. "There's been a wholesale default on the part of virtually all the Northeastern states to put in place vehicle-inspection and maintenance programs and otherwise to identify the kinds of controls that are needed in order to satisfy minimal requirements of the Clean Air Act," Flannery says.

Does electric-utility deregulation pose an additional threat to the environment?

Twenty-four states have loosened longstanding government controls over their electricity markets, and Congress is considering proposals to lift utility regulations throughout the country. [13] With utility deregulation, consumers are being asked to pick their electricity providers, just as they picked their local phone companies after the breakup of the telephone monopoly in the 1980s.

While deregulation may bring benefits to consumers in the form of lower electricity bills, it is forcing utilities to compete for customers for the first time. And some experts worry that in their effort to drive down costs, utilities may cut corners in safety procedures. Those concerns are especially strong with regard to nuclear power.

Like other utilities, nuclear power plant operators are increasing output in the effort to cut unit costs in today's deregulatory environment. Indeed, the 104 nuclear power plants in operation at the end of 1998 generated 17 percent more electricity than the 112 operating units did in 1990. [14]

Industry spokesmen say the increased output does not jeopardize safety at these plants. "Large nuclear plants were designed to run 24 hours a day, 365 days a year, except for coming off-line to refuel the reactor and perform maintenance," says Colvin of the Nuclear Energy Institute. "So running them more hours per year does not correlate in any way to safety. In fact, increasing the capacity of these units focuses more attention on maintaining the plant correctly and therefore increases safety. The industry's performance has been so dramatic that the Nuclear Regulatory Commission (NRC) is revising the way it regulates these plants."

Federal regulators agree that deregulation does not necessarily jeopardize the safety of nuclear plants. "Our primary concern is with safety,

Los Angeles schoolchildren who celebrated Earth Day last year by cleaning up a beach make their environmental stance clear. The 1,500 students sent a message to the world by forming an image of North and South America.

not economics," said Shirley Ann Jackson, former chairman of the NRC. "With sensible cooperation [among regulators] and others with a stake in deregulation, I believe that the nation can continue to enjoy the benefit of safely operated, soundly regulated nuclear-generated electricity, along with the economic benefits of deregulation." [15]

But critics assert that pressure from the nuclear power industry to relax safety standards to help it compete under deregulation is encouraging plant operators to cut corners on safety procedures. They point to a Feb. 15 incident at the Indian Point 2 nuclear reactor in Buchanan, N.Y., where a leak in a steam-generator tube led to the release of radioactive steam into the environment. Although officials said the accident posed no threat, critics say it came as a result of increasingly lax safety standards. "As the Nuclear Regulatory Commission bows to industry pressure to reduce safety standards, more accidents like the one at Indian Point are going to occur," said a statement by Wenonah Hauter, director of Public Citizen's Critical Mass Energy Project.

Deregulation is also prompting other utilities, notably the operators of coal-fired plants, to increase output in an effort to reduce costs. That trend, critics say, has increased emissions of nitrogen oxides and sulfur dioxide, worsening environmental conditions in downwind states. "The problem is growing even worse with the deregulation of the electricity markets," said Sen. Jeffords. "In the five years since deregulation of the wholesale electricity market, increased generation at coal-fired power plants has added the equivalent of 37 million cars' worth of smog to our air." [16]

Like their counterparts in the nuclear power industry, spokesmen for coal-fired power plants say deregulation poses no threat to environmental health. "The Federal Energy Regulatory Commission has concluded that there's virtually no indication that deregulation is going to cause a worsening of the air-quality problems," says Flannery of the Midwest Ozone Group. "That makes sense if you believe, as we do, that it's not these power plants in the Midwest that are causing the Northeast's air-quality problems to begin with."

In the long run, some observers say, deregulation may actually help improve environmental health. "The utility system today is very inefficient, and anything that gets utilities to be more efficient is good for the environment," says Joseph Romm, executive director of the Center for Energy and Climate Solutions and a former assistant Energy secretary.

Many utilities are now establishing unregulated subsidiaries that help industrial plants and other large customers to improve efficiency and thus reduce their electricity bills. "This trend has been incentivized greatly by deregulation because it gives companies choices," Romm says: "I expect that over the next few years deregulation will focus companies' attention on their energy bills. If a utility can offer to not only sell you cheap power but also help you lower your whole energy bill, in five years we should see more efficiency, and therefore slower growth in energy consumption and greenhouse gas emissions than we see today." ∎

BACKGROUND

Clean Air Act

The impact of energy production on the environment has intensified with industrialization and the growth of vehicle traffic in the United States. Throughout the 19th century and well into the 20th, coal, the dirtiest fossil fuel, drove the Industrial Revolution and left its mark as a heavy cloud that darkened the skies over Pitts-

burgh, Detroit and other industrial centers of the Midwest and Northeast.

Development of the gasoline-driven, internal-combustion* engine and the mass production of Henry Ford's Model T in the early 1900s marked the beginning of the ascent of oil as the main source of energy in the United States. Although oil is less polluting than coal, the increase in oil consumption that accompanied the rise in auto traffic more than made up for the difference. By the 1960s, smog caused by auto exhaust combined with coal-fired industrial emissions to foul the air in many American cities.

The federal government first tried to establish uniform air-quality standards with the 1963 Clean Air Act, which required states to curb pollution to protect public health and the environment from the increasingly serious effects of smog and other airborne toxic materials. Building on that law, Congress passed the 1970 Clean Air Act as one of its first responses to the outpouring of public concern for the environment on the first Earth Day, held that year.

The 1970 Clean Air Act set standards for emissions of 189 pollutants that contributed to smog. Factories and power plants were required to install scrubbers to reduce emissions of particulate matter and sulfur dioxide. The law required automakers to install catalytic converters in all cars, and oil companies had to remove lead from gasoline.

Under the provisions of the act and its later amendments, the EPA established national ambient air-quality standards for six "criteria air pollutants," all of which are released by burning fossil fuels and are found to varying degrees throughout the United States:

• volatile organic compounds, carbon-based toxic chemicals, including benzene, toluene and methylene chloride, that escape from gasoline,

mainly as motorists refuel at the pump, and combine with nitrogen oxides to form ground-level ozone in summer;

• nitrogen oxides, commonly found in auto exhaust, which react in sunlight to form ground-level ozone, which causes lung irritation in humans and damages trees and crops;

• carbon monoxide, a colorless, odorless gas produced by burning gasoline that is deadly in high concentrations and causes headaches and dizziness in small amounts;

• particulate matter, dustlike particles released from combustion that cause haze and contribute to respiratory distress in the elderly, young children and other vulnerable individuals such as asthmatics;

• sulfur dioxide, released primarily by coal-fired utilities and industrial plants and the main cause of acid rain, which damages trees and kills aquatic life in rivers and lakes in the Northeast and southern Canada; and

• lead, once added to gasoline to boost octane levels, can damage the brain and central nervous system, especially in children.

Incentives Introduced in 1990

In addition to standards for each of these pollutants and fines levied against violators, the Clean Air Act Amendments of 1990 introduced incentives to encourage compliance with the law. It set emission fees, for example, that prompted many utilities to participate in a system of marketable emission allowances for sulfur dioxide. Under the EPA's Acid Rain Program, begun in 1995, plants that exceed their allowable sulfur-dioxide emissions can now avoid paying fines for violating the law by purchasing emission credits from plants whose emissions are below the limits.

Reductions in these air pollutants

Chronology

1970s
Energy crises and concerns about environmental degradation prompt calls for aggressive steps to slow oil use and air pollution.

April 22, 1970
The first Earth Day garners public support for laws to clean up the environment. Later that year, Congress creates the Environmental Protection Agency (EPA) and passes the landmark Clean Air Act, which requires the EPA to set standards for emissions of air pollutants.

October 1973
The first of a series of oil crises erupts. Oil prices soar following an embargo by the Organization of Petroleum Exporting Countries (OPEC) against the U.S.

March 28, 1979
A leak at the Three Mile Island nuclear power plant near Harrisburg, Pa., triggers a period of decline in the nuclear power industry.

———— • ————

1980s
Lower energy prices slow efforts to improve air quality.

1988
The World Meteorological Organization and the United Nations Environment Program create the Intergovernmental Panel on Climate Change to assess the threat posed by a global warming trend. It concludes that human activities — chiefly the burning of fossil fuels — probably are responsible for the phenomenon.

1990s
Concern over global warming raises new questions about energy use.

1990
Amendments to the Clean Air Act require the use of clean-burning, "reformulated" gasoline in nine cities with the worst air pollution.

1992
The Energy Policy Act sets a goal that alternative fuels replace at least 10 percent of petroleum by 2000.

June 1992
Participants at the Earth Summit in Rio de Janeiro, Brazil, sign the U.N. Framework Convention on Climate Change, agreeing to curb greenhouse gas emissions. The United States and other developed countries agree to cut their fossil-fuel emissions to 1990 levels.

1995
EPA launches Acid Rain Program, allowing coal-fired plants that exceed limits on sulfur-dioxide emissions to avoid fines by purchasing emission "credits" from plants where emissions are below the limits. Environmental commissioners of the 37 states east of the Rocky Mountains set up the Ozone Transport Assessment Group to address air pollution crossing state boundaries.

1997
EPA Administrator Carol M. Browner tightens caps on ozone, forcing state and local governments to adopt costly measures to further reduce industrial and tailpipe emissions.

December 1997
More than 160 countries that signed the 1992 emissions-reduction pact meet in Kyoto, Japan, and agree to curb emissions of carbon dioxide and other greenhouse gases believed to cause global warming.

January 1998
Because of construction delays and environmental concerns, the Department of Energy misses its deadline for beginning to remove spent nuclear fuel from the nation's nuclear plants and transporting it to a permanent repository in the Nevada desert.

November 1998
The United States signs the Kyoto Protocol, committing it and 37 other developed countries to reduce their greenhouse gas emissions by 5 to 8 percent below the 1990 levels by 2008.

September 1999
Leaks of methyl tertiary butyl ether (MTBE), the main additive in reformulated gasoline, from underground storage tanks prompt lawmakers to consider lifting the federal requirement that reformulated gasoline be sold as a way to curb air pollution.

November 1999
The EPA sues seven older Midwestern utilities for violating the Clean Air Act by failing to install pollution-control devices.

December 1999
President Clinton proposes new regulations requiring sport-utility vehicles and other light trucks to meet the same strict emission standards as passenger cars, beginning with the 2004 models.

CQ Photo/Scott J. Ferrell

Carbon-Dioxide Emissions Rose

Energy use in three sectors of the U.S. economy triggered increases of more than 10 percent in carbon-dioxide emissions from 1990 to 1998. Concern about high emissions of CO$_2$ and other greenhouse gases that cause global warming led to the Kyoto Protocol in 1998. The pact commits the U.S. and 37 other developed countries to cut their fossil-fuel emissions by 5-8 percent by 2008.

U.S. sources of CO$_2$ emissions
(in millions of metric tons of carbon)

Sector	1990	1998	1990-1998 Percent Change
Transportation (includes cars and trucks)	431.8	484.9	12.3%
Industrial	453.7	477.7	5.3
Commercial	206.7	238.4	15.3
Residential	253.1	284.5	12.4

Note: Emissions from electric utilities are distributed across all sectors.

Sources: Department of Energy, Environmental Protection Agency

have varied considerably. As lead was phased out of gasoline in the 1980s, cases of lead poisoning in children plummeted. Although particulate-matter standards were tightened in 1996, cases of asthma among children continue to grow. [17] Carbon monoxide emissions have fallen to the point that only six metropolitan areas in the country were still in violation of the standard by 1997, down from 42 in 1991.

"Despite our long-term concern about ozone, overall levels of ozone have been declining," said Robert Brenner, acting deputy administrator for air and radiation at the EPA. "In terms of ozone trends, every year in the 1990s has been cleaner than every year in the 1980s." [18]

Both particulate-matter and sulfur-dioxide emissions from utilities and other plants have been greatly re-duced following the installation in many facilities of smokestack scrubbers. But older coal-fired utilities that were exempted from the Clean Air Act's sulfur-dioxide caps continue to spew these pollutants into the air, and many downwind waterways are still too acidic to support fish and other aquatic life. Utility plants still account for three-quarters of sulfur-dioxide emissions and a third of nitrogen-oxide emissions. [19]

Some areas with heavy smog now require gas-station owners to install special cuffs on gas pump nozzles to reduce the escape of volatile organic compounds. More stringent tailpipe emission standards and incentives to retire older vehicles have helped greatly reduce the emissions of nitrogen oxides, particulate matter and carbon monoxide from each car now on the road. But the rise in auto ownership, together with the huge popularity of light trucks, which are held to weaker standards, has prevented significant gains in curtailing ground-level ozone and smog in many urban areas.

Greenhouse Gases

The action of carbon dioxide and other greenhouse gases on the Earth's surface temperatures has been debated for more than a century. [20] Interest in the subject mounted in recent years as increased concentrations of these gases led scientists to predict a gradual warming of the atmosphere, causing flooding of heavily populated coastal regions, the spread of tropical diseases and food shortages resulting from crop damage.

In 1988, the World Meteorological Organization and the United Nations Environment Program created the Intergovernmental Panel on Climate Change, made up of scientists from many countries, to assess the threat. They concluded that human activities — chiefly the burning of fossil fuels — was likely responsible for the warming trend.

Acting on the panel's findings, participants at the June 1992 Earth Summit in Rio de Janeiro signed the U.N. Framework Convention on Climate Change, agreeing to take steps to mitigate greenhouse gas emissions. As the main consumers of fossil fuels, the United States and other developed countries agreed to reduce their greenhouse gas emissions to their 1990 levels. [21]

In December 1997, representatives from more than 160 countries that had signed the 1992 document met in Kyoto, Japan, to negotiate binding limits on greenhouse gas emissions. The Kyoto Protocol set specific targets, ranging from an 8 percent reduction for members of

Can the Internet Save the World?

T he purchase of a single book from a virtual bookstore like Amazon.com consumes 16 times less energy than buying one at a bricks-and-mortar retail store, according to a new study by an environmental consulting group.

In addition, because the truck that delivers that book contains many other customers' orders, it uses one-tenth the fuel that it would take if all those people had driven to the mall to do their book shopping.[1]

Such findings lead some experts to project that the "new economy" — fueled by the explosive growth of computer technology and e-commerce — could cut the nation's energy usage and help the country slow its contribution to global warming.

"One should not underestimate the impact the Internet has had and will have on the economy," says Joseph Romm, executive director of the Center for Energy and Climate Solutions, which conducted the study.

"It is not a very energy-intensive sector," says Romm, a former assistant Energy secretary whose group advises businesses on how to reduce emissions. "So when you get the kind of growth in it that we now have, you don't get as great a rise in emissions as you would from growth in traditional manufacturing."

Spending on information technology totals about $450 billion a year — more than 60 percent of all capital spending today, according to the Competitive Enterprise Institute, a nonprofit group that promotes government deregulation.[2]

The spread of Internet commerce through such popular Web sites as Amazon.com and eBay.com will continue, experts say, with an inevitable impact on the way Americans buy goods and services and consume energy.

Computer technology and the Internet not only use less energy, Romm says, but also foster efficiency in ways that were not possible before.

"Nothing wastes more energy than making something that nobody is going to buy, shipping it to a warehouse, having

it sit there being heated and cooled and then having to be shipped somewhere else to be scrapped," he says. "Real-time information accessible with the Internet allows you to avoid mistakes, overproduction and excess inventories."

But the digital age's ultimate impact on energy usage and the environment is a matter of some disagreement. Some experts contend that the energy savings realized thus far are small — and the potential for reduction not much greater.

"The digital age, it turns out, is very energy-intensive," concludes an article that appeared last summer in *Forbes* magazine. "The Internet may someday save us bricks, mortar and catalog paper, but it is burning up an awful lot of fossil fuel in the process."[3]

Mark P. Mills, co-author of the *Forbes* story, calculates in a separate study that computers and other information-technology equipment used to power the Internet consume 8 percent of total electricity consumption today.

"With 56 percent of the electricity on the U.S. grid produced by coal-fired generators," he wrote, "the Internet's share of fuel use is on the order of 70 million tons per year of coal, out of the nearly billion tons of coal consumed to make electricity in the U.S. each year."[4]

Clearly, the jury is still out on the subject. "It's a little early to tell what the full impact of the Internet will be," Romm says. "The Internet isn't purely benign, but it does appear that on the whole it is making the country more efficient."

---

[1] Center for Energy and Climate Solutions, "Internet and E-Commerce Unleash Major Environmental and Energy Savings throughout the U.S. Economy," Dec. 10, 1999.

[2] See Mark P. Mills, "Forget Oil. It's the Century of the Electron," *The Wall Street Journal*, Feb. 23, 2000.

[3] Peter Huber and Mark P. Mills, "Dig More Coal — the PCs Are Coming," *Forbes*, May 31, 1999.

[4] Mark P. Mills, "The Internet Begins with Coal," Greening Earth Society, June 1, 1999.

---

the European Union to a 10 percent increase allowed for Iceland. The target for the United States, which signed the protocol, is 7 percent below 1990 levels. If the protocol enters into force, the emissions targets for the developed countries would have to be met between 2008 and 2012.

In order to comply with the Kyoto Protocol, the United States would have to curtail its use of fossil fuels.

Of the 1.6 billion metric tons of carbon equivalent emitted in the United States in 1990, 1.3 billion tons, or 81 percent, consisted of carbon emissions from the combustion of fossil fuels. By 1996, U.S. greenhouse gas emissions had risen to 1.7 billion tons, including 1.5 billion tons of carbon emissions from energy combustion.[22]

Opinion polls suggest that the American public strongly supports the

goals of Kyoto. A majority favors Senate ratification of the treaty, even if developing countries do not agree to reduce or even limit their greenhouse gas emissions.[23] Senators' public statements that they will not ratify a treaty that lacks participation by developing countries have discouraged President Clinton from even submitting the Kyoto Protocol for ratification.

Clinton came under intense criticism from oil, coal, auto and other industries for signing the protocol, which they said would cripple the U.S. economy while letting fast-developing countries such as China and India off the hook entirely. "The problem with the Kyoto Protocol is that if we implement these mandatory emission reductions that have been picked for an arbitrary date less than 10 years from now, it will have a severe economic effect," says Glenn Kelly, executive director of the Global Climate Coalition, an organization of U.S. companies that oppose emission mandates as envisioned in the Kyoto Protocol. "That would merely damage American private companies' ability to continue improving the technologies to reduce greenhouse gas emissions."

Voluntary cuts in greenhouse emissions

President Clinton is asking Congress for a 50 percent increase over last year's $1.1 billion funding of research into clean-fuel technologies and tax breaks for products that incorporate them. Those technologies, together with efficiency improvements, have already enabled companies to reduce their carbon emissions under a voluntary program set up by the 1992 Energy Policy Act. In 1998, 187 U.S. companies undertook 1,507 projects that achieved greenhouse gas emission reductions equivalent to 212 million metric tons of carbon dioxide, or about 3.2 percent of total U.S. emissions for the year. [24]

As scientific data continue to support the notion that global warming is already well under way, the ranks of skeptics appear to be thinning. In December, for example, Ford Motor Co. resigned from the Global Climate Coalition, following the earlier resignations of BP Amoco Corp., Royal Dutch/Shell Group and Dow Chemical Co.

"Ford's position is that we're still not sure all the facts about global climate change are in," says Terry Bresnihan, a company spokesman. "But we're certain that greenhouse gases are being released into the atmosphere, and it's possible that this is having some effect on the environment. So we feel that we should go ahead and start taking a serious look at ways to reduce those emissions." ■

CURRENT SITUATION

Transportation Trends

B ecause auto emissions contribute so heavily to both ground-level smog and greenhouse gas levels, improvements in car design and fuels are a major focus of environmental policies. [25] Since the 1970s, automakers have installed catalytic converters to reduce harmful emissions and improved fuel efficiency to reduce gasoline consumption. Both steps helped improve air quality in heavily populated areas.

But several trends over the past decade have combined to slow further improvements in air quality. Because of population growth and an unprecedented stretch of economic growth, there are more cars on the road than ever before. Even if all the newer cars now in operation were less polluting than older vehicles, the sheer increase in numbers would result in a worsening of air pollution.

But the hottest-selling cars today — sport-utility vehicles, vans and other light trucks — are exempt from the strict emission standards applied to passenger cars. The exemption dates to the 1970s, when light trucks were used primarily by farmers outside the most polluted areas of the country. To reduce costs, automakers built "sport-utes" and vans on light-truck frames, enabling these vehicles to fall under the looser emission standard, even though they are used primarily as passenger cars. Light trucks account for fully half the new cars sold in the United States today and emit up to five times the amount of pollutants as cars.

In December, President Clinton proposed lifting the exemption for light trucks over a five-year period beginning with the 2004 model year. He also proposed a 90 percent cut in gasoline sulfur levels. Sulfur clogs catalytic converters, reducing their ability to trap pollutants in auto exhaust.

"These measures will assure every American cleaner air well into the 21st century," Clinton said. "It will prevent thousands of premature deaths and protect millions of our children from respiratory disease. It will be the most dramatic improvement in air quality since the catalytic converter was first introduced a quarter-century ago. And manufacturers will be able to meet these new standards while still offering the kinds of models popular with consumers today." [26]

The EPA estimates that the new emissions standards would raise the price of a new passenger car by less than $100, a light truck by $200 and a gallon of gas by less than 2 cents. [27]

Another attempt to reduce auto emissions has backfired. To satisfy the requirement of the 1990 Clean Air Act Amendments that clean-burning, "reformulated" gasoline be used in the nine cities with the worst air pollution, petroleum refiners added methyl tertiary butyl ether (MTBE) to boost the oxygen content of fuel sold in most of these markets. It has since been found that cleaner air has come

Big Corporate Polluters Pledge Reductions

Opposition to the Kyoto Protocol, which requires industrialized countries to reduce their emissions of carbon dioxide and other greenhouse gases, still runs strong in the United States — but the corporate winds may be shifting.

When President Clinton signed the treaty in 1998 along with the leaders of 83 other nations, lawmakers in Washington made it clear that support in the Senate was insufficient to gain the two-thirds majority of votes needed to ratify it.

And shortly after Kyoto, large American companies, the biggest consumers of fossil fuels that produce most greenhouse gas emissions, established the Global Climate Coalition to oppose federal mandates aimed at meeting the treaty's terms.

But some corporations' initial, flat-out rejection that heavy reliance on fossil fuels is causing a potentially deadly warming of the Earth's atmosphere gradually is folding — in part because they can profit from reducing greenhouse gas emissions.

Two energy behemoths, the Royal Dutch/Shell Group and BP Amoco, the world's No. 2 and No. 3 oil and gas companies, respectively, have committed to reduce their greenhouse gas emissions by 10 percent over 1990 levels by 2010.

The impact could be huge. The companies generate large quantities of carbon dioxide through oil exploration, drilling, production and petroleum refining. Shell, for example, emitted nearly 115 million tons of carbon dioxide in 1997. One-third resulted from the practice of venting and flaring natural gas in oil fields, which the company plans to phase out by 2002.

"One of the easy things for petroleum companies to do is stop venting and flaring natural gas," says Joseph Romm, executive director of the nonprofit Center for Energy and Climate Solutions, which advises private companies on ways to save energy and reduce greenhouse emissions. "Given that global warming is the biggest environmental problem of the next century, I suspect that there will be a lot of pressure on most companies to adopt good business practices to reduce their contributions to the problem."

The commitments from BP Amoco and Shell to cut emissions, Romm says, can be traced to their corporate headquarters. Both firms are based in Europe, where public sentiment and government support for Kyoto is stronger than in America.

Far more significant, he says, is the recent pledge by DuPont Corp. to reduce carbon emissions by 65 percent over 1990 levels by 2010. "This is a huge commitment," Romm says, "and DuPont has clearly established itself as a leader in the United States."

DuPont's Chambers Works Plant in Delaware, for instance, already has slashed carbon emissions by 45 percent over the past four years by capturing and using the heat produced at its electric-generation plant, a process known as cogeneration.

"Currently, most power plants use coal, natural gas or oil to generate electricity, and they throw away the waste heat, which accounts for two-thirds of the energy generated," Romm says. "Cogeneration technology makes it possible to generate electricity and steam and in fact use the steam to run a chiller, so you can actually have electricity, heat, hot water and cold water from the same equipment."

Romm, who served as assistant secretary of Energy for energy efficiency and renewable energy from 1993 through 1998, is highly optimistic about the potential for greenhouse gas savings through voluntary measures such as these.

"With the exception of companies undergoing rapid expansion, I believe that most businesses, even small businesses, can profitably reduce their greenhouse gas emissions," he says. "If the U.S. economy reduced its carbon dioxide emissions by 4 percent per dollar of gross domestic product every year for the next 12 years, we would meet the terms of Kyoto. That's a reasonable goal."

But other experts are less sanguine. "Romm is a little more optimistic than many people about how many great opportunities there are for companies to make money while reducing their energy consumption," says Paul Portney, president of Resources for the Future, a research organization in Washington.

"The world marketplace is increasingly competitive," Portney says, "and if a utility or manufacturer could save energy by spending a small amount of money, they already have strong incentives to do so. The question is, how many of these $5 bills are lying around on the factory floor."

---

at a heavy cost — water pollution caused by MTBE that has leaked from underground storage tanks.

Legislators from California and some Northeastern states, where MTBE pollution has been most evident, are clamoring for the reformu-lated gasoline requirement to be lifted, as well as a ban or severe restriction on MTBE. A bill cosponsored by Sens. Dianne Feinstein, D-Calif., James M. Inhofe, R-Okla., and Robert C. Smith, R-N.H., would allow states to waive the reformulated-gasoline requirement while continu-ing to meet federal air-quality standards by other means. [28]

Lawmakers from corn-producing states support the MTBE ban, but they want to keep the federal refor-mulated-gasoline requirement. That's because their states stand to profit from increased sales of ethanol, a corn derivative that is the only viable alternative to MTBE. Although it has long been used to boost the oxygen content of gasoline sold in Chicago and Milwaukee, ethanol is hard to transport to distant markets. Opponents of the proposal say that replacing MTBE with ethanol would drive up the cost of fuel in many areas. (*See "At Issue", p. 73.*)

Alternative Fuels

While regulators are tightening air-quality standards, automakers are developing technologies that will enable them to reduce gasoline consumption or even replace it altogether with cleaner fuels.

Natural gas, the cleanest-burning fossil fuel, has been used to power vehicles for more than a decade. Exhaust emissions from vehicles powered by natural gas emit 70 percent less carbon monoxide and 87 percent less nitrogen oxides than gasoline-powered vehicles. Because there are few refueling stations that sell natural gas, however, conversion to natural gas has been largely confined to fleet vehicles such as small buses and business vehicles.

The development of electric cars has been spurred by a California requirement that at least 4 percent of the major automakers' cars sold in the state beginning in 2003 emit no pollutants. One version currently on the market is the "hybrid" car, powered by both gasoline and electricity. These vehicles recharge as they're driven, get twice the gas mileage of conventional cars and can be refueled at any gas station. Because they consume less fuel, hybrids also emit far fewer pollutants than conventional, internal-combustion vehicles.

All the big, international automakers have developed prototypes of hybrid cars, and Toyota Motor Corp. and Honda Motor Co. are marketing models in the United States that get 80 miles per gallon. [29]

The most promising non-polluting energy source for vehicles is the hydrogen fuel cell, which emits only heat and water. [30] Automakers are working with Ballard Power Systems of Canada and other fuel-cell manufacturers to produce marketable fuel-cell vehicles, such as DaimlerChrylster Co.'s NECAR 4, a prototype the company called the first "drivable" hydrogen fuel-cell car in the United States. [31]

The switch to alternative fuels has been much slower than policy-makers had hoped, however. The 1992 Energy Policy Act set a goal of having alternative fuels replace at least 10 percent of petroleum fuels by 2000. The Energy Department's latest estimates suggest that alternative fuels will replace only 0.3 percent of the gasoline used this year. [32]

Industrial plants and utilities are other potential consumers of clean energy. The Clinton administration's 2001 budget request includes $30 million for research and development of renewable-energy sources, including a $4.8 million program to capture underground hot water and steam to generate electricity. The program's goal is to supply 10 percent of the West's electricity with geothermal energy by 2020.

"Geothermal power is a clean, reliable and renewable energy source available in all Western states," said Energy Secretary Bill Richardson. "In fact, it is already a significant supplier of electricity in California, with additional resources in Nevada, Utah and Hawaii. We are confident that this initiative will help to increase the power produced by this existing resource and make it a major contributor to our clean energy mix." [33] ■

OUTLOOK

Nuclear Waste

Amid tightening air-quality regulations, the place nuclear power is likely to assume in the nation's energy mix remains unclear. Efforts to fashion a solution to the longstanding controversy over the storage of spent nuclear fuel foundered on Feb. 10, when a Senate measure failed to garner the 67 votes needed to override a promised presidential veto. As a result, it appears unlikely that Congress will resolve the issue before this fall's elections. [34]

The White House and many environmentalists objected to the measure because it would allow nuclear waste to be stored temporarily above ground at Yucca Mountain and because it would transfer authority for setting radiation-exposure standards at the site from the Environmental Protection Agency to the Nuclear Regulatory Commission.

"Yucca Mountain isn't a very smart place to put this waste," says Shollenberger of Public Citizen. "It's located on fault lines, and there is a possibility that the groundwater would be contaminated because the rock is not as dry as previously believed. The proposal also would reduce the authority of the EPA to set standards to protect health and the environment. The Senate proposal that the EPA would have to reach agreement with the NRC also is not acceptable because the NRC has indicated that it's willing to set less stringent standards in order to be able to license Yucca Mountain. That's just not acceptable."

Meanwhile, radioactive waste continues to build up at power plants, a

At Issue:

Should Congress lift the Clean Air Act's mandate that reformulated gasoline contain 2 percent oxygen?

EDWARD H. MURPHY
Manager of downstream activity, American Petroleum Institute

FROM TESTIMONY BEFORE THE HOUSE SCIENCE SUBCOMMITTEE ON ENERGY AND ENVIRONMENT, SEPT. 30, 1999

mTBE [methyl tertiary butyl ether] has been widely used in gasoline for about 20 years — first, in limited quantities to enhance octane as lead was removed and, more recently, in far greater quantities to add oxygen to cleaner-burning fuels, especially reformulated gasoline.... Oxygen is not added to reformulated gasoline because it's necessary to reduce smog. It's added because the Clean Air Act Amendments of 1990 require it. Before the legislation was passed, refiners stressed that the mandate for oxygen wasn't necessary and urged setting a simple performance standard instead. But their advice wasn't taken.

This, therefore, should not be a debate about MTBE or other oxygenates. It should be a debate about mandates for a gasoline formula — and how they hinder our common objective of working for an even cleaner environment at the lowest possible cost to the economy and the consumer.... [B]anning use of MTBE without repealing the federal oxygenate mandate would create new problems. Leaving the mandate in place would mean substituting another oxygenate, almost certainly ethanol, for the volume of MTBE now used.

But ethanol is not an environmental panacea.... [B]lending of ethanol in gasoline tends to boost emissions by increasing the evaporation rate of gasoline — and it can increase the overall toxicity of emissions. Air-quality regulators are well aware of these shortcomings....

Massive use of ethanol would also present distribution problems, potentially raising costs. That's because ethanol can't be added to gasoline and then shipped in pipelines, as most fuel is transported....

Moreover, expanded use of ethanol would reduce revenues to the Highway Trust Fund by about [$750 million] more each year, owing to a tax break of 54 cents for every gallon of ethanol sold. This is in addition to the roughly $1 billion per year in current government supports to ethanol. Less revenue to the trust fund means [fewer] resources available to build and maintain our highways and bridges — or higher taxes to make up for the shortfall.

Many of our companies use ethanol today, and they will continue to use it to meet their customers' needs. However, banning or phasing down MTBE use without repealing the federal oxygenate mandate would be extremely shortsighted and not in the national interest.

TOM SKINNER
Director, Illinois Environmental Protection Agency

FROM TESTIMONY BEFORE THE HOUSE SCIENCE SUBCOMMITTEE ON ENERGY AND ENVIRONMENT, SEPT. 14, 1999

i would like to acknowledge up front that Illinois is the nation's leading producer of ethanol.... Illinois annually processes 280 million bushels of corn into ethanol. One out of every five rows of corn grown in Illinois goes to the production of ethanol. Illinois is also the largest ethanol consumer in the nation, with approximately 60 percent of the state's fuel blended with 10 percent ethanol....

Section 211(k) of the Clean Air Act requires the use of reformulated gasoline (RFG) in the nation's nine worst ozone non-attainment areas. These cities include Baltimore, Chicago, Hartford, Houston, Los Angeles, Milwaukee, New York, Philadelphia and San Diego....

The use of oxygenates in reformulated gasoline is also required pursuant to the Clean Air Act.... Oxygenates have environmental benefits — they promote more complete fuel combustion resulting in reduced toxic and ozone-forming emissions.

Since the RFG program was introduced in the eight-county Chicago non-attainment area in 1995, more than 95 percent of our RFG has used ethanol as its oxygenate. Ethanol-blended RFG has enjoyed the acceptance of millions of vehicle owners in that area since its introduction....

As a result of recent debates about MTBE, you may at some point be asked to remove the oxygenate requirement from the RFG program altogether. We at Illinois EPA would urge you not to do so for very sound environmental-policy reasons.

The recent study by the National Research Council concluded that the presence of oxygen in gasoline reduces vehicular carbon monoxide emissions by approximately 15 percent. The report also recommended amending the RFG program regulations to account for this impact and concluded that approximately 20 percent of the ozone-forming potential from vehicle exhaust emissions was attributable to carbon monoxide. Therefore, the reduction in carbon monoxide emissions achieved through the use of oxygenates contributes to improved ozone air quality....

[T]he use of oxygenated fuels has contributed to cleaner air in our metropolitan areas, and ethanol, in the final balance, is the environmentally beneficial oxygenate of choice. We seek the support of this subcommittee and the full Congress in assuring that states like Illinois that currently use ethanol should be allowed to continue, and ethanol should be phased in for the rest of the country.

Trees in Cities — They're Really Cool

It's hard for big cities to escape pollution. High population density inevitably means heavy traffic and high levels of tailpipe emissions of smog-producing pollutants. In the summer, those pollutants are transformed by heat and sunlight into ground-level ozone. City dwellers also suffer other consequences of air pollution, such as respiratory distress, eye irritation and the general discomfort that comes with living in a big city on a hot summer day.

Cities also are more likely to suffer brownouts or even blackouts on the hottest days, when electricity-gobbling air-conditioning systems overwhelm the capacity of utilities to satisfy the demand for power. In many cities, especially along the East Coast, the problem is compounded by pollutants that waft in from coal-fired power plants to the west that are running at full steam in an effort to keep up with the demand for cool air.

Demand for air-conditioning is especially high in cities because of the "heat island effect." In natural environments, trees and other plants cool the air by releasing water through the pores in their leaves. As it evaporates, the water draws heat and thus cools the surrounding air. A single tree with a crown 30 feet in diameter can "evapo-transpire" up to 40 gallons of water in a day, which is the equivalent of removing all the heat produced in four hours by a small electric space heater.

But natural air-conditioning systems become less effective as plants are replaced with streets and buildings. Asphalt and other dark building materials absorb solar heat instead of reflecting it away. As a result, it can be up to 8 degrees F hotter downtown than in the surrounding countryside. High temperatures, in turn, worsen air pollution. In Los Angeles, for example, smog increases in intensity by 3 percent for every degree the temperature rises above 70 degrees. [1]

Most efforts to improve urban air quality are directed at the sources of pollution, such as cars, utilities and factories. Regulations issued under the 1970 Clean Air Act and later amendments require automakers to install catalytic converters

on cars and industrial plants to use smokestack "scrubbers" to reduce harmful emissions. But environmental activists in some cities are emphasizing natural solutions to the problem by encouraging city dwellers to plant trees wherever they can. Large trees planted along busy roadways filter out air pollutants in auto exhaust. Their leaves absorb carbon dioxide and ozone, and the trees themselves block the distribution of particulate matter. Careful landscaping also can reduce demand for residential and commercial air-conditioning.

In Los Angeles, one of the country's most intense heat islands, a nonprofit organization called TreePeople recently convinced local officials to abandon plans to spend $200 million to resurface the play yards at city schools with asphalt. "We found $220 million in the budget that was earmarked for new air-conditioning units to cool down the buildings that were being heated by the asphalt," says Andy Lipkis, TreePeople's founder and director. "Then we showed how we could pretty much guarantee to the school district a 12-18 percent annual savings on energy costs by lowering the amount of heat that would be infiltrating in the first place."

After demonstrating that the city could save money by replacing the existing asphalt with permeable materials and planting trees to shade air-conditioning units, windows and classrooms, TreePeople and other community groups won approval to spend $4 million a year to plant and care for about 100 trees at each school in the city. The project, called Cool Schools, also includes educational material to encourage students to help care for their new environments. "The economics of energy savings and urban heat-island reduction made it possible to actually pay for the tree maintenance," Lipkis says. "Once that was clear, it became clear that they couldn't afford not to plant these trees."

Los Angeles children have been planting tree seedlings around their schools in an experiment that experts say could lower the school district's future energy costs by as much as 18 percent.

TreePeople/Becky Villaseñor

---

[1] For more information, see the Heat Island Group, an Energy Department-sponsored research team in Berkeley, Calif., http://EETD.LBL.gov/HeatIsland.

practice that industry spokesmen say cannot continue indefinitely. "Consumers have already paid the government to dispose of this fuel, and now they're having to pay again to

provide storage, monitoring of the waste and security around these sites," says Colvin of the Nuclear Energy Institute. "So there's a significant added cost for what is really no

good reason. There is also concern among the states that if the Department of Energy assumes legal responsibility for the fuel, it may just leave it where it is."

To discourage that outcome, the Minnesota legislature has barred the nuclear facility at Prairie Island from building new on-site storage. "They don't want the site to become a de facto waste-storage site ad infinitum," Colvin explains. "The plant will have to shut down if it doesn't have sufficient space to take the fuel because the state lawmakers don't have any confidence that the federal government will pick it up as promised."

Candidates' Views

The prospects for future policy changes aimed at reducing the environmental impact of energy consumption hinge on this fall's presidential and congressional contests. If the Republican candidate wins the White House and the GOP continues to enjoy majorities in the House and Senate, many of the Clinton administration's environmental priorities, including stiffer air-quality standards and support for the Kyoto Protocol, are likely to be reversed.

But the current front-runners offer few commitments about their environmental priorities when queried by the Sustainable Energy Coalition, a group of about 30 national organizations promoting energy efficiency and renewable-energy technologies. Only Vice President Al Gore, for example, expressed any views on the contentious issue of nuclear power and waste storage, stating that he does "not support an increased reliance on nuclear power for electricity generation," but would "keep open the option of relicensing nuclear power plants" as long as they "can reliably meet strict health and safety standards."[35]

All the candidates voiced support for effective air-quality standards and gains in fuel efficiency. Gov. George W. Bush, R-Texas, said he supports "cleaner gasoline standards across the country," including the need to "look at a national standard for lower sulfide for gasoline," a standard already proposed by the Clinton administration.

Although Bush's rival for the Republican nomination, Sen. John McCain of Arizona, expressed general support for clean air, he said, "it's time to comprehensively review our nation's environmental laws to assure they are relevant to today's needs and capabilities . . . and seek ways to make them more sensible and less costly."

In a separate statement on global warming, McCain reflects the views of many of his Senate colleagues. "If climate change is a bona fide, global environmental problem, the solution must be global as well," he said. "I have serious concerns about the Kyoto treaty because it fails to include the cooperation of countries such as China and India. A problem that is serious enough to require U.S. action should require the responsible participation of other major countries as well."[36]

In answer to the coalition survey, former Sen. Bill Bradley, D-N.J., said he "would support legislation limiting power plant emissions of carbon dioxide [as well as] additional efforts to ensure that all Americans breathe healthful air," including the EPA's most recent standards.

Gore said that "cleaning up grandfathered power plants is a necessary component of any plan to ensure clean, healthy air for all American citizens." Gore, who was recognized as a strong proponent of environmental protection before becoming vice president in 1993, has been criticized by Bradley for his environmental record in the White House.

"To be a custodian of our natural world means more than paddling a kayak for the TV cameras," Bradley said. "The record for prosecutions for environmental crimes during the last seven years is less than half of those prosecuted during the Bush administration. At the same time, many anti-environmental riders have been signed into law. Through all this, the vice president's silence has been deafening."[37]

Whatever the outcome of the presidential election, the winner's environmental policies will be put to the test almost immediately. The next U.N. conference on climate change, which will consider such thorny issues as developing-world participation in global carbon emission caps, is scheduled to convene on Nov. 13 in The Hague.

"This will be the first major issue — and it's not a small issue — that will face the new administration," says Kelly of the Global Climate Coalition. "Just a few days after the election, they will have to get on a plane for The Hague and start negotiating, and there's no way of telling until election night on whose behalf our negotiators will be negotiating." ■

Notes

[1] Quoted in Janelle Carter, "Truckers Protest Soaring Fuel Prices at Capitol," The Associated Press, Feb. 23, 2000.

[2] See David Masci, "Auto Industry's Future," *The CQ Researcher*, Jan. 21, 2000, pp. 17-40.

[3] National Research Council, "Reconciling Observations of Global Temperature Change," Jan. 12, 2000.

[4] Richard Rhodes and Denis Beller, "The Need for Nuclear Power," *Foreign Affairs*, January/February 2000, p. 44.

[5] Energy Information Administration, Department of Energy, "Voluntary Reporting of Greenhouse Gases 1998," December 1999.

[6] From a statement issued Jan. 10, 2000.

[7] Rhodes and Beller, *op. cit.*, p. 38.

[8] Arjun Makhijani, "Decommissioned But Dangerous?" *The Washington Post*, Jan. 24, 2000.

[9] For background on evolving policy on ozone transport, see Tom Arrandale, "Balking on Air," *Governing*, January 2000, pp. 26-29.

[10] Sen. Lieberman addressed the Senate on Nov. 10, 1999.

[11] Sen. Jeffords addressed the Senate on Nov. 10, 1999.

[12] See Matthew Futterman, "Old Test, Short Waits, Big Smiles," *The Star-Ledger* (Newark, N.J.), Feb. 1, 2000.

[13] For background, see Adriel Bettelheim, "Utility Deregulation," *The CQ Researcher*, Jan. 14, 2000, pp. 1-16.

[14] Energy Information Administration, "Monthly Energy Review," January 2000.

[15] Jackson addressed a National Association of Regulatory Utility Commissioners conference on the impact of deregulation on electricity markets on Jan. 23, 1997, in Fort Myers, Fla. She was succeeded as chairman on Oct. 29, 1999, by Richard A. Meserve.

[16] Sen. Jeffords addressed the Senate on Nov. 10, 1999.

[17] For background, see Kenneth Jost, "Asthma Epidemic," *The CQ Researcher*, Dec. 24, 1999, pp. 1089-1104; and Mary H. Cooper, "New Air Quality Standards," *The CQ Researcher*, March 7. 1997, pp. 193-216.

[18] Brenner addressed a meeting of the American Natural Gas Association in Minneapolis, Oct. 5, 1999.

[19] See John Carlin, "Environmental Externalities in Electric Power Markets: Acid Rain, Urban Ozone, and Climate Change," www.eia.doe.gov/cheaf/pubs.

[20] For background, see Mary H. Cooper, "The Politics of Energy," *The CQ Researcher*, March 5, 1999, pp. 185-208; and "Global Warming Update," *The CQ Researcher*, pp. 961-984.

[21] The Kyoto Protocol covers naturally occurring carbon dioxide, methane and nitrous oxide, as well as hydrofluorocarbons, perfluorocarbons and sulfur hexafluoride, synthetic gases released from industrial processes.

[22] Energy Information Administration, "Greenhouse Gases and the Kyoto Protocol," April 28, 1999.

[23] For results of one polling series, see Program on International Policy Attitudes, University of Maryland, Feb. 8, 2000, www.pipa.org.

[24] Energy Information Administration, "Voluntary Reporting of Greenhouse Gases 1998," December 1999.

FOR MORE INFORMATION

Critical Mass Energy Project, Public Citizen, 1600 20th St. N.W., Washington, D.C. 20009; (202) 546-4996; www.citizen.org/CMEP. Founded by consumer advocate Ralph Nader, this organization promotes environmentally safe alternatives to nuclear energy.

Energy Information Administration, National Energy Information Center U.S. Department of Energy, 1000 Independence Ave. S.W., Washington, D.C. 20585; (202) 586-5000; www.eia.doe.gov. EIA provides data, forecasts and analyses to promote sound policy-making, efficient markets and public understanding regarding energy and its interaction with the economy and the environment.

Global Climate Coalition, 1275 K St. N.W., Suite 890, Washington, D.C. 20005; (202) 682-9161; www.globalclimate.org. This coalition of business trade associations and private companies opposes mandated caps on emissions of carbon dioxide and other gases implicated in global warming.

National Petroleum Refiners Association, 1899 L St. N.W., Suite 1000, Washington, D.C. 20036; (202) 457-0480; www.npradc.org. This trade association provides information on the petroleum-refining and petrochemical-manufacturing industries.

Nuclear Energy Institute, 1776 I St. N.W., Suite 400, Washington, D.C. 20006; (202) 739-8000; www.nei.org. NEI promotes expansion of nuclear power as an environmentally friendly alternative to fossil fuels.

Resources for the Future, 1616 P St. N.W., Washington, D.C. 20036; (202) 328-5000; www.rff.org. This environmental research organization examines the benefits and costs of all aspects of environmental policy.

[25] See Mary H. Cooper, "Oil Production in the 21st Century," *The CQ Researcher*, Aug. 7, 1998, pp. 673-696.

[26] Clinton announced the new emissions standards on Dec. 21, 1999.

[27] Environmental Protection Agency, "EPA's Program for Cleaner Vehicles and Cleaner Gasoline," December 1999, www.epa.gov.

[28] See Charles Pope, "Interest Groups Weigh In as Congress Seeks Solution to Gasoline Additive Problem," *CQ Weekly*, Feb. 5, 2000, pp. 253-254.

[29] See Amy Myers Jaffe and Robert A. Manning, "The Shocks of a World of Cheap Oil," *Foreign Affairs*, January/February 2000, pp. 16-29.

[30] For background, see Mary H. Cooper, "Renewable Energy," *The CQ Researcher*, Nov. 7, 1997, pp. 961-984.

[31] See Masci, *op. cit.*, Jan. 21, 2000, p. 32.

[32] Department of Energy, "Alternative Fueled Vehicles in Use and Alternative Fuel Consumption 1998 Through 2000," Jan. 19, 2000, www.eia.doe.gov.

[33] From a Jan. 24, 2000, statement.

[34] See Chuck McCutcheon, "Senate GOP's Compromise on Nuclear Waste Storage Fail to Win Veto-Proof Majority," *CQ Weekly*, Feb. 12, 2000, p. 322.

[35] American Council for an Energy-Efficient Economy, "Presidential Candidates' Views on Energy Policy and Related Environmental Issues," Jan. 18, 2000, www.aceee.org.

[36] From McCain's campaign Web site, McCain2000.com.

[37] From a Feb. 14, 2000, campaign speech in San Francisco, www.billbradley.com.

Bibliography

Selected Sources Used

Books

Easterbrook, Gregg, *A Moment on the Earth: The Coming Age of Environmental Optimism,* **Penguin Books, 1995.**

Despite persistent air pollution and evidence that energy use is behind a gradual warming of global temperatures, efforts to reduce the use of the fossil fuels most responsible for both problems are beginning to pay off in the form of energy-technology improvements, lower alternative fuel prices and voluntary efforts by businesses to curb harmful emissions.

Gelbspan, Ross, *The Heat Is On: The High Stakes Battle over Earth's Threatened Climate,* **Addison-Wesley Publishing Co., 1997.**

As scientific data increasingly support the theory that global warming is already well under way, environmental advocates, countries that are at risk of flooding from rising sea levels and global insurance companies are joining hands in a campaign to support international efforts to slow climatic change.

Articles

Arrandale, Tom, "Balking on Air," *Governing,* **January 2000, pp. 26-29.**

A shaky agreement among states east of the Rocky Mountains to curb the flow of air pollutants across state boundaries has fallen apart. Northeastern states blame Midwestern utilities for dirtying their air, while the Midwest says Eastern politicians are just trying to avoid taking politically costly steps to curb auto emissions at home.

Burtraw, Dallas, Joel Darmstadter, Karen Palmer and James McVeigh, "Renewable Energy: Winner, Loser or Innocent Victim?" *Resources,* **spring 1999, pp. 9-13.**

The shift to relatively clean, renewable energy sources has been slower than once predicted because of their high cost compared with fossil fuels. But the shift may accelerate as new technology makes renewables more efficient and less costly.

Rhodes, Richard, and Denis Beller, "The Need for Nuclear Power," *Foreign Affairs,* **January/February 2000, pp. 30-44.**

Mounting efforts to curb global warming virtually ensure that nuclear power will be an important source of energy in the future, the authors write. Not only does modern technology make nuclear power safe, in their view, it produces virtually no greenhouse gas emissions.

Reports and Studies

Bradley, Robert L., "Renewable Energy: Not Cheap, Not Green," Cato Institute, Aug. 27, 1997.

Despite advances in renewable-energy technology, underwritten largely by government subsidies, renewable energy is still twice as expensive as fossil fuels, the author writes. The report concludes that efforts to include mandates that deregulated electric utilities use renewable energy sources would unfairly raise the cost of electricity.

Energy Information Administration, U.S. Department of Energy, "Greenhouse Gases and the Kyoto Protocol," April 28, 1999.

This exhaustive report describes the scientific evidence pointing to global climate change, the history of negotiations leading to the 1997 Kyoto Protocol and the main sources of greenhouse gas emissions, produced overwhelmingly by energy consumption.

Energy Information Administration, U.S. Department of Energy, "Voluntary Reporting of Greenhouse Gases 1998," December 1999.

Under a voluntary program set up by the 1992 Energy Policy Act, 187 U.S. companies have undertaken 1,507 projects that in 1998 achieved greenhouse gas emission reductions equivalent to 212 million metric tons of carbon dioxide, about 3.2 percent of total U.S. emissions for the year.

National Research Council, "Reconciling Observations of Global Temperature Change," Jan. 12, 2000.

This controversial report concludes that warming of the Earth's surface temperatures is "undoubtedly real" and that the temperature increase has been substantially greater than average in the past 20 years.

Parker, Larry, and John Blodgett, "Air Quality: EPA's Proposed Ozone Transport Rule, OTAG and Section 126 Petitions — A Hazy Situation?" Congressional Research Service, May 14, 1998.

This report by the research arm of the Library of Congress reviews the controversy surrounding the problem of wind-borne transport of air pollutants across state boundaries and the political responses to it. Efforts to curb such emissions, mostly from Midwestern coal-fired utilities, have prompted lawsuits that remain largely unresolved.

5 Regulating Pesticides

DAVID HOSANSKY

Three years after President Clinton signed the sweeping Food Quality Protection Act (FQPA), the bitter debate over the risks of pesticides is as heated as ever.

Now the government is turning up the heat even more. The Environmental Protection Agency (EPA), in one of the most dramatic pesticide actions in years, is announcing sharp limits on two pesticides widely applied to apples, peaches and other produce. At the same time, however, it is declining to tighten restrictions on some other controversial pesticides.

EPA Administrator Carol Browner said the crackdown on methyl parathion and azinphosmethyl stems from concerns that overexposure to the two compounds might cause nervous-system damage and other disorders, especially in infants and small children.

Farmers, who use nearly 1 billion pounds of pesticides a year, worry that such restrictions will put them out of business, but environmentalists and consumer advocates contend that the government is moving too timidly. [1]

Synthetically produced pesticides are highly effective in controlling insects, weeds, rodents and mold. Without these products, growers say they would lose billions of dollars in crops. Food would cost much more, and produce would be full of blemishes.

But environmentalists and public health advocates worry that this intensive chemical use is taking a grave toll on human health and the global environment. Popular fruits and vegetables, and even baby food, contain the residues of dozens of toxic

From *The CQ Researcher,* August 6, 1999.

chemicals, according to reports by such public interest organizations as Consumers Union and the Environmental Working Group. Advocates are particularly concerned over human consumption of two highly potent classes of pesticides that affect the nervous system — organophosphates and carbamates.

Researchers differ over whether low residue levels on produce pose a significant threat to human health. However, an increasing number of studies are linking pesticides on food and in the environment to a number of health disorders, ranging from breast and prostate cancer to aggressiveness and reduced motor skill ability. Infants and children are considered especially vulnerable because they consume greater amounts of fruits and vegetables relative to their body weight than do adults, and they have different metabolic characteristics.

"On any day in the United States, there are several thousand children who are exposed to organophosphates at levels that can be toxic. It is not a rare event," says Philip J. Landrigan, a pediatrician at the Mt. Sinai School of Medicine in New York City, who served as chairman of a National Research Council committee that investigated pesticides in the diets of infants and children. "Even low doses of these chemicals can be quite damaging to the brain."

Farmers, however, say that pesticides are needed to help them produce enough food to support a growing population. It is due in part to pesticides, they point out, that Americans are eating more healthy food with an emphasis on fresh fruits and vegetables.

Furthermore, they contend that the amount of chemical residue on food is far too slight to pose any health threat. "It would be a shame to encourage people to eat less fruits and vegetables because of concern over pesticides," says Scott Rawlins, senior environmental policy specialist for the American Farm Bureau Federation. "We don't see many residues at all, and the residues we do see are very low-level. The risks we see from residues on food is non-existent."

Although much of the controversy has focused on the risk to consumers, scientists also worry about the effect of pesticides on rural workers and residents. Some studies have indicated that farmowners, as well as migrant and seasonal farmworkers, suffer disproportionately from chronic diseases, including certain types of cancer. (*See story, p. 90.*) A study in Mexico concluded that children exposed to pesticides in the womb or at an early age may suffer permanent brain defects. [2]

In addition, groups like the World Wildlife Fund are reporting that pesticides and other toxic chemicals that leak into the environment wreak havoc on the immune and reproductive systems of animals, killing species across the planet. [3] Pesticide spills take an additional toll. In 1991, a train carrying 13,000 gallons of metam sodium derailed in California, dumping its lethal cargo into the Sacramento River and destroying all animal and plant life in the river for 40 miles. [4]

Farmers are hardly the only people who use pesticides. With more than

Pesticide Residues High in Peaches, Apples, Green Beans

Several U.S.-grown products have dangerously high levels of pesticide residues, including fresh peaches, apples, green beans and spinach, according to Consumers Union. Low pesticide levels are found in bananas, broccoli and frozen or canned corn.

Very Low Toxicity	Low to Moderately High Toxicity	High Toxicity
Toxicity Index: Under 10	**Toxicity Index: 11-100**	**Toxicity Index: Over 100**
• Corn (frozen or canned)	• Apple juice	• Apples
• Bananas	• Carrots	• Green beans
• Broccoli	• Peas (frozen or canned)	• Peaches
• Orange juice	• Sweet potatoes	• Pears
	• Tomatoes	• Spinach
		• Winter squash

USDA Agricultural Research Service

Note: The toxicity index indicates the relative amount of pesticide residue.

Source: Consumers Union of the United States

20,000 pesticide products on the market, Americans are exposed to pesticides wherever weeds or insects can be a problem — lawns, homes, office buildings, airplanes, schools. These chemicals play a vital role in keeping down the populations of disease-carrying pests, such as cockroaches and rats. But the products sometimes are used illegally. In 1995, hundreds of homes and businesses required extensive decontamination after unlicensed exterminators used the cheap but deadly pesticide methyl parathion.

Even when such products are used legally, they may pose greater risks than pesticide residues on food. "The somewhat casual use of pesticides in yards, gardens, parks is a much more important target for pesticide reduction," says Sheila Zahm, deputy director of the division of cancer epidemiology and genetics at the National Cancer Institute.

Chemical pesticides, used worldwide since the end of World War II, have stirred up controversy almost

from their inception. Many in the agriculture and health-care communities hailed the new chemicals for spurring the production of food worldwide, thereby helping to alleviate hunger. In addition, the chemicals did much to cut down on insects that carry deadly diseases such as malaria.

Opposition to the use of DDT and other chemical compounds known as chlorinated hydrocarbons crystallized with the publication of *Silent Spring*, the landmark book by Rachel Carson, which linked pesticides with serious damage to the environment and public health. Although DDT was banned in the United States in 1972, health experts remain deeply concerned about the toxic effects of other pesticides still in use — some of which can be traced back to the development of chemical warfare compounds during World War II.

To address consumers' concerns, Congress set up an elaborate system to regulate the sale and use of pesticides. The EPA, established in 1970,

was charged with overseeing the production, labeling and use of all pesticides. The EPA requires manufacturers to conduct extensive testing and safety studies on each pesticide to assure that it doesn't pose undue risks. The agency specifies acceptable application doses and uses for each chemical. It also establishes "tolerances," or maximum acceptable levels, for pesticide residues found in food, with enforcement by the Food and Drug Administration (FDA).

Since laws written in the 1940s and '50s established different tolerances for raw and processed foods, Congress in 1996, after years of debate, passed the FQPA to establish a single standard. The EPA now has to make sure that residues on both raw and processed foods pose a "reasonable certainty" of no harm. For the first time, the agency has to base its tolerances on so-called aggregate risk — taking into account not only dietary exposures but also all non-occupational exposures ranging from drinking water to lawns. In addition, it must account for the increased vulnerability of children and infants.

"I like to think of it as the 'peace of mind' act," President Clinton said when he signed the new law on Aug. 3, 1996. "It'll give parents the peace of mind that comes from knowing that the fruits, vegetables, the grains that they put down in front of their children are safe." [5]

But far from ending the controversy over pesticides, the law has merely moved the highly charged debate from Congress to the EPA. The agency has until 2006 to re-evaluate the more than 9,700 tolerances that it established for pesticides before the new law; one-third of the re-evaluations should be finalized by this month. [6] This complex task means sorting out conflicting scientific claims and determining whether new tests are needed to study the effects of pesticides on the endocrine and immune systems, with a particular emphasis on children and infants.

Public interest organizations are assailing the agency for caving in to pressure from chemical manufacturers and farmers. Seven environmental, consumer and public health organizations resigned from an EPA pesticide advisory group in April, contending that the agency was moving too slowly on implementing the new law.

"We resigned because the pesticide industry and agribusiness lobbyists and their allies in Congress have hijacked this process," said Eric Olson of the Natural Resources Defense Council (NRDC). "Over the past year, the administration has responded to industry pressure. . . . And while the EPA delays action, kids continue to be exposed to clearly excessive residues." [7]

On the other side, farmers are worried the EPA will ban whole classes of chemicals. They say the government is trying to restrict the use of pesticides even when it lacks

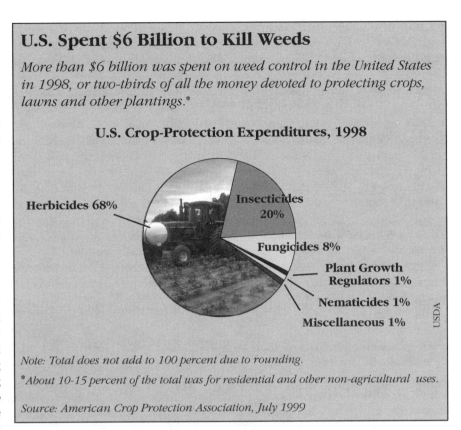

U.S. Spent $6 Billion to Kill Weeds

*More than $6 billion was spent on weed control in the United States in 1998, or two-thirds of all the money devoted to protecting crops, lawns and other plantings.**

U.S. Crop-Protection Expenditures, 1998

Herbicides 68%
Insecticides 20%
Fungicides 8%
Plant Growth Regulators 1%
Nematicides 1%
Miscellaneous 1%

USDA

Note: Total does not add to 100 percent due to rounding.

**About 10-15 percent of the total was for residential and other non-agricultural uses.*

Source: American Crop Protection Association, July 1999

evidence that the pesticides are dangerous in low volumes. To alleviate their concerns, Vice President Al Gore in 1998 urged EPA Administrator Browner to consult with private interests, as well as the Agriculture Department (a traditional ally of farmers), when setting new tolerances. Nevertheless, the American Farm Bureau Federation stepped up the pressure a few months later by releasing a report by several university economists concluding that the elimination of all organophosphates and carbamates would devastate growers, causing the loss of 209,000 U.S. jobs and spurring a surge of imported fruits and vegetables. [8]

"The organophosphates and the carbamates are important to us because they've been around for a long time," says Bill Spencer, a citrus farmer in Yuma, Ariz., who serves on both Farm Bureau and EPA pesticide committees. "They've been proven safe a long time; they're relatively

inexpensive and they allow us to stay in operation."

Spencer says he has done everything possible to cut down on the use of the most controversial pesticides. But environmentalists and health advocates contend that farmers could use newer and safer pesticides to replace many of the most dangerous ones. They also want growers to move more aggressively toward integrated pest management (IPM) tactics, adopting such natural strategies as increasing shade, which blocks sunlight needed by weeds, and luring "good" insects to control pests.

For their part, pesticide manufacturers worry that new regulations will delay the introduction of new products and cost them billions of dollars. The companies say they already are spending, on average, more than $50 million per product to meet a battery of 120 or so tests that the EPA requires to set a tolerance for the chemicals. "The best that all of us in production agriculture, [manufacturers] and growers alike, can hope for is that there is an understanding at the agency that there will be some economic impacts," says Jay Vroom, president of the American Crop Protection Association, a trade group of pesticide chemical manufacturers.

As regulators sort through the many competing claims and implement the new law, these are key questions that are being asked:

Is food treated with chemical pesticides safe to eat?

Doctors and health policy advocates generally agree that the nutritional benefits of eating fresh fruits and vegetables outweigh the risks of ingesting pesticide residues. However, they say the nation's food supply should be far safer than it is.

"I would say that, first, the food supply is generally safe," says Mt. Sinai's Landrigan. "Secondly, a diet rich in fruits and vegetables is far, far better for children than a diet in fats and carbohydrates. With that said, I would argue that there's a need to better improve the safety of the food supply."

Most of the fruits and vegetables Americans eat — be they fresh, frozen or canned — contain minute residues of toxic pesticides. Public interest organizations recommend thoroughly washing and, in some cases, peeling fresh fruits and vegetables to remove as much of the residue as possible. Sometimes, however, the chemical is absorbed deep into a fruit or vegetable and cannot be removed.

The question of whether these residues take a toll on human health is at the heart of the regulatory tug-of-war between health advocates and the agriculture industry. Farmers and chemical manufacturers insist that the pesticide levels on fruits and vegetables are so low that they cannot cause medical problems. "I'm entirely comfortable that these residues are safe," says Vroom. "That isn't meant in any way to say that the new [law] won't make some additional restrictions on the uses of some of our older products a necessity. But in the interim, in terms of any kind of short-term risks, I believe there are none in terms of dietary residues."

On the other hand, organizations such as Consumers Union and the

Farmers say synthetic pesticides are vital to maintaining the nation's food supply, but environmentalists and public health advocates say they are hurting human health and the global environment.

U.S Department of Agriculture

Environmental Working Group have released reports showing that pesticide residues routinely exceed the level that some scientists consider safe for adults. This is especially dangerous for infants and young children, whose developing systems are much more vulnerable to the effects of chemicals.

Last year, the Environmental Working Group concluded that nine out of 10 American children between the ages of 6 months and 5 years are exposed to combinations of 13 different organophosphates. [9] Every day,

more than 1 million children eat an unsafe dose of the pesticide. Other reports by the organization found probable carcinogens and neurotoxins in commercial baby food, and weed killers in rural drinking water.

"Multiple pesticides known or suspected to cause brain and nervous system damage, cancer, disruption of the endocrine and immune systems and a host of other toxic effects are ubiquitous in foods children commonly consume at levels that present serious health risks," an Environmental Working Group report concluded this year. [10]

A report this year by Consumers Union, publisher of *Consumer Reports* magazine, concluded that a number of foods contained potentially unsafe levels of pesticides. The foods presenting the most risk to consumers included fresh peaches, frozen and fresh winter squash, apples, grapes, spinach, pears and U.S.-grown green beans. The report also found that domestic produce frequently contains pesticide residues comparable to — or, in some cases, even exceeding — the levels found on imported produce, despite the common perception that U.S. food is safer. [11]

"The U.S. industry beats its chest like a 1,000-pound gorilla and says, 'We have the safest food supply in the world.' That's tommyrot," says biologist Edward Groth III, who oversaw the January 1999 Consumers Union report.

It remains unclear, however, what, if any, effects these residues have on human health.

The problem is that nobody knows at what level, precisely, pesticides begin to cause subtle health effects.

The EPA, when setting pesticide tolerances, uses a measure known as the "reference dose." This measure is arrived at by taking the highest dose of a particular pesticide that has no observed adverse effect in test animals and dividing it by a "safety factor," which is usually 100. The legal limit for pesticide residues is usually higher than the reference dose because, prior to 1996, government regulators weighed the potential health effects with the economic benefits of pesticides when setting pesticide tolerances for food.

The recent tests by groups such as the Environmental Working Group found that pesticide residues frequently exceeded the reference dose. However, the residues usually did not exceed the legal limit. As a result, the residue on produce often falls somewhere in the range between absolutely safe and potentially unsafe.

But the risk may be greater than ingesting the residue on a single fruit, analysts warn. That is because people are exposed to pesticides from many sources, and the effects of all these chemicals can be additive. "If you're looking at a single chemical, you're probably ignoring that these things have cumulative effects," says David Wallinga, a senior scientist with the NRDC.

Even though the risk for most people is quite low, consumers who eat unusual quantities of certain foods, such as peaches and apples, may be at higher risk — especially in the case of children. "My best guess is we're talking about chronic risks from long-term exposure for people whose dietary patterns are a little more unusual," says Lynn R. Goldman, a former EPA assistant administrator for prevention, pesticides and toxic substances who is now a visiting scholar at the Johns Hopkins University School of Public Health.

Until the uncertainties are resolved, consumers should continue eating fruits and vegetables, but they should take precautions, health experts say. Consumers Union's Groth recommends eating produce that contains relatively low chemical traces, such as broccoli, bananas, apple juice and orange juice. "Pick the foods that have very low residues," he says. "Peel if possible, or wash, and eat in moderation."

Is the government doing enough to regulate pesticide use?

There are many pesticides, such as insecticidal soaps, that pose no known risk to human health. But of the more than 20,000 pesticide products on the market, a large number are toxic. The government faces a Herculean task in ensuring that every potential use is safe.

Despite widespread concerns about pesticides, they continue to be used intensively. Pesticide sales hit $11.8 billion in 1998, according to an industry survey. However, the amount of synthetic pesticides that Americans buy annually has dropped below 900 million pounds, indicating that use of the chemicals may be declining. Although more than 80 percent of the chemicals were sold to farmers, non-farm sales are on the increase. [12]

Americans are exposed to pesticides in their homes, parks, schools, office buildings and airplanes, as well as in the food they eat. A recent study indicated that New York City uses more pesticides to kill rats, roaches and other urban pests than New York's agricultural counties use to protect their crops. [13] Passengers on some overseas flights spend long hours in cabins that have been saturated with pesticides that are designed to linger on seat cushions for weeks. [14] Pesticide spraying in schools from Portland, Ore., to Hartford, Conn., has spurred protests from parents and teachers who are concerned that students are being exposed to toxic chemicals.

To ensure that pesticides do not harm the public health, the EPA registers chemicals and sets the limits, or "tolerances," for their use. Other agencies, including the Food and Drug Administration and the Agriculture and Justice departments, also play a role, checking imported food for pesticide residues, setting standards for pesticide applicators and investigating illegal pesticide use.

Chemical manufacturers bristle at the notion that the government somehow is not regulating the pesticides sufficiently. After all, they point out that each chemical must go through about eight to 10 years of testing and development, including up to four years of review by the EPA. "Very few of our chemicals don't already have batteries of tests," says Vroom.

Environmentalists, however, worry that farmers and chemical manufacturers wield so much clout in Washington that the government has taken an overly sanguine approach to pesticide regulation. They question why the Clinton administration canceled the use of just one pesticide, phosdrin, in its first five years (although it has taken more aggressive steps in recent weeks to curb the use of some pesticides). In contrast, the Reagan administration banned 12 pesticides for food use, and the Bush administration banned four. [15]

Advocates are particularly concerned that the Clinton administration in 1993 agreed to let corn growers use the herbicide acetochlor even though previous administrations had banned its use. By 1997, acetochlor, a probable carcinogen, was detected in numerous tap-water samples in the Midwest and in the ground water of three Midwestern states. Officials in New York state banned the pesticide because of fears of drinking water contamination, even though the federal government continued to allow its use. [16]

The Clinton administration "has done almost nothing to reduce pesticide use or to lower children's ex-

Grape Growers Try the Gentle Approach

After John Ledbetter established himself as a profitable grape grower for various California winemakers, he began in the mid-1980s to think about alternatives to pesticides. Even though he had grown up on a row-crop farm that relied on chemicals to combat insects, weeds and diseases, he wanted to move toward a more environmentally sensitive way of farming.

"We're consumers, just like the people who live in the cities. We breath the same air, drink the same water," says Ledbetter, who farms 8,000 acres in the heart of California's wine country. "It's just kind of a process of coming to the conclusion now that the environment needs to be thought about a little more."

Ledbetter is hardly alone. California grape growers, who lead the nation in producing wine grapes, table grapes and raisins, are making dramatic strides in reducing their use of toxic pesticides. Although exact statistics are hard to come by, one measure of the industry's success can be gauged in a recent report by Consumers Union, which found that the "toxicity index" of pesticide residues on grapes fell by more than 80 percent from 1994 to 1996. [1]

"U.S. grape growers, especially in California, have really made a lot of progress in reducing the use of high-risk pesticides," says Ned Groth III, director of technical policy and public service for Consumers Union.

Throughout the 1990s, organizations of grape growers such as the Lodi-Woodbridge Winegrape Commission have helped educate their members about alternatives to heavy pesticide use. Their goal is not to move farmers to organic techniques, which would bar the use of chemical pesticides even in very small doses. Instead, the emphasis is on "sustainable" agriculture — an approach that strives to balance profits with good environmental stewardship.

Rather than spraying regularly for fungi, for example, farmers hold off unless there are clear signs that fungi are becoming a problem. Farmers also apply special pesticides that pose less of an environmental risk, including insecticides based on natural sources such as nicotine — even though the application of these compounds is often more expensive. And they remove diseased leaves from the vines by hand, thereby exposing the vines to more light and wind, which tends to cut down on disease.

The attitude among many of the grape growers appears to have changed over the last few years. Instead of trying to eliminate as many pests as possible, they now weigh the loss of some grapes against the benefits of not spraying.

"There will be times that I've come to the conclusion that, yeah, I've got a little damage . . . but I'm willing to stand it," Ledbetter says.

Environmentalists hope that this type of approach can be adopted by other farmers across the country. But they concede that grape growers, for a number of reasons, are in a better position to focus on alternative agricultural methods.

For one thing, wine grape growers have enjoyed strong profit margins in recent years, meaning they can afford to spend a little more money on such techniques as applying safer types of herbicides and growing cover crops that provide habitat for "beneficial" insects that eat pests. Another advantage is that grape vines grow in dry, temperate areas where diseases do not pose as much of a threat as in hot and humid areas, which is the type of climate needed for crops that get heavy doses of pesticides, such as cotton. Furthermore, grapes used for wines or raisins don't have to look perfect, so growers, unlike, say, apple farmers, are not obliged to use pesticides for cosmetic reasons.

The move toward sustainable techniques has been spurred in part by the pattern of development in California. Since vineyards are so profitable, grape growers tend to hold on to their lands even while subdivisions spring up all around them — resulting in pressure from nearby residential areas to keep the environment clean.

"That does encourage us to practice good pest-management practices so we are compatible with the people moving in," says Karen Ross, president of the California Association of Winegrape Growers. "A lot of it is quality of life and wanting to be a good neighbor."

But part of the reason for the reduced use of pesticides is the grape growers themselves. Many are transplanted city-dwellers, drawn to the vineyards by the mystique of good wine or the lure of big profits. They are steeped in the environmental movement of the last three decades, not the philosophy of heavy pesticide use that so many other farmers grew up with.

"We're not talking about bib overalls or crusty old farmers," says Andy Beckstoffer, who farms 2,500 acres of wine grapes. "Most of the people grew up in the 1960s, and they don't like that [pesticide] stuff."

---

[1] "Do You Know What You're Eating?" Consumers Union of the United States.

---

posure to pesticides," a 1998 report by the Environmental Working Group concluded. [17]

Marcia Mulkey, director for the EPA's Office of Pesticide Programs, said the agency imposed tight restric-tions on the use of acetochlor and will curtail or cancel the pesticide if it exceeds certain levels in water. She also cautioned against judging the administration by how many chemi-cals it has banned. That is because the EPA in recent years has focused on restricting the uses of the most toxic chemicals while approving newer and safer chemicals, thereby helping to change the mix of pesti-cides on the market without canceling many of them outright, she said.

"The new chemistry coming in, because of this emphasis on reduced risk, is a reason to have a comfort in that regard," she says.

At present, the government cannot say for certain whether pesticides, when used according to legal requirements, have no adverse effect on human health. To be sure, officials know that a pesticide exposure that far exceeds regulatory limits can cause sudden sickness or even death. In 1995, an estimated 79,000 children in the United States suffered pesticide-related poisonings or high exposures, sometimes resulting in hospitalizations, according to the EPA.

Although it is much harder to track the effects of long-term, low-level exposure to pesticides, scientific studies are raising some concern. Research has indicated that very young children who are exposed to pesticides may suffer brain damage and developmental disabilities. For example, a study in Mexico found that children in areas where pesticides were heavily used had trouble performing simple motor skills, such as drawing stick figures or catching a ball.

Other studies have shown that some pesticides can act as endocrine disruptors, increasing the level of estrogen in animals. Laboratory rodents exposed to such chemicals suffer from higher rates of certain types of cancer, and become more aggressive and hyperactive. Females become sexually active at an early age.

Scientists wonder whether such reactions provide clues to current human health and societal issues. "What we're finding is that these low-dose estrogen exposures produce in rodents, at least, a number of effects and syndromes that are human concerns," says Wade Welshons, a pes-

ticides researcher and associate professor of veterinary biomedical sciences at the University of Missouri.

Although scientists cannot duplicate such tests on humans, they are concerned over rising rates of certain types of cancer, such as breast and prostate cancer. In addition, there has been considerable debate over whether pesticides are to blame for reduced sperm counts in men.

Despite such concerns, the EPA generally does not require tests that

The government is charged with regulating the more than 20,000 pesticide products on the market, including a large number that are toxic.

would show whether a pesticide is having a subtle effect on developing immune and endocrine systems, health advocates say. For example, although laboratory animals are observed for obvious adverse reactions to pesticides, such as weight loss or a lack of energy, they are not tested for such syndromes as immune system sensitization — a reaction that could trigger autoimmune diseases such as asthma.

"Unfortunately, these testing requirements have been limited," says David Wallinga, the NRDC's senior scientist. "There are gaps in our understanding."

The EPA's Mulkey said the agency is doing the best it can to keep up with new scientific findings and mandate the appropriate tests. "Science evolves and our knowledge of chemicals evolves," she says. "It's a work in progress."

Can farmers feed the country without using chemical pesticides?

Many environmentalists and consumer advocates believe that farmers can cut down greatly on their use of synthetic pesticides, if not eliminate them altogether. They say growers should rely more on "integrated pest management" methods — using such tactics as crop rotation, natural shade and "beneficial" insects that contain pest populations. "The notion that you cannot do large-scale or production-scale farming without pesticides is absurd," says Gene Kahn, president and CEO of Small Planet Foods, an organic-food processing company.

Conventional farmers, however, beg to differ. In fact, a 1998 study sponsored by the American Farm Bureau Federation concluded that a ban on two of the most controversial groups of pesticides — organophosphates and carbamates — would set back production of crops ranging from apples to wheat. This would result in an increase in imported food and slightly higher food prices, the report concluded. [18]

"The critics who are saying farmers should be using fewer pesticides have never farmed for a living," says Rawlins at the Farm Bureau.

U.S Department of Agriculture

Despite the rhetoric, the two sides may not be as far apart as they appear. Farmers increasingly are turning to natural techniques to control pests, even though they are moving much more slowly than environmentalists would like. On the other side, some environmentalists acknowledge that occasional use of pesticides is critical in keeping down populations of harmful insects and weeds, even though they say that farmers can dramatically cut down on their use.

"There's going to continue to be a significant annual need for pesticides. We're never going to get away from that, nowhere in the world," says Charles Benbrook, a consultant for Consumers Union. "What we hope will happen is there will be a fairly significant move away from the very toxic pesticides that pose a risk to many organisms."

Farmers who want to avoid the use of synthetic chemicals altogether turn to organic farming, which relies on a mix of biological controls and natural pesticides, such as sulfur. Organic farming draws mixed reviews: Although it tends to be more environmentally friendly than conventional farming, some environmentalists worry about the effects of heavy applications of sulfur and other compounds. And economists say techniques such as hand-weeding will always add significantly to its costs.

Still, it is a fast-growing segment of agriculture. Kahn cited statistics indicating that the domestic market for organic foods now exceeds $5 billion in annual sales, while some overseas markets are growing by 20 percent or more per year. "We have no shortage of farmers wanting to switch over," he says.

But the more popular route for conventional farmers is to try to cut down on synthetic pesticides instead of eliminating them altogether. Rather than spraying on a calendar basis — every 10 days during certain times of the growing season, for example — many are hiring specialists to survey their fields to determine pest populations. They spray only when problem pests reach a certain threshold level.

In addition, some farmers are rotating their crops more often. This tends to hold down pest populations because insects multiply when they can feed on the same crop year after year. The 1996 farm law, dubbed "Freedom to Farm," is helping spur such rotations because it lifted longstanding restrictions on subsidized crops.

Another tactic is to plant rows of crops closer together, thereby creating more shade and preventing weeds from growing between the rows. Some farmers also plant cover crops, which serve as habitat for insects that eat pests, or they release such beneficial insects as ladybugs and wasps into their fields.

Such natural methods are getting a boost from new scientific research into the biochemistry of insects. In some cases, farmers can spray female pheromones of certain species at key times of the year, confusing males who are trying to find mating partners. More controversial, however, are biotechnological techniques that create hybrid plants with special resistance to weeds or natural pesticides.

Farmers insist they are doing everything they can to curtail their use of pesticides, both because the chemicals are expensive and because they are concerned about the environment and their own health. "We're the stewards of the Earth," says Bill Spencer, a citrus grower in Yuma, Ariz. "That means you not only take care of the Earth, but you take care of the people who farm it."

There are conflicting signs over whether pesticide use is declining in this country. Manufacturers sold less than 900 million pounds of pesticides in 1998, a drop of about 15 percent from 1993, although their sales in dollar terms are holding steady. [19] But environmentalists worry that chemical use is becoming more intensive, pointing to statistics that show that per-acre applications for insecticides and fungicides increased by 34 percent between 1990 and 1995. [20] The statistics should be evaluated carefully, however, because they do not always differentiate between different types of synthetic pesticides, or even between chemicals and such natural pest control compounds as sulfur.

Some farmers have had notable success in reducing pesticide use. Grape growers in California, for example, who enjoy wider profit margins than many other farmers, have taken advantage of their additional income to spend more on natural pest control methods. (*See story, p. 84.*)

But farmers of many other crops say they have no other viable option for the control of weeds, bugs and diseases. "If the presence of a pest is relatively minor, we don't spray," says Bruce Krenning, an apple and peach grower in Albion, N.Y. "But when they reach a critical threshold, we have to go in." ∎

BACKGROUND

DDT Paves the Way

Farmers have relied on pesticides for thousands of years. As early as the eighth century B.C., the Greek poet Homer referred to the use of fungicides. Popular pesticides in ancient times included sulfur and arsenic, but by the 16th century farmers were also discovering the effectiveness of substances derived from plants, such as nicotine. In the 19th century, farmers in the United States

Chronology

1930s-1950s
Farmers in the United States and across the world use increasing amounts of synthetic pesticides to feed a growing population, while government health agencies seek to control mosquitoes and other disease-carrying insects.

1939
Paul Mueller, a Swiss chemist, discovers DDT's effectiveness as an insecticide. He later wins the Nobel Prize.

1947
The Federal Insecticide, Fungicide and Rodenticide Act (FIFRA) specifies that pesticides must not cause "unreasonable adverse effects on the environment."

1954
The Food, Drug and Cosmetic Act requires regulators to set maximum levels of pesticide residues allowable on raw foods.

1958
Rep. James J. Delaney, D-N.Y., adds an amendment to the Food, Drug and Cosmetic Act prohibiting the use of any cancer-causing pesticides in processed foods.

1960s
Consumers become increasingly concerned about pesticide use.

1962
Rachel Carson's bestseller, *Silent Spring*, links pesticides to widespread damage to the environment.

1970s
Congress strengthens the regulatory system governing pesticides.

1970
Congress creates the Environmental Protection Agency (EPA).

1972
DDT is banned on all U.S. food sources but continues to be used in other countries.

1980s
Congress repeatedly tries, and fails, to resolve inconsistencies in the laws governing admissible levels of pesticide residues in food.

1988
Congress requires the EPA to complete testing of about 600 chemicals in pesticide products; the agency falls well behind schedule.

1989
After the Natural Resources Defense Council identifies Alar, a pesticide commonly used on apples, as a health threat to children, EPA withdraws the chemical from the market.

1990s
As new reports link pesticides with cancer and endocrine system abnormalities, Congress overhauls pesticide laws.

1990
A survey reveals that many farmworkers' children in New York state were exposed to pesticides and experienced health problems consistent with pesticide poisoning.

February 1993
The U.S. Supreme Court upholds a lower court ruling that the EPA must strictly apply the terms of the Delaney clause to processed foods.

June 1993
The National Research Council, releases a study identifying pesticide residue as a potentially grave threat to children.

1994
Lawmakers adjourn without overhauling pesticide laws.

July 1996
The Food Quality Protection Act sets a single health standard for both raw and processed food and is signed into law by President Clinton on Aug. 3.

April 8, 1998
Vice President Al Gore directs the EPA to consult with the Agriculture Department and affected private parties before banning the use of controversial pesticides — a directive that draws fire from environmental groups.

April 26, 1999
Seven environmental, consumer and health organizations accuse EPA of bowing to industry pressure instead of barring the most dangerous pesticides.

Aug. 3, 1999
The EPA bans two key pesticides used on apples, peaches and other produce.

and Europe began relying on more sophisticated combinations of mercury, copper and traditional poisons, using sulfur-based compounds to control mold and arsenic-based compounds to control insects. However, the earlier pesticides were highly toxic, sometimes killing livestock. [21]

Just as in present-day agriculture, however, farmers in ancient days also relied on biological methods to control pests. In ancient China, for example, growers turned to ants to control other insects that ate the leaves of fruit trees — even building bridges of bamboo poles to help the ants travel from one tree to another. Before the era of chemical pesticides, farmers killed weeds manually by pulling them out, while cutting off leaves or buds that were infested with insects. Prior to World War II, farmers also planted a variety of crops and rotated them regularly, which helped to contain pest populations. [22]

Modern pesticides had their beginnings in the years leading up to World War II, when Swiss chemist Paul Mueller, trying to prevent moths from eating holes in clothing, stumbled on a substance that killed insects while appearing to have no effect on humans or other mammals. That chemical, DDT, had first been synthesized in the 19th century by German scientists but had not been recognized at the time for its usefulness as an insecticide. DDT was used widely by both sides during World War II to kill lice and other insects, thereby helping to cut down on malaria and head off a typhus epidemic in Naples. Mueller eventually won a Nobel Prize. [23]

Officials believed DDT was safe because the soldiers, refugees and prisoners who were dusted with the chemical for head lice did not appear to suffer any harm. (In powder form, DDT is not readily absorbed through the skin. It is far more toxic when

dissolved in oil, which was how it was usually applied in later years.) After World War II ended, DDT and many new chemicals developed during the war were deployed in a massive effort to finally win the battle against insect pests. By the 1950s, synthetic pesticides were major pest control agents in the United States, while developing countries used them for controlling insects that spread malaria and other tropical diseases.

In addition to DDT, other powerful chlorinated hydrocarbon insecticides were used during the 1950s and '60s, including BHC (benzene-hexachloride), aldrin, dieldrin and toxaphene. Farmers also began using the first organophosphate insecticide, parathion, which had been developed by German scientists experimenting with nerve gas during World War II. Such potent pesticides enabled farmers throughout the world to dramatically increase their yields and were an important ingredient in the "Green Revolution," the postwar effort to alleviate hunger by improving agricultural methods in the Third World.

Action by Congress

Although there was relatively little concern over the dangers of the new chemicals, Congress set up a regulatory system in the late 1940s. From the beginning, it faced competing pressures. Farmers wanted to use the chemicals to boost crop yields and reduce production costs. Consumers appreciated the resulting quality and low cost of food but also demanded protection from the toxic effects of the poisons. These conflicting interests spawned a hodgepodge of regulations involving several federal agencies.

Congress first addressed the issue of pesticide regulation in 1947, with the

Federal Insecticide, Fungicide and Rodenticide Act (FIFRA). By regulating the sale and use of pesticides, lawmakers tried to satisfy all sides by stating that a pesticide must not cause "unreasonable adverse effects on the environment" when applied as the manufacturer intended. But the law also required regulators to take into account "the economic, social and environmental costs as well as the potential benefits of the use of any pesticide."

The regulatory system set up under FIFRA involves a registration process now administered by the EPA. Each pesticide must be separately registered with the EPA for every intended use. It is the manufacturer's responsibility to provide adequate data from safety tests it runs on each product, including potential effects on the environment and human health. The EPA also must approve the label containing instructions for use and safety warnings before the pesticide can be sold.

The other principal law governing pesticide regulation was the 1954 Food, Drug and Cosmetic Act. It required the appropriate federal agency (eventually the EPA) to establish tolerance levels — or the maximum quantity of pesticide residue that was allowable on raw foods and some processed foods. In 1958, Rep. James J. Delaney, D-N.Y., added language to the law prohibiting the use of all cancer-causing chemicals on commodities used in processed foods. At the time, any detectable residue of a harmful pesticide was a cause for alarm because only relatively significant residues were detectable to instruments. For the next three decades, however, scientific advances enabled regulators to detect increasingly minute traces of residue on foods, making the so-called Delaney clause controversial.

Rachel Carson Sounds the Alarm

The illusion that DDT was a harmless miracle died in 1962 with the

An Illinois Farmer Struggles to Survive

By the traditional laws of nature, Terry Wolf should be able to get by without using any insecticides. The Illinois farmer rotates his corn and soybean crops regularly, a strategy widely used to control a beetle known as the western corn rootworm.

But for the last three years, a remarkable change in rootworm behavior has led to a new rootworm infestation, forcing farmers to return to using insecticides to control the pest and keep their farms afloat.

"We're using the safest products we can, but we don't like the expense and we don't like putting it in the environment," says Wolf, who farms 2,600 acres in east-central Illinois. "But you do have to manage the pests."

Wolf is on the front lines of one of the most extraordinary battles ever waged against an insect. And his inability to wean himself from synthetic insecticides is a cautionary tale for those who believe that simple, biological techniques can easily substitute for synthetic chemicals.

The No. 1 insect threat to Midwestern corn growers, rootworm beetles usually lay their eggs in cornfields in the fall. When the larvae hatch in the spring, they begin feeding on the roots of young corn plants — sometimes damaging them so badly that the plants fall over. A serious infestation can drive down corn yields to 20 bushels per acre or less, compared with normal yields of 160-170 bushels.

Many farmers stopped spraying regularly for the yellow-winged beetles after they discovered that rotating their fields every year between corn and soybeans would naturally control the populations. Although the beetles' eggs were laid in the fall in fields that had grown corn, the larvae would hatch after the fields had been converted to soybeans — and would consequently have no corn roots to eat.

The tactic was successful until a few years ago, when Midwestern farmers began noticing new infestations of the rootworm beetle. Entomologists who were called in discovered an adaptation that may be virtually unequaled in the annals of modern agriculture.

Rather than following nature's script and laying their eggs in cornfields, female rootworms had adapted to the farmers' strategy and were laying their eggs in soybean fields. Thus, when the fields were rotated back to corn, the larvae would have plenty of their natural food — posing once again a severe threat for the farmers.

"It's a rather unique example of insect evolution to a cultural strategy," said Michael E. Gray, a professor at the University of Illinois' Department of Crop Sciences.

To continue a natural war against the beetle, farmers likely would have to go to a three-year rotation, adding another crop, such as oats, to the rotation. That way, eggs laid in a soybean field would hatch in an oat field, and the larvae would perish.

But the market for oats is not big enough to absorb a jump in production. Environmentalists say the Agriculture Department, which has been criticized for its support of conventional farming methods, should take the lead on exploring new uses for oats and other crops, such as mixing them into livestock feed.

"There needs to be some creative thinking about how to enable farmers to farm in a more diversified manner and bring in more crops," says Jennifer Curtis, a consultant to the Natural Resources Defense Council.

In the meantime, Wolf, who prided himself on using no insecticides at all for several years, now starts his planting season by injecting an insecticide known as "Fortress" into the soil. In addition to his distaste for using pesticides, he frets at the cost — at about $18 per acre, the chemical represents more than 10 percent of his annual expenses and cuts significantly into his profits, he says.

He is hoping that researchers soon develop a new strain of corn with roots that will be resistant to the beetles. But if the EPA bans the most effective pesticides — a scenario creating considerable fears in rural America even though it is regarded as implausible in Washington — Wolf says he would have to give up his farm.

"If they take insecticides away, I can't raise corn anymore," he says. "The rootworm can kill me instantly."

publication of Rachel Carson's *Silent Spring*. Carson, a marine biologist, blamed DDT and other chlorinated hydrocarbon pesticides for a dramatic decline in the number of birds and other wildlife that had been poisoned by ingesting contaminated plant material or animals. She also cited government findings of DDT in mothers' milk as evidence that the chemical is passed largely unaltered along the food chain: from contaminated animal fodder to cows and then to their milk and ultimately to human infants.

"Along with the possibility of the extinction of mankind by nuclear war," Carson wrote, "the central problem of our age has therefore become the contamination of man's total environment with such substances of incredible potential for harm — substances that accumulate in the tissues of plants and animals and even penetrate the germ cells to shatter or alter the very material of heredity upon which the shape of the future depends." [24]

About the same time that Carson's bestseller exploded on the scene, growers were observing another unintended effect of pesticides. The longer the chemicals were applied to crops, the more had to be applied to get the job done, creating an ever-

Farmworkers Take Brunt of Pesticides' Punch

I t was a syndrome that appears all too frequently: More than two dozen South Florida farmworkers developed nausea, dry throats and breathing problems in March 1994 after harvesting lettuce in a field that had just been sprayed with Gramoxone Extra, a pesticide that causes damage to human tissues upon contact.

After investigating the incident, state officials issued a warning to the pesticide applicator for allowing unprotected workers into a just-sprayed field, but did not impose a fine. [1]

Neither the incident nor the low-key reaction by the government represented anything but business as usual. The nation's estimated 5 million agricultural laborers — many of whom are migrant and seasonal farmworkers — are more exposed than anyone else in the country to pesticide poisoning. The EPA estimates that they suffer at least tens of thousands of acute illnesses each year due to pesticide exposure, ranging from rashes and nausea to blindness and sudden death. Chronic ailments include cancer and birth defects. [2]

Yet this most threatened segment of the population has scarce protection under federal law. The 1996 Food Quality Protection Act, hailed by President Clinton for protecting consumers from pesticide residues on supermarket produce, contains no provisions for workers. Similarly, the Occupational Safety and Health Administration, which ensures that most workers labor in reasonably safe conditions, does not have jurisdiction over farmworkers.

"They are the group that is the least studied and least taken into consideration," says Marion Moses, a doctor who treats farmworkers and heads up the Pesticide Education Center in San Francisco.

Instead, the workers are covered by a set of EPA pesticide regulations known as the Worker Protection Standard (WPS), which requires such basic safety measures as pesticide training, delayed entry into treated fields and transportation to emergency medical facilities. As weak as these regulations are — workers can get sick even if the rules are followed and their children are routinely exposed to residues — state enforcement is entirely inadequate, critics say.

The Florida Department of Agriculture and Consumer Services, for example, repeatedly fails to thoroughly investigate cases of likely pesticide poisoning and declines to take disciplinary action against employers, according to a 1998 report by two watchdog groups. "The state's handling of pesticide poisoning complaints reveals a pattern of indifference to its obligation to protect the safety and health of Florida's farmworkers," the report concluded. "By failing to issue citations for pesticide poisoning and impose meaningful penalties for serious WPS violations, the state has deprived farmworkers of adequate protection and wholly undermined its effort to deter future misconduct." [3]

The report went on to document cases of workers foaming at the mouth, going into comas or suffering from months of severe abdominal pain and dizziness. One worker had a fatal heart attack after possibly coming into contact with a highly toxic pesticide, methyl bromide.

As much as health advocates are concerned about adult farmworkers, they warn that children may face even higher risks because they are more vulnerable to chemical

increasing spiral. Years later, then-Sen. Al Gore, D-Tenn., wrote in his book, *Earth in the Balance*: "Pesticides often leave the most resistant pests behind as the more vulnerable ones disappear. Then, when the resistant pests multiply to fill the niche left by their dead cousins, larger quantities of pesticides are used in an effort to kill the more resistant pests, and the process is repeated. . . . And all the while, the quantity of pesticides to which we ourselves are exposed continues to increase." [25]

By the late 1960s, the decreasing effectiveness of the chlorinated hydrocarbons, and the mounting evidence of their environmental side effects, led many growers to use alternative pes-

ticides, such as organophosphates and carbamates, which break down more readily in the environment. Public concern about the toxicity of DDT helped spur the creation of the EPA in 1970, which banned DDT on all food sources two years later.

Political Stalemate

B ut the political battles over pesticide use continued to intensify. The EPA came under attack for moving too slowly against harmful pesticides. In one case, for example, the agency did not begin a special review of granular carbofuran until

1985, even though the pesticide, used to kill worms and insects on a variety of vegetables and grains, was blamed for killing birds as early as 1974.

In 1972, Congress amended FIFRA to require the EPA to keep track of all pesticides, including those that had been in use for years. In 1988, it set up a nine-year timetable to complete registration of previously approved products. But the agency, coping with inadequate funding and incomplete scientific data, moved so slowly that one congressman predicted it would take until the year 15,520 A.D. to complete the registration process. [26]

Throughout the 1980s and early '90s, lawmakers faced growing poisoning. In a scathing report last year, the Natural Resources Defense Council (NRDC) warned that children as young as 4 were working on farms, sometimes sprayed directly with crop-dusters or laboring in fields still wet with pesticides. It cited several reports of children dying from pesticide exposure, including a 2-year-old boy who died after playing near flattened pesticide drums and a brother and sister who died after playing in a swing they had made from a burlap sack that was contaminated with parathion.

"We are putting farm children in a situation where they receive some of the highest pesticide exposures in our country," the report warned. "We cannot afford to wait and see if science proves conclusively that illnesses among these children are due to pesticides — particularly since many of the expected health effects occur years or even decades after the exposures." [4]

Farm and pesticide representatives denounced the NRDC report as overly alarmist. Jay Vroom, the president of the American Crop Protection Association, said the industry is concerned about pesticide exposure. But he added that, "the vast majority of farmers and farmworkers take the precautionary steps required by EPA ... to protect themselves, their families and the environments in which they live and work." [5]

Whether such precautions are actually taken, studies indicate that rural Americans suffer from the type of chronic and often fatal health problems associated with pesticide exposure — and the problems are not limited to migrant workers. Farm operators, for example, appear to suffer from unusually high rates of cancer, such as leukemia, lymphoma and brain, prostate and testicular cancer. Preliminary studies indicate that farmworkers — who have less exposure than farm operators to pesticides during the mixing and application of the chemicals but more exposure to residues in the fields — have increased rates of lung, liver and throat cancer. [6]

Some officials in Washington concede that the situation is worrisome. "There are some levels of concern over the exposure to farmworkers," says Marcia Mulkey, director of the EPA's Office of Pesticide Programs.

Moses says the government should do much more to protect farmworkers, but she is skeptical that it ever will. She attributes the government's lack of interest to several factors, including discrimination (most farmworkers are immigrants or members of various minorities) and the power of the agriculture lobby, which maintains that food costs would shoot up if the government imposed new regulations on farming practices.

"Congress knows basically that when you take on farmworker issues, you're taking on social- and environmental-justice issues, and they're just going to have a royal fight on their hands," Moses says. "It's like a third rail."

[1] Shelley Davis and Rebecca Schleifer, "Indifference to Safety: Florida's Investigation into Pesticide Poisoning of Farmworkers," Farmworker Justice Fund and Migrant Farmworker Justice Project, March 1998.

[2] "Enforcement of Farm Worker Pesticide Protection in Washington State," Columbia Legal Services, November 1998.

[3] Davis and Schleifer, op. cit.

[4] "Trouble on the Farm," Natural Resources Defense Council, October 1998.

[5] Glenn Hess, "Pesticide Industry Denies Putting Health of Farm Children in Danger," Chemical Market Reporter, Nov. 2, 1998, p. 1.

[6] Sheila Hoar Zahm and Aaron Blair, "Cancer Among Migrant and Seasonal Farmworkers: An Epidemiologic Review and Research Agenda," American Journal of Industrial Medicine, 1993, Vol. 24, p. 753.

pressure from all sides to amend the law. While environmental and health advocates worried that the EPA was too lax in canceling the use of dangerous pesticides, manufacturers and farmers became increasingly concerned over the Delaney clause, which barred even the most minute portions of cancer-causing pesticides in processed foods — a much tougher health standard than was applied to fresh produce. Since it was impossible to determine which fruits and vegetables would end up in a can and which in the fresh-produce section, regulators started permitting pesticide residues on both types of food as long as the residues posed no more than a "negligible risk" of causing cancer.

As the political deadlock continued, farmers applied more pesticides than ever — some 850 million pounds a year by the early 1990s. But scientists were becoming increasingly concerned over the health risks caused by these chemicals. In 1993, a landmark study by the National Academy of Sciences concluded that children are especially susceptible to the toxic effects of some pesticides. Another study presented new evidence linking DDT, which is still used in some developing countries to control malaria, with breast cancer. Researchers also began warning that pesticides could act as "endocrine disrupters," affecting the reproductive systems of both humans and wildlife, potentially reducing fertility and increasing the rates of certain types of cancer.

President Clinton urged Congress to scrap the Delaney clause and apply a single safety standard to raw and processed foods. Unlike current law, it would not take into consideration the economic effects of pesticides. Lawmakers, however, remained deadlocked until 1996. They were jolted into action only after a federal appeals court ruling required the EPA to apply the stricter standard contained in the Delaney clause to both raw and processed foods. Farmers warned that unless Congress acted they could begin facing widespread losses in 1998 because the EPA would have to revoke the use of as many as 50 common agricultural chemicals. "If the matter is not dealt with, the country is looking at something on the order of a fairly major calamity," warned Rep. John D. Dingell, D-Mich. [27]

To head off such a disaster, lawmakers in both chambers unanimously passed the FQPA in July 1996. The new law, in line with Clinton's recommendation, replaces the Delaney clause with a single health standard that requires the EPA to make sure that the chemicals in both raw and processed food pose a "reasonable certainty" of no harm from all combined sources of exposure. It requires the agency to consider the cumulative effects of different pesticides on human health. The EPA has to take into account the greater vulnerability of infants and children, assuming an additional tenfold safety factor in cases where the science is incomplete. The agency has until 2006 to finish reviewing existing pesticide regulations to make sure they meet the new safety standard. [28]

CURRENT SITUATION

Big Job for EPA

Seeking to keep popular pesticides on the market, farmer organizations and chemical manufacturers are insisting that the EPA amass broad scientific data before canceling the use of any chemical under the 1996 FQPA. The organizations, led by the Farm Bureau and the Crop Protection Association, sued the EPA in June for allegedly basing important decisions about pesticides and food safety on questionable assumptions and incomplete science.

"The lackadaisical, unscientific manner in which the EPA is implementing our nation's food safety law means all pain and no gain for struggling farm families and Ameri-

The EPA's recent ban on methyl parathion, a pesticide applied widely for years on fruits and vegetables, is the first anti-pesticide action intended specifically to protect children.

U.S Department of Agriculture

■ can consumers," said Farm Bureau President Dean Kleckner. "FQPA is a complex but delicate law. The EPA needs to make clear that it is operating under established rules, not whim." [29]

On the other side, environmentalists are assailing the EPA for failing to quickly cut down on the use of the most toxic chemicals, including organophosphates. Seven public interest organizations, including Consumers Union and the NRDC, quit an EPA advisory group in April amid charges that the administration was caving in to industry pressure. They say that even though the EPA is meeting an August deadline to evaluate more than 3,000 chemicals, it is essentially

sidestepping the issue by putting off evaluations of the most dangerous pesticides. However, they praised a recent decision by the EPA to sharply restrict the use of two controversial chemicals, methyl parathion and azinphosmethyl, which are used on apples, peaches and other produce.

"This is long overdue," says Todd Hettenbach, a policy analyst with the Environmental Working Group. "These chemicals should have been pulled out of use a long, long time ago." [30]

While the limits go into effect next year, as a practical matter, officials said, farmers would not use any more methyl parathion this season, because the time for using them is past. Both chemicals are widely used on such a variety of fruits and vegetables that it is difficult for consumers to know if they are present in commercially grown food.

Whipsawed between farmers and consumers, the EPA is in much the same position that Congress was in during much of the 1980s and early '90s. Lawmakers were so deadlocked between the competing demands of powerful interest groups that they failed to create a uniform pesticide policy until 1996, when their hand was forced by court decisions that would have led to the cancellation of many common pesticide uses. But it appears that the remarkable, unanimous passage of the FQPA merely moved the debate to the regulatory front instead of resolving it.

Under the new law, the EPA must make sure that pesticide use on food poses a "reasonable certainty" of no harm — probably meaning that there is no more than a one-in-a-million chance of the residues causing can-

At Issue:

Can farmers cut down on their use of synthetic pesticides without risking the nation's food supply?

JACQUELINE HAMILTON
Senior project attorney, Natural Resources Defense Council

WRITTEN FOR *THE CQ RESEARCHER*, JULY 1999.

chemical manufacturers maintain that we cannot live without synthetic pesticides. The truth is we cannot afford to live with them — at least not the most dangerous ones. Numerous studies have documented a wide variety of severe human health risks from these agricultural poisons, including cancer, birth defects, reproductive harm and nervous system damage. Our children are especially vulnerable to pesticide exposures.

American farmers can provide a safe, affordable and abundant food supply without using massive amounts of highly toxic chemicals. In fact, higher production costs, market demand and health concerns have encouraged increasing numbers of farmers to move away from toxic practices. Wisconsin potato and vegetable growers and suppliers for Gerber and SunMaid Raisin, for example, have successfully reduced their pesticide use, proving that it can be economically viable to use fewer, low-risk chemicals and enhanced biological systems to manage and control pest problems.

At one end of this chemical-reduction spectrum are farmers who apply synthetic chemicals in the most effective, cost-efficient manner possible. Rather than spraying based on the calendar, they monitor their fields to identify pest problems and apply chemicals precisely rather than using a shotgun approach, such as aerial spraying. Next on the continuum are farmers who have used natural systems to further reduce their dependence on chemicals to manage insects, weeds and plant diseases. They build soil systems, plant cover crops, rotate crops, disrupt pest reproduction and foster natural enemies of plant pests. At the other end of the spectrum are the rapidly growing number of organic farmers who shun synthetic chemicals altogether and instead use multiple, actively managed biological systems to prevent pest problems in the first place and to manage problems that do arise.

Farmers need support to wean themselves off synthetic chemicals in the least disruptive way. Most farmers begin by practicing on a small part of their farm and gradually expand the techniques that work best to the rest of their land. But successful transition will require a shift in thinking, and investments in research, training and insurance.

Since the end of World War II, chemical manufacturers have promoted synthetic chemicals as the magic bullet that will take the uncertainty out of farming. These bullets, however, often have gone astray, as in the notorious case of DDT. Without a concerted effort to help American farmers reduce their reliance on dangerous pesticides, these bullets will continue to miss their mark — and head straight for our children.

SCOTT RAWLINS
Senior environmental policy specialist, American Farm Bureau Federation

WRITTEN FOR *THE CQ RESEARCHER*, JULY 1999.

there is a lot of good news for the American food consumer that can be attributed directly to the ability of farmers to control pests. The supply of food is bountiful, quality is unparalleled, variety is ever-expanding and prices are reasonable. Indeed, the U.S. food production system is unrivaled anywhere in the world. This is due in part to the significant benefits our society derives from the safe and judicious use of pesticides:

• Pesticides reduce the risks of crop failure and stabilize food production.

• Pesticides increase yields and allow food to be produced on fewer acres, thereby freeing up land for wildlife habitat and other beneficial uses.

• Pesticides reduce farmers' costs, helping to hold down the price of food and enabling us to compete in world markets.

• Pesticides enable more food to be grown domestically, thereby minimizing the need to import food from other countries, where we have little control over production methods.

All of these benefits would be meaningless if pesticides posed major health risks. But that is not the case. In 1996, the National Research Council released a report, "Carcinogens and Anticarcinogens in the Human Diet," which concluded:

• "The great majority of individual naturally occurring and synthetic food chemicals are present in the human diet at levels so low that they are unlikely to pose an appreciable cancer risk."

• "The synthetic chemicals in our diet are far less numerous than the natural and have been more thoroughly studied, monitored and regulated. Their potential biologic effect is lower."

To improve our food production systems, farmers are continually changing the way they farm. To reduce total pesticide use, the Farm Bureau has advocated research into alternatives such as biological control agents, resistance management and genetic engineering. If new, effective and economical pest control techniques become available, farmers will use them. The fact is, however, that our food is safe now. Forcing farmers to switch to other products would do nothing to improve the health and welfare of Americans.

Agriculture needs a pesticide regulatory system that is balanced, reasonable and understandable, and is based on sound science. Only then will we be able to avoid unnecessary disruptions to our food supply.

cer or other major health problems. Unlike prior laws, the agency cannot take the economic benefits of pesticides into consideration, nor can it apply a stricter standard to processed food. It has until 2006 to reregister more than 9,000 pesticide tolerances, with the first third to be re-evaluated by the end of August.

The task is enormously complex. For the first time, officials must take into account the aggregate effects of pesticides — not only on food but also in the environment. They also have to factor in the susceptibility of young children to chemical poisoning.

EPA officials insist that the process is going well. "It's a big, challenging and difficult job," says Mulkey. "I think we are making very good progress."

It remains unclear, however, whether the result will be the cancellation of a wide range of organophosphates and carbamates, two types of older chemicals that environmentalists and health activists have targeted as the most dangerous pesticides on the market. They are highly toxic, attacking the central nervous system of organisms but also extremely effective in controlling a broad range of pests. Pesticide critics maintain that farmers can use other chemicals that are less harmful to people and wildlife. Farmers, however, say the alternative chemicals for some crops are so much less effective that they might have to be sprayed repeatedly, resulting in higher costs and possibly posing as great a risk to public health as the older chemicals.

Concerned that the EPA might take wide-ranging action against the most controversial pesticides, agriculture lobbyists and some of their allies in Congress appealed to the administration last year. On April 8, 1998, their campaign bore fruit when Vice President Gore sent a four-page letter to EPA Administrator Browner urging her to base any

regulatory decisions on sound science and to consult with the Department of Agriculture as well as industry and environmental groups.

The new directive infuriated pesticide critics. Environmentalists and health advocates charged that "sound science" was being interpreted as "universal science" — an impossible standard that would hamstring agency officials from taking meaningful action against pesticides for years. When they resigned from an EPA pesticide advisory panel this year, representatives of the seven environmental, health and consumer organizations wrote administration officials: "EPA cannot expect to garner consensus in the near term from all stake holders as to the harms resulting from reliance of all pesticides. Faced with uncertainty, EPA must apply the precautionary approach embraced in FQPA." [31]

Failure to take immediate action, the groups contended, would mean that children would continue to be exposed to dangerous levels of neurotoxic chemicals that could have devastating long-term health effects.

For their part, farmers say they would face economic ruin if many chemicals were taken off the market. They also said stricter regulations would not do anything to protect the safety of the food supply, because America will simply have to import more produce, much of which is treated overseas with the same toxic chemicals that are sparking so much debate at home. (Produce cannot be imported into the United States if it has been treated with pesticides that are banned here. However, Farm Bureau officials said such produce would probably make its way across the borders anyway unless government inspectors actually detected the pesticide residues.)

"The way things are heading, America's farmers and consumers will be paying more for poorer nutrition,

less domestic food security and lower confidence in food safety," said the Farm Bureau's Kleckner. "The only winners are foreign farmers, over whom EPA has no control." [32]

The EPA's Mulkey insisted that the agency was not bowing to pressure from either side, but trying to do its job fairly. She said it was unlikely that the agency would take such a drastic step as canceling the use of all organophosphates. "There's just no evidence that any of us have seen that whole classes of chemistry would have to be removed from the market," she says.

She also said that implementation of the new law will guarantee that food will be increasingly safe. "We believe the U.S. food supply is one of the safest in the world," she says. "When we complete the [implementation] process, I think there's no question that the food supply will be even safer."

Will Congress Act?

Not content to sit on the sidelines, House members have introduced two bills designed to protect the pesticide industry. The more far-reaching, by Rep. Richard W. Pombo, R-Calif., and others, would mandate that the EPA use scientific findings before canceling the use of any pesticide. In the absence of scientific data, the agency could not rely on default assumptions, as it has in the past.

Another bill, by Rep. Ray LaHood, R-Ill., would direct the EPA to consider additional data before canceling a pesticide use. But it does not contain as many requirements as the Pombo bill.

"As is often the case, Congress' best intentions can go awry when written into regulations by the administration," LaHood said. If the EPA banned all organophosphates, he added, "Production on fields could drop dramatically and, especially given agriculture's current financial crisis, some farmers could be forced from business."

Lawmakers may be more interested in sending a message to the administration than in trying to amend the pesticide law. After wrestling for the better part of two decades over pesticide regulations, Congress hardly appears eager to reopen such a contentious issue. Furthermore, agriculture supporters on Capitol Hill appear satisfied, at least for the moment, that the EPA is backing off from imposing sweeping restrictions on pesticide use.

"I think the EPA has been acting in good faith over the last year," said Rep. Charles W. Stenholm, D-Texas. "This has to be done right, but it also has to be done in a way that doesn't threaten the food supply, not only of this country but also of the entire world."

But Congress may weigh in on another issue. Pesticide manufacturers are drafting a proposal that would have them pay fees to the EPA for the evaluation of new chemicals. Although businesses hardly ever ask to be taxed, the manufacturers believe that the "fee-for-service" proposal would enable the agency to speed up its pesticide review process. At present, it takes as long as four years for the EPA to give the green light to a new chemical.

The fees would likely be levied on a sliding scale, depending on how much work the EPA estimates it would take to approve a particular product. A pesticide that used a new active ingredient, for example, would probably cost more for the manufacturer to get approved than a new pesticide using active ingredients that had been tested in other formulas.

Manufacturers said the proposal is necessary to help beef up the EPA's registration budget, which has been cut roughly in half from a high of about $30 million several years ago. With older chemicals coming under

increasing scrutiny, they need to start selling replacement products. "This would bring new chemicals into the marketplace and add to the competitive mix," says Vroom of the Crop Protection Association. ■

OUTLOOK

Consumer Education

The way Benbrook of Consumers Union sees it, the government may never take decisive action against pesticide use because the agricultural industry is simply too politically influential. Instead, he thinks the only way to force farmers to cut down on pesticides is for consumers to begin buying fruits and vegetables that contain lower residues.

"The government can't even get into the batter's box, let alone get around the bases," Benbrook says. "If the [1996 pesticide law] slips into gridlock, then consumer-led market invention is probably a safer bet for really accelerating this transition."

So instead of looking to Washington, Benbrook and other consumer advocates are focusing on educating the public about which foods contain the most pesticides. They believe that consumers may begin changing their buying habits, forcing farmers to reduce pesticide use or go out of business.

Benbrook worked with Consumers Union on a report this year analyzing Agriculture Department data on pesticide residues on food. The report, "Do You Know What You're Eating?" found that consumers who do not buy organic produce can still avoid significant residues of the more toxic pesticides by eating bananas, broccoli, sweet potatoes, U.S. and Canadian carrots and tomatoes, winter squash imported from Mexico or

Honduras, apple and orange juice and frozen or canned corn and peas. In contrast, U.S. fresh peaches are loaded with pesticides (Chilean peaches are better), and apples, green beans, spinach, pears and U.S. winter squash also contain significant residues.

Consumers can find out more about pesticides by visiting a Consumers Union Web site on the issue, as well as the EPA's pesticides Web site (www.epa.gov/pesticides). They can also visit an interactive Web site maintained by the Environmental Working Group.

"Despite repeated promises, the government is simply not acting to protect children or anyone else from these toxic chemicals," said Kenneth Cook, president of the Environmental Working Group. "Consumers have to protect themselves." [33]

Changing consumer demand, environmentalists believe, will pressure farmers to adopt alternative agriculture techniques, such as increased shade and the creation of habitat for beneficial insects. Already, farmers are moving slowly in that direction, but they need more support from both the marketplace and Agriculture Department researchers, they say.

Farmers also are looking to cut down on conventional pesticides. They say, however, that consumers are actually driving up pesticide use because of the demand for low prices and unblemished fruit.

"If you don't have a nearly perfect product, you're just not going to get the packers to pack your product," said fruit grower Krenning. "Is the public willing to accept a product that's considerably less — cosmetically anyway — considerably less than they're used to?"

Many farmers believe the trend in the future will be toward genetically engineered crops that will be more insect-resistant and possibly even contain natural pesticides. But such crops are highly controversial because of fears that they could degrade the environment, produce insects that are increasingly resistant to pesticides and even spawn "monster weeds" resistant to the natural herbicides used by organic farmers. [34]

Even though farmers and environmentalists are at odds politically, and also differ over putting more emphasis on biotechnology or on alternative agriculture, people in both camps seem to agree on the need to reduce overall pesticide use. Both hail new approaches that control insect and weed populations through natural methods such as pheromones, and look forward to increasingly sophisticated pesticides that target specific insects or weeds instead of threatening both wildlife and people.

"There's a tremendous amount of common ground between farmers and the environmental community," says Jennifer Curtis, an NRDC expert on alternative-farming methods. "There's so much we can do to cut down on pesticide use by focusing on common ground." ■

Notes

[1] EPA Web site and American Crop Protection Association "Industry Profile," 1998.
[2] Marla Cone, "Pesticides May Harm Brain, Study Finds," *Los Angeles Times*, March 15, 1999, p. A3, and Sheila Hoar Zahm and Aaron Blair, "Cancer Among Migrant and Seasonal Farmworkers: An Epidemiologic Review and Research Agenda," *American Journal of Industrial Medicine*, Vol. 24, 1993, pp. 753-766.
[3] "Persistent Organic Pollutants: Hand-Me-Down Poisons that Threaten Wildlife and People," *World Wildlife Fund Issue Brief*, January 1999.
[4] See Mary H. Cooper, "Regulating Pesticides," *The CQ Researcher*, Jan. 28, 1994, pp. 73-96.
[5] Press release, Environmental Media Services, April 27, 1999.
[6] EPA Web site.
[7] Press release, Environmental Media Services, April 27, 1999.

FOR MORE INFORMATION

American Crop Protection Association, 1156 15th St. N.W., Suite 400, Washington, D.C. 20005; (202) 296-1585; www.acpa.org. The main association of the manufacturers, formulators and distributors of pest control products. It collects industrywide information on pesticide sales and trends.

American Farm Bureau Association, 600 Maryland Ave. S.W., Suite 800, Washington D.C. 20024; (202) 484-3600; www.wsfb.com. A leading organization of farm groups, it issues reports on the importance of pesticides to the economic well-being of the agriculture industry.

Consumers Union of the United States, 101 Truman Ave., Yonkers, N.Y. 10703; (914) 378-2000; www.consumerreports.org. This advocacy organization provides information for consumers seeking to reduce their pesticide exposure and to farmers who want to cut down on their use of pesticides.

Environmental Working Group, 1718 Connecticut Ave. N.W., Suite 600, Washington, D.C. 20009; (202) 667-6982; www.ewg.org. This nonprofit organization issues reports on the prevalence of pesticides in food.

Natural Resources Defense Council, 1200 New York Ave. N.W., Suite 400, Washington, D.C. 20005; (202) 289-6868; www.nrdc.org. This environmental organization issues reports on the hazards of pesticides and proposes agricultural methods that use less chemicals.

[8] "Impacts of Eliminating Organophosphates and Carbamates From Crop Production," Texas A&M University Agricultural and Food Policy Center, April 1999.
[9] "Overexposed," Environmental Working Group, January 1998. See also "Pesticides in Baby Food," Environmental Working Group, July 1995, and "Tough to Swallow," Environmental Working Group, August 1997.
[10] "How 'Bout Them Apples?" Environmental Working Group, February 1999, p. 1.
[11] "Do You Know What You're Eating?" Consumers Union of the United States, January 1999.
[12] American Crop Protection Association, "Industry Profile," 1998, p. 1.
[13] Douglas Martin, "City Said to Use More Pesticides Than Farm Counties," *The New York Times*, Nov. 19, 1998, p. B8.
[14] Linda and Bill Bonvie, "Spraying Risks Remain," *The Boston Globe*, Jan. 10, 1999.
[15] "Same As It Ever Was. . ." Environmental Working Group, May 1998.
[16] *Ibid.*
[17] *Ibid.*
[18] "Impacts of Eliminating Organophosphates and Carbamates From Crop Production," Texas A&M University Agricultural and Food Policy Center, April 1999.
[19] American Crop Protection Association, *op. cit.*, p. 20.
[20] "How 'Bout Them Apples?" *op. cit.*, p. 5.

[21] Cooper, *op. cit.*
[22] Sally Lee, *Pesticides* (1991), p. 11.
[23] *Ibid.*, p. 12-13.
[24] Rachel Carson, *Silent Spring* (1962), p. 8.
[25] Al Gore, *Earth in the Balance* (1992), p. 52.
[26] The lawmaker was then-Rep. Mike Synar, D-Okla., chairman of the House Government Operations Subcommittee on Environment, Energy and Natural Resources.
[27] David Hosansky, "Long-Sought Pesticides Bill Advances Easily After Deal," *CQ Weekly*, July 20, 1996, p. 2031.
[28] EPA Web site.
[29] Quoted in *Farm Bureau News*, June 14, 1999.
[30] Peter Eisler, "Restrictions coming on 2 widely used pesticides," *USA Today*, July 30, 1999, p. 1.
[31] Letter to EPA Deputy Administrator Peter Robertson and Agriculture Deputy Secretary Richard Rominger from the World Wildlife Fund, Natural Resources Defense Council, Pesticide Education Center, Consumers Union, Farmworker Justice Fund, National Campaign for Pesticide Policy Reform and Farmworker Support Committee, April 27, 1999.
[32] Farm Bureau press release, May 11, 1999.
[33] Environmental Working Group, press release, Jan. 11, 1999.
[34] For background, see Kathy Koch, "Food Safety Battle: Organic vs. Biotech," *The CQ Researcher*, Sept. 4, 1998, pp. 761-784.

Bibliography

Selected Sources Used

Books

Carson, Rachel, *Silent Spring*, Houghton Mifflin, 1962

Carson, a marine biologist with the U.S. Fish and Wildlife Service and a gifted writer, sparked a public outcry with her evidence that DDT and other chlorinated hydrocarbons used as pesticides were severely damaging the environment and endangering public health. Her landmark bestseller helped launch the environmental movement and ultimately led to a ban on DDT.

Colborn, Theo, Dianne Dumanoski and John Peterson Myers, *Our Stolen Future*, Dutton, 1996

Picking up where Carson left off, the authors present evidence that pesticides and other synthetic chemicals have severely disrupted the hormonal systems of humans and animals alike, possibly endangering the future of humans by hindering efforts to reproduce.

Gore, Sen. Al, *Earth in the Balance: Ecology and the Human Spirit*, Houghton Mifflin, 1992.

Written before the author became vice president, this volume calls for a more restrained use of pesticides.

Lee, Sally, *Pesticides*, Franklin Watts, 1981

This concise and clearly written book about pesticide uses and controversies by a former special-education teacher provides a thoughtful background about a complex subject.

Articles

Bouma, Katherine, "Did Warnings on Pesticides Go Unheeded?" *The Orlando Sentinel*, March 21, 1999, p. A1

State officials trying to clean up land near Lake Apopka leave such high levels of pesticides that possibly tens of thousands, of birds were killed or severely sickened.

Cone, Marla, "Pesticides May Harm Brain, Study Finds," *Los Angeles Times*, March 15, 1999, p. A3.

Cone summarizes evidence that children exposed to pesticides in the womb or as infants may suffer permanent brain damage.

Robinson, Fred, "Golf Might Be a Toxic Game; Players Unknowingly Can Ingest Pesticides," *New Orleans Times-Picayune*, July 23, 1998, p. D1.

Looks at the controversy over treating golf courses with large amounts of pesticides and fertilizers.

Reports and Studies

Consumers Union, *Do You Know What You're Eating?* January 1999.

Using Agriculture Department data, the consumers' group analyzes pesticide residues in different foods. Among the key findings: U.S. produce is frequently more contaminated than imported produce. The report was summarized in the March 1999 issue of *Consumer Reports*.

Environmental Working Group, *Overexposed*, January 1998

This report, along with a 1995 report by the Environmental Working Group called "Pesticides in Baby Food" and a 1999 report called "How 'Bout Them Apples," concludes that the EPA must greatly restrict the use of the most toxic pesticides on fresh fruits and vegetables to safeguard the long-term health of children.

Environmental Working Group, *Same As It Ever Was . . .*, May 1998

The report concludes that the administration has bowed to influential agricultural interests, allowing new pesticides that threaten drinking water in rural communities while canceling just one pesticide in five years.

National Research Council, *Pesticides in the Diets of Infants and Children*, National Academy Press, 1993

A highly influential report that provides disturbing evidence that children are exposed to potentially harmful levels of pesticides in their daily diets. The report recommends that standards for pesticide residues in foods be set according to their potential damage to children, not adults — a course reflected in the 1996 Food Quality Protection Act.

Natural Resources Defense Council, *Fields of Change*, July 1998.

This report offers a comprehensive analysis of alternative-farming methods, including case studies of farmers who successfully adopted such techniques as rotating crops, monitoring for pests and switching to biologically based pest-control products.

Natural Resources Defense Council, *Trouble on the Farm*, October 1998.

Children in rural areas, especially the children of farmworkers, are exposed to dangerous pesticide levels. The report urges the EPA to consider farm children when setting pesticide-tolerance levels.

Texas A&M University Agricultural and Food Policy Center, *Impacts of Eliminating Organophosphates and Carbamates From Crop Production*, April 1999.

A report by economists warns that domestic production of at least 14 crops would be set back if the EPA eliminated all use of the most controversial pesticides.

6 The Economics of Recycling

MARY H. COOPER

Reduce, reuse, recycle. Since the first Earth Day in 1970, the mantra of the environmental movement has prescribed a simple remedy for the country's growing mountain of waste: If Americans would simply reduce the volume of stuff they buy, reuse what they have and recycle the rest, the depletion of natural resources would be slowed and there would be fewer potentially toxic garbage dumps.

Nearly three decades into the war on waste, however, most Americans have proved reluctant soldiers. There is little evidence that we are reducing our consumption of goods. The U.S. economy is in its eighth year of uninterrupted growth, driven largely by domestic consumption. If Americans were heeding the call to reuse what they have, environmentalists argue, they wouldn't be buying so many new products or tossing so much out. Although the sheer volume of trash is growing more slowly today than it did in the past, the United States remains the world's leading throwaway society. [1]

"Our per-capita waste is just so out of whack," says Michele Raymond, whose firm, Raymond Communications Inc., tracks state recycling efforts. "We're just 20 percent of the people in the world, but we consume 80 percent of the world's resources. Our per-capita waste is the highest in the world and about twice the level of Germany and the United Kingdom. We're just trashing more than anyone else."

The only part of the anti-waste message that has taken hold to any noticeable degree is the call to recycle. Since 1988, when the Environmental Protection Agency (EPA) first set a recycling goal for the United States at 25 percent of total waste, communities across the

From *The CQ Researcher,* March 27, 1998.

country have introduced more than 8,000 curbside recycling programs and more than 3,000 composting facilities, all aimed at reducing the amount of household trash that ends up in landfills and incinerators. Colorful recycling bins are now a familiar sight on neighborhood streets.

"When I announced the 25 percent goal, only about 12 percent of the nation's garbage was recycled," says former EPA Assistant Administrator J. Winston Porter, now president of the Waste Policy Center, a research and consulting firm in Leesburg, Va. "The recycling rate grew pretty rapidly, and our goal was reached in 1995." The nation's overall recycling rate today is 27 percent of the total municipal solid waste stream. Sixteen percent is burned, while the remaining 57 percent ends up in landfills. [2]

Communities have been recycling trash for decades. Most early programs used drop-off points where people could leave their used newspapers, glass bottles and metal cans for a re-

cycler to pick up every week or so. More than 9,000 drop-off centers are still in operation. But lackluster participation in drop-off programs prompted many communities to begin adopting curbside programs in the late 1980s as a way to boost recycling rates. For several years, the supply of recyclable materials was adequate for the infant recycling industry. Indeed, newspaper publishers created such a demand for old newsprint that "garbage rustlers" prowled neighborhood streets to collect junked papers from curbside bins.

But markets for recycled materials, much like those for pork bellies, corn and other commodities, are notoriously volatile. Prices often gyrate when unusual weather, technological advances or other events cause sudden gluts or scarcities of a given commodity. When an oversupply of paper caused the booming market for recycled paper to collapse in the mid-1990s, a number of paper-processing facilities went under, and some recycling operators simply delivered the papers to the local landfill. Since then, recycling has come under closer scrutiny.

Critics blamed the collapse on state and local government goals and mandates for recycling. "Recycling may be the most wasteful activity in modern America: a waste of time and money, a waste of human and natural resources," wrote journalist John Tierney in a scathing criticism of recycling that appeared in *The New York Time Magazine* two years ago. [3] He and other skeptics charge that recycling programs fail to appreciably help the environment while imposing an unwarranted government intrusion into people's lives and disrupting the economy.

Tierney's criticism prompted a flurry of angry responses from readers and experts alike. "If we are serious about lowering the costs of recy-

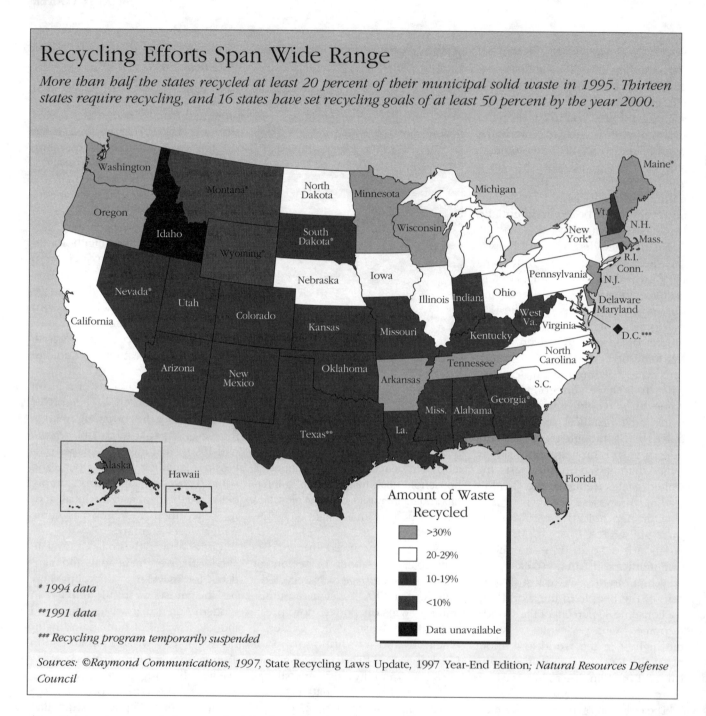

Recycling Efforts Span Wide Range

More than half the states recycled at least 20 percent of their municipal solid waste in 1995. Thirteen states require recycling, and 16 states have set recycling goals of at least 50 percent by the year 2000.

Amount of Waste Recycled

- \>30%
- 20-29%
- 10-19%
- <10%
- Data unavailable

* 1994 data

**1991 data

*** Recycling program temporarily suspended

Sources: ©Raymond Communications, 1997, State Recycling Laws Update, 1997 Year-End Edition; Natural Resources Defense Council

cling, the best approach is to study carefully how different communities improve efficiency and increase participation rates — not to engage in debating-club arguments with little relevance to the real-world problems these communities face," write Richard Denison and John Ruston of the Environmental Defense Fund (EDF).

"By boosting the efficiency of municipal recycling, establishing clear price incentives where we can and capitalizing on the full range of environmental and industrial benefits of recycling, we can bring recycling much closer to its full potential." [4]

Polls indicate that public opinion favors the environmentalists when it comes to recycling. Sixty-three percent of respondents to a recent survey reported that they were "personally doing more now" to help the environment, mainly by recycling. [5]

Skeptics dismiss such statistics, however. "I don't buy them for a second," says Jerry Taylor, director of natural resource studies at the Cato

Institute, a Washington think tank that promotes free-market policies. "If you ask people if they recycle, you're basically asking them if they care about the Earth, or if they like animals. They're going to say 'sure' because they don't want to sound like cretins." Whatever the reason, however, the polls suggest a high degree of public interest in recycling.

Many experts in solid waste management say the debate over recycling has been cast in overly simplistic terms that fail to accommodate the complexities of the markets for different recyclable materials. Whether it makes economic or even environmental sense to recycle, they say, depends on the material in question. "Recycling is like a vacuum cleaner that sucks up dispersed materials and reuses them," says Lynn Scarlett, vice president for research at the Reason Foundation, a nonprofit think tank in Los Angeles, Calif. "Where the material is of uniform quality, collected in large quantities and easy to isolate from contaminants, there are net benefits to recycling."

Steel scrap is one such recycling success story. Used cars, appliances and other goods that end up in junkyards are broken apart to allow giant magnets to separate the steel from plastics and other contaminants; then crushers collapse and bale the metal. Electric arc mini-mills melt the metal down to produce high-quality recycled steel, at less cost than "virgin" steel and ready to be made into new products. Steel has been recycled profitably for years, without the benefit of government support, and now accounts for about half of all steel consumed, Scarlett says.

The economic picture for materials collected in curbside programs is mixed. "Tin" cans, which actually are largely steel, are profitably recycled like steel scrap. Recycled aluminum beverage cans also are a hot commodity because they can be processed into new cans at less cost — and with less pollution — than mining and processing bauxite into virgin sheet aluminum. And despite the market's volatility, there usually is strong demand for old newspapers and cardboard boxes.

But the case for recycled plastics is more complex. There are six major types of plastic resins found in consumer products, only two of which

---

"If you ask people if they recycle, you're basically asking them if they care about the Earth, or if they like animals. They're going to say 'sure' because they don't want to sound like cretins."

— *Jerry Taylor*
Director, natural resource studies,
Cato Institute

---

are relatively easy to recycle. Containers made with these resins often have to be manually separated out of the recycling bin and carefully washed to remove contaminants before they can be reprocessed, an expensive process that is not always cost-effective.

"Environmentalists are right to say there are many opportunities for recycling," Scarlett says. "But for some products, it makes little sense to have any recycled content. Like any manufacturing process, recycling is a way

of making products, an alternative to using virgin feed stocks. The question is whether you can do it and get the product you want at a cost you want. In many cases the answer is yes, in others no. Each product has its own story to tell."

Nonetheless, a growing number of Americans have incorporated recycling into their daily lives and expect curbside service as a basic amenity, like electricity and other utilities. Supporters predict that recycling will keep expanding if Americans are made more aware of the benefits of waste reduction. To that end, more than 1,000 communities participated in the first America Recycles Day last Nov. 15. Sponsored by the EPA and environmental organizations, the event was designed to encourage recycling and the use of products containing recycled materials.

"For many people across the United States, recycling is a matter of habit, something they do in the course of their daily lives, both in the office and at home," says Richard Keller, chief of recycling at the Maryland Environmental Service, a state agency that sorts and markets recycled materials. "But recycling is at a fairly critical crossroads right now. We're already recycling the materials that are easy to recycle. The next step is going to depend on whether we start dealing with materials that are hard to recycle." These include more grades of plastics, as well as organic materials such as food wastes, paper food wrapping, diapers and tissues, which could go to special composting facilities.

The success of recycling programs varies widely according to local conditions. In some highly populated regions of the Northeast and the West,

Our Throwaway Society

• *Every week more than 500,000 trees are used to produce the two-thirds of newspapers that are never recycled.*

• *Americans throw away enough office and writing paper annually to build a wall 12 feet high from Los Angeles to New York City.*

• *Every year Americans dispose of 24 million tons of leaves and grass clippings, which could be composted to conserve landfill space.*

• *Americans throw away enough glass bottles and jars to fill the 1,350-foot twin towers of New York's World Trade Center every two weeks.*

• *American consumers and industry throw away enough aluminum to rebuild our entire commercial air fleet every three months.*

• *Americans throw away enough iron and steel to continuously supply all the nation's automakers.*

• *Americans use up 2.5 million plastic bottles every hour, only a small percentage of which are now recycled.*

Source: Environmental Defense Fund

high fees for landfill dumping make recycling especially attractive. In rural areas of the Rocky Mountain West, the high cost of collecting materials and the low cost of land for dumping waste have hindered recycling efforts. Ultimately, it is up to consumers and their elected officials in state and local governments to decide how best to dispose of their trash. These are some of the issues that shape their decisions:

Do the environmental benefits of recycling outweigh the costs?

Some markets for recyclable materials are strong enough to pay for their collection and conversion into new products. Recycled steel from cars and appliances is one of the most profitable post-consumer materials. Recovery of steel and aluminum cans also tends to more than pay for itself.

But demand for other products is less predictable. Plastics are hard to recycle economically because there are so many types of materials, and most are costly to clean and return to a usable form for new consumer products. Paper is less difficult to recycle, but the market for recycled paper has fluctuated wildly in recent years. After peaking in 1995, prices of recycled newsprint sank so low that some recycling contractors simply dumped the paper they collected in landfills.

On average, curbside recycling programs tend to cost slightly more than they earn from the sale of collected materials. According to Franklin Associates Inc., a Prairie Village, Kan., research firm that conducts solid waste studies for the EPA, residential recycling programs cost on average $2 a month per household. "The cost varies widely from

community to community," says Bill Franklin, the firm's chairman. "But recycling costs are a very small percentage of the total cost of solid waste removal, which averages $10 a month per household." Commercial recycling, which generally is contracted out by businesses to private haulers, probably makes more money than it costs. "We don't have good numbers on commercial recycling," Franklin says. "But it must be cost-effective, or they wouldn't bother to do it."

Environmentalists say the quantifiable financial costs of collecting, sorting and processing recyclable materials are far outweighed by an array of benefits to the environment. Nobody disputes the fact that recycling reduces the amount of trash that ends up in landfills or incinerators. Of the 208 million tons of municipal solid waste generated in the U.S. in 1995, 27 percent, or more than 56 million tons, was recycled. Fifty-seven percent ended up in landfills, and the remaining 16 percent was burned. [6]

But some critics dispute the importance of saving landfill space. "It's not in the least bit true that we're running out of places to put our garbage," Taylor says. He cites a Cato Institute estimate that all the trash generated in the United States over the next 1,000 years would fit into a single, 30-square-mile landfill 1,000 feet deep. "Of course, nobody is going to build that big a landfill," Taylor says. "But this shows the idea that we're running out of places to put garbage is just silly. Anyway, most landfills, when they're retired, are sodded over and turned into golf courses or other public facilities."

Many experts say recycling does far more to help protect the environment than merely preserve land that would otherwise be needed for waste disposal. "The more important goals of recycling are to reduce environmental damage from activities such as strip mining and clear-cutting and to conserve energy, reduce pollution and minimize solid waste in manufacturing new products," write Denison and Ruston of the EDF. "[R]ecycling is an environmentally beneficial alternative to the extraction and manufacture of virgin materials, not just an alternative to landfills." [7]

But some experts say the environmental benefits of recycling depend on the material in question. "Each material has its own tale to tell," Scarlett says. "It takes about 95 percent less energy to make a new can out of recycled aluminum than to make can sheeting by mining bauxite and smelting the ore. But the energy

savings offered by recycled glass are very modest because it takes only slightly less heat to process cullet [recycled glass] than to make glass from silica. And if you have to transport the glass hundreds of miles to a reprocessing facility, those gains may be undone because glass is very heavy and consumes a lot of energy to transport."

Lackluster participation in drop-off programs prompted many communities to adopt curbside collection programs to boost recycling rates.

Even aluminum recycling can harm the environment under some circumstances. "If you have to drive trucks far out into the countryside to pick up the cans, the air pollution generated by the trucks will outweigh the pollution saved by recycling," Porter says. "If you try to get the last squeal of the pig, you end up doing more

environmental damage than good. While the environmental benefits of recycling outweigh the costs for most things, people who treat recycling as a religion haven't considered the whole picture." [8]

Some critics go further, saying the environmental benefits of recycling have been grossly exaggerated. "You'd be hard-pressed to find real environmental benefits in recycling under any circumstances," Taylor says. "If you're recycling glass, what commodity are you saving, sand? We're not running out of sand. We're also not running out of energy — energy prices are the lowest ever, adjusted for inflation. And while, as a general matter, you can argue that energy consumption is a precursor of industrial pollution, if we suddenly started recycling everything instead of using virgin materials, the reduction in energy use wouldn't be all that dramatic."

Do government recycling mandates impede the creation of efficient markets for recyclables?

Most curbside recycling programs now in effect were introduced in the wake of the "landfill crisis" of the late 1980s, when several cities in the Northeast appeared to be running out of space to bury their garbage. Although the perceived crisis never materialized, governments at all levels called for increased recycling. In 1988, when the nationwide recycling rate stood at about 12 percent, then-EPA Assistant Administrator Porter called for Americans to boost that rate to 25 percent by 1993. States followed suit by setting goals of their own, prompting local governments to create or expand curbside residential recycling programs.

Garbage Loaded With Paper, Lawn Trimmings

Cardboard boxes, newspapers and yard trimmings comprised nearly two-thirds of the nation's municipal solid waste recovered in 1995. Some recycled materials, such as batteries and aluminum cans, had high recovery rates but contributed only a small percentage of the total materials recovered.

Recovery of Products in Municipal Solid Waste, 1995

Product	Tons Recycled (in thousands)	Percent of Product Recycled	Percent of All Solid Waste Recovered
Corrugated boxes	18,480	64%	33%
Yard trimmings	9,000	30	16
Newspapers	6,960	53	12
Glass bottles and jars	3,140	27	6
High-grade office papers	3,010	44	5
Major appliances	2,070	61	4
Lead-acid batteries	1,830	96	3
Steel packaging	1,550	54	3
Aluminum beverage cans	990	63	2
Magazines	670	28	1
PET soft drink bottles	300	46	1
HDPE milk and water bottles	190	30	<1
All other products	8,000	8	14
Total recovery	**56,190**	**27%**	**100%**

Source: Environmental Protection Agency, "Characterization of Municipal Solid Waste in the United States," 1996 Update

The majority of recycling mandates are merely goals, with no enforcement provisions. "Most recycling in this country is voluntary," Raymond says. "Some states have mandatory curbside separation, and some have mandatory goals, but most of it is voluntary."

Some jurisdictions, however, including California and New York City, impose fines for non-compliance with recycling mandates. In addition to recycling goals, some governments require agencies to buy a specified percentage of recycled goods, such as office paper, plastic traffic cones or paving materials made of old tires. At the federal level, for example, President Clinton issued an executive order in 1993 requiring all federal agencies to buy printing and writing paper with at least 30 percent recycled content by the end of 1998.

There is little doubt that government mandates have spurred growth in recycling programs. About 40 states have set recycling goals, ranging from 15-70 percent of the waste stream, according to Keller. "Most programs call for 25-50 percent recycling over varying periods of time," he says. "I think that without those mandates, especially on the residential side, you'd see far lower rates of recycling than what you're seeing now."

But critics say mandates distort the markets for recycled materials, possibly impeding their development over time. "Post-consumer material is a resource just like water, energy or any other resource, and a certain amount of it is going to be reused because it makes economic sense to reuse it," Taylor says. "But there's a lot of it that it doesn't make economic sense to reuse, and that's where government mandates come in. It cannot make economic sense to mandate the use of a material that nobody would otherwise use. You can build a nice Potemkin village marketplace out of that, but it doesn't mean you're really helping the economy, because the money used to pay for recycling programs is money that would otherwise have gone to more productive uses."

Many critics blame recycling mandates for the collapse in recycled paper prices in 1995. By suddenly increasing the supply of recycled paper in the early 1990s, this argument goes, governments flooded the market with more material than reprocessors could absorb. But Keller, who finds buyers for his agency's recycled materials, says mandates do not significantly distort the market, at least over the longer term. "In Maryland, which has set recycling goals of 20 percent for large subdivisions and 15 percent for small ones, the marketplace is very resilient," he says. "There may have been some marketplace dislocations when the programs came on line, but as a matter of fact there are some industries that we're working with that are scrambling to find materials. You have to recognize that the markets fluctuate."

Most curbside programs collect recyclables from individual houses, making them most common in urban and suburban neighborhoods as well as residential areas in smaller communities. Typically, apartment houses and commercial businesses are not included in public recycling programs. Some experts charge that by focusing on households, which generate relatively small quantities of trash, governments targeted the least suitable population for efficient recycling programs. "If they had actually studied where the trash was coming from, they would have put the mandates on industrial plants first, then commercial businesses and then multifamily housing units," Raymond says. "Curbside recycling would have come last in order of priority."

Like many other experts, Raymond says mandates have a positive role to play in helping markets for recyclables get started. But in her view, the focus on curbside collection has actually stymied that effort. "Had they phased curbside collection in last, these markets might have stabilized, and they would know what makes sense to pick up and what doesn't," Raymond says. "With commercial re-

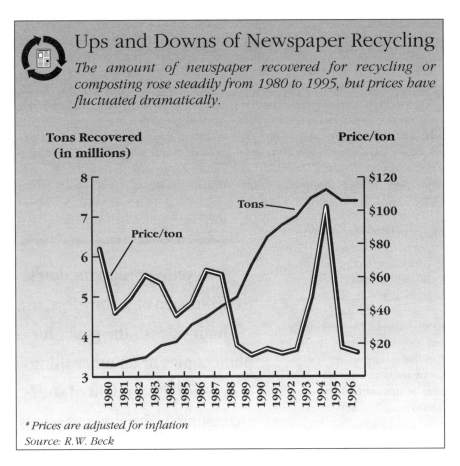

Ups and Downs of Newspaper Recycling

The amount of newspaper recovered for recycling or composting rose steadily from 1980 to 1995, but prices have fluctuated dramatically.

Tons Recovered (in millions) · **Price/ton**

Price/ton · Tons

* Prices are adjusted for inflation
Source: R.W. Beck

cycling, if the market goes bad for paper they simply stop recycling. But you can't do that with curbside recycling because it takes so long to educate people about what stuff to put in their bins. You can't just drop the glass and continue collecting the plastics, even though that probably would be better for the environment in the long run. With residential recycling, once you turn on that spigot you can't turn it off again."

Is a "pay-as-you-throw" system a more rational approach to waste management than other programs?

Experts agree that it is virtually impossible to educate consumers to periodically adjust the list of materials they leave for curbside pickup in response to fluctuations in the markets for recyclables. But program operators have found other ways to make recycling more cost-effective. Costs can be trimmed by shifting pickup schedules from weekly to every other week, investing in automated trucks to reduce labor costs or simply redesigning collection routes to use fewer trucks or reduce the time needed to complete collection.

But the most promising cost-saving measure may be variable-rate waste management. Also known as pay-as-you-throw, this approach replaces the flat fee typically charged households for waste removal, including recyclables, yard trimmings and other trash, with fees that vary according to the amount of trash destined for the landfill or incinerator. "Pay-as-you-throw is an excellent program that bears consideration in most communities," says Lisa A. Skumatz, president of Skumatz Economic Research Associates in Seattle, who found the system raised recycling rates by up to 10 percent in more than 500 communities she studied. [9] "It can be extremely cost-effective, the biggest-bang item you can get to improve recycling and yard-waste diversion." She estimates that more than 5,000 communities have adopted variable-rate programs to date.

Pay-as-you-throw works by charging households for the waste they generate, and so provides an economic incentive to recycle or compost as much trash as possible. Customers usually are charged by the garbage can or by the bag for non-recyclable trash. In Seattle, for example, customers pay by the container. The program is not without glitches: Customers often jam as much as they can into one container — a practice so common it's known as the "Seattle stomp." "Some guy actually hurt his back jamming stuff into his trash barrel and sued the city," Franklin says. "But in general, the pay-as-you-throw system does seem to work. If we know there's a penalty for the second barrel of trash, the economic incentive helps us manage waste better."

Some communities have made the system more accurate by using special trucks equipped with scales to weigh the trash they collect. "The variable-rates approach works for the customer because it says you can do what you want," Skumatz says, "but you'll save real dollars if you recycle."

By placing greater responsibility on the customer, variable rates not only encourage people to recycle but also to reduce their consumption. "Recycling programs, whether they're mandatory or not, in no way encourage source reduction in the

first place," Skumatz says. "They don't encourage you to buy less, use both sides of the paper for photocopies or do other things to reduce the amount of stuff consumed. Variable rates does that — it adds something that even mandatory recycling can't accomplish."

But there is a downside to variable rate-systems. "While unit-based pricing rewards people who are more efficient, it's not a total panacea," Porter says. "People will haul their garbage to the Dumpster in the

> "Recycling programs don't encourage you to buy less, use both sides of the paper for photocopies or do other things to reduce the amount of stuff consumed. Variable rates does that — it adds something that even mandatory recycling can't accomplish."
>
> — *Lisa A. Skumatz, president, Skumatz Economic Research Associates*

McDonald's parking lot on their way to work, or they'll sort their mail in the post office and throw away the junk mail before going home. So there's a lot of trash shifting going on."

Porter also questions the ability of most people to drastically reduce the amount of stuff they consume. "What exactly are you supposed to do, stop buying milk or feeding the dog?" he asks. "You may get a 10 percent reduction in consumption with pay-as-you-

throw, but not much more. People can't change their habits that much."

Variable-rate programs also have limited impact beyond the supply side of the market for recyclables. "Pay-as-you-throw is the best idea we have now because it provides the correct signal to the consumer for wasting less," Raymond says. "The problem is, it doesn't solve the problems we have with recycling right now because it doesn't create markets. It just changes consumers' habits and improves their cooperation in putting all of their recyclables out. Now what are you going to do with them? You've got to have markets for them. Industry has to use recycled materials for the markets to operate properly."

Other critics object to pay-as-you-throw for the same reasons they object to all recycling programs. "I'm suspicious whenever governments at any level think they know exactly the right way to do things," Taylor says. "Some people will be annoyed at having to pay for each bag they throw out and would far rather pay a flat fee for trash removal. I don't think government should be involved in recycling at all. Each household should be allowed to make its own decisions about who's going to collect their garbage and under what terms." ■

BACKGROUND

Birth of a Movement

Throughout history, recycling has been the rule rather than the

Chronology

1940s *The first widespread residential recycling efforts emerge during World War II as consumers contribute scrap metals and paper to wartime industries.*

——— • ———

1960s *Concern builds over the nation's mounting waste stream.*

1962
Author Rachel Carson warns of the dangers of toxic chemicals left in landfills in her best-seller *Silent Spring*.

1965
The Solid Waste Disposal Act launches federal research into the technology of waste disposal and provides technical and financial assistance for state and local waste programs.

——— • ———

1970s *The environmental movement spurs interest in residential recycling.*

1970
The Resource Recovery Act extends federal assistance to recycling programs and waste incineration and requires states to come up with plans for managing their waste.

1975
More than 100 communities across the country have introduced curbside recycling, mostly for newspapers, in an effort to boost recycling. More than a quarter of all aluminum beverage cans, the most valuable post-consumer material, are recycled.

1976
The Resource Conservation and Recovery Act (RCRA) sets national standards for landfills and incinerators. By requiring the use of expensive landfill liners and smokestack scrubbers, the law indirectly encourages recycling.

1978
The Public Utilities Regulatory Policies Act (PURPA) encourages the development of waste-to-energy plants. Support for these alternatives to landfills later wanes, however, because of their emissions of toxic ash.

——— • ———

1980s *Acting on fears that landfill space is running out, communities across the country step up curbside recycling programs.*

1987
The *Mobro 4000*, a garbage barge out of Long Island, attracts national attention as it sails down the East Coast to the Caribbean in the vain search for a place to dump its cargo. The incident prompts concern, largely unfounded, that the entire country faces a landfill crisis.

1988
The Environmental Protection Agency (EPA) sets a recycling goal for the United States at 25 percent of total waste.

1990s *Recycling comes under scrutiny after a series of supply gluts causes upheaval in the markets for recycled materials.*

1991
Manufacturers' demand for recycled materials fails to keep pace with the supply following the sudden increase in curbside programs, causing the first major crash in the market for recyclables.

1993
President Clinton issues an executive order requiring all federal agencies to buy printing and writing paper with at least 30 percent recycled content by the end of 1998.

1995
The nationwide recycling rate reaches 27 percent, exceeding the EPA's 25 percent goal. Prices of recycled newsprint and some other materials reach historic peaks, prompting "garbage rustlers" to raid curbside bins for valuable materials. The Chicago Board of Trade sets up an electronic listing for recycled plastic, paper and glass that helps link buyers and sellers of these materials and thus improves the market's efficiency.

1996
Newsprint prices sink so low that some recycling contractors dump collected paper in landfills.

1997
The pace of new curbside programs begins to slow because most programs already collect the materials that are in demand by manufacturers.

How Germany Copes With Recycling Success

The United States may have launched the recycling movement, but other countries have embraced stricter recycling requirements, notably Germany. German manufacturers must take responsibility for collecting and recycling or reusing the packaging materials for the products they sell. Unlike U.S. recycling programs, which focus on consumers and for the most part rely on their cooperation, the German system embodies the "polluter-pays" principle. It holds that because industry is responsible for choosing what packaging it uses, it should bear the burden of recycling it.

The law was partly a consequence of the collapse of European communism. Before German reunification in 1990, West Germany had "solved" the problem of dwindling landfill space by exporting its trash to East Germany, where landfill regulations were minimal. [1] Meanwhile, West Germany's increasingly influential Green Party helped pass strong environmental protection regulations. With reunification, those regulations were extended to the whole country, and a new solution to Germany's waste problems had to be found.

The Ordinance on Avoidance of Packaging Waste, which took effect in June 1991, required industry to switch to reusable shipping cartons and reduce its use of non-essential "secondary" packaging, such as cardboard boxes containing bottles of aspirin or the plastic "blister" packs used to display many consumer goods. Beverage producers were able to comply with the law by using refillable bottles, a longstanding practice in much of Europe.

But problems quickly arose for essential, "primary" packaging materials, the countless pill bottles, toothpaste tubes and myriad other containers that manufacturers were required to take back and recycle or reuse under the law. Faced with a near-impossible obligation, German industries banded together and created a consortium — the Duales System Deutschland (DSD) — to provide collection and recycling services on their behalf. Manufacturers pay DSD for the right to place a green dot on their packaging, which exempts those items from the law's take-back provision. DSD then pays waste companies to collect those packaging materials from curbside bins or drop-off centers and sells the materials to industry for recycling.

The German system immediately boosted recycling rates.

By 1994, DSD had grown into a multibillion-dollar business and was recycling two-thirds of the country's packaging materials. But the system has also been the victim of its own success, especially in the collection and recycling of plastics. Overwhelmed by a glut of collected plastic packaging, DSD exported much of the excess to other countries where it was often buried or burned.

Despite its drawbacks, the German recycling system is being emulated in other countries, particularly in Europe, where high population densities make landfills less feasible than in the United States. As part of an effort to harmonize regulations throughout the 15-member European Union, the EU in 1994 adopted a Packaging Directive setting both minimum and maximum recycling goals — the latter aimed at avoiding some of the German system's problems. By 2001, all member countries are to recycle from 25-45 percent of their packaging. Germany, which already exceeds the maximum quota for all materials, must either reduce its recycling rate or demonstrate that it can recycle its own materials.

A number of countries have adopted or are considering recycling programs based on the German green dot system. For example, Austria, Belgium and France have introduced similar programs, modified to allow incineration of recyclables as a way to avoid the oversupply of materials that has hampered the German program.

The German model may have little appeal, however, in the United States, where recycling has always been a largely voluntary effort based on individual participation. Additionally, the German approach owes much of its success to the country's high population density and limited geographical area. In the United States, with its vast distances and large tracts of undeveloped land, landfilling is still an option, while transportation costs discourage recycling in many parts of the country.

"Germany's packaging law is the most stringent in the world, and they spend up to $4 billion a year enforcing it," says Michele Raymond, publisher of *State Recycling Laws Update*. "It's a totally different system there."

---

[1] Information in this section is based on Frank Ackerman, *Why Do We Recycle?* (1997), pp. 108-109.

---

exception. Even after the Industrial Revolution ushered in the modern era of mass production and consumption of consumer products, many basic materials continued to be recycled. Until the late 19th century, for example, paper was made from rags, and the demand for rags

upheld a robust market for used clothing and other textile scraps. [10] Scavengers picked garbage dumps for these and other materials that were routinely fed back into the production cycle. Today, the remnants of older types of recycling persist in the form of scrap

dealerships where cars, appliances and other goods are broken up, sorted into their steel and other metal components and sold to mini-mills for use in new products.

Although recycling had always been a common business activity, it was not until the 1940s that people began collecting materials for reasons other than profit. During World War II, Americans voluntarily contributed metals, rubber and other materials for the war effort. More than a third of all paper and paperboard products, as well as other materials, were recovered and recycled by the war industries.

Recycling fell from view after the war, but re-emerged in the 1960s in response to a new concern — the environment. Lady Bird Johnson, the wife of President Lyndon B. Johnson, helped launch a campaign to clean up the trash strewn along the nation's roadways, and Rachel Carson, in her 1962 best-seller *Silent Spring*, warned of the dangers of toxic chemicals left in landfills. Largely unregulated at the time, landfills were frequently used as dumps for hazardous wastes, which leached into the groundwater. [11] Recycling was seen as a way to reduce the amount of trash and thus the need for more landfills.

By the early 1970s, thousands of grass-roots recycling centers had appeared where consumers could drop off newspapers, glass bottles and aluminum cans. In addition, by 1974 more than 100 communities had set up curbside collection services for recyclables, mostly newspapers. Newspaper collection fell off following a slump in the newsprint market in the mid-1970s. But the demand for recycled aluminum remained strong; by 1975, a quarter of all aluminum cans were being recycled.

Federal Role

Although recycling has always been a matter of state and local jurisdiction, the federal government has enacted several laws since the environmental movement's inception in the 1960s that have indirectly influenced the progress of recycling programs. [12] The 1965 Solid Waste Disposal Act launched federal research into the technology of

Of the 208 million tons of municipal solid waste generated in the United States in 1995, 57 percent ended up in landfills.

waste disposal and provided technical and financial assistance for state and local waste programs. The 1970 Resource Recovery Act extended the federal effort to include recycling programs and waste incineration, including waste-to-energy facilities, which generate steam or electricity from burning garbage. [13] The law stopped short, however, of setting standards, and it required states to come up with plans for managing their waste as a condition for receiving the federal aid.

The 1976 Resource Conservation and

Recovery Act (RCRA) set national standards for landfills and incinerators that were strengthened in 1984. While the law did not address recycling directly, its requirements of environmental safeguards, such as landfill liners and smokestack filters, made it more expensive to bury or burn waste and thus encouraged recycling indirectly.

Waste incineration gained support as an attractive source of energy in the wake of the energy crises of the 1970s. In 1978, Congress encouraged the development of waste-to-energy facilities with the Public Utilities Regulatory Policies Act (PURPA), which required utilities to buy power from these plants at favorable rates. Enthusiasm for waste-to-energy facilities soon cooled, however, out of concern over the toxic ash they generate, which must be disposed of in special landfills. As a result, only about 16 percent of municipal solid waste is incinerated. [14]

Landfill 'Crisis'

The administration of Ronald Reagan (1981-1989) enacted no major laws dealing with solid waste. But public perceptions that the country's mounting trash flow posed threats to the environment continued. These fears escalated in 1987, when the *Mobro 4000*, a garbage scow, sailed for days down the East Coast and into the Caribbean Sea in search of a port to dump its fetid cargo. The widely publicized voyage came to symbolize the emergence of a landfill "crisis," in which cities, having run out of space to bury their own garbage, were desperately trying to export it to other jurisdictions.

As it turned out, the *Mobro's* problems had little to do with the lack of landfill space. The barge operator had simply set sail without signing any agreements with landfill operators to dump its garbage, and port authorities turned the scow away, not because local landfills were full but because they feared it carried hazardous wastes. [15] But the *Mobro's* wayward journey bolstered public support for recycling as a solution to the problem.

By this time, recycling operations had expanded in number and in the range of materials collected. Beginning in the early 1980s, recycling operators built "material-recovery facilities" where they could sort, bale and market the recyclable materials they collected in curbside programs. In the absence of federal standards for recycling, states set their own standards. Today, most states have passed laws aimed at reducing the total waste stream and encouraging recycling as well as composting of yard trimmings. [16] ▪

CURRENT SITUATION

An Uncertain Market

C ommunity recycling programs are just the first link in the recycling process. The next role is played by markets for recyclable materials — the paper mills, steel mills, aluminum smelters, glass container makers and plastics reprocessors that transform these materials into new products.

The 1990s have seen both un-

precedented growth in recycling programs and volatility in the markets for recyclable materials. A glut in the supply of recyclables that followed the sudden increase in curbside programs in the late 1980s caused a crash in prices in 1991, as new manufacturing plants failed to keep pace with the supply of raw materials. A so-called "basket" of recyclables that fetched $70 a ton in 1989 went for just $25 a ton by 1992, prompting some communities to pay haulers to cart away the materials they had collected. [17]

Barely two years later, however, prices soared. Old corrugated cardboard rose in value from $25 to $150 a ton during the first six months of 1994, while mixed paper prices skyrocketed from $5 to more than $200 a ton. Prices for old newsprint, plastic soda bottles and milk jugs and aluminum cans also soared. [18] Boom again turned to bust in mid-1995, when prices for paper and plastics plummeted.

Such extreme swings in the market come as no surprise to recycling experts. "After all, these are market commodities, and how they fare depends on what is going on in the overall economy," Keller says. "If the economy goes south and people stop making as many houses and automobiles and buy less retail goods, you'll see a drop-off in the end market for recyclables."

Today, recycling in the United States is a $30 billion industry. As the industry has grown, the market for recyclables has become somewhat more stable, and while prices for most materials are nowhere near their peaks of three years ago, they are close to historical norms. According to R.W. Beck Inc., a consulting and engineering firm that tracks the market in recyclables, the value of a basket of nine materials it measures stood at an estimated $80 a ton in 1997, much lower than the $145

reported in 1995 but higher than the $68 reported in 1996. [19] A closer look shows how different market conditions are for the most commonly recycled materials:

Paper — Almost 40 million tons of paper were recovered from the waste stream in 1996, or nearly 85 percent of all recycled materials. More than half of that was corrugated containers, the single largest item in Beck's index. These are primarily boxes used for packaging and shipping goods from factories to retailers, and most are collected through privately contracted recycling programs. Demand for this material is generally strong.

The glut of old newspapers that sent the market into a tailspin three years ago has abated, in part because growth in newspaper circulation has slowed with the advent and growth of electronic news media. Mixed paper, one of the more recent items included in curbside collection, is expected to be in greater demand as an alternative to corrugated boxes for the production of paperboard, used to make shoeboxes, cereal boxes and other items. Likewise, high-grade paper is in demand, in part because of federal and state purchasing mandates requiring public agencies to buy writing and printing paper with recycled content.

Prices for recycled paper in 1997 ranged between $5.69 per ton for mixed paper to $109 per ton for high-grade paper. With the exception of old newspapers, which fell slightly in 1997 to $15 a ton, prices for recycled paper materials rose slightly from 1996 to 1997.

Although many deinking plants were built in response to the 1995 peak in paper prices, a number of paper recycling manufacturers have been in business for years. Marcal Paper Mills Inc., for example, has been using a variety of waste papers to make 100 percent recycled-content napkins, tissues and paper towels at its Elmwood Park, N.J., plant since 1947.

New deinking technology that can reprocess coated paper, such as old magazines and catalogs, has increased demand for a broader range of paper products than was once collected for recycling. But paper mills still report problems resulting from contamination of the materials, especially from "stickies," or adhesive notes, which raise the cost of producing recycled paper. [20]

Glass — After newspapers, glass containers are the most common item by weight found in residential waste. Although they are rapidly being replaced by plastics for soft drinks, glass bottles and jars are widely used to package beer, other drinks and food products. Recovery of glass containers has fallen slightly since it peaked in 1994. Prices for clear glass — the only type measured in Beck's analysis — fell 20 percent in 1997, to $37 a ton.

Clear, green and brown glass bottles have different properties and must be processed separately. In areas where they are collected together, breakage can quickly contaminate the recovered materials. Another obstacle to reprocessing glass is its weight, which makes it costly to ship, especially in sparsely populated regions such as the Mountain West. Transportation is becoming a greater factor in the cost of reprocessing glass because of consolidation: 127 regional plants have been replaced by 62 larger plants over the past 20 years. [21]

Steel cans — Scrapped appliances as well as steel cans collected curbside account for most steel and iron recovered from municipal solid waste. Almost 60 percent of all steel cans produced in the United States, mostly food cans, are recov-

ered for recycling, and the percentage is growing steadily, thanks in part to the recent inclusion of aerosol cans in many curbside programs. Perhaps reflecting that trend, prices for baled steel cans fell to $50 a ton in 1997, the lowest level reported by Beck since 1980. However, given high demand for scrap steel by the steel industry in the United States and abroad and the recent increase in the number of electric-arc furnaces in

After peaking in 1995, prices for recycled newsprint sank so low that some contractors simply dumped the paper they collected in landfills.

©PhotoDisc

operation, prices for recycled steel are expected to rise in coming months. [22]

Aluminum cans — At 64 percent, the 1997 recycling rate for aluminum beverage cans outstrips that

for steel cans, and amounts to about a million tons a year. But the price of aluminum cans is much higher — $1,090 a ton in 1997 — and has risen by more than half since 1993, making these the most valuable items collected in most curbside programs. Unlike most recyclables, aluminum is relatively unaltered by reprocessing, so it can be recycled over and over again with little sacrifice in quality. Aluminum cans are unusual also because they typically emerge from the recycling process as new aluminum cans, completing the closed loop depicted in the universal symbol designating products with recycled content. Domestic demand for aluminum cans is so high that less than 1 percent of them are exported to overseas processors.

Plastic — More than half of the nation's roughly 32,000 communities have access to programs that collect one or more types of plastic. [23] But plastic recycling has been hampered by the difficulty of separating the different types of containers and packaging materials and reprocessing them into materials suitable for remanufacture. Of the scores of plastic resins used in manufacturing, six are most commonly found in everyday consumer products. Of these, only two have been widely included in recycling programs — polyethylene terephthalate (PET), used to make beverage bottles, and high-density polyethylene (HDPE), used in milk jugs and other containers.*

---

*Plastic containers are numbered from 1-7 depending on which resins they contain.

Prices for old PET bottles, much like those for recycled paper, have fluctuated in recent years, ranging from a record high of $354 per ton in 1995 to $40 per ton in 1996. The main reason for the crash in prices for PET bottles was the opening of numerous factories here and abroad producing virgin resin, which curbed demand for scrap PET. Last year, Beck reports, PET prices rebounded to $118 per ton. There is no lack of capacity to reclaim PET — 27 plants in 18 states processed more than 300,000 pounds of post-consumer PET in 1995. [24]

Both the recovery rate and prices for HDPE bottles have risen in recent years. Many recycling programs have expanded the list of eligible HDPE items to include water and juice bottles as well as pigmented bottles used for liquid detergents. Baled HDPE containers, which totaled 660 million tons, brought $421 a ton last year, almost as much as during the 1995 peak. Recycled HDPE is often used to make new containers, plastic plumbing pipes, leaf bags and plastic "lumber."

The complexity of plastics recycling makes it hard to develop stable markets for products made of resins other than PET and HDPE, however. New technologies are making it possible to break plastic materials down into their original state, so that they are virtually indistinguishable from virgin resins, but most resin producers have not invested in this technology. [25] "Remember, these producers are the Exxons of this world, large, traditional companies that are not likely to spend money for a small niche business like recycling," Raymond says. "Anyway, why should they want to use

less virgin resin? They're selling more and more of it, 40 percent more over the past six years alone. Plastics surpassed steel in the 1970s in terms of volume. Today it's bigger than just about anything."

Most of the plastic that is re-

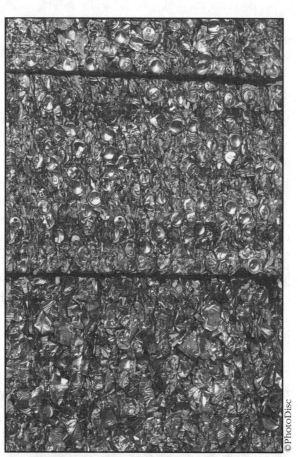

Nearly two-thirds of all aluminum beverage cans were recycled in 1997. About a million tons of aluminum cans are recycled each year.

©PhotoDisc

cycled undergoes only partial reprocessing before it is transformed into new products, products that bear little resemblance to the bottles and packaging materials consumers tossed in the bin. In such an "open-loop" application, plastic bottles are washed, ground up and made into fiber for fleece jackets and carpets, or they are exported. Only about 16 percent is used to make new bottles. [26]

Another obstacle to further plastic recycling is the growing popularity of single-serve PET drink bottles. Because they are often used and discarded away from home, these bottles often elude recycling programs and end up in the trash. Businesses and public agencies are beginning to install special bins to encourage recycling of these bottles.

Compost — Though it is collected separately from other recycled items, yard trimmings are commonly picked up curbside and hauled to a municipal composting facility. Once composted, leaves, grass clippings, branches and some food wastes produce a nutrient-rich soil additive that is purchased by nurseries, landscapers and residential gardeners. But because its value is so low in most parts of the country, the cost of collecting yard wastes is usually borne by consumers and embedded in the bill for solid waste removal.

Some communities provide special bins to encourage households to compost their own organic wastes and keep this material out of landfills. In the Northeast and other areas where landfill operators charge high "tipping" fees to dump trash, yard wastes are actually banned from the waste stream.

Communities Pitch In

The 1990s have seen rapid growth in recycling efforts. Today, about 27 percent of the nation's municipal solid waste is being recovered through

At Issue:

Does recycling make economic sense?

RICHARD A. DENISON AND JOHN F. RUSTON

Denison is a senior scientist and Ruston is an economic analyst at the Environmental Defense Fund

FROM "ANTI-RECYCLING MYTHS," ENVIRONMENTAL DEFENSE FUND, JULY 18, 1996.

*r*ecycling is not just an alternative to traditional solid waste disposal, it is the foundation for large, robust manufacturing industries in the United States that use recyclable materials. These businesses are an important part of our economy and provide the market foundation for the entire recycling process. . . .

Recycling provides manufacturing industries with raw materials that are less expensive than virgin sources, a long-term economic advantage that translates into value for consumers who ultimately spend less on products and packaging. For example, in the area of paper manufacturing, new mills making paper for corrugated boxes, newsprint, commercial tissue products and folding cartons have lower capital and operating costs than new mills using virgin wood. . . . Recycling has long been the lower-cost manufacturing option for aluminum smelters, and is essential to the scrap-fired steel "mini-mills" that are part of the rebirth of a globally competitive U.S. steel industry. . . .

In a recent study examining 10 Northeastern states, recycling was found to have added $7.2 billion in value to recovered materials through processing and manufacturing activities. These activities employed approximately 103,000 people, 25 percent of them in materials processing and 75 percent in manufacturing. . . .

Market prices for materials like polystyrene are set in the near term by supply and demand forces, underpinned by a host of production cost factors, many of which have nothing to do with environmental impact. An entire sub-discipline of environmental economics has developed to address a range of environmental damages, called externalities, that are not reflected in market prices even in the most regulated industries. . . . [When] a coastal wetland in the Carolinas is converted to a pine plantation and results in damage to estuarine fish hatcheries or reduced water quality, such impacts are certainly not captured in the market price of wood taken from the site.

Nor are any of the costs of disposal included in product prices. If someone drains motor oil from a car into the gutter, it may pollute surface water or groundwater. But the price originally paid for the oil does not anticipate its proper or improper disposal. Finally, another major obstacle to incorporating environmental factors into market prices is the difficulty or impossibility of assigning a meaningful economic cost to such "goods," for example, the value of preserving a rare animal or plant species.

JERRY TAYLOR

Director of natural resource studies at the Cato Institute and senior editor of Regulation *magazine*

FROM "MINIMUM CONTENT: MINIMUM SENSE," THE CATO INSTITUTE, April 25, 1997.

*t*en years into America's holy war against garbage, the case for residential curbside recycling has run smack into the harsh realities of economics. If resources are indeed becoming more scarce, they have a funny way of showing it. Prices for energy, minerals and paper have continued to fall as they have over the course of the century. . . . Post-consumer material is less competitive with virgin material than ever before. . . .

"But," you might point out, "what about the environmental externalities of the mining, timber, paper and energy industries? If you accounted for that, wouldn't recycling be competitive?" Again, not necessarily. First, we have no reliable means by which we can "price" those externalities. Second, those industries do spend tens of billions of dollars annually to comply with federal and state environmental regulations. Are the environmental externalities they impose greater than, less than or equal to the regulatory costs they pay to do business? No one knows for sure, but a number of respected economists . . . strongly suspect the environmental externalities of those industries are more than paid for through the cost of regulatory compliance.

Nor are the externalities of recycling's alternative all that impressive. EPA regulations now ensure that solid waste landfills cause only one additional cancer risk every 13 years, and that's assuming we use such worst-case scenarios and assumptions that even that figure, according to most risk assessment specialists, probably overestimates the actual risk by 100 to 1,000 times the actual risk. Likewise, municipal waste incinerators, according to those same worst-case assumptions, pose less than a 1 in 1 million risk to neighboring communities. . . .

Finally, recycling has its own environmental externalities that must be put into the equation. After all, the actual process of extracting usable raw material from a product is an industrial activity every bit as involved as the process of combining various raw materials to make a product. Both are industrial activities. And both create waste. For example, recycling 100 tons of old newsprint generates 40 tons of toxic waste. Is this consequential? Sure. EPA has reported that 13 of the 50 worst Superfund sites are/were recycling facilities.

If recycling makes economic sense, we don't need to mandate it. And if it doesn't, we shouldn't. You can make a silk purse out of a sow's ear . . . but it's usually cheaper to use silk.

recycling, up from just 17 percent in 1990. But because materials that are relatively easy to recycle are already being collected by many programs, the pace of new program start-ups has slowed over the past year, a trend that experts predict will continue.

Recycling often pays for itself in peak years, such as 1995, when communities earn more from selling materials than they spend to collect them. But when the value of recyclables drops, as it did in 1996, recycling often poses a financial burden on local governments, undermining support for the programs.

State and local budget cuts also are forcing many communities to reassess recycling programs. Several cities, including beleaguered Washington, D.C., dropped residential recycling altogether. Miami's City Council planned to do the same until public protests against the move. Many localities have cut back on frequency of collection and taken other steps to reduce costs. [27]

Even in Washington state, one of the leaders in recycling efforts, budget cuts are taking a toll. The Clean Washington Center is a state agency that helped Seattle and Tacoma achieve recycling rates of about half their waste by developing markets for recyclables. But last year the center, which also provides information to recycling programs throughout the country, was cut from the state budget altogether and forced to become an independent organization. ∎

OUTLOOK

No End of Trash

While recycling programs are not growing as fast as they did in the early 1990s, many experts predict that they will continue to expand. "The amount of trash out there is tending to grow at a slower rate than in the past," Franklin says. "Longer-term, we expect the recycling rate to reach 30 percent of the waste stream by 2000 and 35 percent by 2020." He predicts that most of the increase will result from expanding municipal composting facilities to include more yard waste and food waste rather than new materials collected for sale to manufacturers. "We'll see more composting of paper that's too contaminated for traditional recycling, such as food packages, paper napkins, food waste and even wood."

Consumer preference is likely to be a key determinant of recycling's future in the United States. Americans — both manufacturers and consumers — may embrace recycling on the supply side by participating in recycling programs, but they have been less enthusiastic consumers of recyclable materials and recycled-content end products. "Recyclables tend to be the last hired and the first fired," Keller quips. "If the economy is good, more recyclables get used, but if the economy is not going well, people go back to things they're more comfortable with."

In the absence of pressing consumer demand for recycled products, Raymond predicts, manufacturers are unlikely to boost production of these goods. "We don't have a crisis, virgin materials are cheap, energy is cheap and tip fees are very low, so industry has no incentive to use more recycled materials," Raymond says. "That's just corporate behavior as history has always shown it to be."

Many experts say the decade since curbside recycling took off, boosting the supply of recyclable materials, is too short a time to accurately assess the recycling market's full potential. Technological advances continue to broaden the range of materials that can be recycled cost-effectively, and new processing facilities can be expected to boost demand for post-consumer materials. "We will never reach the point where industries will be dependent on recycled materials alone," Keller says. "Although steel can be recycled an infinite number of times, paper loses a little fiber every time it's recycled, so we're going to still need virgin materials. But the technology will continue to improve, and we'll find ways to recycle materials now considered non-recyclable. There's no question that as technology changes, the variety of things we can recycle will improve over time."

Anticipating such an expansion, the Chicago Board of Trade in 1995 set up an electronic listing for recycled plastic, paper and glass that helps link buyers and sellers of these materials and thus makes the market more efficient. "It's not a full-fledged commodities market," Scarlett says, "but it's growing and provides another tweaking mechanism that helps increase information flows and improve recycling markets."

Of course, industry responds to consumer demand as well as the cost of raw materials. And for the most part, Americans remain unreliable end users of products made from recycled materials, which many view as inferior in quality.

"People in the food-processing industry will tell you that as a rule putting the green seal of approval on a product indicating it is environmentally benign is going to cost them market share," Taylor says. "People avoid it because they think it's flimsy, unsanitary or not up to standard performance."

Even active participants in recycling programs overlook recycled-content products. "Sure, there are some 'greens' out there, but the vast majority of us are more sensitive to price and quality than to environmental concerns," Raymond says. "Do I have the time to read the labels on all the products that I buy in the grocery store when I have only 30 minutes to get the shopping done? Get real."

Recent trends suggest those attitudes are slowly changing, however. Environmentally concerned consumers are driving growth in retail businesses such as the Fresh Fields-Whole Foods grocery chain, which specializes in environmentally benign products, including those with recycled content. In any case, consumer demand for recycled-content products may not be necessary for further expansion of this market, which Keller says already accounts for at least $10 billion in sales each year, because so many products include recycled materials even though they don't bear the green seal.

"There is no question that there are still remnants of the population who view recycled materials as inferior," Keller says. "But lots of recycled-content products have been quietly used for decades. There is no steel in the United States that doesn't have a minimum of 25 percent recycled content. There are no paper mills being built in the United States today that depend on virgin materials alone. Even *Air Force One* flies on retread tires." ■

Notes

[1] See Franklin Associates Ltd., *Solid Waste Management at the Crossroads* (December 1997). For background, see "Garbage Crisis," *The CQ Researcher*, March 20, 1992, pp. 241-264.

[2] Franklin Associates Ltd., *op. cit.*, p. 1-16. Franklin Associates provides the EPA with data on recycling. See also J. Winston Porter, *Trash Facts IV*, Waste Policy Center, 1997.

[3] John Tierney, "Recycling Is Garbage," *The New York Times Magazine*, June 30, 1996.

[4] Richard A. Denison and John F. Ruston, "Recycling Is Not Garbage," *Technology Review*, October 1997.

[5] The poll, conducted by American Opinion Research for the now-defunct Council on Packaging in the Environment in 1996, was cited in Bill Noone, "'Closing the Loop' Remains a Priority for Packagers," *Packaging Technology & Engineering*, November 1996.

[6] Porter, *op. cit.*

[7] Denison and Ruston, *op. cit.*

[8] For background on air pollution, see "New Air Quality Standards," *The CQ Researcher*, March 7, 1997, pp. 193-216.

[9] Lisa A. Skumatz, "Nationwide Diversion Rate Study: Quantitative Effects of Program Choices on Recycling and Green Waste Diversion: Beyond Case Studies," Skumatz Economic Research Associates Inc., July 1996.

[10] Information in this section is based on Frank Ackerman, *Why Do We Recycle?* (1997), pp. 14-19.

[11] For background, see "Cleaning Up Hazardous Wastes," *The CQ Researcher*, Aug. 23, 1996, pp. 745-768 and "Water Quality," *The CQ Researcher*, Feb. 11, 1994, pp. 121-144.

[12] For background, see "Environmental Movement at 25," *The CQ Researcher*, March 31, 1995, pp. 288-311.

[13] For background, see "Renewable Energy," *The CQ Researcher*, Nov. 7, 1997, pp. 961-984.

[14] Ackerman, *op. cit.*, p. 18.

[15] *Ibid*, pp. 11-12.

[16] *Ibid*, p. 18.

[17] See Lynn Scarlett, "Roller Coaster Recycling Markets: Down, Up, and What's Next?" *MSW Management*, January/February 1996, p. 51.

[18] *Ibid*.

[19] See Jessica Lucyshyn and Robert Craggs, "A Five-Year History of Recycling Market Prices: 1997 Update," *Resource Recycling*, February 1998, p. 16.

[20] See Franklin Associates Ltd., *op. cit.*, p. 4-8.

[21] *Ibid.*, p. 4-14.

[22] *Ibid.*, p. 4-12.

[23] "'America Recycles Day' to Raise Awareness of Recycling and Buying Recycled Products," *PR Newswire*, Nov. 14, 1997.

[24] Franklin Associates Ltd., *op. cit.*, p. 4-9.

[25] See Susan Warren, "Environment: Polyester Trash Is Pure Plastic after an 'Unzip,'" *The Wall Street Journal*, Nov. 6, 1997.

[26] Franklin Associates Ltd., *op. cit.*, p. 4-9.

[27] See Jim Glenn, "Year End Review of Recycling and Composting," *BioCycle*, December 1997.

FOR MORE INFORMATION

U.S. Environmental Protection Agency, Solid Waste and Emergency Response, 1200 Pennsylvania Ave. N.W., USEPA Ariel Rios (5101); Washington, D.C. 20460; (800) 424-9346 (in the Washington area, (703) 412-9810; http://www.epa.gov. EPA's Solid Waste Hotline offers information on how to contact recycling coordinators at the local level.

Reason Foundation, 3415 S. Sepulveda Blvd., Suite 400, Los Angeles, Calif. 90034; (310) 391-2245; http://www.reason.org. This nonprofit, nonpartisan public policy think tank advocates market solutions to environmental problems. It has done economic studies of recycling.

Waste Policy Center, 211 Loudoun St. S.W., Leesburg, Va. 20175; (703) 777-9800. This independent consulting and research organization analyzes the costs and benefits of recycling.

Environmental Defense Fund, 257 Park Ave. South, New York, N.Y. 10010; (800) 684-3322; http://www.edf.org. EDF provides information on the economic and environmental benefits of recycling.

Solid Waste Association of North America, P.O. Box 7219, Silver Spring, Md. 20907; (800) 467-9262; http://www.swana.org. Representing government officials who manage municipal solid waste programs, this group provides information on recycling, combustion and other alternatives to waste disposal.

U.S. Conference of Mayors, Municipal Waste Management Association, 1620 I St. N.W., 6th floor, Washington, D.C. 20006; (202) 293-7330; www.usmayors.org. This organization of local governments and private firms involved in waste collection and recycling helps communities plan recycling programs.

Bibliography

Selected Sources Used

Books

Ackerman, Frank, *Why Do We Recycle? Markets, Values, and Public Policy*, Island Press, 1997.
The author, a professor at Tufts University's Global Development and Environment Institute, reviews the history and market development of recycling. He argues that environmental as well as economic concerns must be included in any assessment of recycling's value.

Articles

"America's Recyclers: A Funny Sort of Market," *The Economist*, Oct. 18, 1997, pp. 63-64.
Government mandates have skewed the markets for recyclable materials, according to this article, by increasing supply with no concern for demand by industry.

Denison, Richard A., and John F. Ruston, "Recycling Is Not Garbage," *Technology Review*, October 1997.
In this response to an earlier critique of recycling, two researchers at the Environmental Defense Fund point out the economic and environmental benefits of recycling and call for efforts to improve the efficiency of community programs.

Lucyshyn, Jessica, and Robert Craggs, "A Five-Year History of Recycling Market Prices: 1997 Update," *Resource Recycling*, February 1998.
Two recycling analysts with R.W. Beck Inc., a national consulting and engineering firm, point out that markets for recycled materials have become less volatile in the past two years and suggest that program managers may be better prepared to avert the oversupply that buffeted the markets in 1996.

Scarlett, Lynn, "Roller Coaster Recycling Markets: Down, Up, and What's Next?" *MSW Management*, January/February 1996, pp. 50-53.
The gyrations in the markets for recycled materials seen in the mid-1990s are likely to continue, the author writes, because numerous events that are beyond the control of governments will continue to affect demand.

Skumatz, Lisa A., Erin Truitt and John Green, "The State of Variable Rates: Economic Signals Move into the Mainstream," *Resource Recycling*, August 1997, pp. 31-35.
By charging consumers for the amount of non-recyclable waste they generate, the authors write, communities can greatly increase recycling rates. More than 4,400 commu-

nities in the United States and Canada have integrated this approach into their waste collection programs.

Reports and Studies

Franklin Associates Ltd., *Solid Waste Management at the Crossroads*, December 1997.
This research firm, which provides recycling data to the EPA, predicts that the recovery of recyclable materials will continue to grow, though more slowly than in the past, reaching 35 percent by 2010.

Raymond Communications Inc., *State Recycling Laws Update*, Year-End Edition 1997.
State lawmakers enacted a total of 70 recycling bills in 1996, out of nearly 200 bills followed by this annual study. Local governments, however, maintained their commitment to recycling.

Scarlett, Lynn, Richard McCann, Robert Anex and Alexander Volokh, *Packaging, Recycling, and Solid Waste*, Reason Public Policy Institute, July 1997.
This study from a think tank in Los Angeles, Calif., examines the economic costs and benefits of recycling and concludes that government mandates for recycling rates or levels of recycled content in finished products are unlikely to help the environment.

U.S. Environmental Protection Agency, *The Consumer's Handbook for Reducing Solid Waste*, August 1992.
This overview of recycling includes a guide to help consumers understand what types of materials are commonly included in curbside programs as well as community drop-off centers.

U.S. Environmental Protection Agency, *Manufacturing from Recyclables: 24 Case Studies of Successful Recycling Enterprises*, February 1995.
Companies specializing in products containing recycled materials are profiled. Most are small manufacturers in or near the communities generating the recyclables. They include makers of paper, plastic, glass and other products.

U.S. Environmental Protection Agency, *Recycling Works! State and Local Solutions to Solid Waste Management Problems*, January 1989.
This dated but still relevant study examines innovative approaches to recycling — including programs that didn't work — in 14 states and communities.

7 Traffic Congestion

DAVID HOSANSKY

Mary Marshall enjoyed her job at a publishing company in Washington, D.C., but she dreaded her 25-mile commute from the Northern Virginia suburbs. In a daily odyssey that took well over an hour each morning — and often much longer — the 34-year-old editor had to drive along a heavily trafficked section of Interstate 66, then scramble for parking at a suburban Metro station, contend with throngs of other commuters on the train into the city and finally walk several blocks to her office.

"It put wear and tear on my nerves," says Marshall. After a year, Marshall, who has a 3-year-old daughter, got a job closer to home. She now works for an association in a nearby Virginia suburb — a commute of less than 20 minutes each way. "I bought myself two hours a day with my family," she says.

Marshall's experience is hardly unusual. Congestion is worsening across the country, with roads snarled, mass transit systems incapable of handling new suburban travel patterns and time-consuming commutes wearing workers down.

In the last few decades, traffic has grown so heavy that most big cities and their suburbs are gridlocked for much of the workday. Many smaller cities, such as Albuquerque, N.M., and Hartford, Conn., are facing four times the traffic congestion they had in the early 1980s. [1]

Congress approved a huge increase in spending on the nation's roads and mass transit systems in 1998, but many analysts predict that highway congestion will keep getting worse, reaching farther and farther out from cities and threatening to snarl major roadways any time of the day or night.

"It's a serious public-policy issue,"

From *The CQ Researcher,*
August 27, 1999.

says T. Peter Ruane, president of the American Road and Transportation Builders Association, a trade group representing highway engineering and construction firms. "In some cities, it has reached crisis proportions."

Some experts see hope in better suburban planning and new technologies to help control traffic flow. But the more pessimistic doubt that the nation can come up with any long-term solutions.

"Congestion is inescapable," says Anthony Downs, a senior fellow at the Brookings Institution. "Get yourself an air-conditioned car with a stereo radio and a CD player, and commute to work with someone you really like and relax. Because you're not going to escape it."

On the surface, the explanation for the increased congestion is simple enough: The number of miles that motorists drive every year is increasing at a much faster rate than the government is building new roads. From 1980 to 1996, highway usage — measured in vehicle miles traveled — increased by an average annual rate of 3.1 percent. During the same period, highway construction — measured in highway "lane miles" * — increased by an average of just 0.2 percent a year. [2]

---

*A "lane mile" represents one mile of one lane of highway. For example, one mile of a four-lane road equals four lane miles.

Population growth accounts for just a fraction of the increase. Vehicle travel on the nation's highways has increased by 130 percent since 1970, far outstripping the 30 percent population increase. [3] Gone are the days of one car per family; instead, the typical suburban household now owns between two and three vehicles, takes an average of 12 automobile trips a day and logs 31,300 vehicle miles each year. [4]

Americans are far more wedded to the automobile than people in other industrialized nations. About 82 percent of trips in this country are made in private vehicles, according to a 1992 study by the World Resources Institute. That compares with just 48 percent in Germany, 47 percent in France, 45 percent in Britain and 42 percent in Denmark. [5]

Armed with such statistics, advocates of more highway spending say the government has no choice but to satisfy Americans' passion for driving by building more roads. "It's an issue of democracy," says William D. Fay, president of the American Highway Users Alliance in Washington. "People like to drive."

"The whole economy runs on the efficiency of our transportation network," says Ruane of the road and transportation builders association. "The national highway system is the backbone of our economy."

But some analysts question whether Americans are really as tied to their cars as it appears. Environmentalists and other supporters of alternative transportation modes contend that the federal government has focused so much on building and maintaining roads that residents — outside of a few major cities — have no choice but to drive.

"We designed a lot of our suburbs so people have no choice but to use their cars for all their trips, and that makes it very hard to manage growing traffic

Most Congested Urban Areas

Los Angeles, Washington, D.C., and Miami are the most congested cities in the nation, according to annual rankings by the Texas Transportation Institute.

Large Cities	Medium Cities	Small Cities
1. Los Angeles, CA	1. Tacoma, WA	1. Eugene-Springfield, OR
2. Washington, DC-MD-VA	2. Memphis, TN	2. Harrisburg, PA
3. Miami-Hialeah, FL	3. Honolulu, HI	3. Salem, OR
4. Chicago, IL-Northwestern, IN	4. Tampa, FL	4. Allentown-Bethlehem-Easton, PA
5. San Francisco-Oakland, CA	5. Louisville, KY	5. Spokane, WA
6. Seattle-Everett, WA	6. Austin, TX	6. Albany-Schenectady-Troy, NY
7. Detroit, MI	7. Tucson, AZ	7. Brownsville, TX
8. Atlanta, GA	8. Albuquerque, NM	8. Boulder, CO
9. San Diego, CA	9. Nashville, TN	9. Corpus Christi, TX
10. San Bernardino-Riverside, CA	10. Omaha, NE	10. Beaumont, TX
11. Las Vegas, NV	11. Indianapolis, IN	11. Colorado Springs, CO
12. New York, NY-Northeastern, NJ	12. Salt Lake City, UT	12. Laredo, TX

Source: Timothy J. Lomax and David L. Schrank, Urban Roadway Congestion Annual Report 1998, Texas Transportation Institute

problems," says Michael Replogle, federal transportation director of the Environmental Defense Fund.

Land planners also say that the emphasis on highway construction has accelerated the trend toward suburbanization and urban sprawl. As more roads are built, people move farther out, which forces them to drive longer distances to commute or even run minor errands. Given the option, many residents would choose to walk to the store or take a bus to work, the planners say.

"There is ample evidence, both in the history of this country and that of other major cities around the world, that if you have an adequate and appropriate approach to land-use planning, and you provide a balanced transportation infrastructure, people will make smart choices," says Bill Wilkinson, executive director of the National Center for Bicycling and Walking. "What we've got in this country right now is the predictable outcome of 50 years of postwar investment that has virtually ignored any [transportation] mode other than the automobile."

Road construction advocates and environmentalists may be at odds over how to solve the nation's traffic woes, but they agree that congestion is an increasingly expensive problem. Road congestion in 70 major cities cost the nation $74 billion in lost time (4.6 billion hours) and wasted fuel (6.7 billion gallons) in 1996, according to a recent study by the Texas Transportation Institute, an influential research group at Texas A&M University. [6]

In the nation's most congested cities, including Los Angeles and Washington, drivers now spend the equivalent of 1.5 to two workweeks a year stuck in traffic. Gridlock has spread to medium-sized cities as well, including Austin, Texas, and Nashville, Tenn., where drivers now lose an average of more than a workweek every year sitting in traffic jams. [7]

"Congestion is certainly a multi-billion-dollar problem, and this is whether we're talking highways or whether we're talking aviation," says House Transportation and Infrastruc-

ture Committee Chairman Bud Shuster, R-Pa., perhaps the most influential advocate in Washington for more transportation spending. "The evidence is overwhelming that where you have efficient transportation, you increase productivity."

Trying to keep up with transportation needs is costing taxpayers dearly. A recent report by the U.S. Department of Transportation (DOT) estimated that, in 1994, governments at the federal, state and local levels spent $124.5 billion on the nation's transportation system, which amounted to 1.8 percent of the gross domestic product (GDP). That figure — which has almost certainly risen sharply since 1998, when Congress passed the six-year, $217.9 billion Transportation Equity Act for the 21st Century, nicknamed TEA 21 — probably underestimates total transportation funding because it leaves out such indirect costs as state highway patrols and roadside cleanup. [8]

The mounting traffic poses grave challenges for the nation's environmental policies. Building new roads often aggravates air and water pollution problems, fragments wildlife habitats and accelerates the apparent trend toward global warming. Despite gains in air quality in recent years, environmentalists say much more needs to be done.

"Air pollution is damaging our natural environment, killing off forests full of trees, fouling the air in our parks and harming the things that live in them," says Daniel Becker, director of the Sierra Club's global warming and energy program.

Determined to stop relentless road building and force local officials to look at transportation alternatives, environmentalists have filed a number of lawsuits to halt highway construction. In a case that has implications for road projects nationwide, environmental groups in March won a major court victory that forced Atlanta to scrap several dozen federal highway improvement projects that did not meet air quality standards.

The case was settled in June, with the city winning approval to finish about 16 road projects that were already under way. But more than 40 other projects were shelved indefinitely. In response, road-builders are pressing Congress to pass legislation that would amend the Clean Air Act and allow the projects to move forward.

Although it is not a front-burner issue, some administration officials worry that increased motor vehicle traffic is making the United States dangerously dependent on imported oil. The level of imported oil hit an all-time high in 1997, with most of it going to the transportation sector. Some of the increased oil use can be traced to the booming popularity of larger cars and trucks, including sport-utility vehicles. (*See story, p. 125.*)

"U.S. dependence on imported petroleum is more than ever a result of transportation's reliance on oil. . . . There are geopolitical implications,"

warned a 1998 study by the Department of Transportation. [9]

"Transportation and effective logistics are vital to our economic survival as we compete in the global market," Peter "Jack" Basso, DOT's assistant secretary for budget and programs, said at a conference earlier this year. "Therefore, how we meet our needs for transportation in the future is critical." [10]

As government officials wrestle with ways to combat traffic congestion, here are some questions they need to answer:

Does building new roads ease congestion?

At first glance, it would appear that the most likely solution for easing traffic congestion is to build more roads. After all, additional highway lanes would accommodate more cars, enabling Americans to indulge in their driving habits without getting stuck in traffic.

"I think, obviously, we need to continue building new highways," says Kenneth Orski, who heads a transportation consulting firm in Washington, the Urban Mobility Corp., and edits a transportation newsletter, *Innovation Briefs.* "There's just no doubt in most peoples' minds that will be required."

But some analysts say that building too many roads may do more harm than good. They point to studies indicating that new highways gradually induce more traffic, luring drivers who hope to find a less congested route. As more and more drivers use the new route, it may eventually become as crowded as the older roads.

"Building new roads doesn't solve traffic congestion any better than loosening your belt solves obesity," says Replogle of the Environmental Defense Fund.

Environmentalists and urban planners also point out that new roads tend to spur new development, thereby

bringing in more businesses and residents — and creating still more traffic. In fact, as highways are built farther out from the city, they tend to open up outlying land for development, forcing people to drive farther and farther to get to the city. In Atlanta, for example, residents are now driving an average of 36.5 miles a day.

Highway advocates argue just as passionately that it does not make any sense to stop adding road capacity. "We *can* help build our way out of congestion," says Fay of the Highway Users Alliance. "By choosing not to build roads, you worsen congestion."

In advocating increased funding for highway construction, Fay points to congestion in his hometown of Washington as an example of what can happen when road building stalls. Even though the metropolitan area boasts a flagship subway system and a network of bus routes and bike paths, traffic congestion is now second only to Los Angeles, possibly because residents and government officials have turned thumbs down on major road projects, such as a proposed highway that would link Interstate 95 with Interstate 270.

"Washington is an example of a city with an unbalanced transportation plan that relies excessively on alternatives that are not going to be the answer to our problems," Fay says. "It fails to make investments that would accommodate the principal means of travel: the automobile."

The Texas Transportation Institute study notes that two fast-growing Sunbelt cities — Houston, Texas, and Phoenix, Ariz. — have been able to ease traffic congestion slightly in recent years through massive construction programs boosting freeway and street capacity by 50 to 60 percent. But, the report goes on to say, "It remains to be seen whether [the pace of construction] can be sustained in these areas." [11]

If history is any guide, it may be

difficult for the nation to build its way out of its congestion woes. Traffic jams began around 1914, less than a decade after mass production of automobiles began, and highways that were built in the early 1920s were packed within a few years. [12] When New York City built two new bridges in the 1930s to ease congestion on a third span, transportation planners watched in dismay as traffic increased until all three bridges were as congested as the first one had been. [13]

"It's unrealistic to think we're going to have a transportation system where there isn't congestion," says Roy Kienitz, executive director of the Surface Transportation Policy Project, a Washington organization that advocates transportation alternatives. "You have this good. It is there to be consumed."

A broad array of analysts — ranging from environmentalists to road advocates — say the government should pursue an integrated transportation policy that gives people as many options as possible. Although they may disagree over whether to spend more on roads or on mass transit, a wide range of experts support the basic tenets of the 1998 transportation act, TEA 21, which provides funds for roads, subways, commuter rail lines, bike paths, sidewalks and other projects, and gives considerable discretion to local planners.

"So much of what causes congestion and what eases congestion depends on the local situation," says Susan Pikrallidas, managing director of government relations for the American Automobile Association. "To assume that building road capacity is always bad or that building transit is bad, both of those are polarized views. . . . The solution is usually going to be a mix of things."

Is congestion inevitable with urban sprawl?

When Kienitz of the Surface Trans-

portation Policy Project studies the development patterns that are sweeping the United States, he sees congestion inevitably getting worse. The problem, he says, is not merely a growing population or an obsession with cars. Instead, it is sprawling development that forces people to drive longer and longer distances to get to stores and offices.

"When everyone in America has to drive 20,000 miles a year, you just can't build enough highways," Kienitz says. "The reason there's congestion is there's an absolutely insupportable amount of driving. You have to drive 30 or 35 miles to get anything done."

Sprawl has become a fact of life in most U.S. metropolitan areas. [14] Even older cities, such as Washington and Chicago, are surrounded by rings of inner and outer suburbs, with strip malls and office parks that are difficult to get to by mass transit or walking. Newer urban areas, such as Phoenix, are composed largely of subdivisions and malls with limited opportunity for walking, even in downtown areas — a recipe for more driving and more congestion, critics say.

Not everybody agrees that sprawl is a primary culprit in congestion. Fay of the Highway Users Alliance says sprawl can actually ease traffic — if both homes and offices are located in the suburbs, relieving people of the need to commute downtown. "Anyone who doubts that high-density development aggravates congestion should drive through New York," Fay says.

But sprawling development frustrates many urban planners because it requires an inordinate amount of roads and is too spread out to be easily serviced by buses, light-rail or other transit systems. Moreover, suburban zoning regulations tend to separate residential, commercial and business areas — a strategy designed to ensure the peacefulness of residential areas, but that often ends up forcing people

to get into their cars every time they need to run an errand.

"As we spread ourselves farther and farther apart, it becomes inevitable that we must travel longer distances to work, shop, enjoy recreation and visit family and friends," warn the authors of a recent book on urban sprawl published by the Natural Resources Defense Council. [15]

As much as people across the country complain about sprawl, they seem to be seduced into making the same development decisions over and over. Beginning with Los Angeles in the 1950s, one American city after another has expanded outward, rewarding residents with single-family homes, better schools and a temporary respite from the level of traffic that plagues the inner cities — until more subdivisions are built farther out and traffic increases.

Road building and sprawl appear to be tightly linked: New highways spawn new developments, which in turn spawn traffic and demands for still more roads. Some Western communities, such as Salt Lake City, are facing that dilemma head-on. Salt Lake's metropolitan area is growing by 1,000 acres a month, spurring government officials to widen Interstate 15 from six lanes to 12, then begin work on a new, parallel highway to accommodate growing traffic along 100 miles of the Wasatch Range. [16]

Sprawl has become a major target of environmentalists. A recent report by the Sierra Club warned that sprawl is one of the fastest-growing threats to wildlife habitats and everyday quality of life. "The consequences of decades of unplanned, rapid growth and poor land-use management are evident all across America: increased traffic congestion, longer commutes, increased dependence on fossil fuels, crowded schools, worsening air and water pollution, lost open space and wetlands, increased flooding, destroyed wildlife habitat, higher taxes and dying city centers," the report states. [17]

Sprawl also may become an issue in the 2000 elections. Vice President Al Gore is spearheading an administration initiative to help communities preserve open space.

Fay, however, maintains that sprawl is the natural consequence of Americans' desire to live in single-family houses with plenty of space. "The reason we want to move up and out is we want a bedroom for every kid, and we want a large back yard they can play in," he says. "It's the epitome of the American dream."

Dismissing environmentalists' suggestions to limit growth or press people to live in higher-density areas, Fay adds: "The one thing that the public hates more than sprawl is high-density development."

Can mass transit relieve traffic congestion?

Faced with a choice of inching along Interstate 70 to St. Louis in rush hour or taking the new light-rail system, many commuters are opting for the train. In fact, daily ridership on the six-year-old MetroLink system hit 42,500 last year — well ahead of initial projections that ridership would remain under 35,000 until 2010.

"Ridership surpassed estimates, which is unusual," said Les Sterman, executive director of the East-West Gateway Coordinating Council, the metropolitan planning organization for the St. Louis area. "Usually the scandal is that [rail] systems never achieve the estimated ridership," he told *Governing* magazine. [18]

St. Louis is not the only place where light-rail systems are winning unexpected popularity. Dallas, a city where residents traditionally have celebrated their cars, opened the Dallas Area Rapid Transit system three years ago and promptly drew more riders than expected. San Di-

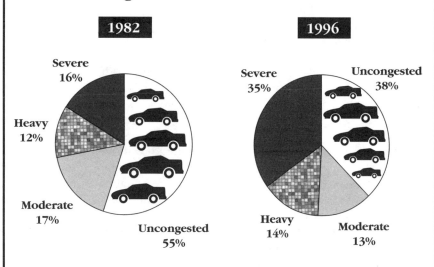

Congestion Is Increasing

The amount of severe traffic congestion in 70 major urban areas more than doubled from 1982 to 1996, according to a recent study by the Texas Transportation Institute.

Congested Travel in Urban Areas

1982

Severe 16%
Heavy 12%
Moderate 17%
Uncongested 55%

1996

Severe 35%
Uncongested 38%
Heavy 14%
Moderate 13%

Source: Timothy J. Lomax and David L. Schrank, Urban Roadway Congestion Annual Report 1998, Texas Transportation Institute

ego, which boasts a commuter rail line, a trolley system and express buses, has become a model of low-cost, high-quality mass transportation. Denver opened a 5.3-mile light-rail system in 1994 and is determinedly adding one new segment at a time.

"If you put good convenient services out there, people will use them," says John Bartosiewicz, the general manger of the Fort Worth (Texas) Transportation Authority, which operates a 10-mile light-rail system that is gradually being expanded.

Despite the success of these new rail systems, it's unlikely that mass transit can solve America's congestion problems. Only about 5 percent of all commuters use mass transit to get to work, compared with 85 percent who commute by car — and most of them drive alone. [19] (The remaining 10 percent walk or use

other modes of transportation, including bicycles.)

Transit ridership nationwide rose from 1996 to 1998, reaching 8.7 billion trips last year, according to the American Public Transit Association. But ridership is actually down slightly from where it stood at the beginning of the decade. [20]

Bus and rail travel is often difficult and time-consuming, especially in suburban areas where offices, stores and houses are built far apart. "It is very difficult to serve dispersed travel patterns with public transportation," says transportation consultant Orski. "While mass transit remains a very viable means of transportation, it serves a very small proportion of trips in the suburbs and in exurbia."

Fay of the Highway Users Alliance says many commuters prefer the convenience — and solitude — of driving themselves. "People support transit, but they don't want to take it," he says. "There are a number of us who really want the morning and evening commute to ourselves."

Even in those areas where a new transit system lures some commuters from the highway, new drivers seem to head for the roads and swiftly tie them up again. "Americans abhor a vacuum and will seek to fill it up," says Amy Coggin, communications director for the public transit association. But, she adds, "Highways would be completely clogged if you didn't have transit."

The federal government is doing what it can to encourage public transit. The 1998 omnibus transportation act, TEA 21, is providing $41 billion in funding over six years for mass transit, boosting its share of the gasoline tax from 2 cents to 2.85 cents and spurring a round of transit expansions across the country, including 166 miles of additional bus routes, 212 miles of various rail systems and eight miles of trolley bus service. The new law also allows employers to deduct more money for public transit subsidies for their workers.

Even though the effects on traffic may be subtle, mass transit officials say that buses, trains and other forms of transit are responsible for taking 5 million cars off the road — thereby reducing the number of accidents and saving Americans an estimated $19 billion in congestion-related costs. "The increased investment in transit is reaping significant returns and helping transit make a difference in the lives of people across the nation," William W. Millar, president of the American Public Transit Association, told a House Appropriations subcommittee in February. [21]

Supporters also note that public transit is a vital option for people who do not have access to cars. "You have to provide means for people who may be too young, too old or

have a disability — who for whatever reason can't drive," says Coggin. "People must have alternatives." ■

BACKGROUND

Rise of the Car Culture

Prior to the 20th century, federal efforts to build national transportation networks focused primarily on canals and railroads, rather than roads. At times, these projects were hampered by the reluctance of some states to relinquish their authority over transportation systems, which were built and maintained by private interests. [22]

Westward migration spurred the development of new roads, including the first federal highway, the National Road. Authorized in 1806, it became the main route west over the Allegheny Mountains into the fertile Ohio River Valley and stretched from Cumberland, Md., to Vandalia, Ill.

Since it relied on federal funding, the National Road set an important precedent, and has been described as "the single most significant act in American transportation, opening the constitutional door to federal support for canals, rails and Interstate highways." [23]

It was not until the late 19th century, however, that government officials began focusing on major road-building efforts. The movement for better roads was spearheaded at first by a powerful network of bicycle enthusiasts, but soon increasing numbers of automobile drivers began demanding paved roads as well. In 1916, the federal government launched its first coordinated program to support state and local road-building projects, attempting to improve mail service to rural areas and the

distribution of crops to the cities. With the 1916 Federal Aid Road Act, the United States embarked on a policy of expanding the national road network that has dominated federal transportation policy ever since.

Spurred by the mass production of automobiles, road and bridge construction continued apace, even during two world wars and the Great Depression. President Franklin D. Roosevelt's public works initiatives of the 1930s, aimed at providing jobs to millions of unemployed Americans, focused on the building of parkways, roads and bridges at a time when the economy ground almost to a halt. Construction of roads for purely civilian use slowed only briefly during World War II.

Road-building escalated with the postwar economic booms of the 1950s and '60s. As more and more working Americans were able to afford a car and a house, they fled the central cities for the suburbs that spread into the surrounding countryside along the new roadways that fanned out from downtown workplaces. With domestic oil supplies still plentiful, low gasoline prices added further impetus to car use and road development.

At the same time that local road networks were expanding, the creation in 1956 of the federal Interstate Highway System ensured the future development of national roadways for passenger travel and freight. To help fund the Interstate system, Congress established the Highway Trust Fund as a repository of federal motor vehicle and gasoline excise taxes to be used for highway construction and maintenance.

As Americans turned decisively toward cars for transportation, privately operated transit systems across the country went into decline. Many bus and rail systems were taken over by local public agencies that in 1961 began receiving federal subsidies to keep

Chronology

1800s-1920s
Early in the nation's history, emphasis is put on highway-based transportation.

1806
Congress authorizes construction of the first federally funded highway, linking the East Coast with the Ohio River Valley.

1916
The first national transportation bill, the Federal Aid Road Act, supports state and local road-building projects in an effort to improve mail service in rural areas and bring crops more quickly to market.

— • —

1930s-1960s
Massive road-building projects during the Depression and postwar boom in suburban development further concentrate federal transportation funds on highway construction.

1956
Congress launches the Interstate Highway System, a 44,000-mile network of federally supported highways. To pay for the Interstate system and other federal roads, the Highway Trust Fund is set up as a repository of revenues raised by the federal tax on gasoline and other fuels.

1961
Privately operated transit systems across the country begin to receive federal subsidies to keep them in operation, as falling ridership leaves them unable to stay afloat from fares alone.

1964
The Urban Mass Transportation Assistance Act authorizes federal funding for local transit authorities and establishes the Urban Mass Transportation Administration, renamed the Federal Transit Administration in 1991.

— • —

1970s-1980s
Despite oil-price increases, Americans continue their overwhelming reliance on cars for transportation

1973
Over the objections of automakers, oil companies and other highway interests, the federal government begins funneling Highway Trust Fund money into financially strapped local transit authorities.

1989
Federal Highway Administration estimates that 250,000 miles of pavement are too damaged to be maintained in a cost-effective manner and that 134,000 bridges are structurally deficient. The agency puts the costs related to traffic congestion at more than $34 billion annually.

— • —

1990s *Federal transportation policy for the first time supports non-highway modes of transportation.*

1991
The Intermodal Surface Transportation Efficiency Act — ISTEA — earmarks a slice of its six-year, $157 billion allocation for investment in non-highway projects, including transit systems, bike and pedestrian facilities and transportation-related historic preservation.

1995
Congress designates a 161,000-mile network of highways to be eligible for federal transportation assistance. Called the National Highway System, the network comprises the 45,000-mile Interstate system and other major highways.

Sept. 30, 1997
Unable to agree on new transportation funding, Congress allows ISTEA to expire. Lawmakers instead pass a stopgap, $9.8 billion measure.

June 9, 1998
President Clinton signs a sweeping, six-year, $217.9 billion measure known as the Transportation Equity Act for the 21st Century, or TEA 21. It boosts spending for both highways and mass transit systems, and guarantees that all revenues raised by the 18.3-cent-per-gallon federal gasoline tax will be spent on transportation.

March 2, 1999
Environmentalists win a landmark federal lawsuit, halting the construction of 61 highway projects in Atlanta that fail to conform to the region's clean air plans. In an out-of-court settlement three months later, environmentalists and state and federal officials agree that about 16 of the projects already under way can proceed. But the ruling throws highway projects across the country in jeopardy.

June 29, 1999
Amtrak unveils its new high-speed train, the *Acela Express*.

them running. Congress established the first formal federal role in urban transit operations with the 1964 Urban Mass Transportation Assistance Act.

Federal subsidies for transit services grew as the cost of building expensive rail systems and operating them as well as bus services outpaced revenues from fares. Beginning in 1973, the federal government began supporting local transit authorities with money from the Highway Trust Fund. This move came despite objections from rural states and localities that claimed it was an unfair use of their constituents' tax dollars.

Mounting Congestion

The nation's dependence on automobiles had grown so great by the 1970s that even the energy crises of that decade failed to slow highway construction.

But just as policy-makers were congratulating themselves on creating a network of Interstates and secondary roads that enabled Americans to drive their cars almost anywhere in the country, transportation in many areas was growing increasingly difficult. By the early 1990s, it was becoming clear that the construction of new roads and new lanes was failing to relieve congestion. Traffic regularly slowed to a crawl in major cities. Rush-hour congestion spread in both space and time, reaching deep into the suburbs and extending for several hours every weekday morning and afternoon. [24]

The suburban sprawl that had started with a booming housing market after World War II came to dominate commuting patterns. As residential development spread farther from downtown, many employers began moving to emerging sub-

urban communities. As a result, commuting routes, once laid out clearly like the spokes of a wheel from the downtown hub, multiplied and shifted direction, resembling more closely a spider web branching from suburb to suburb. Laid out along traditional routes, bus and transit services failed to meet the demand of suburban workers.

Aggravating matters, many existing routes, including the roads and bridges of the Interstate system, began showing their age. Potholes, crumbling bridge supports and eroding shoulders forced bridge and road closings and spurred calls for new federal aid to solve what was called an "infrastructure crisis."

A Shift in Policy

Recognizing that highways alone could not solve the nation's transportation problems, Congress in 1991 passed the Intermodal Surface Transportation Efficiency Act, known as ISTEA. Like prior bills, it authorized a six-year program of federal subsidies. But it broke new ground in several notable ways. Drafted in large part by Sens. Daniel Patrick Moynihan, D-N.Y., and John H. Chafee, R-R.I., the bill reflected the growing consensus that the nation's transportation system needed to be made more efficient, rather than just more road-intensive.

Lawmakers also responded to demands by state and local government officials who wanted a greater say in the way federal transportation funds were to be spent in their jurisdictions, including the option of funding alternative modes of transportation, such as mass transit and bicycles, and the ability to transfer funds among programs. Congress also tried to satisfy the demands by all parties for more money and a fairer

allocation of federal funds based on state and local needs. In all, the complex, 300-page law authorized $157 billion over six years. [25]

The law helped satisfy the demands of planners that the government put more emphasis on building paths for pedestrians and bicyclists, as well as preserve historic places. It also appeased highway builders because of the large amounts of funding included for roads. However, officials in many Southern and Midwestern states complained that, under a complicated funding formula, they were not getting as large a share of transportation spending as the Northeast and West.

As traffic problems grew even more intense during the 1990s, some in Congress said the government needed to do far more for transportation. Among the most determined advocates of increased road spending was Rep. Shuster of Pennsylvania, who took over the helm of the Transportation and Infrastructure Committee in 1995, vowing to direct as much money as possible into the nation's troubled transportation system.

When the 105th Congress convened in 1997, one of the top items on its agenda was reauthorizing the highway act, which was due to expire Sept. 30. But Shuster's determination to raise transportation spending collided squarely with the determination of GOP leaders to restrain budget spending. Shuster's committee approved a six-year, $218.3 billion bill that would have shattered the spending limits established by a landmark balanced-budget agreement. House Speaker Newt Gingrich, R-Ga., refused to bring it to the floor.

Although key senators produced a bill with more modest spending levels, they, too, ran into a plethora of problems. Instead, Congress produced a stopgap $9.8-billion short-

Environmentalists Take on Sport-Utility Vehicles

When word spread that the Ford Motor Co. was designing a new sport-utility vehicle to dwarf all others, members of the Sierra Club held a contest to give the oversized passenger vehicle an appropriate name. They dubbed it the "Ford Valdez" — for the Exxon supertanker that ran aground off the coast of Alaska in 1989.

Ford officials ignored the suggestion, naming the sport-utility vehicle the Ford Excursion. But they haven't been able to ignore all of the bad press their nine-seat behemoth has received. Weighing more than three tons and running just an inch shy of 19 feet — nearly a foot longer than the average parking space — the Excursion has been called the gas-guzzler of the century — and much worse. [1]

The controversy over the Excursion, which arrives in showrooms this fall, underscores the environmental stakes involved in the renewed American appetite for ever-larger vehicles. Just two decades ago, following the oil shocks of the 1970s, energy-efficient subcompact cars dominated the market. Now sport-utility vehicles, light trucks and other large passenger vehicles account for about half of new vehicle sales, making up 50 percent or more of pretax earnings for automakers such as Ford. [2]

Environmentalists worry about the impact these large vehicles are having on air quality. The Sierra Club estimates that the Ford Excursion will emit three times the amount of carbon dioxide as a compact car, such as the Honda Civic, and double that of a midsize car, such as the Ford Taurus. Carbon dioxide emissions have been linked to global warming.

"The auto companies are spending roughly $3 million a year on advertising the biggest, most gas-guzzling vehicles they sell," says Daniel Becker, director of the Sierra Club's global warming and energy program. "They don't mention that while you're enjoying the outdoors, you're polluting it."

Ford officials — who have won kudos from environmentalists for several past initiatives, including voluntarily cutting smog-forming exhaust emissions from their vehicles — point out that it is more energy-efficient to use one Excursion to transport nine people than to use two vehicles. But part of the reason that sport-utility vehicles have drawn the ire of environmentalists is because they so often are used to transport a single driver or just a few passengers.

Spoofing the trend toward ever-larger vehicles, *Miami Herald* humorist Dave Barry recently took up the sport-utility cause. Drivers use their enormous cargo space to transport just a couple of grocery items, Barry wrote, to ensure that "there is plenty of room left over back there in case, on the way home, these people decide to pick up something else, such as a herd of bison." [3]

But the issue is drawing serious review in Washington. The Environmental Protection Agency is weighing new rules that would require light trucks to meet the same stringent emission standards as cars by 2004. The rules would also require oil companies to produce cleaner gasoline. The aim is to greatly improve air quality by reducing the amount of harmful toxins in the air, diminishing acid rain and lessening haze.

The plan is drawing somewhat muted criticism from industry representatives, who worry that it would add greatly to their manufacturing costs. They question why the government is so focused on tightening clean air regulations when air quality has improved dramatically since the early 1970s.

"I'm not sure we're going to be able to squeeze a whole lot more out of tailpipes," says William D. Fay, president of the American Highway Users Alliance. "I tend to look at the good news: how much cleaner the air is."

Critics of sport-utility vehicles also worry about their safety. For one thing, larger vehicles tend to cause extensive damage to other cars in collisions, because of their size, height and stiff frames. Federal regulators said the design of sport-utility vehicles, vans and pickup trucks was responsible for about 2,000 fatalities in 1996.

The increasing use of light trucks "presents a growing safety problem that needs to be addressed," said Thomas Hollowell, a senior researcher at the National Highway Traffic Safety Administration. [4]

Another problem with sport-utility vehicles is that they are more likely than cars to roll over because their center of gravity is much higher. This has prompted the federal government to require warning stickers on many sport-utility vehicles stating that they don't perform like cars.

Despite such controversies, the light truck market has boomed in recent years. That's why Ford officials — who have dedicated themselves to helping the environment by using more recycled materials in their vehicles and seeking new ways to improve fuel-efficiency — say they have little choice but to keep manufacturing them.

"These are our most competitive vehicles," says Susan Skerker, senior director of worldwide public policy for the automaker. "People have the money, and they're paying for convenience and comfort. . . . We feel that our job is to meet customer choice, but in a responsible way."

---

[1] See "Gas Guzzlers," *The Philadelphia Inquirer*, March 6, 1999, p. A8.

[2] See "Ford's Green Dilemma," *Business Week*, Dec. 21, 1998, p. 97.

[3] Dave Barry, "Wit's End," *The Washington Post*, March 28, 1999, p. W36.

[4] Quoted in Keith Bradsher, "Study Cites Fatal Design of Sport-Utility Vehicles," *The New York Times*, March 1, 1999, p. A12.

term reauthorization of the highway act, and pledged to return to the fray in 1998. [26]

The following year, with budget concerns fading because of the strong economy and increased revenues, Shuster and other transportation advocates in Congress won a remarkable victory. They amended the law to ensure that all revenues collected from the 18.3-cents-per-gallon federal gasoline tax be spent on transportation, rather than allow the government to continue to reserve a portion for deficit reduction. Studding the transportation bill with projects for key lawmakers, they won broad support to raise transportation spending levels by 40 percent over the 1991 bill. This enabled lawmakers to increase spending for states across the country, while guaranteeing every state a minimum 90.5-cent return on every dollar it pays to the federal government in gasoline taxes.

Critics said the funding levels were simply too high and dubbed the bill a prime example of "pork-barrel" spending because it included nearly $18 billion devoted to specifically designated highway, rail and bus projects favored by members of Congress for their districts. Budget hawks led a mostly unsuccessful effort to scale back the funding. Although President Clinton opposed the special projects and wanted tougher provisions aimed at drunken driving, he signed the bill into law because he said it would pay for needed transportation improvements without threatening other spending priorities. "It does a lot more good than harm, much more," Clinton said. [27]

Overall, the $217.9 billion Transportation Equity Act for the 21st Century included $174.6 billion for highways, $41 billion for mass transit and $2 billion for safety programs. Whereas the 1991 law emphasized building alternatives to highways and creating links between different modes of transportation, the new bill provided huge increases in funding for both highways and mass transit.

Lawmakers also gave state and local governments more flexibility to use federal funds to help them reduce a backlog of repairs and needed projects. The law also provided support for innovative financing, or loans and lines of credits, designed to encourage a mixture of private and public funding to help pay for big construction projects, such as high-speed rail. [28] ∎

CURRENT SITUATION

Battle in Atlanta

Long associated with its doomed struggle against Union forces led by Gen. William Tecumseh Sherman, the city of Atlanta has become another national battleground — this time in the war against congestion. Soaring economic growth and virtually unchecked development have come at a high price. Atlanta's residents spend more time in their cars than residents of any other city in the world, driving 100 million miles per day, or 36.5 miles per capita.

"Our region has become the poster child for sprawl," Jack L. Stephens Jr., executive vice president for customer development of the Metropolitan Atlanta Rapid Transit Authority, told the Senate Environment and Public Works Committee July 14. "We have become the victims of our own success."

But Atlanta's unflagging efforts to build new roads came to a screeching halt on March 2, when a federal appeals court, siding with environmentalists, ruled that the construction of 61 highway projects failed to conform to the region's clean air plans. In an out-of-court settlement three months later, environmentalists and state and federal officials agreed that about 16 of the projects already under way could proceed. The others would be shelved, at least until they passed environmental muster. Meanwhile, local officials began putting a greater emphasis on funding transit systems and other transportation alternatives.

By imposing stricter requirements on state and local transportation officials, the ruling has thrown highway projects across the country in jeopardy, exposing the increasingly acrimonious battle between preservationists and developers — and threatening to draw Congress into the fray. "All of a sudden we now have projects in late stages of planning or under construction that are being stopped," says Fay.

The Atlanta lawsuit is just one of several instances in which environmentalists and preservationists have succeeded in at least temporarily halting the construction of major highways, and it may portend increasingly fierce local struggles over the future of transportation development. In a high-profile case that could affect traffic in the nation's capital, a federal district judge in April halted plans to replace the aging Woodrow Wilson Bridge on Interstate 95, a vital East Coast transportation link, because of insufficient environmental reviews.

Road advocates, fresh from their victory in capturing billions of additional highway dollars in the 1998 transportation spending legislation, are furious that environmentalists now are stopping new construction on a local level. "We call it an environmental *jihad*. They're trying to demonize the highway industry,"

Life in the Slow Lane: Bikers Enjoy Their Commute

There is something unusual about Lyra Halprin: she actually enjoys her commute.

The senior public information officer for the University of California's Sustainable Agriculture Research and Education Program in Davis, Halprin rides her bike to work almost every morning, regardless of the weather. "I like biking; it's good exercise, and it's beautiful," she says. "I don't do so well with coffee, so I need something else to get my body going so I'm ready for work."

When it comes to commuting choices, Halprin is distinctly in the minority in this country. A 1992 Federal Highway Administration report estimated that just 0.4 percent of all workers in this country commute by bicycle. Even walking to the office ranked far higher, at 3.9 percent of all workers. [1]

But there was a time at the end of the 19th century when bicyclists were a powerful political force in transportation circles, dominating government road-building decisions. [2] Now, they again are winning some transportation funding battles with the argument that bike paths can give people an important alternative to sitting on congested roads.

"What we really need to do is reduce the demand and need for highways while we provide people with a much wider range of choices," says Bill Wilkinson, executive director of the National Center for Bicycling and Walking, a Washington-based advocacy group. "It's a lot cheaper to build transit and bike paths. The return on investment will be greater and it has a much better impact on the quality of life in our communities."

Both to provide people with more transportation choices and to improve the quality of life in this country, Congress agreed to a provision in the 1998 omnibus transportation bill — the Transportation Equity Act for the 21st Century, known as TEA 21 — to set aside about $3.3 billion for transportation "enhancements." Depending on the needs of local communities, these enhancements may include sidewalks, preservation projects, scenic byways or bicycle paths.

Although the 1991 omnibus transportation act also dedicated money to enhancements, highway lobbyists urged Congress in 1998 to end the practice. Since most people use their cars to commute and run errands, the road advocates argued that the government should spend as much money as possible on roads, not bike paths.

Some transportation analysts doubt that biking will ever do much to ease congestion in this country. "The use of bicycles is, by and large, limited to recreational use," says Kenneth Orski, a Washington-based transportation consultant. "Their use for commuting for work is negligible. That is not to say that we ought to forget biking as a means of transportation, but biking will never solve our transportation problems."

Wilkinson, who commutes about 10 miles by bike from his suburban Maryland home to his Washington office, believes far more people will use bike paths if developers begin laying out communities in more traditional ways. Retail centers, offices and homes should be built fairly close together, he believes, and linked by bike and pedestrian paths, instead of being separated by many miles of roads.

"I don't think we can build trails to give people the opportunity to hike and walk anywhere they want to go," Wilkinson says. "But I don't think we can build highways so people can drive 55 mph everywhere they want to go either. We've got to rethink what we need to do in terms of land-use planning and zoning."

One of the few places in this country that has put an emphasis on bike trails is Halprin's hometown of Davis. Halprin says that most of her co-workers bike to work. Although her own commute is just two miles each way, she has friends who take advantage of bike paths to pedal 20 miles each way to Sacramento.

The way Halprin sees it, more Americans would commute the Davis way if they had bike paths to follow. "It's really peaceful," she says. "People will use them if they build them."

Just 0.4 percent of all workers in the U.S. commute by bicycle.

Corbis Images

---

[1] Federal Highway Administration, "New Perspectives in Commuting," 1992.

[2] See David Hosansky, "As the Wheel Turns," *CQ Weekly Report*, April 26, 1997, p. 955.

Amtrak Looks to the Future . . .

As planners search for ways to modernize the nation's overburdened transportation network, they are increasingly looking "back to the future." They see the humble railroad train, which helped shape the Industrial Revolution 200 years ago, transforming life in the 21st century.

But the sleek trains the planners envision are barely related to their smoke-belching forebears. Some species of this highly evolved breed, known as high-speed rail, can go nearly 200 mph.

High-speed rail has been in commercial service in Europe and Japan for decades. Japan's famed "bullet" trains began operating in 1964, just before the start of the Olympic Games in Tokyo. France's high-speed TGV trains began regular passenger runs in 1981. [1]

Now, high-speed rail seems to be picking up steam in the United States. On June 29, Amtrak officials unveiled the fastest train in North America — the *Acela Express*. Amtrak will begin running the electric-powered trains between New York and Boston before the end of the year. Initially, the new trains will travel at a maximum speed of 150 mph, but they have the ability to go up to 165 mph. [2]

Amtrak will also use the *Acelas* (pronounced ah-Cell-ahs) on the busy New York-Washington route, where its high-speed Metroliners have been operating since 1969.

Transportation officials hope the new trains will lure harried travelers from congested roadways and air corridors in the Northeast. They also hope the trains will attract enough passengers to impress transportation officials in other parts of the country.

"You're going to have congressmen and senators saying, 'New York's got that, why can't I have it?'" Wisconsin Republican Gov. Tommy G. Thompson, chairman of Amtrak's board, said at the ceremony in Washington to unveil the train. "This is the synergism that's going to open it up." [3]

An artist's rendition shows the new high-speed Amtrak passenger train, the Acela Express.

Reuters/Amtrak

Already there are about a dozen other high-speed routes on the drawing board, some of which would be operated by Amtrak. The most ambitious is a 676-mile project in California that would link San Diego, Los Angeles, San Francisco and Sacramento with trains reaching speeds of 200 mph or higher. Other possible high-speed corridors include a Midwestern route between Chicago and Milwaukee, a Pacific Northwest route between Eugene, Ore., and Vancouver, B.C., Canada, and a Gulf Coast route from Birmingham, Ala., to Houston, Texas.

"Once you have high-speed rail in one place in America, then you have opportunities in other places," says Rep. Bud Shuster, R-Pa., chairman of the House Transportation

---

says Ruane of the road and transportation builders association. "They want to force everyone into dense urban areas and give them no choice where to live."

Ruane warns that blocking construction of new roads will further snarl traffic and create increasingly dangerous highway conditions. Furthermore, he contends that it makes little sense to impose the Clean Air Act so restrictively when motor vehicle-related pollution has dropped dramatically since the early 1970s. [29]

Seeking to override the lawsuits,

the road builders are backing legislation sponsored by Sen. Christopher S. Bond, R-Mo., that would amend the Clean Air Act. Bond's bill would allow the "grandfathering" of road projects that received preliminary environmental approval years ago. That approach had been used by the Environmental Protection Agency before the March court decision, but it drew fire from environmentalists because it permitted the construction of numerous highways in cities that were failing to meet clean air requirements.

"I'm not going to let extremist

environmental interest groups stop highway improvements," Bond said. "The unacceptable condition of our states' highways literally means that lives are at stake."

But Bond's bill may face tough going on Capitol Hill, in part because lawmakers could come under fire for trying to pare back clean air standards. "It's an uphill battle with that legislation," Fay concedes.

Environmentalists argue that strictly enforcing clean air rules will improve transportation, not hurt it, by forcing state and local governments to em-

... Its New High-Speed Train Is About to Debut

and Infrastructure Committee. "I think there's going to be a future for high-speed rail."

But whether such systems can attract significant ridership or make a profit is uncertain. Most are likely to cost more than $100 million to build; the California project has a projected price tag of $23.3 billion. [4]

Funding for some of the projects remains uncertain, but presumably could be raised from a combination of government and private sources. The federal government would likely contribute through a provision in the 1998 surface transportation reauthorization act that uses federal funds to help leverage private investment in major transportation projects.

"These systems may be an effective alternative in corridors where travel is increasing and it is difficult to expand highway and airport capacity," Phyllis F. Scheinberg, the General Accounting Office's associate director of transportation issues, stated in a Jan. 14 letter to the House Budget Committee. "However, high-speed rail systems are costly, and thus ridership levels may not be high enough in the United States for systems to recover their costs."

In part because of such concerns, Florida Republican Gov. Jeb Bush announced in January that he was ending state financing for a proposed 320-mile high-speed rail project that would have linked Miami, Orlando and Tampa.

At some point, officials in congested regions may find themselves with few alternatives but to turn to high-speed rail. That is because it is increasingly expensive and difficult to expand roads and airports, due to the scarcity of open land in high-density areas.

High-speed rail "is a heck of a lot cheaper than the never-ending business of widening highways and expanding airports," says Amtrak spokesman John Wolf.

Another advantage of high-speed rail is that it promises to be more convenient than airplanes for business travelers, since it would link one downtown with another and offer amenities for people who want to work comfortably while they travel. The new *Acela* has electrical outlets for laptop computers (which do not have to be turned off during takeoff and landing, as on an airplane) and considerable legroom. Leisure travelers can take advantage of such features as diaper changing stations in the bathrooms and beer on tap in the cafe cars.

Amtrak's future may depend on the success of the new high-speed trains. Since its creation by an act of Congress in 1971, the national passenger railroad has needed $22.7 billion in operating and capital subsidies from the federal government. Under the 1997 Amtrak Reform and Accountability Act, the railroad cannot use government funds to cover operating expenses after 2002.

Recent General Accounting Office reports have warned that Amtrak may not meet that deadline, even though it has made strides in such areas as privatizing food service and creating an express package delivery service. Amtrak has failed to meet similar deadlines in the past and has received extensions from Congress.

"We are very hopeful that high-speed rail in the Northeast Corridor is going to be a success," Shuster says. "The solutions to Amtrak lie in part in high-speed rail."

---

[1] For background, see Richard L. Worsnop, "High-Speed Rail," *The CQ Researcher*, April 16, 1993, pp. 313-336.

[2] See Matt Swenson, "The Very Big Engine that Could," States News Service, June 29, 1999.

[3] Quoted in Matthew L. Wald, "High Speed Plus Luxury on the Rails," *The New York Times*, June 30, 1999, p. A16.

[4] Edward Epstein, "S.F., San Jose Win Preliminary OK for Planned Bullet Train," *The San Francisco Chronicle*, June 17, 1999, p. A22.

---

phasize public transit, sidewalks and other alternatives to cars.

"Atlanta has been a poster child of what's gone wrong with American transportation, but it's also an emerging success story of how the Clean Air Act has worked to help local and state officials get back on track when land use and transportation have conflicted with air quality," says Replogle of the Environmental Defense Fund. "Since March, the region has redirected several hundred million dollars from sprawling roads into purchasing new clean buses [that use

cleaner-burning fuel], building park and ride lots, building sidewalks and bike paths and developing HOV [high-occupancy vehicle] lanes and highway safety projects that will either help, or at least not hurt, the air quality problem."

Some Atlanta officials agree. "I think it is clear that [the lawsuit] took the region in the right direction for solving its clean air problems," Stephens said in his July 14 testimony.

Whether or not the lawsuit will help or hinder Atlanta's traffic problems, the city is breaking new ground

in transportation planning. Even before the suit was settled, Georgia Democratic Gov. Roy Barnes was on his way to winning unprecedented power from the legislature to control growth by heading up a new super-agency known as the Georgia Regional Transportation Authority. The agency — whose acronym, cynics joke, might as well be "Give Roy Total Authority" — has the power to stop new highways and shopping malls, and force counties to pay for mass transit systems.

Surprisingly, this approach has

won the support of many local business leaders and developers who are concerned that Atlanta's traffic problems, if left unchecked, could become a major liability.

"We have to interconnect people again," John A. Williams, a developer who chairs the Metro Chamber of Commerce, told *Governing* magazine. "Restore the sense of neighborhood, all the things that humans feel comfortable in. We need sidewalks, and we need to get people out on those sidewalks. . . . We can't have a shopping center dropped in the middle of a field somewhere anymore." [30]

Life in the Fast Lane

Drivers in the San Diego area who commute on their own are being given a unique choice: They can drive slowly along heavily trafficked lanes of Interstate 15 for free, or pay up to $4 to cruise in uncongested lanes that are normally reserved for high-occupancy vehicles. It is part of a pilot Department of Transportation program aimed at easing congestion without building additional roads.

So far, so good, San Diego officials report. About 3,000 drivers a day take advantage of these so-called hot lanes, apparently willing to pay a toll, at least occasionally, if it gives them the opportunity to drive faster. To keep the lanes moving smoothly, officials vary the toll from 50 cents to $4, depending on the level of congestion, and are prepared to raise the toll to as high as $8 to keep too many people from using the lanes.

"It's a very popular program," says Kim Kawada, a senior regional planner for the San Diego Association of Governments. "Commuters appreciate the opportunity to pay to use an uncongested roadway."

Such tolls may be the prelude to more controversial traffic-regulation plans known as "congestion pricing." Some planners and environmentalists want drivers who use certain high-density highways to pay for the privilege, especially in rush hour, because it would encourage commuters to find alternative means of transportation.

At first glance, such an approach may seem like an additional tax on drivers who already help support roads through state and federal gasoline taxes. "This is a scheme by people who want to punish those who like to drive," says Fay. "I can't stand for that."

But environmentalists have a different perspective. They argue that current gasoline taxes do not cover all highway construction and maintenance costs. Instead, road expenses are subsidized by local property taxes, as well as state and local general taxes that help pay for such auxiliary services as highway patrol officers. Free parking also is subsidized — either by the government or private businesses.

"I think we have to be aware of all those hidden costs and how our failure to price transportation fairly has contributed to our traffic congestion problems," says Replogle of the Environmental Defense Fund.

The concept of congestion pricing, though controversial, is not entirely new. For years, the densely developed island nation of Singapore has charged drivers for entering a central zone, with the toll rising during the morning and evening rush hours. Several cities in Norway adopted the idea, charging motorists in downtown areas a relatively high toll in the morning, a lower one through the afternoon and no toll at all in the evening.

New technology is helping to spur such variable-pricing schemes because officials no longer need to rely on tollbooths. In San Diego, for example, drivers who want to use the restricted lanes have transponders installed in their cars that can be read automatically whenever they use the hot lanes. The fees are then withdrawn from a prepaid or other designated account.

In addition to earning good reviews from environmentalists, congestion pricing also has won support from some conservatives, who see it as a way of bringing order to traffic through the traditional approach of economic supply and demand. "Only by making drivers pay for the costs they impose on society can the demand for motoring be brought into line with restricted supply," the *Economist* magazine editorialized in 1997. [31]

In the United States, however, there appears to be little political support for imposing widespread tolls on downtown drivers. Instead, officials are more interested in taking the limited, and politically safer, step of charging for the privilege of using certain lanes. At present, there are only a handful of places like San Diego where motorists can pay tolls to drive on less-congested lanes. Maryland highway planners are considering introducing the concept to some of the congested lanes in the Washington area.

Critics of the concept, who sometimes dub the toll lanes "Lexis lanes," worry that it allows the more affluent to buy their way around gridlock. "It's giving the rich people an advantage," one motorist told *The Washington Post*. "Everybody paid for it [the road]. Everybody should wait the same." [32]

In San Diego, however, officials say the criticism has been muted. One reason is that the money raised by the toll is used to bolster public transportation, which is viewed as helping low-income residents. Another reason is that low-income residents can benefit just as much as the rich by using the lanes. Consider, for example, a cash-strapped single

At Issue:

Should the United States continue to build highways in order to ease traffic congestion?

TAYLOR BOWLDEN

Vice president for policy and government affairs, American Highway Users Alliance

FROM STATEMENT TO SENATE ENVIRONMENT AND PUBLIC WORKS TRANSPORTATION AND INFRASTRUCTURE SUBCOMMITTEE APRIL 15, 1999.

*t*he evidence is strong that public investments in alternatives to highway travel are unlikely to relieve traffic congestion or improve air quality. Between 1980 and 1990, the only mode of commuting that realized an increase in the percentage of workers was "driving alone." During that time period, there were 19 million net additional workers but 22 million more people driving to work alone. Essentially, that means every new member of the work force chose to drive alone, plus three million workers switched from some other mode of travel to driving by themselves.

Why? Is it because Americans hate biking, walking or mass transit? No. It's simply because those alternatives often don't work for them. The majority of new single-occupant-drivers in the last decade were working women. Most of them run family errands on the way to or from work, and driving their own car is the only workable solution. . . .

For that reason, it is highly unlikely that traffic congestion problems will be solved by diverting funds away from road improvements and into transportation alternatives instead. In many fast-growing regions, additional highway capacity is desperately needed and the only effective way to address the transportation demands of busy suburban commuters.

The Washington, D.C., metropolitan area offers a good illustration of this point. Over the last two decades, Washington has built an excellent rail transit system and invested heavily in the construction of high-occupancy vehicle (HOV) lanes. As a result, we have the nation's third highest percentage (13.4 percent) of commuters who use [mass] transit and easily the highest percentage (16 percent) of commuters who carpool. Yet, according to the Texas Transportation Institute's annual report on traffic congestion, Washington now has the second worst congestion in the country. And a 1997 transportation study conducted by the Greater Washington Board of Trade concludes that the problem lies in an insufficient metropolitan road network. . . .

We all want less traffic congestion, cleaner air and more livable communities. Good public policy, however, should take into account observable patterns in housing and commercial development as well as demographic and technological changes that make further decentralization seem likely. In many cases, traffic flow improvements and additional highway capacity will be the only effective means to address the transportation demands in fast-growing areas.

ROY KIENITZ

Executive Director, Surface Transportation Policy Project

WRITTEN FOR *THE CQ RESEARCHER*, AUGUST 1999.

*c*ommunities across the United States are learning the hard truth: Road building cannot prevent congestion or even keep up with the growth in driving that results from our auto-oriented development patterns. In fact, evidence shows new roads fuel the already explosive growth in the amount we drive. New and wider roads bring only short-term relief, at very great expense.

In 70 of our major metropolitan areas, transportation officials are already making sure that road building stays ahead of population growth. Between 1982 and 1996, the amount of space on major roadways per resident actually increased by more than 9 percent. But at the same time, these metro areas spread out so fast that the number of miles covered by each driver each day increased by 31 percent. All those traffic jams are the result of sprawling growth and the driving it requires.

Far from relieving congestion, new roads in busy metropolitan areas generate even more traffic, and as a result they quickly fill to capacity. New and wider roads open up new areas to auto-oriented strip malls and subdivisions, which create even more car trips. Across the country, new roads are jammed long before their 20-year design life. A study by UC-Berkeley researchers found that in metropolitan areas, up to 90 percent of new road capacity is filled with new traffic within five years. The Federal Highway Administration estimates that up to 50 percent of added road capacity is used up by new driving trips.

Even if it worked, trying to relieve congestion with new roads would break the bank. In order to keep up with the annual increase in the amount of driving, states and cities would have to add 2-3 percent to their road capacity each year. In 1996, a 3 percent increase in road capacity would have meant building 184,664 additional miles of roadway. This would have cost almost $130 billion. Right now, under the largest such spending bill ever passed, the federal government has allocated about $32 billion annually for all surface transportation projects.

Congestion may be here to stay, but we can make sure people are not trapped by it. We can start by building communities where a car is not necessary for every errand. State and local governments can give travelers alternatives to the clogged highways, such as good transit systems and conveniently designed communities with neighborhood stores close by and streets that are safe for biking and walking. In the long run, these strategies will do more to fight congestion than all the roads we can build.

mother who spends a couple of dollars to use a hot lane in order to avoid paying a much larger penalty for picking up her child late from a day-care center.

"It's a broad range of economic classes that use [the toll lanes]," says Dan Beal, manager of technical resource and policy for the American Automobile Association of Southern California. "People of limited means value their time also." ■

OUTLOOK

High-Tech Solutions

As counterintuitive as it might seem, a pair of physicists believe that some congested highways do not have enough cars. Bernardo Huberman of the Xerox Palo Alto Research Center in California and Dick Helbing of the University of Stuttgart in Germany concluded from a study of Dutch highways that, with enough cars on the road, traffic can reach a "synchronized" state that moves very efficiently.

When cars are packed at the right density, the physicists observed, they cannot abruptly swerve around each other or suddenly change speed. Instead, they essentially merge into a single, fast-moving unit. "The traffic collapses into a solid thing," Huberman told *New Scientist* magazine. "It's moving like a solid block." [33]

Whether or not this theory has practical applications remains to be seen. But it is already clear that science is beginning to help alleviate congestion in the United States and other countries.

For years, transportation engineers have been touting the development of "intelligent transportation systems" that use new technologies to better

direct drivers or remove traffic obstacles. For example, engineers at the Texas Transportation Institute have developed a series of software programs to ensure that traffic signals on road networks are synchronized with prevailing traffic patterns. The signals can "talk" with each other, adjusting their timing to minimize the number of cars that have to slow down or stop at an intersection and to ensure that the heaviest traffic at any time of day gets the longest green light. "What we have, in essence, is the ability to create a smart person on top of the [traffic light] pole," says Timothy J. Lomax, one of the institute's engineers.

Other innovations include large electronic signs on urban highways warning drivers of accidents or heavy traffic ahead. Entrance ramps onto these highways have signals to regulate merge areas that would otherwise become bottlenecks.

Engineers also are taking aim at tollbooths. Instead of having to wait in long lines at a tollbooth, drivers now have transponders in their cars that are automatically read on such toll routes as New York's Tappan Zee Bridge, allowing them to pay through a credit card or alternative account instead of having to stop and hand cash to a tollbooth attendant.

"Tollbooths ought to be abolished," says Replogle of the Environmental Defense Fund. "You can send a transponder with every motor vehicle registration and even give people $20 of free toll value with that tag as an incentive to introduce it. This would cut traffic congestion right away and reduce air pollution from cars waiting to go through tollbooths."

Some of the most ambitious efforts to beat traffic through technology are being designed in Tokyo, where officials hope to transmit information from the city's traffic computers to the guidance systems of specially equipped cars. The cars would auto-

matically be guided to the least congested routes.

Transportation Secretary Rodney Slater asked Congress this year for $271 million for the Intelligent Transportation System Program, which helps fund such technological innovations. Slater said the goal is to "expand existing [road] capacity with technology." [34]

But others are not sure that new highway technology will do much good at all. The problem, they say, is that the more engineers can regulate traffic flow, the more drivers will swarm to the most efficient routes and snarl them up again.

"There is no difference between road space created by adding another lane to the highway and road space created by cramming twice as many cars in a lane," says Kienitz of the Surface Transportation Policy Project. "They're asking the wrong question: How can I use existing roads to get four times as many cars on them, and get four times as many cars in the city and create four times as much pollution?" The real question, he says, is how do we get people to drive less — not more.

Telecommunications technologies may provide some of the answers. Innovations such as E-mail and the Internet allow many people to "telecommute" from their homes without getting on the roads at all — as well as shop and perform such tasks as renewing library books. [35]

This may not be enough to solve the ever-worsening problem of rush-hour congestion. But to experts wrestling with the seemingly intractable problem of squeezing more and more motor vehicles onto the roads, it offers a rare ray of hope.

"Personally," says Orski, the Washington consultant, "I think that the growing use of telecommunications is going to contribute more to this than anything else." ■

Notes

[1] Texas Transportation Institute fact sheet, undated, on the institute's Web site, http://tti.tamu.edu/.

[2] U.S. Department of Transportation, Bureau of Transportation Statistics, "Transportation Statistics Annual Report 1998," p. 2.

[3] February 1999 fact sheet from The Road Information Program, a nonprofit research group affiliated with businesses and labor unions that support highway construction.

[4] F. Kaid Benfield, Matthew D. Raimi and Donald D.T. Chen, *Once There Were Greenfields*, Natural Resources Defense Council, 1999, p. 32.

[5] James J. MacKenzie, Roger C. Dower and Donald D.T. Chen, "The Going Rate: What It Really Costs to Drive," World Resources Institute, 1992, p. 1.

[6] Timothy J. Lomax and David L. Schrank, "Urban Roadway Congestion Annual Report 1998," Texas Transportation Institute.

[7] *Ibid.*

[8] U.S. Department of Transportation, *op. cit.*, p. 66.

[9] *Ibid.*, p. 109. For background, see Mary H. Cooper, "The Politics of Energy," *The CQ Researcher*, March 5, 1999, pp. 185-208, and Mary H. Cooper, "Oil Imports," *The CQ Researcher*, Aug. 23, 1991, pp. 585-608.

[10] Remarks from a Jan. 26, 1999, conference reprinted in General Accounting Office, "Surface Transportation: Moving Into the 21st Century," May 1999, p. 12.

[11] Texas Transportation Institute, *op. cit.*, p. 11.

[12] See W. Wayt Gibbs, "Transportation's Perennial Problems," *Scientific American*, October 1997, p. 54.

[13] MacKenzie, Dower and Chen, *op. cit.*, p. 2.

[14] For background, see Mary H. Cooper, "Urban Sprawl in the West," *The CQ Researcher*, Oct. 3, 1997, pp. 865-888.

[15] Benfield, Raimi and Chen, *op. cit.*, p. 30.

[16] See Timothy Egan, "Freeways, Their Costs and 2 Cities' Destinies," *The New York Times*, July 14, 1999, p. A1.

[17] "The Dark Side of the American Dream," Sierra Club, August 1998, p. 1.

[18] Quoted in Ellen Perlman, "The Little Engine That Might," *Governing*, August 1998, p. 36.

[19] See Alan Ota, "Mass Transit in Growth Mode," *CQ Weekly*, May 16, 1998, pp. 1270-1271.

[20] See American Public Transit Association Web site, www.apta.org.

[21] Testimony before the Transportation and Related Agencies Subcommittee of the House Appropriations Committee, Feb. 10, 1999.

[22] Background drawn from Mary H. Cooper, "Transportation Policy," *The CQ Researcher*, July 4, 1997, pp. 577-600, and J.F. Hornbeck, "Transportation Infrastructure: Economic Issues and Public Policy Alternatives," *CRS Report for Congress*, Congressional Research Service, Jan. 26, 1993.

[23] See I. Mei Chan, ed., *Building on the Past, Traveling to the Future: A Preservationist's Guide to the ISTEA Transportation Enhancement Provision*, Federal Highway Administration and National Trust for Historic Preservation, undated, p. 28.

[24] For background, see Charles S. Clark, "Traffic Congestion," *The CQ Researcher*, May 6, 1994, pp. 385-408.

[25] For background, see *1991 CQ Almanac*, pp. 137-151.

[26] See "Issue: 1991 Intermodal Surface Transportation Efficiency Act Reauthorization," *Congressional Quarterly Weekly Report*, Dec. 6, 1997, p. 2996.

[27] See Alan K. Ota, "What the Highway Bill Does, *CQ Weekly*, July 11, 1998, pp. 1892-1898.

[28] See "Issue: Surface Transportation Reauthorization," *CQ Weekly*, Nov. 14, 1998, p. 3123.

[29] For background, see Mary H. Cooper, "New Air Quality Standards," *The CQ Researcher*, March 7, 1997, pp. 193-216.

[30] Quoted in Alan Ehrenhalt, "The Czar of Gridlock," *Governing*, May 1999, p. 20.

[31] "Jam today, road pricing tomorrow," *The Economist*, Dec. 6, 1997, p. 15.

[32] Quoted in Alan Sipress, "Paying for Space In the Fast Lane; Md. Plan Targets Congestion," *The Washington Post*, May 18, 1999, p. A1.

[33] Quoted in Charles Seife, "Jam Packed," *New Scientist*, Jan. 30, 1999, p. 7.

[34] Testimony before the Senate Transportation Appropriations Subcommittee, March 4, 1999.

[35] For background, see Kathy Koch, "Flexible Work Arrangements," *The CQ Researcher*, Aug. 14, 1998, pp. 697-720.

FOR MORE INFORMATION

American Highway Users Alliance, 1726 M St. N.W., Suite 401, Washington, D.C. 20036; (202) 857-1200. The alliance's membership includes the oil, auto, trucking and highway construction industries and other interests that want to maximize funding on road construction and maintenance. An affiliated group, The Road Information Program, posts information on the Web at www.tripnet.org.

Federal Highway Administration (U.S. Transportation Department), 400 7th St. S.W., Washington, D.C. 20590; (202) 366-0660. The agency administers federal highway programs authorized by the 1998 Transportation Equity Act for the 21st Century (TEA 21) and funded with money from the Highway Trust Fund. Statistics on highways can be obtained from the Transportation Department's Bureau of Transportation Statistics at the same address, (202) 366-3282, http://www.fhwa. dot.gov.

Surface Transportation Policy Project, 1100 17th St., N.W., 10th Floor, Washington, D.C. 20036; (202) 466-2636; http://www.transact.org. An umbrella group that represents environmentalists, bicycle riders, historic preservationists and other interests that oppose sprawl and support alternative modes of transportation, such as bike and pedestrian facilities and public transit.

Texas Transportation Institute, CE/TTI Building, Texas A&M University, College Station, Texas 77843-3135; (409) 845-6002; http://tti.tamu.edu/ A research organization at Texas A&M University, the institute issues annual reports on road congestion and examines strategies to ease traffic problems.

Bibliography

Selected Sources Used

Books

Benfield, F. Kaid, Matthew D. Raimi, and Donald D.T. Chen, *Once There Were Greenfields*, Natural Resources Defense Council, 1999.

The authors contend that the American dream of home ownership in the suburbs is in danger of turning into a nightmare because it is generating sprawl. The book documents the consequences of sprawl, including increasingly congested highways and ever-longer commutes. It advocates "smart growth" development with an emphasis on communities and transit-oriented development.

Downs, Anthony, *New Visions for Metropolitan America*, The Brookings Institution, 1994.

According to Downs, Americans have yet to come to grips with their responsibility for the problems associated with suburban sprawl and the emptying of inner cities — decades of migration to outlying areas, emphasis on low-density housing and reliance on cars for transportation.

Articles

"Living With the Car," *The Economist*, Dec. 6, 1997, p. 21.

Charging drivers who use heavily congested roads is becoming an increasingly popular way for governments in industrialized countries to contain traffic problems, according to this package of articles.

Egan, Timothy, "Freeways, Their Costs and 2 Cities' Destinies," *The New York Times*, July 14, 1999, p. A1.

Massive road-building projects in Salt Lake City could lead to unbridled development and the type of problems that larger cities are wrestling with, such as sprawl, congestion and pollution. In contrast, Milwaukee is tearing down a half-built section of urban highway in a bid to cut down on sprawl.

Gibbs, W. Wayt, "Transportation's Perennial Problems," *Scientific American*, October 1997, p. 54

Every time there is a breakthrough in transportation technology, Americans expect to cut their traveling time — and they usually are disappointed. This comprehensive article looks at traffic problems since automobile innovations in the 1890s, concluding that congestion and pollution are virtually inevitable.

Reports and Studies

Department of Transportation, "1997 Status of the Nation's Surface Transportation System: Condition and Performance."

Brief overview of the nation's highway and transit systems. It provides estimates on the amount of money required to maintain or upgrade them.

Department of Transportation, Bureau of Transportation Statistics, "Transportation Statistics Annual Report," 1998.

Indispensable summary of the nation's transportation system. Evaluates the condition and performance of roads, railroads and other modes of transportation, as well as safety issues, freight movement, long-distance travel trends and the interaction between transportation and the economy.

General Accounting Office, "Surface Transportation: Moving into the 21st Century," May 1999

This comprehensive report features analyses by 15 transportation experts, drawn from Congress, academia, government transportation agencies and private companies. It summarizes current trends and puts forth a diversity of proposals for accommodating increased demands on the transportation system.

Lomax, Timothy J., and David L. Schrank, "Urban Roadway Congestion Annual Report, 1998," Texas Transportation Institute.

Statistical analysis reveals that the total cost of congestion in 70 major U.S. cities amounts to $74 billion. The study also concludes that congestion problems are no longer limited to big cities, since the amount of time that commuters have spent stalled in traffic in small and medium-sized cities has more than quadrupled since 1982.

MacKenzie, James J., Roger C. Dower and Donald D.T. Chen, "The Going Rate: What It Really Costs to Drive," World Resources Institute, 1992.

Private motor vehicle use in the United States is heavily subsidized, thereby encouraging people to use their cars more and more. This report for an environmental organization concludes that the tangible costs of driving, such as highway patrols and routine street maintenance, and the intangible costs of driving, such as air pollution, are great enough to raise the price of gasoline by several dollars per gallon.

Moretti, Frank R., "Smart Growth: A Wolf in Sheep's Clothing," The Road Information Program, March 1999

This report for an industry-oriented group warns that regional growth policies that attempt to impose growth boundaries or limit road construction are likely to decrease the quality of life. Instead, it advocates that regional leaders should accept that growth is inevitable and plan for it in an integrated manner.

8 Population and the Environment

MARY H. COOPER

Two hundred years ago, an English cleric named Thomas Robert Malthus wrote an essay that would forever change the secure view people had of their place on Earth. Like other animal species, Malthus wrote, humans can reproduce faster than the natural resources they require to survive. As a result, he postulated, humans eventually would overwhelm the environment, possibly resulting in their extinction.

"Famine seems to be the last, the most dreadful resource of nature," Malthus wrote. "The power of population is so superior to the power in the Earth to produce subsistence for man, that premature death must in some shape or other visit the human race." [1]

Malthus wrote his treatise in response to the prevailing optimism of the time, which saw population growth as an unqualified boon to mankind. The Marquis de Condorcet, a French mathematician and pioneering social scientist, and William Godwin, an English social philosopher, held that man was perfectible, headed toward a future free of all evil, discomfort and disease. As mankind approached immortality, Godwin predicted, population growth would cease altogether because sexual desire would be extinguished.

Two hundred years later, the debate continues — but amid profound changes. In Malthus' day, there were fewer than 1 billion people on Earth. More recently, global population has mushroomed, growing from 1.6 billion to almost 6 billion in the 20th century alone, numbers that surely would have been taken by 18th-century thinkers as confirmation of the Malthusian nightmare. But technological changes, equally unimaginable to observers at the dawn of the Indus-

From *The CQ Researcher,*
July 17, 1998.

trial Revolution, have vastly increased global food supplies, giving credence to Malthus' optimistic critics. [2]

What hasn't changed over the past two centuries is the distance separating the two sides in the ongoing debate over human population. On the one side are Malthus' intellectual heirs, dubbed doomers or Cassandras. They see the continuing rise in global population as a recipe for disaster. The crash will come not only because of food shortages, they say, but because of myriad insults to the environment humans exact by their sheer numbers. *(See graph, p. 150.)*

"I certainly think we face an environmental crisis, whether it amounts to a Malthusian outcome or not," says Leon Kolankiewicz, coordinator of the Carrying Capacity Network, which promotes sustainable development. Rather than the global collapse of food supplies that Malthus envisioned, Kolankiewicz foresees any number of localized crises, similar to that which may have struck Easter Island in the Pacific Ocean, whose inhabitants are believed to have died out after exhausting the island's natural resources.

"For a time, people can exceed the long-term carrying capacity for an area, but this eventually leads to collapse," he says. "In a given region, if not the world, not only will the population collapse, but there also will be such damage to the natural capital — the resources that sustain life — that for a long time to come the environment will no longer be able to support human life."

On the other side of the debate are Godwin's successors — the boomers or Pollyannas — who say more people mean a larger pool of human ingenuity to discover new ways to thrive on planet Earth. They point to the successes of the Green Revolution, an international drive to increase crop yields in the 1950s and '60s, as evidence that humans will always come up with a technological fix to accommodate their growing numbers.

Several new developments have colored the population debate in recent years. One is the discovery that human activities — especially in the developed world — affect the atmosphere, long considered a relatively inexhaustible asset of Earth's environment. When scientists demonstrated that the release of chlorofluorocarbons from man-made coolants and aerosols had eroded Earth's protective ozone layer, world leaders agreed in 1992 to ban the chemicals.

More recently, scientists have concluded that burning fossil fuels may cause a gradual but potentially catastrophic warming of the atmosphere. Fear of so-called global warming resulted in last December's agreement in Kyoto, Japan, to curb the burning of oil, coal and natural gas.

Malthus' supporters point to these and other strains on the environment as signs that human population has exceeded Earth's "carrying capacity," its ability to sustain life indefinitely. Other signs

Childbearing Is Greatest in Africa and Asia

The fertility rate — the average number of children that women in a country have — is generally higher in Africa and Western Asia and lower in North America, Europe and Eastern Asia. In the future, according to United Nations projections, small differences in childbearing levels will result in large differences in global population. If women average a moderate two children, population would rise to 11 billion in the 21st century and level off. If women average 2.5 children, population would pass 27 billion by 2150. But if the fertility rate fell to 1.6 children, population would peak at 7.7 billion in 2050 and drop to 3.6 billion by 2150.

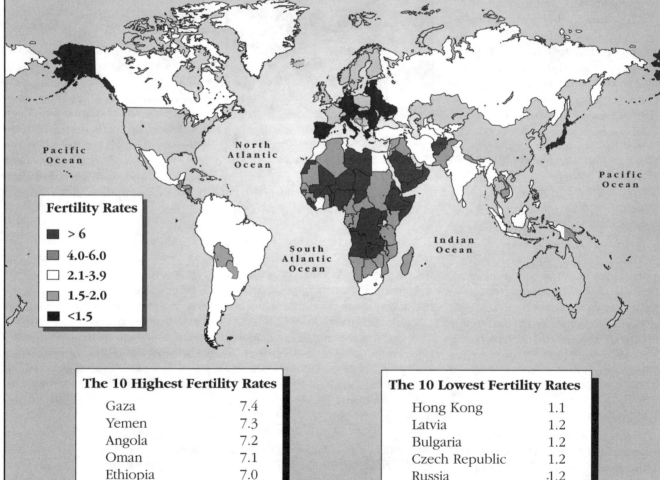

Fertility Rates

- ■ > 6
- ▨ 4.0-6.0
- □ 2.1-3.9
- ▨ 1.5-2.0
- ■ <1.5

The 10 Highest Fertility Rates	
Gaza	7.4
Yemen	7.3
Angola	7.2
Oman	7.1
Ethiopia	7.0
Somalia	7.0
Uganda	6.9
Western Sahara	6.9
Burkina Faso	6.9
Togo	6.8

The 10 Lowest Fertility Rates	
Hong Kong	1.1
Latvia	1.2
Bulgaria	1.2
Czech Republic	1.2
Russia	1.2
Italy	1.2
Spain	1.2
Greece	1.3
Slovenia	1.3
Estonia	1.3

Source: "1998 World Population Data Sheet," Population Reference Sheet include the rapid disappearance of plant and animal species as humans settle in once-remote parts of the world, a sharp decline in certain fish from overfishing, water shortages as agriculture and industry outpace existing water reserves and land degradation resulting from the relentless spread of agriculture onto land that is ill-suited to cultivation.

Although these strains have not yet precipitated a global environmental collapse, ecologists say we are living on borrowed time. "There is tremendous momentum in population growth," says Brian Halweil, a research fellow at the Worldwatch Institute, which studies global environmental problems. "Even if the total fertility rate were now at replacement level, world population growth would still be a problem." *(See map, p. 136.)* Halweil points to regions that are fast approaching a food crisis, such as the Nile River basin, whose current population of 110 million is expected to more than triple to 380 million by 2050. "With so many people being added," he says, "the per capita availability of resources will zoom down."

It's not that women are having more babies than their grandmothers. In fact, fertility rates have fallen in much of the world, especially where women have gained access to education and economic opportunities that make bearing large numbers of children less attractive. What has happened is that more children now survive to adulthood, thanks to vaccines, improved hygiene and more reliable food supplies.

Optimists in the population debate point to other statistics to refute Malthusian predictions of impending doom. While population growth continues, the rate of growth has slowed considerably in recent years as births in a growing number of countries are falling below 2.1 children per couple

— the "replacement level," below which population begins to decline. This trend has forced the United Nations Population Division to lower its projections of future population growth. Under the "low" variant of its most recent projection, the U.N. agency expects human population to peak at 7.7 billion around the middle of the next century before starting a slow decline. Under its "high" variant, however, there would be 27 billion people on Earth by 2150, with no end of growth in sight.

But some optimists in the debate focus on the low numbers and conclude that the real threat today is the prospect that there will be too few people in coming decades — a virtual birth dearth.

"Predictions of a Malthusian collapse have been vastly exaggerated over the last few decades and continue in the face of new evidence that fertility rates are falling worldwide," says Steven W. Mosher, president of the Population Research Institute, in Falls Church, Va. "This is happening not only in the developed world but also in many developing countries, such as Thailand and Sri Lanka, which are already below replacement level, so that their populations will shortly be declining. The world's population will never double again."

Indeed, say optimists in the population debate, the real problem humanity faces is the coming loss of population, especially in Europe, where births have fallen far below replacement level. *(See story, p. 144.)* Ironically, Italy — homeland of the Vatican, contraception's archenemy — has the lowest fertility rate in the world: Each woman has an average of just 1.2 children in her lifetime. "If you built a fence around Europe, which has an average fertility rate of 1.35, the last European would turn out the lights in 300 years," Mosher says. "If current trends continue, the continent's population would go from 860 million today to zero."

But the Cassandras say it's too soon to start mourning the loss of

European civilization. For one thing, they say, no one can predict with any certainty how many children future generations of people will choose to have. Moreover, because of high birthrates in earlier decades, the large number of women entering their child-bearing years will ensure that population continues to grow despite falling fertility rates. The fastest growth will come in the very countries that are least able to support more people — poor countries of sub-Saharan Africa and South Asia. "Population dynamics are like a supertanker," says Robert Engelman, director of the program on population and the environment at Population Action International. "They don't go from zero to 60 in 30 seconds, and they don't stop so fast either. So while total population growth has slowed more than demographers had expected, it's wrong to say the trend is irrevocable or permanent."

For 200 years, worldwide food production defied Malthusian predictions of global starvation. But now there are ominous signs that worldwide grain production will be unable to keep up with the population growth that is expected to continue for at least the next several decades. According to Worldwatch President Lester R. Brown, impending water shortages will soon force China to begin importing vast quantities of grain to feed its 1.2 billion people. This will drive up grain prices, Brown predicts, leaving developing countries in Africa and elsewhere unable to import enough to meet their food needs. The result: Malthus' nightmare.

"The jury's still out on Malthus," said Robert Kaplan, author of numerous articles on population and environmental issues. "But 200 years later, some people still agree with him. I think that's his ultimate success." [3]

In this bicentennial of Malthus' essay, these are some of the key questions being asked about population growth and the environment:

Will World Population Keep Climbing?

The world's population reached nearly 6 billion in 1997, more than double the 1950 level.

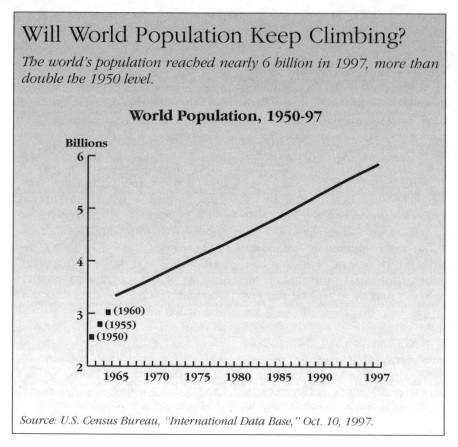

World Population, 1950-97

Source: U.S. Census Bureau, "International Data Base," Oct. 10, 1997.

Can agricultural productivity increase without causing irreversible damage to the environment?

In the 1950s and early '60s, a time of unprecedented high population growth in the developing world, demographers and policy-makers in the industrial countries realized that global food supplies — much provided by exports from developed nations — would soon fall short of demand. Agricultural researchers embarked on an urgent project to develop better-yielding grains in an attempt to avert widespread famine.

The results of this effort, later dubbed the Green Revolution, were stunning. Hybrid strains of rice, wheat and other grains were developed that produced more food per plant and shortened maturation periods so that more than one crop could be cultivated each growing season. In some instances, crop yields tripled.

The Green Revolution's success leads some experts to conclude that further advances in agronomy will suffice to feed the world's growing population. According to Mosher of the Population Research Institute, researchers at the United Nations' Food and Agriculture Organization (FAO) are confident that, even using current technology, enough food could be produced to feed as many as 14 billion people — well above most projections of Earth's population at its peak.

"There is a curious dichotomy between the world's political leaders, who are talking famine, and the researchers who are running the numbers," Mosher says. "The experts aren't being listened to by their own political bosses." In his view, the reason no one is listening to scientists who are confident in the world's ability to feed so many more people comes down to self-interest. "Popu-

lation programs have been generously funded for the past 30 years, and there are a lot of researchers who have benefited from these programs and don't want to see them ended," he says. "As the Chinese would say, they don't want to see their own rice bowls broken."

While other experts agree that further improvements in food production are possible, they worry about the environmental effects of intensifying agriculture much beyond current levels. "I suspect that there is more the Green Revolution can do, that there are more opportunities to increase the yield of a set unit of land," says Engelman of Population Action International. "The important point is that almost all agricultural experts agree that the vast majority of all food will be produced on land we're now cultivating. There just isn't a whole lot of new farmland out there."

Intensifying output on existing farmland can only continue so long before the land is seriously degraded, Engelman warns. "I worry that we may not be able to increase output generation after generation without irrevocably damaging the resources we depend on for food." These include the soil, fresh water and the whole complex of systems that produce food, including organisms in the soil that facilitate the uptake of nutrients in plants.

Each year, an estimated 25 billion metric tons of nutrient-rich topsoil are blown or washed away, largely as a result of intensive agriculture. The soil that is left is denser, making it less able to retain water and allow root penetration. Irrigation produces another problem, salinization, or the buildup of salt and other waterborne minerals in the soil, which can destroy the land's productivity over time. [4] According to David Pimentel, an agricultural expert at Cornell University, soil degradation poses an even more serious threat to the environment than global warming. "It takes 500 years to produce one inch of soil," he said. "Erosion is a slow, gradual problem, but considering that 99 percent of our food comes from the land, it's one that's basic to the survival of the food system." [5]

Besides depleting the soil, irrigation and other modern agricultural techniques pose additional environmental hazards. "Inherent in Green Revolution technologies is the dependence on greater quantities of water, pesticides and fertilizers," says Kolankiewicz of the Carry Capacity Network. "The environmental effects of this kind of agriculture are numerous and far-reaching, including pesticides that can be bioaccumulated and affect whole species and the drawdown of aquifers and depletion of stream flows by irrigation. So we're already robbing Peter to pay Paul."

Drawing on his experience as a Peace Corps volunteer in Latin America during the 1980s, Kolankiewicz also points to the damage caused as more and more marginal lands are brought into cultivation. "Very steep land is being stripped of trees because of the desperate need for food, population growth and inequitable land distribution," he says. "In many countries the best land for sustainable agriculture is owned by just a few people, who hold it idle, raise cattle on it or grow grain for export."

Some experts see a way out of this quandary through a more efficient global economy. "In an ideal, future world, there would be a number of places where people farming today would trade their labor for food produced elsewhere," says Nicholas Eberstadt, a Harvard University demographer and scholar at the American Enterprise Institute for Public Policy Research. "The environmental implications of such specialization are positive, however, because marginal lands would be under less pressure" from cultivation.

But a key condition for this outcome, Eberstadt says, is broader access to property rights. Environmental degradation occurs "when nobody feels they

own a common resource, and everyone feels they can plunder it," he says, citing desertification in the Sahel in southern Sahara — caused by trying to turn marginally productive land into farmland — and severe industrial pollution in China, where property rights are severely limited. "Both a clear and rational framework of property rights and a more relaxed regimen of international trade could be facilitating mechanisms for ensuring sustainable food supplies in the future."

Should the U.S. government support international efforts to curb population growth?

The United States has led the industrialized nations in funding programs that provide family-planning services to developing countries since the late 1960s. At that time, the U.N. Population Fund was set up to coordinate programs aimed at slowing rapid population growth. The federal government provides funding through the U.N. fund as well as through the U.S. Agency for International Development (AID), which helps other governments and non-governmental organizations (NGOs) in voluntary family-planning projects that provide information, services and supplies to communities throughout the world.

U.S. population assistance has been controversial, however. Anti-abortion activists charge that many overseas programs are coercive, forcing women to be sterilized or undergo abortions against their will. China's one-child policy — the toughest population-control policy in the world — has been especially criticized for allegedly forcing pregnant women who already have a child to have abortions, even late in pregnancy.

In response to the critics, President Ronald Reagan initiated the so-called Mexico City policy — named for the 1984 international population conference. Federal law already barred the use of U.S. funds to pay for abortions performed under international family-planning programs. Reagan took the

ban a step further, issuing an executive order that prohibited federal funding of any NGO involved in abortion activities, even if U.S. funds were not used specifically to pay for abortions. [6]

As one of his first acts after taking office, President Clinton reversed the Mexico City policy, sparking a renewed debate over funding of international population programs. Supporters of these programs say they are largely responsible for the fall in fertility rates over the past three decades. "These programs are absolutely effective," says Carl Haub, senior demographer at the Population Reference Bureau. "A lot of countries can't get started [on cutting population growth] without outside help."

While many countries with high population growth can afford to pay for family-planning clinics, medical personnel and supplies such as birth control pills and condoms, U.S.-funded AID personnel help governments coordinate their programs, Haub says. "AID personnel provide continuity in countries with unstable local governments," he says. "They basically keep the ball rolling by providing the social marketing needed, especially in illiterate societies where it's hard to educate people on how to use birth-control methods like the pill."

Critics say that despite the existing ban on funding programs that provide abortion services or abortion-related lobbying or research, part of the $385 million AID budget earmarked for family-planning services inevitably finds its way into such programs. "Population-control programs in Third World countries involve various forms of coercion," says Mosher, who spent a year studying life in a commune in China in 1979, as the one-child policy there began to be enforced. "China is the worst case in terms of the sheer number of women who are brutalized, but it's not alone," he says. His institute has documented instances of abuse in 38 countries, including sterilizations performed

High Fertility Means Low Development

Regions with high fertility rates like Africa and Latin America have a lower per capita gross national product (GNP) and greater annual population increases than more developed areas, such as North America and Europe. Indeed, Europe's 1.4 fertility rate is below the replacement level, and its population is declining by 0.1 percent a year.

Major Regions of the World

	Population mid-1998 (millions)	Natural Population Increase (Annual %)	Projected Population (millions) 2010	Projected Population (millions) 2025	Total Fertility Rate	1996 GNP Per Capita
World	5,926	1.4%	6,903	8,082	2.9	$5,180
More Developed Nations	1,178	0.1	1,217	1,240	1.6	20,240
Less Developed Nations	4,748	1.7	5,687	6,842	3.3	1,230
Africa	763	2.5	979	1,288	5.6	650
North America	301	0.6	333	376	2.0	27,100
Latin America & the Caribbean	500	1.8	591	697	3.0	3,710
Oceania	30	1.1	34	40	2.4	15,430
Asia	3,604	1.5	4,235	4,965	2.8	2,490
Europe	728	-0.1	731	715	1.4	13,710

Source: "1998 World Population Data Sheet," Population Reference Bureau, 1998

without informed consent, coerced abortions and unhygienic conditions in clinics.

"In countries like Mexico, Peru, Bangladesh and Indonesia, agents of the state are going to people's homes and telling women what they should do," Mosher says. "Imagine U.S. Health and Human Services agents coming to your home and telling you to take contraceptives. You would be outraged, yet this is the nature of population-control campaigns overseas."

But supporters of continued U.S. funding of international family-planning programs point instead to the gradual fall in fertility rates as evidence that women are voluntarily embracing the opportunity to

have fewer children. "There's almost nothing rational about the debate over whether the United States is somehow contributing to abortions overseas," Engelman says. "We see the fall in fertility rates in developing countries as great news. It shows that population assistance is having the impact it was designed to have — more women are wanting fewer children."

Haub fears that the recent warnings about the dangers of population decline in the industrialized world will further erode support for U.S. funding of population programs. "This trend most definitely can have an effect on people's opinions about these programs," he says. "But fertility trends in Europe have

absolutely nothing to do with trends in developing countries, which have very young populations and account for 80 percent of world population and 98 percent of the population growth."

Haub points to Mali, where the fertility rate has remained unchanged from around 7 children per woman for the past decade or more. "It's ridiculous to say that fertility rates in Africa are plummeting." Indeed, AID surveys suggest that more than 100 million married women in developing countries have an unmet need for family-planning information and contraceptives. [7]

But support for population programs remains weak in Congress, where the abortion controversy remains the primary focus of the debate on population. In April, for example, Congress added a stipulation to a State Department authorization bill (HR 1757) to pay nearly $1 billion in back dues to the U.N. that would bar U.S. aid to any international groups that lobby for abortion rights. President Clinton threatened to veto the measure. [8]

Some experts say the abortion debate in Washington undermines the progress made by family-planning efforts to date. "The U.N. estimates that if there isn't an immediate stepping up of international family planning there will be 3 billion more people in 50 years," says Halweil of Worldwatch. "That's 9.5 billion people by 2050. But reports that the population explosion is over, combined with pressure from groups that oppose abortion, are eroding domestic support for international family-planning efforts."

Should immigration be limited to protect the U.S. environment from overpopulation?

Like most industrialized countries, the United States has experienced a decline in fertility rates in recent decades, as the postwar baby boom was replaced with the baby bust of the 1970s and '80s. Today, American women have, on average, 2 children. That's slightly below the 2.1 level demographers identify as replacement level fertility, since it allows for the replacement of both parents, with a small allowance for children who die before reaching adulthood.

But the U.S. population, now 270 million, is expected to grow almost 50 percent by 2050, to 387 million. [9] With fertility rates steady among native-born American women, experts say the increase is largely due to immigration. More than 800,000 immigrants legally enter the United States each year (1.1 million, if illegal immigrants are included). That level

is almost triple the average annual immigration of 255,000 from World War II until 1970.

Almost as controversial as using abortion to control population growth is cutting immigration levels to slow environmental degradation. Indeed, although many environmental groups identify population growth as a threat to the environment, and most population growth in the United States today is a result of immigration, few of these organizations actually advocate capping immigration levels.

Earlier this year, the Sierra Club, one of the oldest and most respected environmental groups in the United States, ignited controversy among its members: It asked whether the group should abandon its neutrality on immigration or advocate caps on the number of people admitted each year in the interest of protecting the environment from the effects of overpopulation. When the votes were counted in April, the membership chose by a 3-to-2 margin to continue to stay out of the immigration quagmire altogether.

"This is a resounding defeat for a misguided policy," said Carl Pope, the Sierra Club executive director and a strong proponent of the group's neutral position on immigration. "Through this vote, our members have shown they understand that restricting immigration in the United States will not solve the environmental problems caused by global overpopulation. The common-sense solution to overpopulation is birth control, not border patrols." [10]

But supporters of immigration caps say the vote was little more than a politically correct cop-out encouraged by the group's leaders, who fear alienating the Hispanic and Asian immigrant population of California, its main political base. "There's no way we can stabilize population without reducing immigration," says Kolankiewicz, a Sierra Club member who was involved

in the effort to bring the issue to the vote. "The Sierra Club tried to step very delicately around a very controversial domestic issue. But it's duplicitous to suggest that with continued international family-planning measures we'll be able to stabilize our population."

Over the past 45 years, Kolankiewicz says, U.S. immigration levels have quadrupled at the same time global fertility has declined by 40 percent. "We have the right and the responsibility to control our own population," he says.

While acknowledging the link between population growth and environmental degradation, some experts dispute the value of capping immigration levels in the United States. Of the 800,000 foreigners who legally enter the United States each year, all but about 120,000 gain entry because they are related to current residents or citizens. A significant reduction in immigration levels, says Haub, "would mean we'd have to tell the people who are already legal residents they can't bring over their immediate relatives. That's a political impossibility."

For its part, the Clinton administration has not taken a clear position on the issue of immigration's impact on the environment. A 1996 report by a White House task force concluded that "reducing immigration levels is a necessary part of population stabilization and the drive toward sustainability." [11] But the president recently defended immigration, calling immigrants "the most restless, the most adventurous, the most innovative and the most industrious of people."

Clinton condemned "policies and ballot propositions that exclude immigrants from our civic life" and praised the United States' tradition as an immigrant nation. "Let me state my view unequivocally," Clinton said. "I believe new immigrants are good for America." But he sidestepped the question of whether current immigration levels are appropriate. ∎

Background

A Radical Idea

When Malthus launched the ongoing debate over population growth in 1798, Europe was on the threshold of a radically new era. The Industrial Revolution was just getting under way, opening the way for dramatic shifts in Europe and North America from an agricultural to a modern industrial economy.

Malthus graduated from Cambridge University and later became an Anglican priest. In 1805 he became what is considered the world's first professor of political economy, a position he held at the college of the East India Company until his death in 1834.

The essay that made him famous arose from a friendly argument with his father over man's place in the world. Daniel Malthus espoused the optimistic view that prevailed at the time — no doubt inspired by the rise of democracy and technological progress — that man's ability to improve his lot is unlimited.

Two philosophers were the main purveyors of this view. In France, the Marquis de Condorcet welcomed the revolution in his country as evidence of mankind's ceaseless progress toward perfection. Even after he was imprisoned for criticizing the new Jacobin constitution, Condorcet never lost his optimism. Before starving to death in prison, he completed his writings, which were published posthumously in 1795. [12]

In England, social philosopher William Godwin shared Condorcet's views. In "An Enquiry Concerning Political Justice, and Its Influence on General Virtue and Happiness" (1793), Godwin took Condorcet's utopian thinking even further, calling for the abolition of all governmental and social institutions, including religion, school and family. All such associations, Godwin wrote, were oppressive and would no longer be needed when mankind reached its inevitable goal of perfection. At that point, he predicted, population growth would cease to be a concern. "The men who exist when the earth shall refuse itself to a more extended population will cease to propagate, for they will no longer have any motive, either of error or duty, to induce them. In addition to this they will perhaps be immortal." [13]

In refuting Condorcet and Godwin, Malthus argued that the notion that all people can live in ease and comfort defies laws of nature. Because population will always tend to grow faster than food supplies and other natural resources required for human survival, he wrote, humankind will always be afflicted with "misery and vice," such as war, famine, disease and abortion. "Famine seems to be the last, the most dreadful resource of nature," Malthus wrote. "The power of population is so superior to the power in the earth to produce subsistence for man, that premature death must in some shape or other visit the human race." [14]

Godwin's prediction that population growth will cease as people stop reproducing, Malthus wrote, defies another of the "fixed laws of our nature." "[T]owards the extinction of the passion between the sexes, no progress whatever has hitherto been made," he wrote. "It appears to exist in as much force at present as it did two thousand or four thousand years ago. . . . Assuming, then, my postulata as granted, I say that the power of population is indefinitely greater than the power in the earth to produce subsistence for man." [15]

Malthus modified his views slightly in later essays on the subject, suggesting that population growth could be slowed somewhat by delaying marriage and childbirth. But his basic thesis that there are natural limits to population growth was to greatly influence thinkers of his time and later. Charles Darwin acknowledged a debt to Malthus in devising his theory of evolution, published in 1859. Karl Marx, who published *Principles of Political Economy* the same year, denounced Malthus as a pawn of conservatives because his theory ruled out the Marxist ideal of the classless society. [16]

20th-Century Concerns

Record population growth in the 1960s and '70s sparked renewed interest in Malthus. The burgeoning environmental movement also raised concern about the effect of population growth on fossil fuel supplies and other natural resources. As in Malthus' time, optimists dismissed such worries, arguing that technological advances would provide for virtually limitless numbers of people.

Throughout this century, no voice has been more influential in rebutting Malthus than the Roman Catholic Church. In 1968, Pope Paul VI declared in an encyclical, "Humanae Vitae," that "each and every marriage act must remain open to the transmission of life," effectively banning all forms of birth control short of abstention. Population growth is not the problem among poor nations, the pope implied, but poor government and a lack of social justice. He called for humanity to undertake "the efforts and the sacrifices necessary to insure the raising of living standards of a people and of all its sons."

The same year the encyclical was

Chronology

1700s *The debate over the impact of population growth begins.*

1793
English social philosopher William Godwin calls for the abolition of all governmental and social institutions as oppressive obstacles to human perfection. He predicts that population growth will eventually cease.

1795
Posthumously published writings by the Marquis de Condorcet, a French philosopher, argue that mankind is evolving toward perfection.

1798
Thomas Robert Malthus, an English cleric, warns in *An Essay on the Principle of Population* that unlimited population growth will overwhelm food supplies.

——— • ———

1950s-1960s
The Green Revolution greatly increases crop yields, quelling fears that famine will halt Earth's rapid population growth.

1960
The International Rice Research Institute (IRRI) is created to increase rice yields. Research eventually leads to a doubling and tripling of yields, averting famine in Asian countries with high population growth.

1968
Pope Paul VI issues an encyclical entitled "Humanae Vitae," banning all artificial methods of birth control and ensuring the Roman Catholic Church's position as the most influential opponent of international population-control efforts.

——— • ———

1970s *Record population growth renews Malthusian fears, while China launches its controversial one-child policy.*

1971
The Consultative Group on International Agricultural Research (CGIAR) is set up to coordinate the improvement of food production worldwide. Its 16-member research organization helps boost crop and fish yields.

——— • ———

1980s *U.S. support for overseas family-planning programs wanes amid anti-abortion sentiment.*

1980
Stanford University biologist Paul Ehrlich bets University of Maryland Professor Julian Simon that commodity prices will rise as a result of population growth. Ten years later, Ehrlich loses the bet to Simon, who argues that technological progress will increase commodity supplies and lower prices.

1984
President Ronald Reagan initiates the so-called Mexico City policy — named for the population conference held there — prohibiting federal funding of any non-governmental organization involved in abortion activities.

1990s *Forecasters alter their future projections in the wake of an unexpected slowing of population growth.*

January 1993
Shortly after taking office, President Clinton overturns the Mexico City policy.

1996
A White House task force calls for curbs on immigration to stabilize the U.S. population and protect the environment.

November 1996
The World Food Summit sets a goal of cutting in half the number of undernourished people on Earth from 800 million to 400 million by 2015.

——— • ———

2000s *Population growth is expected to continue, albeit at a slower pace.*

2000
After a century of rapid growth, Earth's population is expected to reach 6 billion, up from 1.6 billion in 1900.

2050
The population of the United States is expected to reach 387 million, up from 270 million in 1998. According to the United Nations Population Division's "middle" variant, world population is expected to peak at 7.7 billion before starting a slow decline.

Falling Fertility Rates Threaten ...

The population debate usually focuses on the impact of overpopulation on food supplies, health and the environment in developing countries. But scores of developed nations face an equally ominous threat: dwindling populations caused by low fertility.

Falling fertility rates have helped slow population growth throughout the world in recent years, but in some 50 countries the average number of children born to each woman has fallen below 2.1, the number required to maintain a stable population. Nearly all of these countries are in the developed world, where couples have been discouraged from having large families by improved education and health care, widespread female employment and rising costs of raising and educating children.

Conservative commentator Ben Wattenberg and others who question the value of family-planning programs have seized on this emerging trend to shift the terms of the population debate. "Never before have birthrates fallen so far, so fast, so low, for so long all around the world," Wattenberg writes. "The potential implications — environmental, economic, geopolitical and personal — are both unclear and clearly monumental, for good and for ill."[1]

According to Wattenberg, the implications are particularly dire for Europe, where the average fertility rate has fallen to 1.4 children per woman. *(See map, p. 136.)* Even if the trend reversed itself and the fertility rate returned to 2.1, the continent would have lost a quarter of its current population before it stabilized around the middle of the next century. With fewer children being born, the ratio of older people to younger people already is growing. "Europe may become an ever smaller picture-postcard continent of pretty old castles and old churches tended by old people with old ideas," Wattenberg writes. "Or it may become a much more pluralist place with ever greater proportions of Africans and Muslims — a prospect regarded with horror by a large majority of European voters."[2]

Some European governments are clearly concerned about the "birth dearth" in their midst. With fewer children being born, they face the prospect of shrinking work forces and growing retiree populations, along with slower economic growth and domestic consumption. Italy, whose fertility rate of 1.2 children per woman is among the lowest in the world, stands to suffer the most immediate consequences of shrinking birthrates. "Italy's population will fall by half over the next half-century, from 66 million now to 36 million," says Steven W. Mosher, president of the Population Research Institute. "The Italian government warns that the current birthrate, if it continues, will amount to collective suicide."

Like Italy, France and Germany have introduced generous child subsidies, in the form of tax credits for every child born, extended maternal leave with full pay, guaranteed employment upon resumption of work and free child care. Mosher predicts that the European Union will likely extend these and other policies to raise birthrates throughout the 15-nation organization in the next couple of years because all members are below replacement level.

"Humanity's long-term problem is not too many children being born but too few," Mosher says. "The one-child family is being chosen voluntarily in many European countries like Italy, Greece, Spain and Russia, which are already filling more coffins than cradles each year. Over time, the demographic collapse will extinguish entire cultures."

Although it is most pronounced in Europe, the birth dearth affects a few countries in other parts of the world as well. Mosher calculates that Japan's population will fall from 126 million today to 55 million over the next century if its 1.4 fertility rate remains unchanged. The trend is already having a social and cultural impact on the country. "In Japan, which boasts the longest lifespans of any country in the world, it's now common for an elderly

---

issued, Stanford University biologist Paul Ehrlich issued an equally impassioned plea for expanded access to birth-control services in *The Population Bomb*. In this and other warnings about the dangers of population growth, Ehrlich and his wife, Anne, also a Stanford researcher, predicted that the resources on which human survival depends would soon run out. "Population control is absolutely essential if the problems now facing mankind are to be solved," they wrote.[17]

At the same time, Worldwatch's

Brown began warning of an impending food crisis. "As of the mid-1970s, it has become apparent that the soaring demand for food, spurred by both population growth and rising affluence, has begun to outrun the productive capacity of the world's farmers and fishermen," he wrote. "The result is declining food reserves, skyrocketing food prices and increasingly intense international competition for exportable food supplies."[18]

The voices of alarm were dismissed by some free-market economists,

who, echoing Godwin's view of man's perfectibility, asserted that human ingenuity would resolve the problems of population growth. The late Julian Simon, a professor at the University of Maryland, declared that Earth's natural resources will never be completely exhausted because human intellect, which is required to exploit them, is infinite.[19] To prove his point, Simon bet Paul Ehrlich that between 1980 and '90 the prices of several minerals would fall as technological progress raised their supply. Ehrlich bet that growing resource scarcity,

... Dire Consequences for Europe

person to hire a family for a day or a weekend to experience family life and enjoy interaction with young people," Mosher says. "It's sad to have to rent a family for a weekend, but this is a way of life that is no longer available to the Japanese because the country is dying."

The birth dearth has geopolitical implications, as well. "As the population plummets, you can say goodbye to Japan as a world power," Mosher says. "And this trend is very hard to reverse. Every young couple would have to have three or four kids to stop the momentum, and that's not going to happen."

Apart from encouraging childbirth, the only way governments can halt population loss is to open the doors to immigrants. In the United States, where the 2.0 fertility rate is just below replacement level, the population is growing by 160,000 people a year, thanks to immigration.

While immigration has always played a prominent, if controversial, role in the United States and Canada, it is a far more contentious issue in the rest of the developed world. Most European countries have more homogeneous societies than those of North America, and deeply entrenched resistance to immigration, especially by people from non-European countries, has fueled support for right-wing politicians like France's Jean-Marie Le Pen. Anti-immigrant sentiment has occasionally escalated into violence, such as the firebombings of housing for Turkish "guest workers" in Germany during the 1980s.

Still, immigration has become more acceptable throughout much of Europe in the past decade, and many of the "guest workers" who come from North Africa, Turkey and other places in search of jobs have stayed and even gained citizenship. "Immigrants are continuing to move to Europe, bringing their cultures and their religions with them," Mosher says. "Intermarriage also is increasing." Japan has been much less hospitable to foreigners.

"Immigration is a very sensitive subject in Japan," Mosher says, "and it is unlikely to be used in the short term to address the growing shortfall of workers there."

Advocates of population-control programs dismiss the concern over shrinking birthrates. "We are delighted to see falling birthrates in our lifetimes, and will continue to encourage the trend," says Robert Engelman, director of Population Action International's program on population and the environment. "I don't want to minimize the problems associated with aging populations. But because this is a slow process, societies will have plenty of time to adjust to the economic and political stresses by increasing immigration from parts of the world where population will continue to rise for some time."

Of course, immigration will be a viable solution to depopulation only as long as humanity continues to grow in number in other parts of the world. Those who worry about falling population point to the United Nations' most conservative projections, which suggest that global population could begin to shrink as early as 2040. But others see little cause for concern.

"If world population starts to fall in 2040, so what?" Engelman asks. "Please identify the danger of population decline that starts at a level much higher than today's and at worst may bring population down to levels seen earlier in the 20th century. There's only so much fresh water, so much atmosphere to absorb the waste greenhouse gases we inject into it every day, so much forest, so much land that can be cultivated. When you consider the enormity of these problems, there's nothing to be afraid of with gradual population decline."

[1] Ben J. Wattenberg, "The Population Explosion Is Over," *The New York Times Magazine*, Nov. 23, 1997, p. 60.

[2] *Ibid.*

stemming in part from population growth, would drive prices up. Simon won the bet.

Green Revolution

Acting on concerns that rising populations in developing countries were outstripping the world's capacity to produce enough food, leaders of NGOs, foundations and national governments launched an international agricultural-research effort to avert famine. In 1960, the International Rice Research Institute (IRRI) was created to increase the yield of rice, the basic food for more than half the world's population. Within a few years, IRRI developed the first of several dwarf breeds that enabled farmers to grow more rice on limited land, using less water and fewer chemicals.

Under the leadership of the Consultative Group on International Agricultural Research (CGIAR), set up in 1971, biologists and agronomists from 16 research centers around the world have since produced hundreds of hybrid strains of staple grains, such as rice, wheat and corn. They have recently extended their efforts to improve yields of potatoes, fish and other basic foods.

These efforts have been so successful that they are known as the Green Revolution. Indeed, although world population has almost doubled since 1961, per-capita food production has more than doubled. The FAO estimates that people in the developing world consume almost a third more calories a day than in the early 1960s. As a result, experts say, there are fewer deaths from

Population Programs Depend . . .

The International Conference on Population and Development, held in Cairo, Egypt, in 1994, laid out a formula for stabilizing the world's growing population. Adopted by 180 nations, the plan called for improvements in women's health and job opportunities and greater access to high-quality reproductive health care, including family planning.

As the following examples show, countries that embraced the Cairo conference's "program of action" are at varying stages in population planning, due to varying levels of development, status of women and religious beliefs:

China — In 1971 Mao Zedong acknowledged the threat posed by China's more than 850 million people and launched a family-planning policy urging later marriage, increased spacing between children and a limit of two children per couple. The policy was later intensified into the radical "one-child" policy, which attracted international condemnation for its practice of forced abortions. The policy has since been relaxed, however. According to firsthand reports, it never covered most of rural China, where many families have three or more children. Still, the fertility rate has plummeted, from 5.8 children per woman in 1970 to 2 today. China's 1.2 billion people makes it the most highly populated country in the world. [1]

India — In 1951 India launched the world's first national family-planning policy. Although almost half of the nation's married women use family planning, and birthrates have come down, most of the slowdown has come in the more developed southern part of the country. "The real story in the past 20 years has been in the large illiterate states of the north known as the Hindi belt," says Carl Haub, senior demographer at the Population Reference Bureau. "In Uttar Pradesh, with a population of 150 million people, women still have an average of five children." That compares with 3.9 children for the country as a whole. With 989 million people, India today is the second most populous country in

the world. With an annual growth rate of almost 2 percent — twice that of China — India may surpass China by 2050. [2]

Pakistan — Just across India's northwestern border, Pakistan has been much less aggressive in its population program. The fertility rate has fallen only slightly, from 6.6 children per woman in 1984-85 to 5.6 children today. A number of factors have contributed to the slow fall in fertility, including official indifference, inadequate funding of population programs and the country's Islamic traditions, which grant women little status, give men the leading role in family decisions and place a high value on sons. [3]

Bangladesh — When Bangladesh won independence from Pakistan in 1971, it had roughly the same population — 66 million people — and the same population growth rate — 3 percent a year — as Pakistan. But the new leaders of Bangladesh, unlike Pakistan, made family planning a top priority. As a result of a sweeping education program and widespread distribution of contraceptives, the fertility rate has dropped from more than 6 children per woman to three. Today, the population of Bangladesh is 120 million, compared with 140 million in Pakistan. [4]

Thailand — Population-control advocates consider Thailand a major success story. Its strong government program is credited with raising contraceptive use from 8 percent to 75 percent of couples over the past 30 years. As a result, the fertility rate has plummeted from 6.2 to 2 births per woman, slightly below the replacement level of 2.1. The relatively high status of Thai women, an extensive road network facilitating access to health clinics and low child mortality are cited as reasons for the program's success. [5]

Rwanda — Since the bloody civil war in 1994, when as many as 750,000 Tutsis were slaughtered by rival Hutus, members of both tribes have set about what one doctor calls "revenge fertility" — a competition to procreate in

famine and malnutrition than ever before. [20] The famines that have occurred in the past 35 years, such as those in Ethiopia and Somalia in the 1980s, and now in Sudan, have been largely the result of war and civil unrest rather than scarcity of global food supplies.

A little-mentioned side effect of the Green Revolution, however, was the environmental damage that accompanied the astonishing increase in crop yields. Some of the new strains were more sus-

ceptible to insect infestation than traditional breeds. Pesticide use in rice production, for example, increased sevenfold, threatening the safety of water supplies. Some insects have developed resistance to the chemicals, resulting in yet heavier pesticide use. Green Revolution crops also require fertilizer, in some cases up to 30 times the amount used on traditional crops. With prolonged use, fertilizers can damage the soil. Finally, because many new plant

strains require irrigation, the Green Revolution has been accompanied by increased erosion and water run-off, further harming land productivity.

"The reduced productivity requires added fertilizer, irrigation and pesticides to offset soil and water degradation," write David Pimentel and Marcia Pimentel of Cornell University. "This starts a cycle of more agricultural chemical usage and further increases the production costs the farmer must bear." [21] ■

. . . On Wide Range of Factors

what is among Africa's most densely populated countries. With fertility at about 7 children per woman and population growth of 3.5 percent, the population of this impoverished country roughly the size Maryland is expected to grow from 7.2 million people today to 25 million by 2030. [6]

Kenya — Although it was one of the first African countries to introduce family-planning services, Kenya saw its fertility rate continue to grow for some time, from 5.3 children per woman in 1962 to 8 children per woman by 1977. In 1982, however, the government strengthened the program, providing community-based services in isolated areas that have increased the use of contraceptives among rural populations. As a result, the fertility rate has fallen to 4.5 children per woman — a rate that ensures continued population growth for decades but one that places Kenya well below the average rate of 6 children per woman in all of sub-Saharan Africa. Kenya's success in lowering fertility rates is now being mirrored in several other countries in the region, including Zimbabwe, Ghana, Nigeria and Senegal. [7]

Tunisia — Since 1957, Tunisia's population has doubled from 4 million to 8 million. While that's a huge increase, it pales in comparison with neighboring Algeria, which also started out in 1957 with 4 million inhabitants but now is home to 57 million. The difference, according to journalist Georgie Ann Geyer, is culture. "Thirty percent of the budget in Tunisia goes to education," she said. "Also, population control is part of the culture." [8] The government population program provides free family-planning services in most parts of the country, and mobile units serve rural areas. The program also is sensitive to religious customs: Rather than urging new mothers to use birth control methods right after delivery, for example, health personnel schedule a return visit to hospital 40 days later — the day new mothers return to society from seclusion, according to Islamic custom. [9]

Iran — Since the 1979 Islamic revolution, Iran's population has jumped from 35 million to 60 million, fueled in part by official encouragement for large families. In 1993, the government adopted a strict family-planning program that encourages vasectomy and other means of birth control — though abortion remains illegal in most cases — and denies subsidized health insurance and food coupons to couples with more than three children. As a result of these efforts, the population growth rate has dropped from 4 percent a year in the 1980s — among the highest in the world — to about 2.5 percent in 1996. [10]

Peru — To stem its 2.2 percent annual increase in population, the government of Peru in 1995 stepped up its population-control program, with the additional goal of raising the status of women in the country. Since then, the program has come under fire, as health workers are accused of offering gifts to illiterate women to undergo sterilization in often unhygienic conditions. [11]

[1] See Mark Hertsgaard, "Our Real China Problem," *The Atlantic*, November 1997, pp. 96-114.

[2] See "India's Growing Pains," *The Economist*, Feb. 22, 1997, p. 41.

[3] Population Reference Bureau, "Pakistan: Family Planning with Male Involvement Project of Mardan," November 1993.

[4] See Jennifer D. Mitchell, "Before the Next Doubling," *World Watch*, January/February 1998, pp. 20-27.

[5] Population Reference Bureau, "Thailand: National Family Planning Program," August 1993.

[6] See "Be Fruitful," *The Economist*, Feb. 1, 1997, p. 43.

[7] See Stephen Buckley, "Birthrates Declining in Much of Africa," *The Washington Post*, April 27, 1998.

[8] Geyer spoke at "Malthus Revisited," a conference held May 8-9, 1998, by the Warrenton, Va.-based Biocentric Institute, which studies ways to enhance the quality of life for all peoples.

[9] See Population Reference Bureau, "Tunisia: Sfax Postpartum Program," March 1993.

[10] See Neil MacFarquhar, "With Iran Population Boom, Vasectomy Receives Blessing," *The New York Times*, Sept. 8, 1996.

[11] See Calvin Sims, "Using Gifts as Bait, Peru Sterilizes Poor Women," *The New York Times*, Feb. 15, 1998.

CURRENT SITUATION

Population Explosion

The 20th century has seen by far the fastest population growth in human history. For the first million years or so of man's existence on Earth, global population probably did not exceed 6 million — fewer than New York City's current population. With the beginning of agriculture some 10,000 years ago, population expanded gradually until it approached 1 billion by 1700 and 1.6 billion by 1900. Population growth never exceeded 0.5 percent a year over that 200-year period. [22]

By 2000, global population is expected to reach 6 billion. The unprecedented population explosion of the 20th century peaked in the 1970s, when the growth rate reached 2 percent a year. It has since slowed, thanks to improved access to family-planning information and contraceptives and expanded educational and employment opportunities for women in developing countries.

As couples become less dependent on children to help in the fields and take care of them in old age, the value of large families decreases. The same medical advances that helped fuel the population explosion by reducing infant mortality also enable couples to have fewer children in the knowledge that they will survive to adulthood.

As a result of these changes, fertility rates of most developing countries are following those in industrialized countries, where fertility rates have fallen dramatically in recent decades. As more people move to the cities, the cost of raising children — housing, food, clothing and schooling — is a powerful inducement to reducing family size. "Birthrates in a large number of countries in the developing world, except for Africa, Pakistan and some countries in the Persian Gulf, have come down to a degree," says Haub of the Population Reference Bureau. "The big question is whether they will come down to the 2.1 level seen in developed countries. That would bring the population growth rate to zero."

But while fertility rates are slowly falling in many developing nations, the population momentum of the earlier boom ensures that population growth will continue in these countries for years to come. While population growth rates have dropped in industrial nations, in the developing world more than 2 billion young people under age 20 are entering or will soon enter their childbearing years, according to the Population Reference Bureau. This trend is especially significant in sub-Saharan Africa, the region with the highest fertility rate in the world — an average of 6 births per woman. With 45 percent of the inhabitants of sub-Saharan Africa age 15 or younger, population growth will likely continue, no matter what the birthrate may be in the next few decades. [23]

The difference in fertility rates between industrialized and developing countries has implications for the future. Today, there are four times as many people in developing countries as in industrial countries. Because 98 percent of global population growth is taking place in developing countries, that gap is likely to widen. If current trends continue, many industrial nations will soon begin to lose population, especially young, working-age people. [24] As developing countries struggle to support and employ their growing number of youth, many more young people from the developing world may migrate to other regions, including the developed countries.

Norman Myers of Oxford University, in England, puts the number of "environmental refugees" at 25 million, primarily in sub-Saharan Africa, China, the Indian subcontinent, Mexico and Central America, who are fleeing drought, erosion, desertification, deforestation and other environmental problems.

"The issue of environmental refugees is fast becoming prominent in the global arena," Myers writes. "Indeed it promises to rank as one of the foremost human crises of our times." Myers foresees increased resistance to immigration in industrial nations. "Already migrant aliens prove unwelcome in certain host countries, as witness the cases of Haitians in the United States and North Africans in Europe. No fewer than nine developed countries, almost one in three, are taking steps to further restrict immigration flows from developing countries." [25]

Environmental Impact

As global population continues to mount, so does the strain on the environment, as people move into previously uninhabited areas and consume ever-increasing amounts of natural resources. In recent times, the first signs of population's impact on the environ-

ment were regional food shortages in the 1960s and '70s. Initially, the Green Revolution resolved the shortages by introducing high-yield grains and innovative farming techniques. But the more intensive methods of agriculture required to boost food production in many parts of the world have since produced environmental damage of their own. "You can't fertilize crops without fresh water," says Halweil. "If you increase fertilizer use, you have to increase water use. As a result, large areas of Latin America, Africa and China are now suffering water shortages."

Another result of intensified irrigation and fertilizer use is the buildup of salt and other minerals that are left in the soil after the water evaporates. After prolonged irrigation, land also tends to become waterlogged and no longer suitable for growing plants. Even before land degradation sets in, there are limits to the benefits of fertilizers. "You can't just keep putting fertilizer on the land indefinitely," Halweil says. "Eventually the yield increases cease."

With economic development, more people around the world are consuming poultry, beef, pork and other meat products. As demand for such foods rises, cattle ranches are occupying land once used for agriculture, pushing farmers onto marginal lands such as steep hillsides and virgin forests. The deforestation that results, most evident recently in tropical South America and Africa, promotes erosion and has been implicated in global warming.

Biologists recently warned that a "mass extinction" of plant and animal species is now taking place, the result of human destruction of natural habitats. [26] Even the oceans are showing signs of strain from population growth. Overfishing and pollution have caused sudden decreases in fish catches, prompting temporary bans in many fisheries that only a few decades ago seemed limitless. [27]

Population growth has also been accompanied by air and water pollution. While developed countries have made

At Issue:

Has economic development proved Malthus wrong?

JAMES P. PINKERTON
Lecturer, Graduate School of Political Management, The George Washington University

JOHN F. ROHE
Attorney and author of **A Bicentennial Malthusian Essay** *(1997)*

*i*n 1798, a 32-year-old minister from England published, anonymously, a 54,000-word "Essay on the Principle of Population." In it, he argued that "the power of population is indefinitely greater than the power in the Earth to produce subsistence for man." And so, he concluded in his famous formulation, "Population, when unchecked, increases in a geometrical ratio. Subsistence increases only in an arithmetical ratio." Neither the author nor his essay stayed obscure for long. Yet for all the renown of Thomas Robert Malthus, it is hard to think of an idea that has been simultaneously more influential and more wrong.

On the bicentennial of his famous treatise, Malthus lives on as adjective; a Nexis database search for the word "Malthusian" just in the last year found 138 "hits." Indeed, Malthusianism has become an intellectual prism for explaining the world, like Marxism or Freudianism — even for those who have read little or nothing of the original texts. Just as Marxists explain everything as a consequence of class structure or Freudians interpret behavior by identifying underlying sexual impulses, so Malthusians start with an inherent presumption of scarcity and impending doom. And so Malthus stands as the patron saint of pessimists, those who see the glass as half-empty, not half-full. As he wrote then, his view of the world had "a melancholy hue."

Interestingly, the first Malthusians were on the political right. The landed gentry from which Malthus sprang looked upon the swelling population of the big cities with fear and even loathing . . . .

Today's Malthusians, of course, are on the environmental left. Once again, the dynamic is that many among the elite look upon their fellow humans as liabilities. And once again, they have been mostly wrong.

The leading Malthusian today — if you don't count Vice President Al Gore — is Stanford Professor Paul Ehrlich. His landmark book, *The Population Bomb*, published in 1968, began with an alarm. "The battle to feed all humanity is over," he declared, predicting worldwide famine. A more recent book, *The Population Explosion* (1990), co-written with his wife Anne, carries on the same doom-gloom argument. Praising, of course, the memory of Malthus, the Ehrlichs prescribe a long list of control on virtually every aspect of human activity . . . .

Ironically, toward the end of his life, Malthus altered his views. In "Principles of Political Economy" (1820) he acknowledged that economic growth would improve the prospects of the populace. But as so often happens, the original outrageous assertion is remembered forever, while the subsequent revision, even if it is closer to the truth, fades away quickly.

*p*hilosophers at the dawn of the Industrial Revolution . . . suggested that prosperity and wealth were dependent on more people. In his essay, "Of Avarice and Profusion" in 1797, William Godwin states, "There is no wealth in the world except this, the labor of man . . . ." While serving as an ordained priest in the Church of England, Thomas Robert Malthus questioned these findings. He pondered basic mathematical principles. If parents had four children, and if the population continued to double every generation, the exponential progression would be as follows: 2, 4, 8, 16, 32, 64, 128, 256, 512, 1024, 2048. The numerical surge becomes explosive. Malthus determined a finite planet could not accommodate perpetual growth . . . .

Thomas Robert Malthus unlocked the door to one of nature's best-kept and most formidable secrets. He discovered a universal law of biology. For every plant and animal, there are more offspring than the ecosystem can sustain. And we are just beginning to grapple with the ethical dilemma resulting from his humbling conclusion: This universal law even applies to us.

The view from a seemingly lofty perch on nature's food chain can be deceptive. We enjoy but a brief reprieve from universal biological principles. The prescient message of a pre-scientific era has not been rendered obsolete by modern technology.

Our planet now experiences a daily net population gain of 250,000 people (total births minus deaths), and approximately 1.3 billion go to bed hungry every night. Several hundred thousand slip beyond the brink of malnutrition every year.

While the Earth's natural capital is systematically dismantled, efforts to discredit Malthus persist. For example, Julian Simon claims the world's resources can continue to accommodate human growth for 7 billion years! By then, the unchecked human biomass would fill the universe.

Efforts to discredit Malthus do not always plummet to such overt absurdities. Subtle efforts to refute him are exhibited every time a politician promises to add more exponential growth to the GNP. Proponents of growth are implicitly found in every financial report, business forecast and economic news publication. An abiding faith in growth has become the unexamined conviction of our age. Notions of sustainability are not on the table. The talismanic affinity for growth is an implicit rejection of Malthus . . . .

We were not exempt from the laws of biology unveiled by Thomas Robert Malthus in 1798. And we are not exempt now. At the bicentennial anniversary of his essay, Malthus deserves recognition for predicting the cause of today's most pressing concerns and most challenging ethical challenges. We discredit him at our peril.

Developed Nations Use the Most Resources

The United States accounts for only 5 percent of the world's population but uses a third of its paper and dumps three-quarters of the hazardous waste. Similarly, other developed countries account for a small fraction of Earth's population but use the largest percentage of its metals and paper.

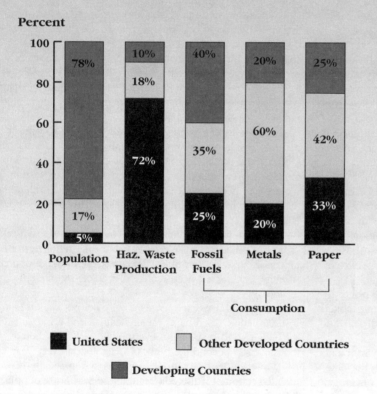

Share of Population, Waste Production and Resource Consumption

Sources: *"New Perspectives on Population: Lessons from Cairo," Population Bulletin,* March 1995; Natural Resources Defense Council

the Rhine River and has greatly improved air quality. Mankind is capable of creative solutions."

Even more controversial is the link between population growth and global warming. Consumption of coal, oil and natural gas has been implicated in the gradual heating of the atmosphere that scientists fear will cause melting of polar ice caps, rising water levels and flooding of crowded coastal areas. Warming may also speed desertification and the spread of malaria and other insect-borne diseases. Although carbon-fuel consumption can be expected to continue to rise with economic development, many scientists predict that the growth in human population alone will increase demand for these fuels until cheap alternatives are developed.

But optimists in the population debate firmly reject this argument. "The odd suggestion that babies are somehow responsible for pollution tends to be the mindset of people who blame problems on the sheer number of people who exist," says Mosher, reflecting the view of many critics of the Kyoto Protocol, which was endorsed last December by the United States and 167 other countries. "But this view is wrong and was also rejected at Kyoto.

When the developed countries asked developing countries to further decrease their total fertility rates as part of the treaty, they were rejected outright, and rightly so. There is no necessary connection between the number of children being born and the level of carbon dioxide in the air."

Critics also charge that the global-warming theory rests on shaky scientific evidence. Consequently, they oppose U.S. participation in the treaty, which they say would cost more than 3 million jobs as businesses curb production to comply with its requirement to cut carbon emissions. The Clinton administration, which strongly supports the treaty, faces an uphill battle in the

strides in these areas, industrializing countries are facing mounting problems. China, for example, which uses coal for industry, as well as for heating and cooking, has among the worst air pollution in the world. Taiyuan, in northern China, has seven times as much particulate matter as Los Angeles, by far the most polluted city in the United States. Beijing and other Chinese cities are also blanketed by pollutants.[28]

Optimists in the population debate

reject the notion that population growth by itself causes environmental damage. "I don't think there is a direct link between population and the environment," says the Population Research Institute's Mosher, who blames misguided government policies. "You can create environmental problems in a lightly populated country by failing to control pollution, just as you can have a very clean environment in a densely populated country, such as Germany, which is cleaning up

Senate, which must ratify it by a two-thirds majority before it will take effect in the United States. [29] ■

OUTLOOK

Grain Crunch?

For the past several decades, the Green Revolution has largely discredited the Malthusian prediction of imminent collapse of the global food supplies needed to feed a rapidly expanding population. But the environmental degradation that has continued apace during that time may have laid the groundwork for just such a calamity in the not too distant future. According to Worldwatch, rapid industrialization in China is reducing the supply of water farmers use to irrigate their grain crops. Because 70 percent of the grain consumed by China's 1.2 billion inhabitants comes from irrigated land, the diversion of water for industrial use may soon force the country, now largely self-sufficient, to start importing grain.

Because of its sheer size, China would quickly overwhelm the global supply of grain, driving up prices and forcing less affluent grain-importing countries, such as those of sub-Saharan Africa, out of the market. The result, Worldwatch warns, would be widespread famine. "For the 1.3 billion of the world's people who live on $1 a day or less, higher grain prices could quickly become life threatening," write Brown and Halweil. [30]

Brown has made similarly dire predictions in the past that have proved wrong, drawing the scorn of optimists in the Malthusian debate. But now, the situation he describes is sufficiently alarming to have drawn the attention of the U.S. National Intelligence Council, which calls

for greater U.S.-China cooperation in agricultural production and technology. Brown and Halweil endorse the idea.

"If the world's two leading food producers can work closely together to protect their agricultural resource bases, while the world works to stabilize population," they write, "it will benefit not only each of those countries, but the rest of the world as well." [31]

Although the implications of China's water shortage are especially alarming, it is hardly the only country faced with competing demands on dwindling water supplies. According to Population Action International, some 80 percent of the world's population lives in countries facing problems with fresh water supplies. Population growth will lead to more widespread water shortages, the group predicts, heightening the risk of conflict over water supplies in areas such as the Tigris-Euphrates basin, where water rights are already a source of tension among Iraq, Syria and Turkey. [32]

Meanwhile, the CGIAR continues trying to ward off famine with further improvements in crop yields as well as fish and meat production. In an effort to halve the number of undernourished people on Earth to 400 million by 2015 — the goal set by the World Food Summit in November 1996 — the international research organization is studying the potential of bioengineering as the next weapon in its arsenal to continue the Green Revolution into the next century. [33]

Consumption to Blame?

Today's consumer society has added a new twist to the warning issued by Malthus about inadequate food supplies. Latter-day Malthusians warn that the economic systems prevalent in most of the world today can only accelerate that end by encouraging consumption of resources without regard to its impact on the environ-

ment. In the United States, advertisements promise consumers that buying an endless array of products will bring greater happiness. With the end of the Cold War and the demise of the Soviet Union, the Western model of economic life is being pursued throughout most of the world.

Some experts say the combination of population growth and rising consumption do not threaten Earth's carrying capacity. "The long-term trend for inflation-adjusted prices of commodities has been going down, not up," Eberstadt says. "This suggests to me that natural resources are less scarce today than they were when there was less demand. In any case, we're heading toward a knowledge-and-service economy, so the direction of our development is less resource-intensive and more reliant on human skills. That gives me hope that we may be able to manage our resource demands in the future."

But many environmentalists say Malthus' nightmare will become reality that much sooner if the rest of the world adopts the consumption-based model developed in North America and Western Europe. In their view, economic growth has become a fundamental, but flawed, barometer of well-being. "Every news report, every business forecast assumes that growth is good and that more growth is better," says attorney John F. Rohe, author of the 1997 book *A Bicentennial Malthusian Essay*. "But the issue is not how we grow. It's how we can develop sustainably." *(See At Issue, p.149.)*

In this view, current efforts to protect the environment fall far short of the changes that are required to ensure sustainability. "People wonder whether the economy can continue to grow if we stop excessive consumption of oil and polluting goods," Halweil says. "They say we can shift to solar energy, fuel cells and biodegradable plastics. But the answer isn't having a hybrid-fuel car in everyone's garage. It's having fewer people driving and more taking public transportation."

The only answer to having more people on the planet, Halweil says, is to drastically cut consumption. "We are addicted to consumption, and we have to be slowly weaned off it," he says. "I don't know what it will look like, but the economic system will have to be different if the environment is to be protected." ■

Notes

[1] Thomas Robert Malthus, *An Essay on the Principle of Population* (1798), cited in Philip Appleman, ed., *An Essay on the Principle of Population* (1976), p. 56. For background, see "World Hunger," *The CQ Researcher*, Oct. 25, 1991, pp. 801-824.

[2] See "Population Growth," *The CQ Researcher*, July 16, 1993, pp. 601-624.

[3] Kaplan spoke at "Malthus Revisited," a conference held May 8-9, 1998, by the Warrenton, Va.-based Biocentric Institute, which studies ways to enhance the quality of life for all peoples.

[4] See Population Action International, *Conserving Land: Population and Sustainable Food Production*, April 1995.

[5] Pimentel spoke at the May conference on Malthus (see above).

[6] See "International Population Assistance," *Congressional Digest*, April 1997.

[7] See "What Birth Dearth? Why World Population Is Still Growing," *Population Action International Fact Sheet*, 1998.

[8] See "Clinton Uncaps Veto Pen As State Department Bill Clears," *CQ Weekly*, May 2, 1998, pp. 1167-1168.

[9] See James P. Smith and Barry Edmonston, eds., *The New Americans* (1997), p. 95.

[10] Quoted in William Branigin, "Sierra Club Votes for Neutrality on Immigration," *The Washington Post*, April 26, 1997.

[11] President's Council on Sustainable Development, "Task Force Report on Population and Consumption," 1996, p. iv.

[12] Condorcet's last work was *Esquisse d'un tableau historique des progrès de l'esprit humain.*

[13] Quoted in Gertrude Himmelfarb, "The Ghost of Parson Malthus," *Times Literary Supplement* (London), Jan. 23, 1998.

[14] Malthus, *op. cit.*, p. 56.

[15] *Ibid*, p. 19-20.

FOR MORE INFORMATION

Carrying Capacity Network, 2000 P St. N.W., Suite 240, Washington, D.C. 20036; (202) 296-4548; http://www.alternatives.com/lmspg/ccc.htm. An advocacy group that focuses on population stabilization, immigration reduction, economic sustainability and resource conservation to preserve the quality of life.

World Bank, 1818 H St. N.W., Suite S9035, Washington, D.C. 20433; (202) 473-8729. The bank provides member countries with loans and technical advice for family-planning projects designed to slow population growth.

Population Action International, 1300 19th St. N.W., Second Floor, Washington, D.C. 20036; (202) 659-1833; www.populationaction.org. This organization promotes population stabilization through public education and universal access to voluntary family planning.

Population Reference Bureau, 1875 Connecticut Ave. N.W., Suite 520, Washington, D.C. 20009-5728; (202) 483-1100; www.prb.org. An educational organization that provides information on family planning and international development programs and U.S. population policy.

Population Research Institute, 5119A Leesburg Pike, Suite 295, Falls Church, Va. 22041; (540) 622-5226. The institute focuses on human rights abuses in population programs and promotes economic development without recourse to these programs.

Zero Population Growth, 1400 16th St. N.W., Suite 320, Washington, D.C. 20036; (202) 332-2200; www.zpg.org. ZPG supports expansion of family-planning programs and women's access to abortion and family-planning services.

[16] For more information on Malthus and his time, see David Price, "Of Population and False Hopes: Malthus and His Legacy," *Population and Environment*, January 1998, pp. 205-219. See also Keith Stewart Thomson, "1798: Darwin and Malthus," *American Scientist*, May-June 1998, pp. 226-229.

[17] Paul R. and Anne H. Ehrlich, *Population Resources Environment* (1972), quoted in Appleman, *op. cit.*, p. 240.

[18] Lester R. Brown, *In the Human Interest* (1974), quoted in Appleman, *op. cit.*, p. 243.

[19] See Julian Simon, *The Ultimate Resource* (1981).

[20] See "Environmental Scares: Plenty of Gloom," *The Economist*, Dec. 20, 1997, p. 20.

[21] David Pimentel and Marcia Pimentel, "The Demographic and Environmental Consequences of the Green Revolution," *The Carrying Capacity Briefing Book* (1996), p. XII-101.

[22] *Ibid.*, p. XII-97.

[23] Population Reference Bureau, *1998 World Population Data Sheet*, May 1998.

[24] See Michael Specter, "Population Implosion Worries a Graying Europe," *The New York Times*, July 10, 1998, p. A1.

[25] Norman Myers, "Environmental Refugees," *Population and Environment*, November 1997, pp. 175-176.

[26] See William K. Stevens, "One in Every 8 Plant Species Is Imperiled, a Survey Finds," *The New York Times*, April 9, 1998.

[27] See "The Sea," *The Economist*, May 23, 1998, Survey section, pp. 1-18.

[28] See Elisabeth Rosenthal, "China Officially Lifts Filter on Staggering Pollution Data," *The New York Times*, June 14, 1998.

[29] See "Fresh Focus on Global Warming Does Not Dispel Doubts About Kyoto Treaty's Future," *CQ Weekly*, June 6, 1998, pp. 1537-1538.

[30] Lester Brown and Brian Halweil, "China's Water Shortage Could Shake World Food Security," *Worldwatch*, July/August 1998, p. 10.

[31] *Ibid.*, p. 18.

[32] See Tom Gardner-Outlaw and Robert Engelman, "Sustaining Water, Easing Scarcity: A Second Update," *Population Action International*, Dec. 15, 1997.

[33] See Consultative Group on International Agricultural Research, "Nourishing the Future through Scientific Excellence," Annual Report 1997.

Bibliography

Selected Sources Used

Books

Appleman, Philip, ed., *An Essay on the Principle of Population: Thomas Robert Malthus*, W.W. Norton, 1976.
This volume contains not only the writings of Malthus and his contemporaries but also those of 20th-century thinkers who joined the debate over Earth's ability to support a rapidly growing population in the 1970s.

Brown, Lester R., Michael Renner and Christopher Flavin, *Vital Signs 1998: The Environmental Trends That Are Shaping Our Future*, W.W. Norton, 1998.
Among the trends featured are population growth and grain yields, two essential ingredients in the Malthusian prediction of famine. Though population growth has slowed, it continues, and further increases in grain yields may be hampered by dwindling water supplies.

Easterbrook, Gregg, *A Moment on the Earth: The Coming Age of Environmental Optimism*, Penguin Books, 1995.
The author claims that prevailing concerns over a number of environmental issues are overstated. The recent slowing of population growth, he writes, marks the beginning of an era when man's impact on the environment will be insignificant: "Human overpopulation, which environmental orthodoxy today depicts as a menace of unimaginable horror, will be seen by nature as a minor passing fad."

Rohe, John F., *A Bicentennial Malthusian Essay: Conservation, Population and the Indifference to Limits*, Rhodes & Easton, 1997.
The author attributes many of today's problems, from famine to road rage, to the same overpopulation that concerned Malthus 200 years ago. Compounding the problem, he writes, is the quest for economic growth regardless of its impact on natural resources.

Articles

Ashford, Lori S., "New Perspectives on Population: Lessons from Cairo," *Population Bulletin*, March 1995.
The International Conference on Population and Development, held in September 1994 in Cairo, Egypt, produced a list of goals for family-planning programs. This article presents an overview of these programs around the world and identifies policies that have had the most success in reducing population growth.

Brown, Lester R., and Brian Halweil, "China's Water Shortage Could Shake World Food Security," *Worldwatch*, July/August 1998, pp. 10-18.
Rapid industrialization and population growth are depleting China's water supplies so fast that the country's farmers may soon be unable to meet domestic food needs. If China is forced to buy its grain, global grain prices will rise, perhaps beyond the means of poorer developing countries that depend on imports to meet their food needs.

Hertsgaard, Mark, "Our Real China Problem," *The Atlantic*, November 1997, pp. 97-114.
During a trip through rural China, the author found that the country's infamous one-child policy has been largely abandoned and that continuing population growth is compounding China's serious environmental pollution.

Mann, Charles C., "Reseeding the Green Revolution," *Science*, Aug. 22, 1997, pp. 1038-1043.
The Green Revolution prevented widespread famine in recent decades, but many scientists worry that the potential for increasing crop yields is reaching its limit. Bioengineering and other breakthroughs may provide the tools to achieve another major leap in agricultural productivity.

Price, David, "Of Population and False Hopes: Malthus and His Legacy," *Population and Environment*, January 1998, pp. 205-219.
The author, an anthropologist at Cornell University, presents an excellent overview of the life and times of Thomas Robert Malthus on the bicentennial of his essay on population and the relevance of his ideas to modern concerns about Earth's carrying capacity.

Smail, J. Kenneth, "Beyond Population Stablization: The Case for Dramatically Reducing Global Human Numbers," *Politics and the Life Sciences*, September 1997.
A Kenyon College anthropology professor opens a roundtable presentation by 17 population experts who support greater efforts to curb population growth.

Reports and Studies

Gardner-Outlaw, Tom, and Robert Engelman, *Sustaining Water, Easing Scarcity: A Second Update*, Population Action International, 1997.
Water supplies are threatened in many parts of the world by rising population. By 2050, the authors report, at least one person in four is likely to live in countries that suffer chronic or recurring water shortages.

Population Reference Bureau, *World Population Data Sheet: Demographic Data and Estimates for the Countries and Regions of the World*, 1998.
This pamphlet presents a country-by-country assessment of population, fertility rates, life expectancy and other statistics that help demographers forecast future population growth trends.

9 Protecting the National Parks

RACHEL S. COX

Ah, the grandeur of our national parks. The awe-inspiring Grand Canyon . . . spoiled by thick air pollution and the drone of tourist planes. The spectacular thermal pools of Yellowstone . . . fouled by untreated waste from an aging sewage system. The winter stillness of Yosemite . . . shattered by the roar of snowmobiles.

Like the Declaration of Independence, America's national parks embody a noble idea. They conjure images of freedom and integrity, of an enduring, priceless patrimony to be protected for the common good and enjoyed by all people.

Although the National Park System remains the nation's premier recreation attraction and the envy of the world, the system is troubled. Many national parks, once seen as retreats from life's daily pressures, are now beset by many of the same pressures themselves. When the Florida Everglades joined the roster of the National Park Service (NPS) in 1947, for example, it was a vast, largely unspoiled ecosystem of watery marshlands and numberless wild creatures. Rampant development in South Florida, however, has taken its toll. The wetlands have been reduced in size to half their original area, and the number of nesting wading birds, for example, has declined 70 percent — from 265,000 birds in the 1930s to just 18,500 in the early 1990s. [1]

In addition to outside development pressure, vastly increased visitation has created immense pressure on the parks from within. In 1996, 40 million more tourists visited the national parks than in 1978. [2] By 1998, park visits had reached nearly 300 million. [3] Crowding has become such

From *The CQ Researcher,*
June 16, 2000.

Tourists ride mules through Grand Canyon National Park, which is coping with growing pains and will prohibit most private vehicles by 2002.

UPI Photo/Jack Kurtzt

a problem that many parks now charge admission and maintain long waiting lists for campgrounds and cabins.

The scope of Park Service responsibilities also has grown enormously since Congress anointed Yellowstone as the first national park in 1872. After 35 more parks had been added, the NPS was created in 1916 to oversee the growing system. Today there are 379 "units" in 20 "National" categories, including Parks, Monuments, Battlefields, Cemeteries and Trails. Together, the parks encompass 83.3 million acres in 49 states and four U.S. territories. There are no NPS units in Delaware.

Meanwhile, the system's aging infrastructure is at the breaking point in many parks. Yosemite's sewage system is among scores of early systems in need of reconstruction and expansion. At the same time, many Park Service structures themselves have come to be seen as historic resources, redoubling the urgency, and sometimes the complexity, of proper maintenance. According to federal guidelines, a structure is eligible for designation as a historic landmark when it becomes 50 years old. Thus, in addition to the many old buildings needing maintenance, the modern-style structures erected during a building push in the 1950s

and '60s now must be cared for not only with an eye toward their functionality, but also with consideration for their historic attributes.

But Park Service supporters say that despite their growth in numbers, usage and complexity, the parks have not received similarly expanded funding from Congress. Park Service supporters point out that in constant dollars, annual funding has decreased by more than $600 million over the past two decades. They consider the investment level to be woefully low and argue that it is unreasonable to expect the Park Service to manage its resources successfully when it lacks adequate financing.

"Given limited appropriations, the Park Service has done a remarkable job of managing its parks," says Brian Huse, senior director of the National Parks Conservation Association's Pacific region. "In the last 20 years, at least 80 new parks have been added, but appropriations haven't increased much more than inflation. The public doesn't truly understand how dire the condition of the parks is: lack of funding, backlog of maintenance and emphasis on building [rather than maintenance]."

Others see the problems as predictable evidence of governmental inefficiency or as byproducts of management decisions made on the basis of skewed priorities. In the most drastic proposals, property-rights advocates take issue with the very notion of national parks, arguing that the federal government should divest itself of public lands.

Underlying the discussion is the general question of what purpose Park Service lands should serve. The legislation that established the Park Service directed it "to conserve the scenery and the natural and historic

Blue Ridge, Smoky Mountains Most Popular

Ten Most-Visited National Parks, 1999

Rank	Park	Location	Visits (in millions)
1.	Great Smoky Mountains	N.C.; Tenn.	10.3
2.	Grand Canyon	Ariz.	4.6
3.	Yosemite	Calif.	3.5
4.	Olympic	Wash.	3.4
5.	Rocky Mountain	Colo.	3.2
6.	Yellowstone	Mont.; Idaho; Wyo.	3.1
7.	Grand Teton	Wyo.	2.7
8.	Acadia	Maine	2.6
9.	Zion	Utah	2.4
10.	Haleakala	Hawaii	2.0

Corbis Images

Golden Gate National Recreation Area is the second most popular destination in the National Park System.

Ten Most-Visited National Recreation Sites, 1999

Rank	Site	Location	Visits (in millions)
1.	Blue Ridge Parkway	N.C.	19.8
2.	Golden Gate National Recreation Area	Calif.	14.0
3.	Great Smoky Mountains National Park	N.C.; Tenn.	10.3
4.	Lake Mead National Recreation Area	Nev.	9.0
5.	George Washington Memorial Parkway	D.C.	7.0
6.	Gateway National Recreation Area	N.Y.	6.8
7.	Natchez Trace Parkway	Miss.	6.4
8.	Statue of Liberty National Monument	N.Y.	5.4
9.	Delaware Water Gap National Recreation Area	Pa.	5.0
10.	Cape Cod National Seashore	Mass.	4.9

Source: National Park Service

objects and the wildlife therein and to provide for the enjoyment of same in such a manner and by such means as will leave them unimpaired for the enjoyment of future generations."

In the beginning, the dual goals of the Park Service — to conserve and to promote enjoyment — were not viewed as contradictory. But as environmental science established itself as a discipline beginning in the 1930s, it became increasingly evident that the Park Service itself, through decisions about use and development of the parks, had destroyed the original flora and fauna of many parks. In recent decades, the conviction has grown that the first duty of the Park Service is to the ecosystems that sustain the parks.

In this view, the key to solving many park problems lies in scientific research. With data in hand, Park Service managers say they could, in effect, serve the resource base, using scientific information about the effects of air pollution on flora and fauna to plan transportation solutions, for instance. And while human activities might play second fiddle to the requirements of nature, the natural systems that inspired protection in the first place would endure for generations to come. [4]

"The central dilemma of National Park management has long been the question of exactly what in a park should be preserved," wrote national parks historian Richard Sellars. "Is it the scenery . . . or is it the integrity of each park's entire natural system? [A] kind of 'facade' management became the accepted practice in parks: protecting and enhancing the scenic facade of nature of the public's enjoyment, but with scant scientific knowledge and little concern for biological consequences." [5]

No one argues today that the Park Service has succeeded in managing its lands so as to leave them "unimpaired." Indeed, it is one of the ironies of the Park Service's dilemma that both conservative private-property advocates and left-leaning conservationists agree that the Park Service has not effectively managed its properties. But the solutions they suggest differ markedly.

As lawmakers, conservationists and Park Service officials plan for future visitors to the parks, here are some of the questions they are asking:

Does America need more national park land?

In his 1999 State of the Union address, President Clinton affirmed his intention to increase the amount of "conservation land" protected by the federal government. For the National Parks, the president's Lands Legacy Initiative has taken the form of a hoped-for increase in funding through the Land and Water Conservation Fund, which was established in 1964 to buy additional public lands using income generated by oil and gas leasing on the Outer Continental Shelf (OCS).

By 1980, Congress had authorized expenditures from the fund of up to $900 million a year, but actual appropriations generally have been far lower. Park supporters and conservationists have long argued that the intent of the original law has been subverted by diverting OCS income from making land purchases to un-

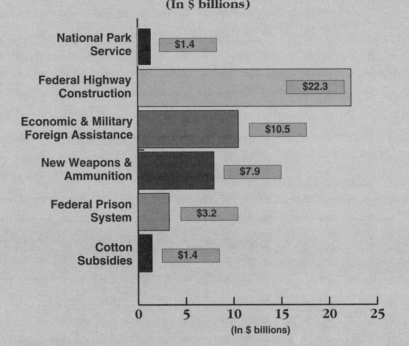

More Spent on Federal Prisons Than Parks

Contending that the nation's funding priorities are skewed, supporters of more spending on national parks note that the United States spends as much on cotton subsidies as it does on the park system and twice as much on federal prisons.

Comparing the National Park Service Budget, 1997
(In $ billions)

National Park Service	$1.4
Federal Highway Construction	$22.3
Economic & Military Foreign Assistance	$10.5
New Weapons & Ammunition	$7.9
Federal Prison System	$3.2
Cotton Subsidies	$1.4

(In $ billions)

Source: National Resources Defense Council and National Trust for Historic Preservation, "Reclaiming Our Heritage: What We Need to Do to Preserve America's Parks," 1997.

derwriting the national debt.

On May 1, the House passed a major land-conservation bill known as CARA — the Conservation and Reinvestment Act (HR 701). Backed by 315 Republican and Democratic cosponsors, the bill calls for setting aside $2.8 billion of the roughly $4 billion in annual gas and oil drilling fees for land acquisition and other environmental activities.

Of the total, some $450 million would be earmarked for federal land purchases, with an equal amount being made available to states through a grant program. The federal portion still would require an annual appro-

priation, but some supporters of the legislation argued that since the funds could be spent for nothing else, they likely would be appropriated.

CARA opponents contended that the bill would "infringe on private property rights and transfer power to federal officials," according to *The Washington Post.* "CARA stands for Congress Abdicating the Rights of Americans," said Rep. Jack Kingston, R-Ga. Rep. Helen Chenoweth-Hage, R-Idaho, asked rhetorically, "Why does the government need more land when they can't even take care of what they have?" [6]

Proponents of parks expansion

argue that land purchases are needed to protect resources and to prevent inappropriate uses, such as mining or housing development, not only near the parks but also within the parks. In the Mojave National Preserve, for example, "there are thousands of acres that are still privately owned inside the park. These lands could become pockets of development that could ruin the remote desert setting the preserve was created to protect," Thomas C. Kiernan, president of the National Parks Conservation Association (NPCA), told the Senate Committee on Energy and Natural Resources in May 1999.

The NPS estimates that it needs $1.5 billion just to acquire private inholdings within established park boundaries and otherwise complete existing National Parks within the continental U.S. and Hawaii, according to a 1997 report by the Natural Resources Defense Council (NRDC) and the National Trust for Historic Preservation (NTHP). The figure covers more than 349,000 acres in 102 different park units. When Alaska is included, the total of privately held land within National Park boundaries jumps to 4.75 million acres. [7]

"Unless Congress appropriates more of the funds it has committed to deliver, the Park Service cannot hope to come close to meeting the acquisition needs at the nation's parks," the report concludes. "Until it does, the public is not getting what it was promised when parks were established. Instead, mining, grazing, logging, and other commercial development incompatible with resource protection will continue to occur within and near the nation's

treasured parks."

Unlike the purchase of inholdings, creation of a new national park requires an act of Congress. The California Desert Lands Act created the last big park established by Congress. "Now, you can't get a good-sized park designated," says John Echeverria, director of the Environmental Policy Project at Georgetown University Law School. President Clinton has angered many lawmakers opposed to more parklands by creating National Monuments — a class of governmentally protected lands that does not require congres-

A herd of bison grazes in Yellowstone National Park, which the National Parks Conservation Association lists as one of the 10 most endangered national parks because of snowmobile incursions and air pollution.

Corbis Images

sional approval.

But Congress has continued to add about three smaller park units per year over the last two decades says Park Service spokesman David Barna. In 1998, Clinton signed the National Underground Railroad Network to Freedom Act, which protects dozens of sites associated with the secret escape routes used by slaves. Two sites connected with the Civil Rights Movement—Little Rock Central High School in Arkansas and Tuskegee Airmen National Historic Site in Alabama—were added in 1999, along with Min-

utemen Missile National Historic Site in South Dakota, which interprets the history of the Cold War. This May, the Park Service proposed special protection for a 1,500-acre site in Colorado to memorialize the massacre of 150 peaceful American Indians, mostly women and children, by 700 U.S. soldiers at Sand Creek in 1864. [8]

"If the National Park is to preserve history," Barna says, "absolutely, the system is going to grow." New historic sites will be added as America broadens its view of its history. "The Park Service sees itself as the teacher of democracy," Barna says. It begins with the Revolutionary War sites and presidents' homes. But, just as the Park Service has been seeking to add diversity to its employee base and broaden the diversity of the visitors it attracts, Barna says, it has a responsibility to include cultural and historical sites that tell the stories of all the peoples of the nation.

Periodically, lawmakers consider shrinking the National Park System. In 1996 a de-accessioning commission was proposed, but not approved, similar to that created for surplus military bases. In the mid-1990s, the 104th and 105th Congresses considered bills to facilitate the transfer of federally owned parklands to private interests. [9] Many critics of the park system contend that the system includes too many units that do not pass the test of national significance because they were created as pet projects of legislators, rather than for their overriding value to the nation.

Proponents of privatization argue that the Park Service should divest itself of its parks. Conservative economist Randal O'Toole of the Thoreau Institute invokes former Park Service Director James Ridenour. Ridenour coined the term "park barrel" to refer to parks created more as local economic-development projects than as legitimate additions to the National Park System."

O'Toole promotes radical decentralization of the parks, with each individual unit operating as a private business. He proposes that any site unable to cover its costs out of user fees and other income should be sold to nonprofit organizations or other federal or state agencies.

The Cato Institute goes further still. Arguing that "both environmental quality and economic efficiency would be enhanced by private rather than public ownership," the free-market think tank proposes that "all federally owned lands should be auctioned over the next 20 to 40 years, not for dollars, but for certificates to be distributed equally to all Americans." [10]

Proponents of the existing federally managed system, on the other hand, argue that expanding park boundaries, and having funds available to purchase adjacent land when development threatens, are essential to protecting the parks themselves.

"Purchasing and conserving additional available land and water resources remain an urgent need," concluded a recent report by seven conservation organizations, among them the National Audubon Society, the National Parks Conservation Association, and the Defenders of Wildlife. [11]

Ecologists contend that park boundaries do not generally correspond to the limits of the ecosystems of which the parks are a part. Consequently, they argue, activity adjacent to a park — such as the mining operation proposed in 1996 for a site that bordered Yellowstone — would produce runoff that would prove nearly as damaging to park resources

as if it had been built inside park boundaries.

"When we speak of our magnificent National Park System, we should recognize that what happens outside the parks is just as important as what happens inside," the NPCA's Kiernan testified in May. "If we are serious about preserving these places, we should be prepared to defend them from all threats, internal and external, even if it inconveniences us or requires economic sacrifices."

Will additional federal funding solve the National Park Service's problems?

For the past five years, since the end of budget cutting associated with deficit reduction, the NPS has enjoyed fairly steady budget increases, says Chuck Clusen of the NRDC. The funding includes about $1 billion a year for operating expenses, visitor services and resource protection. The administration's fiscal 2001 budget request is $2.04 billion, which is $233.5 million above the fiscal 2000 enacted level, but the Republican-dominated House reduced the level to $1.7 billion.

Yet the Park Service is often limited in how much it can spend on maintenance backlogs and scientific research. New construction projects and park purchases often take a big chunk of the budget, and, as one Park Service official said, those appropriations tend to be "very political."

"From fiscal year 1981 to fiscal year 1996," reports the NRDC and the NTHP, "Congress required the Park Service to complete $1.1 billion worth of projects it had not planned to do. Often these congressional add-ons are for new construction. As a result, not only does the backlog of existing repairs grow, but new maintenance responsibilities are added without additional funds to cover them."

In a 1997 story cataloging such "park barrel" projects, reporter Frank

Greve of Knight Ridder Newspapers pointed out that the projects also tend to be located in the districts of Congress members with clout. "While adding hundreds of millions of dollars for their own favored projects since 1994, lawmakers haven't been so kind to the Park Service," he wrote. "They've trimmed, on average, about a third of the money for construction and land-buying initiatives that the Park Service proposed." [12]

Rep. Ralph Regula, R-Ohio, chairman of the House Appropriations Interior Subcommittee, defended the practice. "We're the policy-makers," he told Greve. "There's nothing in the Constitution that says that a project requested by the administration is legitimate, and a project recommended by a member is not."

To Clusen of the NRDC, appropriation levels are simply too low. "When you stack appropriations up against so-called needs, this backlog of $8.5 billion, we'll never get it paid down. We won't even come close."

The NPCA has recommended that Congress give the Park Service more than $600 million annually in additional funding "to meet ongoing operational requirements, including visitor services and interpretive needs, public safety, research, and natural, recreational, and cultural resource management.

"We do not accept the assumption that the American public cannot pay for its parks with tax revenue. Parks are a quintessential governmental function, and the American public overwhelmingly supports funding parks through appropriations." [13]

Yet the NPCA is not averse to some of the many supplementary funding schemes that have emerged in response to federal budget capping and the growing push for privatization.

One experiment widely considered a success is the Recreation Fee Demonstration Program, established un-

Parks Funding Lagged Behind Visitor Demand

The number of visitors to America's national parks has increased by more than 64 million over the past two decades. But parks supporters say that funding actually has declined by about $635 million when funding increases are adjusted for inflation.

Visitors and Funding at U.S. National Parks, 1978-1998

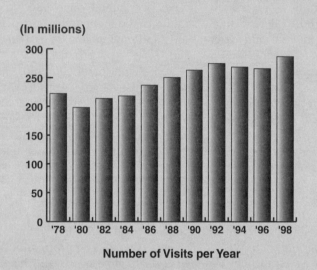

(In millions)

Number of Visits per Year

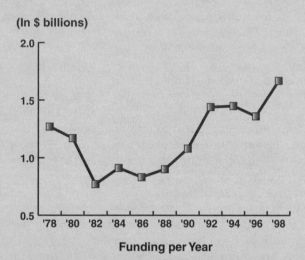

(In $ billions)

Funding per Year

Source: National Park Service

der the fiscal 1996 Omnibus Appropriations bill. The five-year program authorizes 100 Park Service units to increase or add new entrance or user fees, with the new income being returned to the parks instead of being added to general Treasury revenues. The estimate for NPS Demonstration Program receipts next year is $148.4 million. [14]

The demonstration program allows individual parks to keep 80 percent of the new revenue generated, with the other 20 percent going into a fund that benefits all units in the park system. The Park Service hopes to increase the percentage of fees that will go into the general NPS budget kitty from 20 to 40 percent, Barna says. For the life of the program, more than $600 million in additional funds will have been available to the Park Service to protect resources and infrastructure and to improve visitor services. [15]

The new fees have not deterred visitors, but expansion of the fee program to new parks also has not been suggested. It is considered more suitable for large, usually Western parks with complex infrastructure requirements, such as campgrounds, roadways and sewage and utility systems. And some observers worry that the system could lead to funding inequities among rich and poor parks, depending on visitation numbers and on which ones could raise fees.

In April, the NPS began selling a new National Parks Pass, which it projects to yield $168 million for the parks over five years. The $50 pass is available on-line from the NPS Web site and through the American Automobile Association and retail partners such as L.L. Bean.

Additional funds may be generated by raising the fees charged by the parks to commercial filmmakers,

who have used the parks as favorite settings since Westerns ruled the screen. As the law now stands, the Park Service can recoup only the cost of monitoring the filming, a negligible application fee and any cost of damage remediation. Hollywood paid just $300 when parts of "Star Trek" were shot in Yellowstone. The film went on to gross more than $50 million.

"It is simply unreasonable to ask the visiting public to pay increased entrance and user fees while at the same time fees for commercial uses of the national parks — from concessions to commercial filming — have remained astonishingly low, or even free," said Philip H. Voorhees, director of national programs at the NPCA. [16]

In 1998, Congress passed legislation to ensure that the government will receive a better return from concessionaires operating in the parks. That same year, both houses passed legislation giving the Park Service the authority to increase filming fees, but it was not enacted. Similar legislation has been proposed in the current 106th Congress.

However, Voorhees warned, "As with all user fees, whether derived from visitor entrance and use of the resources or commercial uses of the parks, it is vitally important that the Congress be mindful of the risk of creating perverse incentives for filming and other park activities. No matter the origin, fee streams should not be allowed to drive or otherwise influence park management decisions. Congress should be wary of 'incentivizing' commercial filming fees for park managers to the degree that the attraction of the additional revenues colors decision-making." [17]

But 'incentivizing' might be a good word for precisely what free-market advocates prescribe. "If we are to improve the condition of our parks," write Donald R. Leal and Holly L. Fretwell, "the incentives governing our parks must change. The goal should be to make them financially self-sufficient, supported by those who use them." [18]

The first step in getting there, they argue, is setting realistic fees. The National Center for Policy Analysis, a conservative research group based in Dallas, calls the current new fees "still dirt-cheap." The $20 per carload fee good for a week's stay at Yellowstone, they say, still is "only about one-eighth of what it cost, adjusted for inflation, when Woodrow Wilson was president."

To Fretwell and Leal, making each

national park self-sufficient, allowing it to charge for services and use the income for maintenance, would solve the problems of overuse and underfunding. "Self-sufficiency would give park managers an incentive to provide more services and maintain parks in good condition," they argue. "In contrast, a tax-financed park offers limited service, fails to collect fees and encourages park overuse by subsidizing goods and services."

Fretwell rejects the argument that higher fees will have an exclusionary effect. First, he says, even with any increases most parks will remain a

Environmentalists fear that a landfill being created adjacent to Southern California's Joshua Tree National Park will harm the site by depositing 20,000 tons of garbage a day in the desert.

bargain. Moreover, he says, visitation to the parks is already limited to those who can afford the transportation to get there, and the additional fees are a marginal addition that is unlikely to discourage visitors.

Fretwell and Leal also argue that fees would "free park managers from a major obstacle to protecting park resources — politics." Fretwell points to what she sees as egregious examples of government extravagance — $333,000 to build self-composting latrines in Delaware Water Gap National Recreation Area and $1 million

for a generator-equipped self-composting outhouse in Glacier National Park's back country. She contends the Glacier outhouse was built with the support of Montana Congress members despite the fact that less than 1 percent of park users will ever see it.

While most traditional park advocates are opposed to a financing system that they contend could bankrupt small and out-of-the-way parks and parks offering few obvious "services," they are not against free enterprise. Since passage of the National Parks Omnibus Management Act of 1998, park concessionaires are now required to return a larger percentage of their profits to the Park Service. Since 1990, the fastest growth in private support to the National Park Foundation has come from corporate partners. In 1996 alone, innovative partnerships with corporate donors generated nearly $4 million for national parks. The underwriting of Washington Monument restoration work by Target Stores is perhaps the most visible example. Log Cabin Syrup is donating $1 million toward the upkeep of log cabins in the park system.

In the mid-1990s, the Park Service even considered licensing its name to corporations. Conservation organizations wary of creating "the SUV of the National Park Service" or "Park Ranger Barbie" jumped on the enabling legislation and killed it, however. Today, Park Service spokesman Barna says, "We do not in any way allow contributors to advertise in the parks."

Another innovative proposal promoted by such organizations as the NRDC and the NTHP is to create a capital improvement fund financed through the sale of National Park bonds insured by the federal government. While the idea is still under consideration in Congress, the NRDC's Clusen says, the Treasury Department and Office of Management and Budget have registered strong opposition to the notion of federal bond issues pegged to specific purposes. "It would be a big precedent," Clusen concedes.

Can the Park Service protect both natural resources and cultural monuments?

The Park Service actively preserves America's historic landmarks. It maintains the National Register of Historic Places — a catalog of the country's structures, parks and neighborhoods, and objects with architectural or historical significance. The NPS also reviews federally funded projects to assess their effects on historic resources; maintains the Historic American Engineering Record and the Historic American Buildings Survey; and oversees grants to states for preservation activities, among numerous other responsibilities.

Within the national parks themselves, Park Service Director Robert G. Stanton said at the 1999 National Preservation Conference in Washington, D.C, "almost 60 percent [of the units] exist mainly to preserve and interpret to the public our nation's cultural resources. We are also doing more than ever before to preserve and interpret cultural resources in our largely natural and recreational parks." [19]

But to many critics, the Park Service still is not doing enough. "We

have found that within some of the big national parks there has been a lack of protection of cultural resources," says Barbara Pahl, the director of the National Trust's Mountains/Plains Office. With financial resources short, management decisions often seem to require trade-offs, Pahl says, noting that "the staff has a lot more biologists, etc., than it has architectural historians." [20]

In Elkmont, Tenn., preservationists have been fighting for years to prevent the Park Service from demolishing some 60 old bungalows in Great Smoky Mountains National Park

Grand Teton National Park represents the ruggedness of the West. But the National Park Service fears tourists may be a little too rugged on it. Scientists are studying the impact of visitors and pollution on this and several other national parks.

that reflect the area's history as a summer resort. Ironically, the Park Service itself prepared and approved the application to list the properties in the National Register.

The Park Service has become more sensitive to the value of cultural resources "since the 1930s, when it tore down hundreds of buildings and moved them around to save a specimen here and there," says John Hildreth, director of the Trust's Southern Office. But, he says, "there's still a heavy bias against cultural resources. They're definitely a second-

tier resource within the minds of many Park Service officials."

Cumberland Island National Seashore provides a good example of the management issues that emerge when cultural- and natural-resource values clash. Much of the property within the reserve was donated by the owners of elaborate summer "cottages" there — Rockefellers, Vanderbilts and the like. One of the most outstanding, "Plum Orchard," stands in a remote setting surrounded by wilderness. How are visitors to access the historic house without negatively impacting its fragile coastal environment? "It's a very difficult management issue," Hildreth concedes.

At an April hearing of the Senate Appropriations Subcommittee on the Interior and Related Agencies, Interior Secretary Bruce Babbitt voiced support for the demolition of Many Glacier Hotel, a National Historic Landmark. Sen. Conrad Burns, R-Mont., quickly responded with a press release saying that "Glacier National Park and its historic buildings hold a very dear place in the hearts of Montanans, and I think it's very premature and irresponsible for Secretary Babbitt to be discussing [its] destruction."

Given the millions of dollars needed to repair a large, old structure like Many Glaciers, cultural resource advocates see salvation in the promotion of creative partnerships that could harness private dollars for rehabilitation without compromising preservation standards or natural resource goals. One such experiment is now under way at Rocky Mountain National Park, where the Park Service an-

Making the Presidio Self-Sufficient

When the federal government decided in 1989 to close the Presidio, the vast U.S. military base overlooking San Francisco's Golden Gate, the National Park Service drew up plans to manage it along with the adjacent Golden Gate National Recreation Area.

It seemed to many a natural next step. The Presidio's windswept, 1,500-acre site commands stunning vistas of San Francisco Bay and contains a wealth of natural resources. In addition, some 550 buildings are listed in the National Register of Historic Places. Other cultural and historic resources reflect the site's occupation by the native Ohlone people, by Spain and Mexico, as well as its service to the U.S. military from the Revolutionary War to the present.

But the plan to add it to the National Park System encountered a formidable obstacle. The 104th Congress included numerous staunch opponents of expanding the federal parks realm. Indeed, legislation was being considered that would have divested the government of the national parks, even sold off the public lands to help balance the federal budget. The legislative compromise that saved the Presidio launched a unique experiment in park management — one that critics say never should be repeated.

"I'm wildly opposed to it as a model," says Johanna Wald, director of the land program at the Natural Resources Defense Council (NRDC) in San Francisco. "This might actually be self-sustainable because of the reservoir of opportunity to earn money. But 99.9 percent of our parks aren't like that at all."

While the Presidio is considered a national park, the Park Service controls only the coastal fringe. The rest is managed by the nonprofit Presidio Trust, which is responsible not to the U.S. Department of the Interior but directly to Congress. The park must be self-supporting by 2013 or the land and buildings will be sold off.

"The site and the Presidio Trust [managers] are under heavy scrutiny," says Courtney Damkroger, assistant director of the Western Regional Office of the National Trust for Historic Preservation. "They're charged with a delicate balancing act of meeting the self-sufficiency mandate while also operating a national park."

Observers say that the Presidio's financial goal is probably attainable. Unlike any other national park, the Presidio contains 3.5 million square feet of usable building space amid one of the tightest real estate markets in the country.[1] Renters already occupy many of the buildings. Some 80 historic structures have been refurbished and leased.

Recently, officials approved plans for filmmaker George Lucas to build a 23-acre Digital Arts Center on the site of the historic Letterman Hospital. The facility will contribute about $5 million per year toward the estimated $36 million annual cost of maintaining the park. The Lucas proposal touched off a controversy that underscored complaints about the Presidio's unusual management structure, most of them focusing on uncertainty about the board's overall plans for the property.

"This is the largest single development decision the trust will be making," says Wald. "It will have significant environmental impacts on traffic, water use, visitor experience, trees and nearby historic resources."

Wald contends that the Presidio Trust, while stressing the pressure to achieve financial self-sufficiency, has provided little information to allow the public to evaluate the proposal.

A detailed plan does exist for the park, one drawn up by the Park Service when it expected to take over management. Those plans call for the park's historic structures to be leased to private companies, nonprofits and government agencies dedicated to solving global problems, such as environmental degradation.

The Presidio, a decommissioned military base in San Francisco, has been turned into a national park.

KRT Photo/Tracy Everbach

Many current tenants do fall into that category, but increasingly, newer occupants do not. A recent agreement leases 62,000 square feet to the Hambrecht Co., which handles Internet stock trades. Park advocates question whether creating a haven for dot-com companies is appropriate for a national park. But under the legislation that created the Presidio Trust, such decisions are left to the trust's Board of Directors.

"They're mandated to preserve resources, but first and foremost they're mandated to achieve self-sufficiency," says Brian Huse, Pacific Region director of the National Parks and Conservation Association. "Major stakeholders and the National Park Service have been cut out of the process. The financial mandate creates a lot of stress."

---

[1] Johanna H. Wald, "The Presidio Trust and Our National Parks: Not a Model to be Trusted" *Golden Gate University Law Review*, Vol. 28.

nounced in the early 1990s that it would demolish the buildings of McGraw Ranch, which it had purchased in the late 1980s. Now the Park Service is working with a non-profit organization to convert the buildings into a research center. A mammoth experiment in private-public cooperation at the Presidio in San Francisco has become a more controversial example. (*See sidebar, p. 163.*)

But given the number of structures in national parks that the Park Service values primarily as wilderness and wildlife habitat, even preservation supporters like Rheba Massey see a problem. A former historian and preservation planner with the Wyoming State Historic Preservation Office, Massey surveyed the historic ranch structures in Grand Teton National Park. Some have been used by the Park Service for housing or offices, and a Wilderness School has been allowed to reuse some others.

"There are a lot of beautiful, old dude ranches that could be re-used," she says. But, she concedes, finding uses for so many historic structures is a legitimate problem, especially when the roads that provide access to the structures have been closed in the interests of wildlife preservation. ■

BACKGROUND

A New Concept

America's national parks were born when the country itself was still largely wilderness, and the federal government was busily divesting itself of the public domain—assigning lands obtained through purchase and conquest to homesteaders, miners, railroad men and other 19th-century "developers."

Congress created the world's first national park in 1872, setting aside more than 2 million acres for Yellowstone Park, mostly in what is now northwestern Wyoming. Eight years earlier, however, lawmakers had set a precedent for reserving scenic lands for public enjoyment, transferring ownership of the beautiful Yosemite Valley to California for "public use, resort and recreation . . . inalienable for all time." (In 1906 the state lands would be returned to become part of Yosemite Park as we know it today.) [21]

No sooner had President Abraham Lincoln signed over the Yosemite Valley and the Mariposa Grove of Giant Sequoias to California then private landowners like James Mason Hutchins, who had led the first tourist expedition to Yosemite in 1855, began complaining about their claims being nullified by legislation. The never-ending conflict between government and Western property owners had begun.

Yet the relationship between public and private interests would not always be antagonistic. As historian Sellars notes, the creation of Yellowstone set the tone and image of national parks that endure to this day: "Vast and spectacularly beautiful, Yellowstone provided . . . the most enduring image of a national park: a romantic landscape of mountains, canyons, abundant wildlife, and fantastic natural phenomena." [22]

Yellowstone also reflected a complex intermingling of corporate, governmental and altruistic motivations that similarly has characterized the national parks ever since. In the case of Yellowstone, it was the Northern Pacific Railroad that promoted the park's creation. "By preventing private land claims and limiting competition for tourism in Yellowstone," Sellars writes, "the federal reservation of the area

served, in effect, as a huge appendage to the Northern Pacific's anticipated monopoly across southern Montana Territory."

Sequoia and Yosemite (1890), Mount Rainier (1899) and Glacier (1910) national parks also were "to a large degree the result of the railroads' political pressure," according to Sellars. Railroad interests did not always get their way—in the mid-1880s Congress defeated a proposal by rail and mining interests to build a railroad through northern Yellowstone and reduce the park in size. But creation and promotion of the parks gave the railroads an enticing marketing device. Tourism became a powerful new economic engine shaping the face of the West. Meeting travelers' needs for transportation, food, lodging and diversion would become a controlling concern for the parks' federal managers. [23]

An Expanding Mandate

The Antiquities Act, passed by Congress in 1906, extended the umbrella of federal protection to cover not only resources of great scenic and natural splendor but also lands of historic, prehistoric and scientific value. Provoked by concern about the destruction and looting by pot hunters of Native American ruins in the Southwest, the act established fines for looting and injuring prehistoric artifacts on public lands. Just a few days earlier, Mesa Verde Park had been created to protect the extraordinary cliff dwellings in southwestern Colorado.

The Antiquities Act also provided a legal mechanism by which lands could be set aside as federal reserves without congressional authorization. President Theodore Roosevelt, the national voice for the country's grow-

Chronology

1870s *As the federal government divests itself of public lands, railroad interests and nature lovers press for creation of a scenic reserve.*

1872
Congress passes the Yellowstone Park Act to provide for the "preservation, from injury or spoliation, of all timber, mineral deposits, natural curiosities, or wonders within said park." President Grant signs the bill on March 1, 1872, creating the world's first national park.

1900s *As the number of national parks grows, the federal government expands its purview to include resources of concern to anthropologists and archeologists.*

1906
Concerned about vandalism at prehistoric cliff dwellings, Congress creates Mesa Verde National Park. The Antiquities Act makes it a crime to take artifacts from federal lands.

1910s *With creation of the National Park Service, a philosophy of developing the parks as scenic attractions takes hold.*

Aug. 25, 1916
President Woodrow Wilson signs the National Park Service Act, creating the new bureau within the Department of the Interior.

1930s *Under the New Deal, Park Service responsibilities expand. Wildlife biologists for the first time propose to perpetuate and even restore natural conditions in the parks.*

1933
President Franklin D. Roosevelt gives the Park Service responsibility for managing numerous relatively small sites notable for their historical associations.

1950s *After wartime cutbacks, funding for the Park Service expands to meet the demand from young.*

1956
In February, Park Service Director Conrad Wirth formally announces Mission 66. The 10-year program produces more than $1 billion of new, usually modern-style construction.

1960s-1970s *A growing conservation movement wins legislative victories, and the Park Service notes its scientific shortcomings.*

1962
The Leopold Commission charts a course of "natural regulation" for Park Service wildlife management and calls for an infusion of science into park management.

1964
The Wilderness Act authorizes federal land managers, including the Park Service, to designate protected areas.

1970
The National Environmental Policy Act requires resource-management decisions to be based on scientific analysis and prescribes public review of environmental impact statements.

1980s *Reagan administration gives opponents of federal land control greater access to government.*

1983
Interior Secretary James Watt resigns after less than three years during which the economic exploitation of lands near the parks is encouraged, along with easier public access to the parks.

1990s-2000s *Despite the efforts of some legislators to shed national parks, the Clinton administration fights to expand them.*

March 1995
The Park Service releases gray wolves in Yellowstone despite the protests of nearby ranchers.

1998
National Parks Omnibus Management Act adds three large, new Park Service units in California: Death Valley, Joshua Tree and the Mojave National Preserve.

May 2000
A controlled "burn" in Bandelier National Monument destroys hundreds of homes and 50,000 acres of New Mexico land.

ing conservation movement, applied it enthusiastically, setting aside numerous monuments that would eventually be designated as national parks, among them Devils Tower, Chaco Canyon and Grand Canyon.

The Organic Act creating the NPS in 1916 brought together 36 disparate parks under one bureaucratic roof. Two of the leading advocates of the new agency — Chicago businessman Stephen T. Mather and lawyer Horace M. Albright — served as the NPS's first and second directors, respectively. Throughout their tenure, from 1916 to 1933, they would continue to seek public acceptance and political support for the parks by opening them to ever-greater public use.

"In the administration of the parks the greatest good to the greatest number is always the most important factor determining the policy of the Service," Mather said in 1920. [24]

As if in anticipation of conflict to come, Mather also founded in 1919, along with Park Service official Robert Sterling Yard and 100 other business leaders, scientists and scholars, the National Parks Association, now the NPCA, in order "to defend the National Parks and Monuments fearlessly against assaults of private interests and aggressive commercialism."

With the 1926 addition of Great Smoky Mountains National Park, more than 500,000 acres in Tennessee and North Carolina, what had begun as a mostly Western Park Service took on national scope. And beginning in the 1930s, the Park Service became increasingly involved in preserving America's historic as well as its natural, treasures.

Postwar Expansion

President Franklin D. Roosevelt re-organized and expanded the responsibilities of the National Park Service. Among 56 sites added were Jamestown and Yorktown in Virginia, the birthplaces of Presidents Washington and Lincoln, an array of Civil War battlefields and the National Capital Parks in Washington, D.C. Since 1933, a majority of the areas added to the National Park System have been recognized largely for their cultural significance. [25]

The NPS also oversaw the operations of some 600 camps of the Civilian Conservation Corps (CCC), Roosevelt's scheme for providing employment to more than 120,000 Depression-idled men while contributing countless new projects to the national infrastructure.

A total of 118 CCC camps were located in the national parks, where workers constructed bridges, roads, buildings and hundreds of recreational facilities, many still in use. [26]

CCC funding also paid for the first sizable group of biologists to work in the parks. The Park Service's commitment to scientific study of its natural resources had until then been limited to survey work by a small band, led and paid for by George Wright, a wealthy biologist.

By 1936, the number of professionally trained wildlife biologists had grown from the original three-man survey team to 27 biologists. But by January 1940, the biologists had been transferred out of the Park Service.

Not surprisingly, World War II brought a severe reduction in Park Service funding. Appropriations dropped from $21.1 million in 1940 to $4.6 million in 1944. Once war ended, however, they recovered quickly, with appropriations back up to $26 million by 1947. [27]

After the war, with the number of young families booming and more and more of them owning cars, visi-tors to national parks shot up. Visitation levels had returned to the pre-war high of 20 million-plus by 1946, then doubled by 1952. Despite facilities that had suffered badly from the neglect of the war years, the parks welcomed more than 70 million visitors per year by 1960.

To meet the growing visitor demand, Park Service Director Conrad L. Wirth in 1956 proposed a 10-year reinvestment and development program called Mission 66. President Dwight D. Eisenhower endorsed it, and Congress provided funding of more than $1 billion.

"When facilities are adequate in number, and properly designed and located, large numbers of visitors can be handled readily and without damage to the areas," Wirth said. "Good development saves the landscape from ruin, protecting it for its intended recreational and inspirational values." [28]

The program repaired or built more than 3,000 miles of roads and 1,800 parking areas; opened 575 new campgrounds; and erected more than 1,200 employee-housing units and 114 visitor centers.

Wilderness Act of 1964

Despite Wirth's eco-friendly rationale for his new building program, which favored modernist glass-and-steel structures over the traditional rustic Park Service style, Mission 66 encountered stiff opposition from the growing conservation movement, particularly the newly activist and confrontational Sierra Club.

"A lot of environmentalists cut their teeth fighting Mission 66 projects," says the NTHP's Pahl.

The Wilderness Act of 1964 demonstrated the burgeoning strength of the environmental movement. The tough, new law established a process

The Fight to Save the Everglades

Few national parks are more at the mercy of the surrounding lands than Everglades National Park. Although the vast 1.5-million-acre park is the third largest outside Alaska, it is only the southern tip of a swampy ecosystem that covers roughly the southern third of Florida.

"Most national parks don't have the luxury of taking in the whole ecosystem on which they depend," says Rick Cook, the park's public affairs officer. "But just a quick glance at a map will show you that we're at the bottom of the watershed here. We depend almost totally on actions taken outside the park."

For nearly 50 years, government and commerce seem to have been working, often with the best intentions, to deprive the Everglades of its lifeblood — unpolluted water. As urbanization and agriculture have consumed land to the north and east, drainage, flood control and water-supply projects have re-directed the age-old flow of fresh water, leaving some areas of the park inundated and others parched. Runoff from agricultural operations and other pollutants has altered water chemistry, disrupting the natural plant cover and sparking huge algae blooms in Florida Bay.

Now, efforts are under way to undo the damage. It's a project "unprecedented in world history," says National Parks Conservation Association (NPCA) Vice President Ron Tipton, "to try to restore a significant part of a major ecosystem."

The Clinton administration made restoration of the Everglades and the South Florida ecosystem one of its highest environmental priorities in 1993, when federal agencies established the South Florida Ecosystem Restoration task force to coordinate their activities in the area. The Water Resources Development Act of 1996 formalized the Task Force under the chairmanship of the secretary of the Interior and expanded membership to include state, local and tribal representatives. According to General Accounting Office estimates, the federal government allocated more than $1.2 billion to restoration efforts between 1993 and 1999.[1]

In July 1999, the Army Corps of Engineers issued a plan to re-engineer the hydrologic system of the South Florida basin so as to capture, store and move a larger percentage of fresh water from Central Florida into the Everglades.

A boater slips through a recently opened section of the threatened Florida Everglades.

Newsmakers/Tim Chapman

The projected cost was $7.8 billion over the next 20 years.

Funding the massive effort awaits congressional approval. Legislation now being considered would fund 11 out of the 60-odd projects planned at an overall cost of $1 to $2 billion. Gov. Jeb Bush, R-Fla., recently signed a bill committing $2 billion over the next 10 years.

Success will require extraordinary cooperation among agencies and interests that have often found themselves at odds in the past. "It's kind of unusual to find the Army Corps of Engineers leading a green parade," says Tipton. But, as Chuck Clusen of the Natural Resources Defense Council points out, "Having a national park there is not just very nice; it's essential to the preservation of our urban life."

Environmentalists see a major threat in a current proposal to build a new commercial airport on the former site of Homestead Air Force Base to the east of the park. "In my opinion, it's completely incompatible with restoration," says Ken Collins of the NPCA. "If you're going to spend $8 billion to restore the natural ecosystem, it doesn't make sense to build a major airport next door."

The Air Force is currently completing a Supplemental Environmental Impact Statement for the airport, and a decision is expected from the White House this fall or winter. The Department of the Interior favors an alternative proposal calling for mixed use at the site.

Park supporters also worry that after the engineering is done to redirect water to the Everglades, day-to-day water-management decisions will continue to shortchange natural resources. "How can we be assured the Everglades will get its share?" Tipton asks. "It never has. When you get to the point where people are turning the spigot off and on, choosing among agriculture, flood control, easing a water shortage, they just say, 'Too bad Everglades.'"

The key to success, according to Tipton and Cook, is including "assurances language" in federal legislation funding the restoration. "So much has been done in the name of Everglades restoration that has later been turned around and operated for other purposes," Cook says. "Especially for the costs involved, this should really assist the Everglades."

[1] General Accounting Office, "South Florida Ecosystem Restoration: An Overall Strategic Plan and a Decision-Making Process are Needed to Keep the Effort on Track," April 22, 1999.

for federal land managers, including the Park Service, to study and then designate protected, road-free wilderness areas. Soon afterward, the 1970 National Environmental Policy Act required all federal agencies to assess the environmental impacts of proposed actions. "Besides the Park Service Organic Act," says Park Service historian Dwight Rettie, "no single law has probably had such profound and enduring influence on the work of NPS."

Meanwhile, Park Service personnel were slowly beginning to consider the state of the resource base itself. In 1962, Secretary of the Interior Stuart Udall persuaded A. Starker Leopold, a professor of biology and the son of famed ecologist Aldo Leopold, to head a "blue ribbon" committee of wildlife specialists to study the service's wildlife-management practices. They concluded that "within reason" the Park Service should conserve and restore wildness "by allowing natural processes to proceed unimpeded." The adoption of management by "natural regulation" that ensued would, in turn, provoke its own critics. [29]

In 1971, Congress created a process that would add vast acreage to the National Park System. The Alaska Native Claims Settlement Act permitted the president to set aside up to 80 million acres in Alaska for national parks and forests, wildlife refuges or wild and scenic rivers systems. After years of study and political wrangling, including the unilateral creation of 15 new national monuments by President Jimmy Carter, the Alaska National Interest Lands Conservation Act of 1980 added more than 47 million acres to the National Park System. Since World War II, the National Park System had more than doubled in acreage, and by 1980 visitation had risen from about 20 million to nearly 300 million. ■

CURRENT SITUATION

Legislative Initiatives

The Reagan presidency briefly stanched the conservationist tide. The short but controversial tenure of Interior Secretary James Watt afforded a hearing for Western proponents of private development in and around the public lands and a less biocentric approach to their management. Nonetheless, Park Service appropriations first exceeded $1 billion in fiscal 1989, the second year of George Bush's presidency.

Debate about how to run the Park Service has been influenced by the calls for a more businesslike approach to government that began during the Reagan era. A $34 million budget shortfall in 1993 caused the first highly visible cutbacks in public services, such as campground closings, and undoubtedly raised public awareness of budget issues within the Park Service. Free-market environmentalist Fretwell considers the closings as a form of grandstanding. "If you can show a really popular park is going to close," she said, "Congress will increase the budget." [30]

But belt-tightening in the mid-1990s by President Clinton and the Republican Congress added impetus to efforts to make the Park Service less dependent on federal funding. Many of the resulting initiatives — a fee system, for example, and expansion of the number of parks for which reservations are required — were welcomed by conservationists and privatization advocates alike.

Legislation sponsored by Sens. Craig Thomas, R-Wyo., and Dale Bumpers, D-Ark., and passed on Nov.

13, 1998, enabled the Park Service to increase its share of the revenue from hotels, restaurants and countless other businesses operated within the parks. And private funding sources are being expanded, notably through the congressionally chartered National Park Foundation.

At the same time, pleas continued for improving the Park Service's scientific capabilities. In 1992, a National Research Council committee warned, "The nation cannot afford to wait any longer for NPS to move toward a new mandate for science. The Park Service is entrusted to manage some of the nation's most treasured resources, and science is an indispensable tool in that process." [31]

Babbitt, a former Democratic senator from Arizona, brought a reputation as a strong environmentalist to his post as secretary of the Interior under President Clinton, and on his watch the Park Service has aggressively supported park ecosystems, sometimes to the displeasure of nearby landowners. When grey wolves were reintroduced in Yellowstone and central Idaho in 1995, for example, a move intended to restore a natural balance to animal populations by returning the ecosystem's largest predators, ranchers complained that the wolves posed a threat to their livestock.

Throughout the park system, new emphasis has been given to controlling and, when possible, removing invasive, non-native plants and animals. The tamarisk shrubs in the Grand Canyon, for example, have overtaken much of the diverse, native vegetation along the Colorado River. But even with invasive plants, politics sometimes comes into play. In the Great Smoky Mountains, hunters opposed Park Service efforts to remove the descendants of European wild boars, which have wrought havoc with native vegetation. The

At Issue:

Should national parks become self-supporting entities run like businesses instead of funded by Congress?

DONALD R. LEAL AND HOLLY L. FRETWELL
From "Back to the Future to Save Our Parks"

POLITICAL ECONOMY RESEARCH CENTER, JUNE 1997

*p*ark management continues "as is" in spite of the parks' deterioration only because the money to operate parks comes from taxes, not customers. If we are to improve our parks, the incentives governing [them] must change. The goal should be to make them financially self-sufficient, supported by those who use them.

Self-sufficiency means relying on park visitors, not Congress, for operating support. (True self-sufficiency would mean covering . . . capital improvements, too, but self-sufficiency in operations would be an important start.) Attaining self-sufficiency will require . . . charging higher fees and practicing greater diligence in fee collection.

There are several reasons why our park systems should move toward self-sufficiency. First, self-sufficiency would give park managers an incentive to provide more services and maintain parks in good condition. Park managers who depend on visitors for funds want them to have a memorable experience that brings them back. Unhappy customers will be less likely to return.

Self-sufficiency would also encourage more realistic pricing . . . and careful attention to collecting lawful fees. In contrast, a tax-financed park offers limited service, fails to collect fees and encourages park overuse by subsidizing goods and services.

Self-sufficiency would also give park management an incentive to balance costs and benefits. Since costs must be covered out of revenues, managers would add services that covered costs and eliminate those that didn't. In contrast, when park operations are mostly funded by taxes, management can ignore such economic realities. . . .

Self-sufficiency would also free park managers from a major obstacle to protecting park resources — politics. Because most national park funding is controlled by Congress, park managers must cater to politicians and special interests. . . . And when public funds are appropriated, they tend to flow to bureaucratic support and not to the parks themselves.

The great benefit of self-sufficiency is that it is a spur to provide more services. While it is difficult to say whether a park with many services is "better" than a park with fewer services, revenues tend to grow. This indicates that the parks with more services are pleasing their customers. At the same time, we have found no evidence that greater services damage the environment of the parks. Indeed, the greater flexibility and availability of funds suggest the opposite.

LISA A. GUIDE
Deputy Assistant Secretary for Policy and International Affairs, U.S. Department of the Interior

WRITTEN FOR *THE CQ RESEARCHER*

*t*he proponents of national parks "self-sufficiency" want America's crown jewels to resemble businesses more than public resources. What kind of business would our parks look like if their wishes came true? Try McDonald's, Taco Bell or Disney World.

Let's imagine a visit to Grand Canyon National Park for a family of four: After paying a $300 entrance fee, our visitors would drive by a strip of chain hotels, fast-food restaurants and souvenir stands. Private vendors would abound, hawking everything from Vishnu schist — one of the oldest kinds of canyon rock — to photos with a life-size cardboard cutout of President Teddy Roosevelt, who created the park in 1919. The nearby theme park would feature a harrowing water ride to simulate the effects of a canyon flash flood. Phantom Ranch, the comfortable lodge at the canyon's base, would become a four-star resort. And it would be too expensive for most Americans.

Such a fanciful description of a for-profit park does not belittle the idea of effective government spending. National parks should be run efficiently. But parks are not businesses — they were not created to return a profit. They were created as a resource for the public.

We don't expect our nation's highway system should pay for itself — why would we expect that of our parks? Americans value the quiet beauty of parks — something that can't be expressed in dollars.

People respect and enjoy national parks because they are authentic, irreplaceable. Ask yourself: Could the Frederick Douglass National Historic Site, the Women's Rights National Historical Park or George Washington's birthplace exist as money-makers? No. Are these pieces of history to be honored and preserved? Absolutely.

The National Park Service is addressing a serious maintenance and improvements backlog. It has started a successful pilot project to determine if Americans are willing to pay greater fees to support parks. Since 1996, the Park Service has collected more than $323 million extra from 100 of those sites — all going to direct park improvements.

In 1912, James Bryce, the British ambassador to the United States, said: "The national park is the best idea America ever had." He's still right today. The fundamental concept behind that idea is the protection of our country's incomparable beauty, while making it available to all.

animals were introduced by a commercial hunting operation early in the 20th century. Now the Park Service is trying another approach, reintroducing captive red wolves into the park.

In 1997, Robert G. Stanton, a career NPS official, replaced Park Service Director Roger Kennedy. In August 1999, Stanton released a plan to strengthen scientific research and natural resource programs in the parks. The document begins with a startling acknowledgment: "The lack of information about park plants, animals, ecosystems and their interrelationships is profound. If we are to protect these resources into the far future, we must know more."

The plan's overriding goal "is to preserve park resources." To support the effort, it calls for a five-year effort that doubles funding levels for natural-resources management.

The Bandelier Burn

Another volatile issue came to the fore in May when an attempt to set a controlled "burn" in Bandelier National Monument got out of control and destroyed hundreds of homes and some 50,000 acres of New Mexico land. Efforts to place blame for the fire will doubtless have serious repercussions for Park Service personnel. But it is instructive, too, to consider the fierceness of the fire as a logical outcome of decades of Park Service policy that suppressed natural processes in the service of human goals.

Left to itself, a ponderosa pine forest contains a mixture of tall, old-growth trees and low vegetation and brush. Natural fires, sparked usually by lightning strikes, burn the brush and grasses without damaging the trees. Suppress the fires—as the Park Service did for decades in the interest of human safety—and the brush accumulates, along with underbrush and young trees that act like tinder in the event of a fire, burning so

much hotter that the trees themselves go up in flames.

The NPS has practiced prescribed burning for decades. But as with other policies where human pursuits, from snowmobiling to hunting to simply driving through a spectacular landscape, conflict with naturally occurring phenomena, decisions about managing those pursuits become freighted with conflicting goals. ■

OUTLOOK

Resources First

On March 27, Babbitt unveiled a new long-range plan for the Yosemite Valley that clearly embodies the Park Service's current philosophy of resource-first management. Twenty years after the Park Service stopped stocking the Yosemite's rivers with nonnative fish, the plan aims to limit infrastructure, reduce congestion and restore fragile ecosystems.

The plan responds to a natural event in 1997 that did what the Park Service itself would probably not be able to accomplish — it washed away two major, popular campsites along the Merced River in Yosemite. Now the Park Service hopes to revive the rare, oak woodland habitat that the campgrounds had replaced and allow native aquatic wildlife to recover, a goal that requires the removal of a dam and three bridges. The 10-year project will cost some $300 million.

But with the Merced running deeper and colder to support fish populations, it will also become less hospitable to swimmers and rafters. That sets up the age-old conflict between preservation and recreational use of National Park resources that was embodied in the Park Service's

Organic Act of 1916 continues to play itself out, and will continue to do so.

Current conflicts focus on snowmobile and Jet-Ski use in the parks. Following a lawsuit alleging environmental damage from snowmobiles in Yellowstone and Grand Teton national parks, the Park Service issued a proposed winter use plan for Yellowstone that is expected to ban use of the vehicles, which opponents contend emit a thousand times as much pollution as cars. In April, the Park Service announced that it would ban nearly all snowmobile traffic in 25 national parks and other areas.

"Industry representatives and snowmobile advocates blasted the decision as hasty, unwarranted, and overreaching," *The Washington Post* reported. [32] Edward Klim, president of the International Snowmobile Manufacturers' Association, invoked the specter of governmental exclusionism. "This may be happening to snowmobiles today, but I tell you, tomorrow it will be campers, and the next day it will be sport utility vehicles," he said. "It's part of a planned campaign by this administration to limit public access to public lands." [33]

But environmental groups point out that regulations have been on the books since 1972 that should have prevented snowmobilers from using the parks years ago and that the ban is necessary to protect public resources, including peace and quiet, from pollution, damage to wildlife and other environmental degradation.

During his last year in office, President Clinton has, indeed, sought to establish his legacy as an environmental president. But his power has been checked by the Republican congress, which has proved unreceptive to large new land reservations. Instead, Clinton has resorted to the time-honored tactic of creating National Monuments under the Antiquities Act. In April he declared Giant Sequoia National Monument in Central California—the fifth of his administration. His opponents in the House responded by amending an appropriations bill to forbid federal agencies to develop management plans for four of the monuments.

In its formative years, the National Park Service pursued development of the parks for human enjoyment and tourism—stocking rivers with non-native fish, for instance, wiping out predatory animals, and building lodges and roadways intended to promote the parks' scenic, rustic atmosphere. In 1922, the superintendent of Sequoia National Park, John White, summed up the dilemma, stating that the Park Service's "biggest problem" was to develop the parks "without devitalizing them; to make them accessible and popular, but not vulgar; to bring in the crowds and yet to maintain an appearance of not being crowded." [34]

The crowds White envisioned were puny by contrast with today's visitation figures, but the push and pull of competing values and uses remains. Privatization advocates believe that the market should be allowed to decide which ones carry the day. Historic preservationists worry that environmentalists overlook cultural values in their devotion to the value of the ecosystem.

With a national election coming up, the personnel who will supervise decision-making are sure to change. Whether decision making will occur in the presence of more or less financial resources will largely turn on the outcome of that political struggle. ∎

Notes

[1] National Parks Conservation Association, "Strategic Agenda," p. 3. For background, see Richard L. Worsnop, "National Parks," *The CQ Researcher*, May 28, 1993, pp. 457-480.
[2] Sharon Buccino, Charles Clusen, Ed Norton and Johanna Wald, "Reclaiming Our Heritage: What We Need to Do to Preserve America's National Parks," Natural Resources Defense Council and National Trust for Historic Preservation, 1997.
[3] National Park Service, "Statistical Abstract," 1998.
[4] For background, see Mary H. Cooper, "Energy and the Environment," *The CQ Researcher*, March 3, 2000, pp. 161-184 and Mary H. Cooper, "New Air Quality Standards," *The CQ Researcher*, March 7, 1997, pp. 193-216.
[5] Richard Sellars, *Preserving Nature in the National Parks* (1997), p. 4.
[6] Quoted in *The Washington Post*, May 2, 2000.
[7] Buccino et al, *op. cit.*, p. 15.
[8] *The New York Times*, May 10, 2000.
[9] National Parks Conservation Association, "Park Policy Agenda," p. 8.
[10] Terry L. Anderson, Vernon L. Smith and Emily Simmons, "How and Why to Privatize Public Lands," 1999, The Cato Institute.
[11] NPCA, *op. cit.*, p. 15.
[12] Frank Greve, "Senior Legislators Claim Park Funds for Pet Projects," *The Washington Post*, Dec. 1, 1997.
[13] National Parks Conservation Association, "Park Policy Agenda," *op. cit.*, p. 25.
[14] National Park Service, "Bureau Highlights," BH-59.
[15] *Ibid*.
[16] Testimony of Philip H. Voorhees before House Subcommittee on National Parks and Public Lands, Feb. 4, 1999.
[17] *Ibid*.
[18] Donald R. Leal and Holly L. Fretwell, "Back to the Future to Save Our Parks," Political Economy Research Center, 1997.
[19] National Trust for Historic Preservation, *Forum Journal*, winter 2000, p. 28.
[20] For background, see Richard L. Worsnop, "Historic Preservation," *The CQ Researcher*, Oct. 7, 1994, pp. 865-888.
[21] For a discussion of the first national park, see Dwight F. Rettie, *Our National Park System* (1995), footnote, p. 9.
[22] Quoted in Sellars, *op. cit.*
[23] *Ibid.*, pp. 12, 15.
[24] *Ibid.*, p. 31.
[25] Quoted in National Trust for Historic Preservation, *op. cit.*, p. 28.
[26] Rettie, *op. cit.*, p. 251.
[27] *Ibid.*, p. 7.
[28] Quoted in Sellars, *op. cit.*, p. 181.
[29] T.H. Watkins, et al., "National Parks, National Paradox," *Audubon*, July/August 1997, p. 58.
[30] Quoted in Leal and Fretwell, *op. cit.*
[31] National Research Council, Committee on Improving the Science and Technology Programs of the National Park Service, "Science and the National Parks," 1992.
[32] *The Washington Post*, April 27, 2000.
[33] *The New York Times*, April 27, 2000.
[34] Quoted in Sellars, *op. cit.*, p. 64.

FOR MORE INFORMATION

National Park Foundation, 1101 17th St., N.W., Suite 1102, Washington, D.C. 20036-4704; (202) 785-4500; www.nationalparks.org. Chartered by Congress and chaired by the Interior secretary, the foundation encourages private-sector support of the National Park System.

National Parks Conservation Association, 1300 19th St., N.W., Suite 300, Washington, D.C. 20036; (202) 223-6722; www.npca.org. A citizens' interest group that seeks to protect national parks.

National Trust for Historic Preservation, 1785 Massachusetts Ave., N.W., Washington, D.C. 20036-2117; (202) 588-6000; www.nthp.org. A membership organization that actively works to preserve historical, architectural and cultural landmarks through lobbying, fund-raising and educational programs.

U.S. Army Corps of Engineers, 20 Massachusetts Ave., N.W., Washington, D.C. 20314-1000; (202) 761-0001; www.usace.army.mil. The corps provides local governments with disaster relief, flood control, navigation and hydroelectric power services.

Bibliography

Selected Sources Used

Books

DiIulio, John J. Jr., Gerald Garvey and Donald F. Kettl, *Improving Government Performance: An Owner's' Manual*, Brookings Institution, 1993.

Three scholars at the Brookings Institution, a liberal think tank, offer suggestions on improving the National Park Service and other government agencies.

Rettie, Dwight F., *Our National Park System*, University of Illinois Press, 1995.

A former chief of the Park Service's policy development office, Rettie takes a detailed, insider's look at the structure and functioning of the large, federal bureaucracy and argues for a more coherent vision of the National Park System.

Sellars, Richard West, *Preserving Nature in the National Parks*, Yale University Press, 1997.

Through detailed historical documentation, this highly influential volume illuminates the history and culture of the Park Service in light of the historical conflict between the pursuit of increased tourism and the scientific management of natural resources.

Wagner, Frederic H., et al., *Wildlife Policies in the U.S. National Parks*, Island Press, 1995.

Drawing on the results of a five-year study of wildlife-management policies in the national parks, the authors recommend changes in policy formulation, management and scientific research procedures.

Articles

Conaway, James, "Our Collapsing Legacy," *Preservation*, November/December 1997.

In an evocative discussion of several of the National Park Service's most intriguing historic sites, Conaway illuminates the tensions and stresses that define the Park Service's struggle to care for them appropriately.

Sharp, Bill, and Elaine Appleton, "In Search of the Early Everglades," *National Parks*, January/February 1993.

By evoking the bounty of the unspoiled Everglades and detailing the losses caused by intense land development in South Florida, the authors make a case for increased funding of scientific research within the National Park Service.

Watkins, T.H., Jon Margolis, Ted Williams and Ted Karasote, "National Parks, National Paradox," *Audubon*, July-August, 1997.

To mark the 125th anniversary of Yellowstone, the first national park, this group of articles traces the evolution of the Park Service's conservationist approach to managing its resources.

Reports and Studies

"National Parks for the 21st Century: The Vail Agenda," National Park Service, 1992.

This prescription for parks management and growth was prepared in the form of a "Report and Recommendations to the director of the National Park Service."

"Natural Resource Challenge: The National Park Service's Action Plan for Preserving Natural Resources," Department of the Interior, 2000.

In this brief document, the Park Service spells out its commitment to improving scientific-data gathering in the national parks to improve natural-resource management.

Anderson, Terry L., Vernon L. Smith and Emily Simmons, "How and Why to Privatize Federal Lands," The Cato Institute, 1999.

The authors make a case for the federal divestiture of the public lands.

Buccino, Sharon, Charles Clusen, Ed Norton and Johanna Wald, "Reclaiming Our Heritage: What We Need to Do to Preserve America's National Parks," Natural Resources Defense Council, National Trust for Historic Preservation, 1997.

This plea for strengthening the national commitment to preserving and maintaining both cultural and natural resources includes profiles of the problems facing individual parks and proposals for increasing national funding levels.

Hass, Glenn E., "National Parks and the American Public: A National Public Opinion Survey on the National Park System," National Parks and Conservation Association, 1998.

This survey, conducted at the University of Colorado, found that Americans highly value their parks but are concerned about their future.

Leal, Donald R., and Holly L. Fretwell, "Back to the Future to Save Our Parks," Political Economy Research Center, 1997.

Two free-market environmentalists argue that the national parks should each be self-sufficient, citing state parks in Texas and South Dakota as examples of how such a system can work.

10 Saving the Rain Forests

I n Indonesia, desperate fishermen burn lush forests to trap turtles, which they sell for food in Hong Kong and other Asian ports. In Ivory Coast, impoverished peasants invade state-owned nature preserves, burning and cutting trees to carve out small farms. In Brazil, cash-strapped landowners hack away at the last remnants of the Atlantic rain forest to create pasture and cropland.

The world's last rain forests are vanishing. Despite a determined international campaign waged for years by an array of conservation and government organizations, the irresistible forces of population growth and rural poverty are consuming the lush tropics as never before.

The crisis has intensified in recent years, with unprecedented fires destroying millions of pristine acres in Latin America and Asia and economic crises spurring governments to scrap environmental protections and open up more forests to development. And now, portending more destruction, Asian logging firms are beginning operations in Latin America, and U.S. oil companies are surveying the Amazon.

"All indications are that the extent and rate of loss are increasing," says Bruce J. Carbarle, director of the World Wildlife Fund's global forest program. "There may be positive indications in terms of the political dialogue, but in terms of action on the ground, we haven't seen that yet."

Scientists fear that the loss of the forests will have major worldwide consequences, including global climate change and the massive extinction of plant and animal species. In tropical areas, floods and droughts are having catastrophic effects where trees no longer protect the soil. In Nicaragua, the entire side of a de-

nuded volcano collapsed during Hurricane Mitch in 1998, burying 2,000 subsistence farmers in an avalanche of mud. [1]

Already, more than half of the forested belt around the tropics — once about 5.5 million square miles — has been lost. [2] Pristine tropical forests in West Africa, Madagascar, the Philippines and Brazil have been reduced to less than 10 percent of their natural areas. India has virtually no original forests remaining. [3]

Moreover, scientists estimate that at least 34 million acres of tropical forests are still being cleared yearly due to the insatiable global demand for land, timber, crops and such valuable commodities as gold and oil; millions more acres are partially logged. [4]

In the early 1990s, amid much publicity about the need to save the rain forests, the pace of deforestation appeared to slow somewhat. [5] But then came massive forest fires in 1997 and '98 and an economic crisis that spurred indebted individuals and governments to strip the forests anew. In Indonesia, for example, the government began clearing millions of acres for oil-palm plantations, and village traders showed up in the

capital, Jakarta, selling rare monkeys in tiny cages for pets. Brazil slashed funds for rain forest preservation as part of a fiscal-austerity package to win overseas loans.

"It's going to take a lot to slow the current rate of destruction," says Randy Curtis, director of conservation finance and policy at The Nature Conservancy's Latin American/Caribbean division. But, he adds, "We don't have any choice, so we just have to keep churning forward."

Deforestation is hardly unique to the tropics. For thousands of years, human progress in Europe and other temperate regions has gone hand-in-hand with clearing land. But the uniqueness of tropical ecosystems suggests that destroying rain forests may have tragic consequences.

Rain forests play a vital role in regulating water flow and stabilizing soil. Take away the trees, which act as sponges, and the land is vulnerable to flooding and erosion in the wetter months, and to drought in the dry season.

Perhaps nowhere have the effects of tree-cutting been as severe as in Haiti, a once lush country that loses an estimated 36 million tons of topsoil each year and is slowly turning into a desert. Caught in a maelstrom of economic and political turmoil, Haiti may portend the future for other severely deforested countries from the Philippines to El Salvador. [6]

To make matters worse, rain forest soil generally is too poor to grow crops for more than a few years, forcing farmers to constantly clear new land — until no more is left. Ivory Coast, which has cleared most of its forests for cocoa and coffee plantations, faces imminent economic disaster because the soil is expected to give out. "The situation is dramatic," said Jean-Michel Pavy, a World Bank biodiversity expert. "We are talking about a matter of years." [7]

From *The CQ Researcher,* June 11, 1999.

Saving the Rain Forests 173

The toll has been greatest on the indigenous people who have inhabited the forests for hundreds or even thousands of years. Many tribes have been wiped out entirely because of disease, battles with settlers and the loss of their traditional homelands.

But the effects of deforestation are also reaching the United States and other wealthy nations. Since rain forests are thought to harbor about half the world's species of plants and animals, researchers worry that destruction of the globe's genetic library will hamstring efforts to create new medicines and more productive crops.

In addition, the forests act as "carbon sinks," absorbing some of the excess carbon that is pumped into the atmosphere by industry. Thus, clearing the rain forests is likely to aggravate global warming, possibly causing coastal flooding and unpredictable weather patterns.

"We cannot escape the effects of global climate change, biodiversity loss and unsustainable resource depletion," the U.S. Agency for International Development (AID) warns. "The quality of life for future generations of Americans will in no small measure be determined by the success or failure of our common stewardship of the planet's resources." [8]

On the surface, the causes of deforestation appear fairly straightforward. Logging companies, including multinational firms with little interest in the long-term health of the forests, strip the forests of mahogany and other valuable trees. Local farmers penetrate the forests on logging roads, while plantation owners clear swaths of forest for cocoa, coffee and other crops. Cattle ranchers use the land for pasture.

"The pattern in Latin America is well-established," said Anthony Coates, deputy director of the Smithsonian Institution's Tropical Research Institute in Panama. "A road goes in, the loggers and farmers move in, they slash and burn and then move on to repeat the process." [9]

In addition, miners are swarming to the Amazon and other rain forests in search of gold and other minerals, and oil companies increasingly are exploring the vast reserves beneath Latin America's forests.

But more complex factors are also at work in developing countries, including overpopulation, poverty, inequitable land distribution, corrupt or inefficient government agencies and burgeoning debt. The destruction is being driven both by impoverished people who exploit forest resources simply to survive, and by corporations and wealthy planters seeking to meet the worldwide demand for lumber, crops and minerals.

Not surprisingly, straightforward conservation strategies have failed to stem the tide. Protected preserves, for example, are often invaded by slash-and-burn farmers who view them as unnecessary playgrounds for the rich. "I have 10 children and we must eat," said Sep Djekoule, an Ivory Coast farmer. "There is no way they can keep me away from my livelihood." [10]

Efforts by affluent nations to protect the forests often have met with failure. Throughout the decade, a World Bank policy against giving loans for logging projects in virgin forests failed to stop companies from finding other funding sources. A 1998 initiative by the Group of Seven leading industrialized nations, or G-7, to fund 90 percent of a $250 million rain forest conservation project in Brazil had a rocky start when the government, in the midst of a fiscal austerity program, temporarily turned down the money. [11]

"You're dealing with places with a lot of human misery, a lot of economic problems," says Mark Plotkin, president of the Amazon Conservation Team, in Arlington, Va.

Undaunted, environmental organizations are working with govern-ment agencies on a three-pronged offensive to save as least a portion of the forests. Their main tactic is to place land in protected preserves that are overseen by local conservation organizations or government agencies. About 5 percent of Earth's rain forests currently are off-limits to development, but biologists believe that figure must be at least doubled if a substantial portion of rain forest animals and plants are to be saved from extinction. In 1998, Conservation International scored a major success in South America when it persuaded Suriname to put one-tenth of its area off-limits to development. [12]

Second, environmentalists want to increase the economic value of rain forests so there will be more profit from leaving them alone than destroying them. They have helped turn several rain forest preserves into ecotourism destinations. They are persuading tropical countries to subsidize forested states that supply drinking water to cities, thus encouraging them to preserve the forests, which soak up precious water. They also are working with power companies in the United States and other industrialized countries that are beginning to contribute money to forest preservation efforts aimed at slowing down global warming.

Third, environmentalists are advising industries how to minimize the impact of development. Loggers, for example, are encouraged to avoid denuding steep hillsides by cutting only selected trees. And coffee growers are urged to grow coffee under the rain forests' natural canopy, instead of clearing forests to create coffee plantations. Increasingly, consumers are becoming interested in "rain forest-friendly" products.

But these are imperfect strategies. Developing countries frequently lack either the desire or the means to protect parks from poaching or legal development. Moreover, making a profit from an intact forest is so elusive that some economists believe it is a losing battle. And it remains unclear whether logging and other such activities can be conducted without badly damaging the forest.

Still, environmentalists are cheered by the growing worldwide concern over deforestation. Brazil, the Philippines and other nations have recently imposed partial or total bans on logging old-growth forests The World Bank committed itself to helping establish 125 million acres of forest preserves and 500 million acres of "sustainable" forestry projects. And in a widely publicized announcement in 1998, Brazilian President Fernando Henrique Cardoso promised to put 10 percent of the country's rain forests — 240,000 square miles — into protected preserves. [13]

Even though it is not clear how much more parks and laws will help — after all, 70 percent of tropical forest logging in Brazil already is done illegally — the United Nations Food and Agriculture Organization predicts the situation will improve. "There is a global commitment to improving the management of forests," it says in a 1999 report. [14]

As efforts intensify to save the rain forests, conservationists and officials must confront these questions:

Are the rain forests doomed?

The Rev. Gerald Hanlon, a priest in Peru, recently described the environmental destruction around him — a new highway slashed through a once pristine ecosystem, trees cut down to fire a brick kiln, a lake polluted by a timber mill. Doubtful of

Threatened Frontier Forests of South America

Large-scale resettlement and agricultural and resource development projects claimed much of the 645,000 square kilometers of forest lost in South America between 1980 and 1990. However, the continent still retains vast areas of frontier forest, or large tracts of original forest cover. Logging currently is the main threat to the continent's tropical and temperate frontier forests.

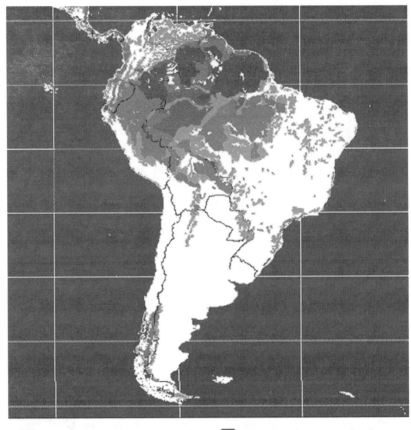

■ Frontier forests under medium or high threat

■ Frontier forests unassessed for threat

■ Frontier forests under low or no threat

■ Non-frontier forests

Source: World Resources Institute, May 1999

the Amazon's survival, Hanlon pledged to leave a small piece of forest near his own house untouched. "If I live to a great age and all this passes into history," he wrote, "at least I shall be able to say that I once saw the rain forest." [15]

Many scientists share Hanlon's pessimism. The world's population — now about 6 billion — is growing yearly by about 90 million people. The unprecedented growth subjects the forests to hordes of slash-and-burn farmers and subsistence hunters, swelling cities and creating ever-increasing demand worldwide for lumber, palm oil, coffee and other tropical products. At the current rate of destruction, the forests have perhaps 50 years left, after which there may be just a few remnants left in national parks and steep, inaccessible regions. [16] Fire, which has devastated forests in recent years, may destroy most of the remaining tropical tracts even sooner, taking with it millions of species of plants and animals, many still undiscovered.

"We're destroying our biodiversity," said Garo Batmanian, head of the Brazilian office of the World Wildlife Fund. "Humanity is becoming poorer." [17]

Underscoring the grim outlook, a joint European research group, Tropical Ecosystem Environment Observations by Satellites (TREES), concluded in 1998 that conservationists should consider abandoning efforts to save "hot spots" — areas rich in biodiversity that are threatened by development — and focus instead on the few remaining areas that are not yet facing encroachment. "The pressures to remove the forests are too great to be stopped," said study coordinator Frederic Achard. [18]

Even the last great areas of virgin rain forest, including large tracts in the Amazon and Congo, are coming under growing pressure by multinational logging companies that have already cleared most of the original forests in Southeast Asia.

To save a significant portion of the rain forests' animals and plants, conservationists are pressing developing countries to put at least 10 percent of the remaining forests in protected preserves. "What makes the most sense is to first protect what's left," says Plotkin of the Amazon Conservation Team.

Even if they meet their 10 percent goal, scientists predict an extraordinary wave of extinctions. That's because the destruction of just 50 percent of a forest tends to cause the immediate loss of 10 percent of its species and the gradual extinction of countless additional plants and ani-

mals. [19] Many undiscovered species are thought to have already disappeared, and such familiar rain forest creatures as orangutans are becoming perilously rare.

But figuring out the rate of extinction when only 10 percent of a rain forest is saved may be an irrelevant exercise. At present, just 5 percent of the forests are designated as protected, and the pace of creating new parks in the tropics has diminished. Some experts conclude that, in the end, no more than about 7 percent of Earth's rain forests will be protected unless there are major policy changes. [20]

Even more problematic, many existing forest preserves are "paper parks" that are virtually unguarded. Governments lack the resources to patrol them, and impoverished residents view them as unreasonable barriers to development. In "protected" lands in Southeast Asia, for example, poachers hunt the few remaining rhinoceroses for their horns and deplete the rivers by fishing with dynamite, poison and electric shocks. "The final bulwark erected to shield tropical nature from extinction is collapsing," warned a 1997 study. [21]

Parks aside, conservationists are rushing to minimize the effects that logging, oil extraction and other activities would have on the surviving rain forests. They believe that significant portions of rain forests may survive with only moderate damage if companies are willing to use such techniques as leaving intact strips of trees along rivers and on hillsides and transporting mining equipment by helicopter instead of building roads. In addition, the conservationists are trying to promote more environmentally benign uses of the rain forests.

"You want to preserve both areas that are very rich in species and being cleared very rapidly, and also save intact areas," says Dirk Bryant, a senior associate with the World Resources Institute. "That way, you can

maximize biodiversity."

Conservation organizations are scoring some notable victories. Mobil Oil Corp., for example, consulted with Conservation International when conducting preliminary oil explorations in a biologically rich section of the Peruvian Amazon without substantially damaging the environment. The company cleared minimal forest areas, used small underground seismic charges instead of drilling exploratory wells and took steps to prevent watershed contamination.

Due to the growing awareness worldwide about the importance of biodiversity, environmentalists say they may yet be able to preserve significant portions of the rain forest. "Overall, I am very optimistic," said Glenn Prickett, vice president of corporate partnerships for Conservation International. "I think you have a new generation of leaders who recognize the environmental problems and the very valuable assets they have in these untouched areas."

But every environmental victory seems to be accompanied by a setback. A new policy in China, for example, to ban most logging is merely creating more demand for Indonesian lumber. A policy initiative in Brazil to put 10 percent of the rain forests into preserves has been thrown into doubt by the need for budget cuts.

Even though saving the rain forests may be in the long-term interest of humanity, it has little short-term economic appeal to impoverished countries that need the forests to sustain their swelling populations. Duke University biologist John Terborgh warns that, despite the best efforts of conservation-minded leaders, "There are going to be a few successes and more than a few failures."

Can people profit from rain forests without destroying them?

In a landmark 1989 article, Yale

University economist Robert Mendelsohn and two fellow researchers advanced the bold claim that more money could be made by collecting plants in the rain forests than by destroying them. They demonstrated that fruits, nuts, latex and wild chocolate on a 2.5-acre plot in the Peruvian Amazon could produce a net profit of $422 and, over time, generate two to three times the per-acre return earned by cattle ranchers. [22]

The article helped spark a new school of thought among environmentalists: The best way to save the rain forests was to demonstrate the potential profits of leaving them intact. As Harvard University biologist Edward O. Wilson wrote in his 1992 book, *The Diversity of Life*: "The race is on to develop methods to draw more income from the wild lands without killing them, and so to give the invisible hand of free-market economics a green thumb." [23]

Unfortunately, conservationists early in the decade who pushed the benign harvesting of natural forest products found themselves facing two problems: Few rain forests contain products of great economic value. And second, when there are valuable products, the harvesting tends to be so intense that it degrades the environment. The Peruvian example seems to be an exception — profitable in part because the land studied was along a river that provided a natural transportation route.

"If something is worth doing at a fairly low intensity of operation," says economist David Simpson, a fellow at Resources for the Future, "it's even more worth doing at a high intensity of operation, which would definitely cause environmental impacts."

Consider some of the rain forests' most well-known agricultural products. Coffee, which grows wild under the rain forest canopy, is now grown more profitably on cleared plantations. Rubber, which continues to be tapped from trees in the Amazon by workers scratching out a subsistence living, is more economically grown on Asian plantations or produced synthetically. Trees can be harvested without widespread damage to the environment, but much higher profits result when less environmental care is taken.

The very diversity of the rain forests is an economic barrier, since the one species that produces a desirable fruit or other product is often mixed in with dozens or hundreds of other plant species. "Rather than grabbing some nuts from one tree and going off 100 yards and finding the next tree, people just line them up in a field," says Ohio State University agricultural economist Douglas Southgate.

To be sure, there are niches for non-forest timber products. In Peru, for example, local people sell seeds from native trees to organizations planning reforestation projects. But such activities tend to generate either just enough revenue to preserve a relatively small section of land or so much revenue that crowds of harvesters clear away the non-profitable plants, gradually altering the ecosystem. "What people tend to do is sort of weed out the other things, so you end up with something like an orchard," Southgate says

Refusing to be deterred, however, conservationists in recent years have come up with more innovative and promising incentives to preserve rain forests. One of the most touted is "carbon sequestration," which takes advantage of the ability of forests to store vast amounts of carbon dioxide and reduce the effects of global warming. Companies in industrialized countries, hoping to earn carbon "credits" to offset their greenhouse gas emissions, pay developing countries to set aside tracts of forest. In one of the most notable instances, an agreement between U.S.-based energy companies, environmental groups and government officials led to the protection of about 1.5 million acres in Bolivia, including the expansion of the spectacular Noel Kempff Mercado National Park.

Drinking water also is emerging as a possible source for profits. Rain forests act as natural sponges, storing groundwater that is needed by growing cities in developing countries. Since destroying forests for plantations or industrial operations would mean losing the water, governments are experimenting with different ways of encouraging the preservation of watershed areas. In Brazil, for ex-

The Nature Conservancy is working with local environmental organizations to protect and manage more than a million acres in Ecuador's vast Condor Bioreserve.

Greg Miller/The Nature Conservancy

Most Original Forests Have Disappeared

Only about one-fifth of the world's original forest cover remains in large, relatively undisturbed tracts, or frontier forests.

Region	Original Forest (000 KM²)	Total Remaining Forest (Frontier and Non-Frontier Forest) (000 KM²)	Total Frontier Forest (000 KM²)	Frontier Forest as a Percentage of Total Original Forest
Africa	6,799	2,302	527	8%
Asia	15,132	4,275	844	6%
Central America	1,779	970	172	10%
North America	10,877	8,483	3,737	34%
South America	9,736	6,800	4,439	46%
Europe	4,690	1,521	14	0.3%
Russia	11,759	8,083	3,448	29%
Oceania*	1,431	929	319	22%
World	**62,203**	**33,363**	**13,500**	**22%**

* *Oceania consists of Papua New Guinea, Australia and New Zealand*

Source: "The Last Frontier Forests," World Resources Institute, 1997

ample, 5 percent of the sales tax collection in Parana is earmarked for municipalities with sources of drinking water, thereby rewarding them for keeping the water-producing areas uncontaminated. [24]

Another economic incentive is using rain forest plants for pharmaceutical purposes. More than half the prescription drugs used in the United States are derived from natural sources, and researchers believe that clues to curing such diseases as cancer and AIDS may be found in the rain forests. Several U.S. pharmaceutical companies are investing millions of dollars in rain forest research, even working with local officials to preserve natural areas. (*See story, p.179.*)

In recent years, ecotourism also has become an incentive to preserving rain forests. (*See story, p. 180.*) Travelers who want to visit undisturbed places helped preserve portions of the African savanna, and

conservationists believe the same approach can work for rain forests. Costa Rica, for example, has preserved about 25 percent of its land and is becoming an increasingly popular destination for tourists seeking pristine beaches and forests.

However, no economic incentives are surefire barriers to deforestation, and some even have environmental drawbacks. Carbon sequestration, for example, may simply encourage large companies to keep polluting. "It's a risky strategy," says the World Wildlife Fund's Cabarle. "There's no way you can create enough forest to even begin to compensate for the amount of carbon we're pumping out."

Moreover, recent economic studies indicate that so-called bioprospecting by pharmaceutical companies pays too little economic return in this age of synthetically produced drugs to justify setting aside huge sections of virgin forest. And

ecotourism sometimes spawns environmentally damaging development while doing little to help the lot of impoverished local communities. [25]

The situation is frustrating for scientists who say rain forests contain a wealth of riches that could enhance everyday life. Harvard's Wilson cites hundreds of tropical fruits, grains and tubers that are savored by local people but not marketed worldwide. And Plotkin has devoted his life to working with traditional medicine men, or shamans, uncovering numerous promising remedies, such as a painkiller from the skin of a poison-dart frog.

Despite the mixed marketing results, many conservationists still believe that economics is the key to saving the rain forests. "In the final analysis," Plotkin says, "they are going to have to pay for themselves."

Are wealthy nations contributing to tropical deforestation?

Visiting Brazil in 1997, President Clinton announced that the United States would contribute $10 million to a program to protect the rain forests. But the following year, Brazilian officials cut the program as part of a budget austerity deal, worked out with U.S. approval, to get a much-needed $41.5 billion loan package from the International Monetary Fund. [26]

Stephan Schwartzman of the Environmental Defense Fund denounced

Bioprospecting Has Yet to Strike It Rich

With its pink, five-petaled flowers, the rosy periwinkle of Madagascar looks like just another pretty tropical plant. But it produces two alkaloids that are highly effective in treating children with lymphocytic leukemia and adults with Hodgkin's disease — two of the deadliest forms of cancer. [1]

The rosy periwinkle is just one of many plants that have been used for medicinal purposes. A recent study sponsored by the National Institutes of Health and other agencies found that 40 percent of the most commonly prescribed drugs were developed from natural sources. [2] These range from traditional painkillers such as aspirin to the potent anti-cancer drug Taxol, which is derived from the bark of the Pacific yew tree. This year, researchers are looking at Australian frog secretions that contain antibacterial properties and a compound from the bark of a Samoan tree that may help with AIDS treatments. In addition, scientists who have found evidence that the AIDS virus was originally contracted from chimpanzees in African forests believe the same forests hold the key to treating the disease.

There are doubtless far more cures waiting to be found in tropical rain forests and other natural places: Of the approximately 1.8 million species that have been catalogued on the planet, only a minute fraction have been closely examined for their medicinal value. And biologists believe that tens of millions more may yet be discovered — more than half of them in tropical rain forests. These species can yield leads for promising drugs, insecticides or other products because they produce highly complex molecules, such as plant toxins that repel insects.

"Certainly the destruction of the rain forests would jeopardize our future discoveries," says David G. Corley, a tropical-species researcher at Monsanto Corp. "Our future ability to bring innovative products to the market and meet human needs depends on biodiversity."

As recently as the early 1990s, environmentalists viewed the search for natural medicines, or bioprospecting, as perhaps the most promising incentive to stop deforestation. When pharmaceutical giant Merck & Co. struck a million-dollar deal with Costa Rica in 1991 to search for usable new species, it appeared at last that there was an economic reason, as well as a social imperative, to save the forests. Two years later, the National Institutes of Health and other government agencies launched a $12 million grants program to evaluate tropical species and work with indigenous people who use natural products for medicine.

Although these initiatives have developed promising research leads, they have yet to produce a single drug in the marketplace. Instead, like so many other conservation initiatives, bioprospecting is failing to live up to the early expectations, and some former advocates of the approach, such as Shaman Pharmaceuticals, now are pulling back.

One problem is economics. It is so rare to find an organic sample with important medicinal properties — an estimated one in 250,000 samples will lead directly to a commercial drug — and it takes so long to develop a product from such a sample — often 10-20 years — that many drug companies are reluctant to make large investments in the process. [3] Moreover, each square mile of protected tropical rain forest has so many unexamined plant and animal species that there is little economic incentive to set aside vast new regions.

Another problem is the divisive issue of who should profit from bioprospecting. Since developing countries contain a major portion of the world's biological resources, they want considerable compensation for their plants and animals. Finally, there is also a trend in the pharmaceutical industry toward synthetic compounds, which can be screened at a rate of close to 100,000 molecules a day to check for possible medicinal effects. [4]

Small wonder, then, that economists warn against relying on bioprospecting to save the rain forests. "To be sure, society as a whole, either now or in later years, might attach a very high value to the lives saved because specimens can be gathered in the wild," economist Douglas Southgate writes. [5] "But none of this has much of an impact in the marketplace."

More promising, some researchers say, is the use of tropical species for research into better food supplements or the development of more productive crops. Indeed, a wild species of Mexican maize, nearly extinct when examined in the 1970s, is being used to develop disease-resistant types of corn.

As for the health-care industry, the increasing emphasis on using new techniques should help develop drugs much more quickly. But scientists still believe that the natural world could give invaluable guidance when it comes to developing entire new classes of treatment. The problem, they warn, is that the rate of extinction is increasing just as they are developing more sophisticated techniques to study plants and animals for their medicinal values.

"The greatest tragedy," says Joshua Rosenthal, program director of biodiversity at the National Institutes of Health's Fogarty International Center, "is that there is so much we don't even know that we're losing."

[1] Edward O. Wilson, *The Diversity of Life* (1992), p. 283.

[2] Interview with Joshua Rosenthal, program director of biodiversity at the National Institutes of Health's Fogarty International Center.

[3] Janet N. Abramovitz, "The Complex Realities of Sharing Genetic Assets," *Nature*, April 9, 1998.

[4] "Ethnobotany: Shaman Loses Its Magic," *The Economist*, Feb. 20, 1998, p. 77.

[5] Douglas Southgate, *Tropical Forest Conservation* (1998).

Ecotourism Offers Exotic Travel and Hope

The opportunities appear limitless: hiking in Costa Rica, birdwatching in the Amazon, canoeing down a remote African river or just relaxing in a spacious tent cabin under the rain forest canopy. For countless nature-starved travelers, such activities have an irresistible appeal.

Ecotourism is booming. Exact statistics are hard to come by, but ecotourism has become a multibillion-dollar industry in the United States, where most tour operators are based. Outdoor magazines are filled with ads for adventure and natural history trips to every continent, even Antarctica.

For environmentalists struggling to save the remaining rain forests, ecotourism offers salvation. Environmental activists tell stories of pristine patches of forest snatched at the last moment from chainsaws or bulldozers by investors seeking to make money while saving the environment. In Ghana, a tourism project that involved the creation of a visitor center, canopy walkway and trails at Kakum National Park was credited with generating 2,000 local jobs and saving much of the forest from logging and farming. It won the British Airways Tourism for Tomorrow awards. In Brazil's Atlantic region, climbers used bows and arrows to shoot ropes over 100-foot-high trees to build a canopy walkway, creating a park for tourists and ensuring an intact habitat for such rare species as the golden-faced lion tamarind.

"Ecotourism is probably one of the best options we have," says Oliver Hillel, who oversees ecotourism initiatives for Conservation International and helped set

Lamb Studios/Conservation International

Ghana's Kakum National Park features a walkway above the forest canopy.

up the Brazilian reserve.

But far from being a reliable tool, ecotourism often has damaged the very thing it was designed to save. In a Mexican cloud forest reserve for monarch butterflies, for example, crowds of visitors litter the grounds and sometimes trample the butterflies. And in Ecuador's famed Galapagos Islands, tourism revenues have sparked a sevenfold population increase since 1960, spawning crime and pollution, along with a wave of invasive species such as wasps and fire ants that are threatening the local ecosystems. "Tourism is a curse in disguise," an island scientist told *National Geographic.* [1]

Indeed, there may be something of a contradiction in bringing people to natural areas in order to keep them undisturbed. Even in the United States, the Grand Canyon and other popular national parks are affected by millions of visitors and bumper-to-bumper traffic. In developing countries with little tourism experience, the impact can be devastating. Megan Epler Wood, president of the nonprofit Ecotourism Society in Bennington, Vt., cites areas of Nepal where all the trees were cut to provide firewood for trekkers, and unspoiled Costa Rican coastal areas that were bought by foreign developers. [2]

Still, Wood and other ecotourism advocates say the new industry on balance has been a positive force. A prime example is Costa Rica, which has set aside 25 percent of its land for preservation partly because of the huge influx of tourist dollars.

Seeking to curtail the negative impacts of travel in natural areas, the Ecotourism Society runs programs to

the agreement as "an insignificant step towards balancing Brazil's budget and a giant step toward the destruction of Brazil's ecological patrimony."

Even though Brazilian officials restored much of the funding early in 1999, the effectiveness of their environmental programs remained in question because of the ongoing need for budget cuts. "The [budget] crisis has made me even more pessimistic about the future of the environment here," said Paulo Paiva, a Brazilian environmental official. [27]

The episode in Brazil illustrates the complex role that the United States and other wealthy nations play in tropical deforestation. On one hand, government and corporate leaders contribute millions of dollars toward rain forest conservation. And concerned consumers pitch in by buying such products as Ben & Jerry's Rain Forest Crunch ice cream, which teach tour operators about environmentally friendly practices, such as working closely with local people, limiting the amount of travelers on each trip and using rustic facilities with such features as kerosene lighting instead of electricity. Wood believes that tour operators are becoming better environmental stewards. Travelers looking for environmentally aware tour operators can check the group's Web site, www.ecotourism.org.

"The capability of delivering sustainable development benefits in all these biologically diverse rain forests is great," Wood says. "It is one of the main choices for local people in the rain forests. They find it more compatible with the existing natural environment than other forms of development."

Still uncertain, however, is whether the tourism potential for rain forests compares with East Africa, where conservation efforts have been spurred by worldwide interest in seeing large animals in the wild. But trekking through the rain forest, where many creatures live hidden in the dense canopy, may be less alluring.

Some also wonder whether it is possible to provide facilities that satisfy the tastes of less intrepid tourists without degrading the fragile rain forest ecosystem. "There's not a whole lot of money to be made from a handful of people who are willing to rough it and willing to be eaten by wild animals or bitten by mosquitoes as opposed to staying in a luxury hotel," says David Simpson, an economist at Resources for the Future. Too often, he adds,

the formula for drawing tourists is: "Spray DDT and kill mosquitoes; get rid of predatory animals; build a road; build a nice hotel."

Conservation International's Hillel, however, says it is possible to strike a balance between the needs of travelers and the goal of environmental protection. Ideally, he says, an ecotourism destination is divided into different zones, including a developed area with hotels, an accessible natural area with trails and rustic accommodations and a mostly untouched wilderness area. Furthermore, at least 30 percent of the tourism revenues should go to local people, who can operate the facilities and work as guides.

Perhaps the biggest benefit of ecotourism is that it can motivate local people to protect their resources, Hillel says. He cites an example in Bolivia, where poor residents who used to scratch out a living from illegal logging and hunting are now making money from an ecotourism lodge and emerging as the most effective defenders of a nearby preserve.

"In this area, you can imagine the government doesn't carry a lot of weight," Hillel says. "But when the community says 'Don't do it,' this is something that the people really respect."

[1] Peter Benchley, "Galapagos: Paradise in Peril," *National Geographic*, April 1999, p. 30.

[2] Megan Epler Wood, "Monitoring the Global Challenge of Community Participation in Ecotourism: Case Studies and Lessons from Ecuador," The Nature Conservancy and U.S. AID, 1998.

uses Brazil nuts and cashews collected by indigenous people in the Amazon to promote non-destructive uses of the forest.

On the other hand, U.S. economic and trade policies sometimes indirectly accelerate the rate of deforestation. And consumers, who use prodigious quantities of lumber, oil, coffee and other products also spur more tropical development.

"A major force [behind deforestation] is the growing demand for forest products, stoked mainly by rising affluence," writes Janet N. Abramovitz, senior researcher at the Worldwatch Institute. "Today, less than one-fifth of the world's population living in Europe, the United States and Japan consumes over half the world's industrial timber and more than two-thirds of its paper," she wrote in a 1998 report. "To reduce their consumption and waste by even a small fraction

would ease pressures on forests significantly." [28]

To be fair, governments and conservation organizations in Europe and the United States spark the creation of new rain forest preserves every year and encourage loggers and industrial companies to minimize the environmental effects of their actions. And the governments of developing countries are hardly blameless, since they regularly sponsor initiatives to clear land for farming and housing.

But despite pledges on all sides to preserve the rain forests, economic policies by wealthy nations often cause more environmental damage. For example, the International Monetary Fund (IMF) — which is controlled primarily by the U.S. and other wealthy nations — regularly pressures debt-burdened countries to cut their budgets, including environmental programs, to qualify for loans. In

one recent case, Indonesia ended restrictions on foreign investment to clear forestlands as part of a $43 billion agreement with the IMF. [29]

"The IMF has the idea that they have the answer to any macroeconomic question, and the impacts on people and the environment are basically secondary," says environmentalist Marijke Torfs, who worked with Friends of the Earth and other organizations in 1998 to try to cut U.S. funding for the IMF.

The debt-burdened countries face further pressure to exploit their natural resources to pay off the debts. The four countries with the most rain forest — Indonesia, Congo, Brazil and Peru — owe the United States about $5 billion. The huge debt has spurred calls in Congress to forgive part of the debt to encourage rain forest preservation. In the meantime, Indonesia is burning millions of acres of untouched forest to create palm oil, rubber and coffee plantations to shore up the economy.

Consumer demand also fuels deforestation. In Latin America, so many trees have been felled to create coffee plantations that migratory songbirds are losing vital winter habitat. As consumers of fully one-third of the world's coffee, Americans contribute to such environmental degradation.

"When coffee is produced in a way that's not sustainable, it pollutes streams, it gets rid of forest cover, it increases erosion and reduces the amount of carbon dioxide the plants take out of the air," said Russell Greenberg, director of the Smithsonian Institution's Migratory Bird Center in Washington. [30]

The situation recalls an earlier wave of deforestation in the 1960s and '70s, when U.S. demand for beef contributed to the conversion of vast Central American rain forests into ranchlands. Now that large oil reserves are being found in the Amazon, oil imports by the United States, Europe and Japan may indirectly spur more deforestation.

Because the causes of deforestation are so complex, the United States sometimes can hardly avoid contributing to the problem. By propping up the price for domestically grown sugar, for example, Washington has undermined a main export market for the Philippines, causing tens of thousands of displaced Filipino sugarcane workers to stream to upland forests where they engage in slash-and-burn farming.

Sometimes, however, the U.S. role is more direct. Indigenous people in Ecuador sued Texaco Inc. over its part in oil operations that spilled as much as 19 billion gallons of toxic waste into the environment. The company, which is no longer operating in Ecuador, paid $40 million for an environmental cleanup but claims much of the damage was caused by other companies. [31]

"Our life in the Amazon is being twisted and ruined," Humberto Piaguahe, leader of the 400-member Sequia tribe of Ecuador, told reporters. We are being done in by the contamination. We are disappearing." [32]

Conservationists looking for a silver lining believe they can harness the U.S. economy to help the environment, rather than create more harm. For example, the Audubon Society and the Migratory Bird Center believe consumers can encourage reforestation efforts by buying only shade-grown coffee. Since 1996, shade-grown coffee advocates have made uneven progress, partly because the beans tend to be more expensive.

But the advocates won a convert in 1999 when the Rainforest Café chain announced it would sell only shade-grown coffee and encouraged other restaurants to adopt the policy. "This is environmentally friendly," says company President Kenneth Brimmer. "It's part of what Rainforest stands for." ■

BACKGROUND

A Profusion of Life

The tropical rain forests that have spurred worldwide conservation efforts girdle the globe, mostly between the Tropic of Cancer and the Tropic of Capricorn. They are the richest ecosystems on Earth, believed to harbor at least one-half of the estimated 30 million or so organisms on the planet. Scientists still struggle to explain how rain forests regulate local weather patterns and spawn such a profusion of life. Along with the boreal forests of Canada and Russia, they are the largest remaining intact forests, since most of the original temperate forests in the United States, Europe and Asia have been cleared.

Stepping into a tropical rain forest is a memorable experience. It is like walking into the semidarkness of a long tunnel, for the overhead canopy is so thick that it blocks most of the sunlight from hitting the forest floor. Tree trunks typically reach straight up 100 feet or higher before branching out, their interwoven limbs sheltering the forest from harsh drying winds and nurturing a consistently humid climate.

Scientists believe the rain forests began developing during a warm, moist period about 200 million years ago. The vegetation typically requires at least 80 inches of annual rainfall and thrives in equatorial regions where the average temperature is 75 degrees. [33] Powerful entities that create their own weather systems, the forests send up columns of white vapor after a rainfall that form brooding clouds, diffusing the sunlight and eventually releasing more rain on the trees.

When most people think of rain forests, what they have in mind are lowland forests. These are the most prolific of the world's plant communities, with profusions of hanging vines and creepers that wind around and sometimes connect giant evergreens that soar 200 feet or higher. In *Heart of Darkness*, Joseph Conrad described the foreboding sense of journeying on a river into such a rain forest in Africa: "Going up that river was like going back to beginnings, when vegetation rioted . . . and the trees were kings." [34]

The largest intact lowland forests are in the Amazon and Zaire river basins. But fragments of once extensive lowland forests still exist in Southeast Asia, Central America and West Africa.

At higher altitudes, tropical mountains are covered with montane rain

Chronology

1970s *The World Bank and regional development banks provide loans to developing countries for massive projects that result in widespread deforestation. Demand by U.S. consumers for beef spurs the "hamburgerization" of Central America.*

1977
Amid mounting alarm over rain forest loss, an environmental movement in Kenya begins employing women to plant trees in deforested areas.

———— • ————

1980s *The pace of deforestation accelerates, with as much as 1.8 percent of the rain forests destroyed yearly.*

1980
The "Global 2000" report, commissioned by President Jimmy Carter, identifies deforestation as the biggest environmental threat for the next two decades.

1982
Brazil, with World Bank funding, launches the vast Polonoroeste project, a controversial road-construction and resettlement campaign in the Amazon basin.

1984
Brazil completes the Tucurui Dam, spanning 12 miles on the Tocantins River, a tributary of the Amazon. It floods 800 square miles of virgin forest.

Mid-1980s
As a result of a relocation project in Indonesia, 2.5 million Javanese inhabit the undevel-oped outer islands. More than 1.7 million forested acres are cleared, the highest deforestation rate in Southeast Asia.

1985
World Bank helps launch the Tropical Forestry Action Plan with the goal of establishing sustainable forest management in every tropical country.

December 1988
Brazilian rubber tapper Chico Mendes is assassinated following his extensively publicized campaign to curtail forest clearing in the Amazon.

———— • ————

1990s *Threats of global warming heighten concern about deforestation. The annual loss rate of tropical rain forests dips early in the decade before sharply increasing in the late 1990s.*

1990
The Group of Seven leading industrialized nations (G-7) agree to work with Brazil to develop a $250 million pilot program for rain forest conservation. Funding is delayed for years due to bureaucratic red tape and disagreement over how to disburse the money.

1991
Amid concerns that sustainable forestry goals are spurring new rates of destruction, the World Bank withdraws support from the Tropical Forestry Action Plan and institutes a policy of no new loans for tropical logging.

1993
Foresters, timber companies and environmental groups from around the world launch the Forest Stewardship Council with the goal of certifying logging operations that minimize environmental damage.

1994
The newly created Global Environment Facility, a multilateral group that works closely with the U.N. and the World Bank to promote environmental initiatives, receives pledges of $2 billion from 34 nations to aid worldwide conservation programs.

1997-1998
Fires destroy millions of acres of pristine rain forests in Mexico, the Amazon and Indonesia due to droughts caused by El Niño.

April 1998
Brazilian President Fernando Henrique Cardoso creates four protected rain forest areas, totaling more than 1 million acres, as part of a commitment to triple the amount of protected Amazon land by 2000.

June 17, 1998
Suriname announces it will set aside one-tenth of its land for conservation purposes.

July 29, 1998
President Clinton signs legislation to forgive some debts of developing nations that undertake conservation initiatives. Congress provides no funding for the plan in 1998 but considers a $50 million appropriation in 1999.

February 1999
Preliminary figures from Brazil indicate that deforestation in the Amazon increased by almost 30 percent from 1997 to 1998.

forests, sometimes called "cloud forests" because of the mists that engulf the treetops. The height of the canopies of these forests decreases as the elevation increases. Lichens hang like beards from the upper branches of the gnarled and twisted trees, and the floor is covered with damp, green mosses. Another type of rain forest is the mangrove forest, which flourishes along sheltered shores in tropical regions.

Tropical rain forests cover about 3 million square miles, or 6 percent of Earth's land surface, and contain a greater variety of life than any other region. [35] Harvard's Wilson counted 43 different species of ants on a single tree in the Amazon — about the same number of ant species in all of Great Britain. [36] Whereas an entire temperate forest may contain only a handful of tree species, a single acre of rain forest can boast more than 100. [37] In Borneo, home to one-third of the world's flowering plants, a few acres of rain forest contains more species of trees than all of Europe. [38]

But this web of life is so fragile that, in some cases, a single species of plant can be pollinated by just one type of insect. In perhaps the most remarkable case of this interdependence, there are about 900 species of fig trees in the world and 900 species of tiny wasps that pollinate them — one for every species. [39]

Rain forests are so complex that researchers divide them into vertical strata, each containing multitudes of plant and animal species. On the forest floor are networks of fungi and swarms of insects, along with such unusual creatures as the bird-eating tarantula. The next layer up, the understory, is composed of shrubs, immature trees and dwarf palms that are laden with orchids and other epiphytes — plants that grow on other plants — and bound with a profusion of woody vines that reach toward the sun.

It is the top layer, the canopy, that has most intrigued naturalists in recent years. Bathed in strong sunlight and bursting with fruits, nectars and seeds, the canopy supports the spectacular animals that most people associate with rain forests — agile monkeys, brightly colored toucans, gliding geckos, sluggish sloths — as well as uncounted species of insects. Many canopy inhabitants spend their whole lives in the trees, hidden from observers on the ground.

The canopy shelters most of the species in the rain forest, and possibly the majority of all life forms on Earth. In fact, scientists are revamping their theories about species diversity because of the rain forest canopies. Until the early 1980s, scientists believed there were no more than a few million species in the world — perhaps 5 million at most. [40] But then they began exploring the canopy with a new technique, fogging the foliage with a biodegradable pesticide and counting the insects that fell. Fogging enabled Smithsonian entomologist Terry Erwin to count more than 650 beetle species in a single tree in Peru and as many as 60,000 insect species in a 2.5-acre plot in Ecuador. Now many scientists believe there are as many as 30 million species in the world, although estimates range from 10 million to 100 million. [41]

Disastrous Schemes

For thousands of years, forest-dwellers wove themselves into the diversity of rain forest life. Although few relics survive from the early inhabitants — wooden arrowheads, woven baskets and other natural materials quickly rot in the tropics — anthropologists believe the first people in the rain forests lived off fish and game as well as fruits, nuts and tubers. In fact, anthropologists say that some peoples — the Pygmies of Africa, the Semang of Malaysia and others — gradually evolved smaller statures that made it easier to move through the dense brush and to climb trees. [42]

Scientists believe the early inhabitants may have relentlessly hunted some species into extinction, such as giant kangaroos and marsupial wolves in New Guinea and Australia. However, the indigenous people lacked the sophistication, or the desire, to destroy the rain forests. To this day, their farming techniques are held up as models of sustainable agriculture, in part because they relied on so many crops that they did not deplete any single source.

The first major assaults on the rain forests were launched in the early to mid-19th century by European and North American nations seeking hardwood, rubber and other commodities. But it was not until the middle of this century, when tropical populations began to boom, that the rain forests began suffering widespread destruction.

Seeking to relieve overcrowding, developing countries conceived disastrous schemes to move poor people out of the cities and into the sparsely populated forests. Brazil's ambitious and ill-fated Operation Amazonia, for example, destroyed large swaths of rain forest to make room for the country's new capital, Brasilia, and a network of roads linking the coast to the interior. The government also built dams, created gigantic colonization projects in the Amazon and encouraged environmentally damaging cattle and mining operations. Similarly, Indonesia in the 1980s moved 2.5 million landless people to underdeveloped islands, clearing forests at a higher rate than anywhere else in Southeast Asia. [43]

By 1990, Earth's tropical rain forests had shrunk to little more than half of their original area of 5.5 million square miles, with about 1.8

percent more cleared each year and environmentalists warning that the ancient forests could not endure more than another few decades. Yet, much of the cleared land proved of little value to the new inhabitants, because the soil of rain forests is often too poor to sustain farming for more than a few years.

Amid warnings of catastrophic damage to the global environment, conservation organizations and national governments began seeking to stem the tide in the 1980s and '90s. The World Bank cut off funding for logging projects in undisturbed forests; a consortium of nations set up a $1.3 billion global environmental fund and U.S. government agencies worked to set aside land and to explore the rain forests for possible medicinal uses. Across the world, conservation groups and indigenous peoples joined forces to plant trees in deforested areas, create preserves and popularize sustainable uses of the forest, such as harvesting fruits and latex.

But they were too late to save many of the indigenous peoples who had lived in the rain forests for millenniums. Beset by disease, pollution and settlers determined to kill them for their land, at least 90 Amazon tribes have been wiped out of existence this century — nearly one per year. [44] In the latest setback, a pilot program to survey Brazil's rain forest and mark off 40,000 square miles for indigenous people is threatened by the Brazilian economic crisis.

The worldwide conservation efforts also may be failing to preserve the forest plants and animals. Wilson estimated in 1992 that the destruction of the rain forests was dooming at least three species to extinction every hour, or about 27,000 a year. "Clearly, we are in the midst of one of the great extinction spasms of geological history," he wrote. [45]

Despite such warnings, the defor-estation has continued. If Wilson's estimate was correct, the world has lost about 189,000 species in the seven years since he published his book. ∎

CURRENT SITUATION

Government Initiatives

As a deeply divided Congress this year debates plans to cut taxes and boost spending, Republicans and Democrats are finding themselves in agreement on at least one issue: Appropriating money for rain forests.

President Clinton's fiscal 2000 budget proposes spending $50 million on a much-touted plan to forgive debts by developing nations in exchange for those nations undertaking certain conservation efforts. Congress passed the plan overwhelmingly in 1998, but provided no funding for it.

The proposed "debt-for-nature" swap builds on earlier U.S. initiatives and brings together an unusual group of political leaders, including Clinton and one of his arch-rivals, House Budget Committee Chairman John R. Kasich, R-Ohio. It is perhaps the most closely watched rain forest initiative in Washington in years, winning praise from Nature Conservancy President John C. Sawhill as "a means for preserving millions of acres of tropical forests."

The unlikely sponsor of the plan is Rep. Rob Portman, R-Ohio, a conservative best-known for his work on the Ways and Means Committee. Portman, who does not serve on the Resources Committee and has almost no experience on environmental bills, usually focuses on such matters as pension reform, tax collection methods and restricting the ability of Congress to impose mandates on state and local governments. But he is an avid kayaker and outdoorsman who has visited the rain forest in Costa Rica, and he believes preserving the rain forests should be a major U.S. priority. "By protecting these far-off tropical forests," he says, "we are also protecting our own air quality, food supply and the medicines we use to cure disease."

Portman believes the legislation can spur major conservation efforts without costing U.S. taxpayers much money. He notes that about half of the world's tropical forests are located in four countries — Brazil, Congo, Indonesia and Peru — that have more than $5 billion of outstanding U.S. debt. Given their economies, they are unlikely to repay much of the debt anyway. So, he asks, why not forgive it in exchange for such initiatives as the creation of funds to preserve and restore forested areas? "This is one case where, for a very small subsidy, there can be a huge return," he says. "It's a common-sense approach to a major problem that affects all of us, not just the countries that have tropical forests."

In addition to the $50 million this year, the plan would spend $125 million in the two years on the debt-for-nature swaps. [46]

But with lawmakers pursuing competing plans to cut taxes, boost military spending and shore up the Social Security and Medicare trust funds, it remains uncertain whether they will find the money for the rain forest initiative. Indeed, rain forest conservation efforts generally have received limited attention in Congress. In recent years, for example, funding for AID programs to protect rain forests have either remained stable or slightly declined. At present, the agency spends about

$15 million to $20 million annually on forestry initiatives.

On the other hand, the United States is stepping up initiatives with other industrialized nations. It joined more than 30 other nations in pledging a total of $2.75 billion in 1998 to the Global Environment Facility, a multilateral group that works closely with the United Nations and the World Bank to promote environmental initiatives worldwide. Of that money, $300 million or more is expected to be spent assisting countries to protect their rain forests.

The G-7, meanwhile, has launched additional initiatives throughout the decade, including pledging most of the funding for a $250 million pilot project to save the remaining Brazilian Amazon. President Clinton in October 1997 promised an additional $10 million, saying: "We share Brazil's determination to conserve the Amazon, one of the world's most wondrous and biologically diverse environmental habitats."

But facing an economic crisis, Brazil cut much of its environmental budget in 1998, leaving the fate of the new program in doubt. Also uncertain is whether President Cardoso will follow through on his 1998 pledge to set aside 10 percent of the rain forest, or 240,000 square miles.

Market-Based Solutions

Even as world leaders appear stymied over rain forest conservation efforts, country music is moving to bridge the gap. Gibson Musical Instruments in Nashville, Tenn., has released a new line of guitars made from wood that is harvested using environmentally friendly techniques and certified by the Forest Stewardship Council. Although guitar makers normally rely on mahogany and other rare tropical woods, they are concerned about the growing scarcity of certain woods.

"If we keep using the forests at the rate we're currently doing and not paying any attention to maintaining them, there won't be any more left," says Gene Nix, a Gibson wood specialist.

While Washington officials focus on the rain forest battle overseas, some environmentalists are looking for success in the consumer products arena. They believe that a key to saving the rain forests will be generating consumer demand for environmentally friendly versions of wood, coffee and other rain forest products. And consumers appear to be on their side: a poll cited by the Rainforest Alliance showed that 66 percent of consumers would switch brands to favor corporations that demonstrate environmental responsibility. [47]

Many businesses are trying to cultivate images as environmental stewards. After protests by the Rainforest Action Network, for example, retailing giant Home Depot promised early this year to emphasize selling wood that is harvested from carefully managed forests. Similarly, Seattle-based Starbucks entered into a three-year

A ground orchid reflects the rich biodiversity of the rain forest in East Madagascar.

O. Langrand/World Wildlife Fund

agreement with Conservation International (CI) in 1999 to help farmers grow coffee in the shade of forest canopies, instead of cutting down trees. The partnership will focus initially on coffee growers adjacent to one of the world's most threatened and environmentally diverse ecosystems: the El Triunfo Biosphere Reserve in Chiapas, Mexico.

"Starbucks and CI share an interest in ensuring that coffee production does not harm the world's rich and fragile tropical forests," said Starbucks President Orin Smith.

At the forefront of the lumber effort is the Mexico-based Forest Stewardship Council, an international organization that certifies well-managed forests and their wood products. To win certification, a logging company must do minimal harm to animal habitats and local cultures. Logging must be limited to a pace that allows a forest to replenish itself. Since its founding in 1993 by a coalition of logging companies and environmental organizations, the council has certified more than 37 million acres worldwide. [48]

"It allows consumers to make an intelligent choice and choose products that come from well-managed forests," says Richard Donovan, president of SmartWood, a Vermont-based conservation organization that works with the council to certify wood.

The idea seems to be gaining acceptance in the logging community. Even though unrestricted logging techniques can frequently be more economical, Donovan said that 200 logging operations around the world have become certified, with the loggers in many cases approaching the environmental community, rather than the other way around. "They feel they either want to do it for their own

At Issue:

Is it economically viable to look for natural cures in rain forests?

JOSHUA ROSENTHAL
Program Director for Biodiversity, Fogarty International Center, National Institutes of Health

WRITTEN FOR *THE CQ RESEARCHER*, MAY 1999.

ompounds derived from plants, animals and micro-organisms always have been and will continue to be important sources of medicinal agents. Forty percent of all drugs approved by the FDA between 1983 and 1994 were derived from natural products. Currently, major new pharmaceuticals derived from natural products are in clinical trials for treatment of extreme pain, cancer, AIDS, malaria, obesity, Alzheimer's and heart disease, among other therapeutic needs.

Tropical forests contain more than half of the species on the planet. These rich ecosystems historically have been an important source of many of these drugs, and yet we have analyzed only a tiny fraction of their species for pharmaceutical potential. In recognition of this potential the National Institutes of Health, most of the world's major pharmaceutical companies, hundreds of biotechnology companies and many other public and private organizations support natural products discovered from rain forests. Most scientists believe that it pays to look for natural cures in rain forests.

Perhaps a more debatable question is whether new drugs from tropical forests will pay for conservation of these endangered habitats. It would be unrealistic to depend on any single income source to counter the enormous economic pressures responsible for tropical forest destruction, and most conservation programs employ a variety of approaches.

In fact, we have seen already that combining drug-discovery research with conservation — bioprospecting — can be very powerful. This year the government of the small Amazonian country of Suriname set aside 4 million acres of tropical rain forest for preservation. In part, this occurred because supporters in Suriname were able to point to an active bioprospecting program in their country that is yielding a variety of benefits to local communities as well as scientific and government institutions. In the process, a piece of rain forest has been conserved that provides all of us with many benefits, including potentially new treatments for diseases, replenishment of global oxygen supply, recreational opportunities and many others.

Perhaps the greatest irony of today's dramatic rates of tropical deforestation and associated species extinction is that this process coincides with explosive growth in our scientific and technical ability to explore and develop the biochemical riches of those forests. Discovery of new medicines is not the only reason for, nor the singular means of, preserving these unique, irreplaceable treasures — just one of the best we have.

R. DAVID SIMPSON
Fellow, Resources for the Future

WRITTEN FOR *THE CQ RESEARCHER*, APRIL 1999.

ome people argue that every time we lose biodiversity-rich habitat we lose a treasure trove of potential cures for AIDS or cancer or a disease yet-to-be-identified. Since cures depend on having as many leads as possible, so the argument goes, we must conserve as many genes, species and ecosystems as we can. If pharmaceutical researchers only realized how much money they could be making from biodiversity, the argument concludes, they would conserve habitat.

Regrettably, the argument doesn't hold water. Saving more tropical rain forests will have little effect on the chance of finding the next miracle drug or of making a bundle.

Economically speaking, a species' value lies in the added chance it creates that researchers will find what they are looking for. With millions and millions of species in existence, sources of useful products are either so common as to be redundant, or so rare as to make discovery unlikely. Either way, the sheer numbers of wild plants and animals available to sift through mean no wild area is worth much as the potential source, say, of a chemical that will treat cancer.

Research by Resources for the Future has shown that pharmaceutical companies would be willing to pay, at most, only a couple of dollars per hectare to preserve some of the most imperiled, biodiverse regions on Earth. The money to be made isn't enough to overcome the pressures for metropolitan expansion in such "hot spots."

One needn't appeal only to rarified economic theory to see that the economic case for biodiversity preservation through bioprospecting remains bleak. The British science journal *Nature* documented the dearth of ventures as the cover feature of its April 9, 1998, issue. The rush of interest, contracts — and, eventually, revenue — that many early advocates hoped for has failed to materialize.

Biodiversity does matter — for commercial, ecological, esthetic, ethical and spiritual reasons. No substitute exists for it as a whole. Still, bioprospecting is no key to conservation. In terms of profit, preservation for the purpose rarely beats out other land-use options. In terms of success in finding useful products, this enterprise doesn't depend on the vastness of virgin habitat. By insisting otherwise, we may be diverting attention — and funds — from more promising conservation strategies.

The Limits of Reforestation

The volcanic island of Krakatoa was about the size of Manhattan and covered with lush rain forests before its eruption in 1883. But all life and most of the island was destroyed in an explosion that was of such force — equivalent to about 100-150 megatons of TNT — that the resulting airwave circled the Earth seven times, stirred seas as far away as France and created ash-colored sunsets worldwide for years. A series of tidal waves killed some 40,000 people on the nearby islands of Java and Sumatra. [1]

As for Krakatoa, it virtually ceased to exist. All the explosion left behind were four fragments — small lifeless islands covered with volcanic ash up to more than 300 feet deep. Naturalists working in nearby Indonesia began surveying the island, wondering if it would reveal how a rain forest emerges from total destruction.

It soon became clear that the islands were not destined to remain devoid of life. Just nine months after the explosion, a French expedition discovered a single animal: a microscopic spider. It apparently had floated in on a strand of silk. [2] Other forms of life gradually arrived, including insects and the seeds of plants that were carried by wind and water from islands 25 miles away. Just 10 years after the eruption, explorers found a few saplings; by the 1920s, the island was largely covered by forest. [3]

But nature has yet to entirely recover. Few of the new trees are found in the mature rain forests of Java and Sumatra, and recent surveys have found just five species of butterflies. It may be hundreds or even thousands of years before the forest, sustained by a cycle of numerous species of insects and birds scattering the pollen and seeds of a great variety of plants, recovers its former luxuriance. Still, the island's thick tree cover "offers testimony to the ingenuity and resilience of life," according to Harvard University biologist Edward O. Wilson. [4]

For conservationists dismayed by the current worldwide destruction of rain forests, Krakatoa offers both hope and caution. Certainly, nature is a resilient force, and rain forests that are partially logged or used for small-scale slash-and-burn farming can recover. In some cases, small clearings may help rare species that have trouble contending with dominant tree competitors.

On the other hand, badly damaged rain forests may take centuries to regain their onetime glory, and rain forest land that is cleared altogether for such activities as cattle ranching may never grow a wealth of plants again. Furthermore, even minor deforestation can cause the extinction of endemic species.

For all their profusion of growth, rain forests are far more fragile than the temperate woods in the United States and Western Europe. In temperate zones, the soil typically contains the nutrients necessary for life and remains hospitable to trees.

But rain forests are a very different type of ecosystem. Nutrients and carbon are generally stored in the tissue and dead wood of vegetation, while the soils tend to be heavily acidic and poor. Although some rain forest soils are rich with volcanic minerals, they are more commonly so sandy that scientists sometimes refer to the areas as "wet deserts." Moreover, the seeds of tropical trees tend to be fragile, germinating within weeks instead of lying dormant for long periods until the right conditions of temperature and humidity occur, as do seeds in temperate regions.

"In some areas, where the greatest damage is combined with low soil fertility and no native forest exists nearby to provide seeds, restoration might never occur without human intervention." Wilson wrote. "Ohio, in a word, is not the Amazon." [5]

There are other worrisome indications that much of the rain forests will never come back, even if large-scale restoration efforts are attempted. The forests interact in mysterious ways with the weather, bringing down the rain that they need for sustenance. Cutting down trees reduces humidity, potentially drying the land. Also, heavily logged forests tend to lose their genetic variation, resulting in trees that may be more susceptible to disease and stunted growth. A recent study indicated that trees left standing in pastures can dominate the reproduction in remnant forests, creating a "genetic bottleneck," because the seeds from the pasture are more easily spread by birds and other animals. [6]

Because of such barriers, conservation organizations focus on warding off destruction before it happens. To be sure, they point to minor restoration projects, such as tree-planting programs that create natural corridors for wildlife to move from one patch of forest to another. But the sense generally is that once a rain forest is destroyed, there is little hope it can return.

"Once they're lost, they're gone," says Bruce J. Carbarle, director of the World Wildlife Fund's global forest program. Noting that the rain forests have been evolving steadily since the last Ice Age 8,000 years ago, he adds: "It would be inconceivable to think we could re-create that."

---

[1] Edward O. Wilson, *Diversity of Life*, (1992), p. 16.

[2] *Ibid*, p. 19.

[3] Mark Collins, *The Last Rain Forests* (1990), p. 51.

[4] Wilson, *op.cit.*, p. 23.

[5] *Ibid*, p. 274.

[6] University of Georgia press release, July 2, 1998. The study is by Prof. James Hamrick.

internal credibility reasons or there's a market for it," he said.

Some environmentalists, however, have misgivings about whether it makes sense to focus on sustainable logging. With scientists struggling to understand the basic biology of rain forests — the growth rate of different species and the ways in which seeds are dispersed and pollinators work — conservationists disagree over what methods may be used to log a forest without greatly damaging it. In fact, reports by Conservation International warn that repeatedly logging a forest for one species of tree, such as mahogany, can create severe ecological damage, especially if logging companies clear out competing vegetation to spur growth of the desired tree. A more effective approach, according to CI researchers, would be to purchase already logged areas that may cost as little as 5 percent of the pre-logging price. [49]

But Donovan believes it is possible to strike a balance between the demand for lumber and the need to protect forests. To ensure an adequate level of protection, he said the Forest Stewardship Council may request a complete logging ban in such areas as steep hillsides where there is a chance of severe erosion or where the last vestiges of a rain forest may harbor endangered species. "Every forest is different, and you have to look at the circumstances," he said. "It's got a great potential for success." ■

OUTLOOK

A Question of Money

Loggers, cattle ranchers, plantation owners, developers and miners— all have been blamed for the destruction of the rain forests. But even if they were to stop their activities tomorrow, British environmentalist Norman Myers believes it would do little to save the forests. He identifies the growing number of landless peasants, desperate to feed their families, as the driving force behind clearing away trees.

In the Philippines, for example, he says forested areas have dropped from about two-thirds of the nation's land area in 1945 to one-sixth or less at present. Landless peasants, driven from the fertile lowlands by rapid population growth and the concentration of agriculture into large farms and plantations, have migrated by the millions to formerly unpopulated upland forests. Using machetes and matches, farmers desperately try to clear a few acres of land and stave off starvation for another couple of years.

The number of slash-and-burn, or shifting, farmers in the developing world has been estimated at between 200 million and 600 million — meaning they could account for as many as one-in-10 people on the planet. "Shadowy figures to Western eyes, they are precipitating the most rapid global change in land use in history," Myers warned. [50]

For all their efforts to set aside preserves and persuade multinational corporations to adopt environmentally friendly practices, conservationists know they cannot turn the tide without confronting poverty and population growth. Already estimated at 6 billion, the world's population is projected to surpass 10 billion by the year 2050. [51] As the flood of people exhausts the nutrient-poor soil of the rain forests and exposes the land to more erosion and watershed contamination, the poverty can only become more intense.

To compensate, some analysts believe developing countries should try to improve their crop yields from existing farmlands. Since the rain forests tend to be too poor for sustained farming, agricultural economists such as Southgate of Ohio State University say the focus should be on making existing farmland more productive, thereby alleviating food shortages and the need to clear more land. In addition, they promote such initiatives as agroforestry — using land for crops, pasture and trees — and the creation of tree plantations so loggers will have little incentive to blaze roads into remote areas.

But such proposals are not without a downside. More intensive agricultural methods can harm the environment because of soil erosion and possible water contamination by fertilizers and pesticides.

Others call for more emphasis on creating preserves and patrolling them to stop illegal logging and poaching. Two professors at the Center for Tropical Conservation at Duke University, Randall Kramer and Carel van Schaik, recently concluded that law enforcement should be "a fact of life" in many parks, since that may be the surest way to guarantee the long-term survival of vital ecosystems — and perhaps the future well-being of nearby communities. [52]

But it is not clear whether parks can be fully protected, even with vigilant patrols. Noting that Salvadoran peasants pushed their way into Honduras and the United States despite the best efforts of law enforcement, Southgate asked: "If rural people who are desperate to support themselves and their families pay little heed to national frontiers, how much respect are they ever likely to show for park boundaries?" [53]

Similarly, Southgate and others question the long-term benefits of such economic gambits as carbon sequestration and a tax structure offering incentives for conserving land

and water. Unless both the poor as well as the wealthy profit from conservation, the rain forests will continue to be besieged.

In the end, the solution may come down to money. If the industrialized nations believe it is in their best interests to save the rain forests, they may have to dig into their budgets and pay for it. "What you have to do is provide enough money to make it worthwhile for people who normally destroy the forests not to destroy the forests," said economist Simpson of Resources for the Future. "Basically, you've got to pay them off." ■

FOR MORE INFORMATION

Conservation International, 2501 M St., N.W., Suite 200, Washington, D.C. 20037; (202) 429-5660; www.conservation.org. CI promotes rain forest preservation through economic development, including the exchange of debt relief for conservation programs that involve local people.

World Resources Institute, 10 G St. N.E., Suite 800, Washington, D.C. 20002; (202) 729-7600; www.wri.org. WRI is an independent center for policy research and technical assistance on global environmental and development issues.

World Wildlife Fund, P.O. Box 97180, 1250 24th St., N.W., Washington, D.C. 20037; (202) 293-9211; www.wwf.org. WWF conducts scientific research and analyzes policy on environmental and conservation issues and supports projects to promote biodiversity and save endangered species and their habitats.

Worldwatch Institute, 1776 Massachusetts Ave., N.W., Washington, D.C. 20036; www.worldwatch.org. This research organization focuses on interdisciplinary approaches to solving global environmental problems.

Notes

[1] "Devastation of Denuded Hillsides," *Los Angeles Times*, Nov. 22, 1998.

[2] Mark Collins, *The Last Rain Forests* (1990), p. 96.

[3] Randall Kramer, Carel van Schaik and Julie Johnson, *Last Stand* (1992), p. 19.

[4] United Nations Food and Agriculture Organization, "Report on the State of the Forests," 1997.

[5] *Ibid.*

[6] "As Trees Go, Haiti Becomes a Caribbean Desert," *Reuters*, Dec. 15, 1998.

[7] Glenn McKenzie, "West Africa Faces Grim Choice; Ivory Coast Families Killing Precious Rain Forests for Lucrative Crops," *Chicago Tribune*, Feb. 15, 1999, p. 4.

[8] From AID's Web site, www.info.usaid.gov/environment, April 6, 1999.

[9] "Canal Ecology Endangered; Rain Forest Needs More Protection," *The Washington Times*, Jan. 13, 1999, p. A1.

[10] McKenzie, *op. cit.*

[11] Diana Jean Schemo, "Brazil Slashes Money for Project Aimed at Protecting Amazon," *The New York Times*, Jan. 1, 1999, p. A9.

[12] Kramer et al, *op. cit.*, p. 32.

[13] Schemo, *op. cit.*

[14] Cambridge International Forecasts, February 1999.

[15] Gerald Hanlon, letter to *The Guardian*, Feb. 14, 1999.

[16] Kramer et al, *op. cit.*, pp. 16, 19.

[17] Diana Jean Schemo, "Data Show Recent Burning of Amazon is Worst Ever," *The New York Times*, Jan. 27, 1998, p. A3.

[18] Fred Pearce, "No Hope for Rain Forests," *Fort Lauderdale Sun-Sentinel*, Nov. 1, 1998, p. 28A.

[19] Kramer et al, *op. cit.*, p. 21

[20] *Ibid*, p. 23.

[21] Carel Van Schaik, John Terborgh and Barbara Dugelby, "The Silent Crisis: The State of Rain Forest Nature Preserves," in Kramer et al, *op. cit.*, p. 64.

[22] Douglas Southgate, *Tropical Forest Conservation* (1998), p. 45.

[23] Edward O. Wilson, *The Diversity of Life* (1992), p. 283.

[24] "Water, We Can Care For It!", The Nature Conservancy, p. 5.

[25] Janet N. Abramovitz, "The Complex Realities of Sharing Genetic Assets," *Nature*, April 9, 1998.

[26] The Associated Press, Nov. 25, 1998.

[27] Anthony Faiola, "Killing the Forest for the Trees," *The Washington Post*, March 23, 1999, p. A11.

[28] Worldwatch Institute, *Taking a Stand*, (1998), pp. 7-8, 32.

[29] Fred Pearce, "Economy Turns Turtle," *The Guardian*, Feb. 25, 1999, p. 7.

[30] Sara Silver, The Associated Press, Dec. 15, 1998.

[31] "Reinventing the Well," Conservation International, p. 18, and National Public Radio, Feb. 7, 1999.

[32] Richard Pyle, The Associated Press, "Texaco Says Ecuadorian Indian Lawsuit Doesn't Belong in U.S. Courts," Feb. 2, 1999.

[33] Roger Thompson, "Requiem for Rain Forests?" *Editorial Research Reports*, Dec. 20, 1985, pp. 945-964.

[34] Collins, *op. cit.*, p. 14.

[35] *Ibid*, p. 96.

[36] *Ibid*, p. 13.

[37] *Ibid*, p. 39.

[38] Karen Catchpole, "Welcome to the Jungle," *Escape*, April 1999, p. 44.

[39] Laura Tangley, *The Rain forest* (1992), p. 46.

[40] *Ibid*, p. 37.

[41] Virginia Morell, "The Variety of Life," *National Geographic*, April 1999, p. 16.

[42] Collins, *op. cit.*, p. 93.

[43] Mary H. Cooper, "Saving the Forests," *The CQ Researcher*, Sept. 20, 1991, pp. 681-704.

[44] Tangley, *op. cit.*, p. 98.

[45] Wilson, *op. cit.*, p. 280.

[46] Testimony before House Appropriations Subcommittee on Foreign Operations, Export Financing and Related programs, March 1, 1999.

[47] Rainforest Alliance fact sheet.

[48] *Ibid.*

[49] Laura Tangley, "Sustainable Logging Proves Unsupportable," *U.S. News & World Report*, June 29, 1998, p. 63.

[50] Norman Myers, "Pushed to the Edge," *Natural History*, March 1999, p. 20.

[51] Kramer et al, *op. cit.*, p. 16.

[52] *Ibid*, p. 215.

[53] Southgate, *op. cit.*, p. 149.

Bibliography

Selected Sources Used

Books

Collins, Mark, ed., *The Last Rain Forests*, Oxford University Press, 1990.

A beautifully illustrated book that details the life of the rain forests, including the people who live there and the many plant and animal species that make these forests. The book also discusses the reasons for deforestation and urges action to save the forests.

Kramer, Randall, Carel van Schaik and Julie Johnson, eds., *Last Stand*, Oxford University Press, 1992.

This collection of essays by economists and conservationists about the myriad threats facing the rain forests includes a final chapter on strategies to save the forests.

Southgate, Douglas, *Tropical Forest Conservation*, Oxford University Press, 1998.

This academic treatment of the main economic issues facing Latin America's forests contains in-depth analyses of such conservation strategies as bioprospecting, ecotourism, marketing of non-timber forest products and more intense agricultural use of already-cleared land.

Tangley, Laura, *The Rainforest*, Chelsea House, 1992.

A leading environmentalists has written an easy-to-read introduction to the rain forests. Tangley discusses the devastating effects of deforestation on local people and the environment, and proposes alternatives to destroying them.

Wilson, Edward O., *The Diversity of Life*, Harvard University Press, 1992.

In this landmark book, one of the world's leading biologists warns that the Earth may face a massive extinction of plant and animal species unless major conservation steps are undertaken. Wilson focuses much of his discussion on the rain forests, detailing the many ways that they can enrich future generations if left intact.

Articles

"The Complex Realities of Sharing Genetic Assets," *Nature*, April 9, 1998.

A series of articles examining the economic and scientific issues of trying to use plant and animal species to create new drugs.

Morell, Virginia, "The Variety of Life," *National Geographic*, February 1999.

This package of five articles captures the stunning diversity of Earth's plant and animal species and spells out the threat of a major wave of extinctions.

Pearce, Fred, "Playing with Fire," *New Scientist*, March 21, 1998.

A detailed examination of the causes and devastating consequences of forest fires in Indonesia.

Reports and Studies

Bryant, Dirk, Daniel Nielsen and Laura Tangley, "The Last Frontier Forests," World Resources Institute, 1997.

This landmark report and concludes that just 20 percent of the Earth's original forest cover still remains in large, relatively undisturbed tracts.

Forests for Life, World Wildlife Fund, 1998.

The fund's annual global forest report summarizes major conservation efforts as well as environmental threats and forest destruction.

Gordon, Debra L., Marianne Guerin-McManus and Amy B. Rosenfeld, "Reinventing the Well," Conservation International, 1997.

This report by a conservation group that seeks to minimize the environmental effects of industrial development in the Tropics focuses on oil development. It provides case studies of companies that have used "best practices" to protect the environment as well as examples of the environmental and social damage caused by careless industrial development.

State of the World's Forests, United Nations Food and Agriculture Organization, 1999.

A biannual report that surveys deforestation and conservation initiatives worldwide. Despite finding evidence of continuing deforestation, the report concluded that more and more countries were taking steps to protect their forests. The report is perhaps the most widely quoted source for statistics on the destruction of rain forests and other types of forests, but environmentalists believe it understates the crisis facing forests by reporting only on areas that have been entirely cleared of trees, rather than areas that have been just partially cleared.

Wood, Megan Epler, "Meeting the Global Challenge of Community Participation in Ecotourism: Case Studies and Lessons from Ecuador," The Nature Conservancy, 1998.

The president of the Ecotourism Association analyses the benefits as well as the drawbacks of ecotourism, with specific recommendations about how to make travel more environmentally friendly in Ecuador.

How to Write a Research Paper

This guide to writing a research paper is arranged in five parts: the first section outlines six steps that will help you write a paper—from getting ready to choose a topic to writing and revising. The second part discusses library research, and the third and fourth give tips on using the Web to conduct research. Finally, you will find a list of links to useful online resources. The Internet is constantly changing. Be aware that some of the resources noted here may no longer be available; however, you should be able to find most of them and what is included here will give you a good idea of the information that is available.

Six Steps to Writing a Research Paper

Step 1   Getting Started

Goal: Preparing for the assignment and getting ready to choose a topic

UNDERSTAND THE ASSIGNMENT. Read over the instructions for the assignment to make sure you fully understand what the instructor has in mind and on what basis you will be graded.

CONSIDER THE PROCESS YOU'LL USE. The paper is your final *product,* but a research paper involves an extensive *process* before you can generate the product. If you focus too quickly on the end product, you may miss some of the important research steps and find yourself writing a paper

Adapted, with permission, from *A+ Research and Writing for High School and College Students,* copyright 1997 by Kathryn L. Schwartz. Published by the Internet Public Library: http://www.ipl.org.

without enough understanding of the topic. Browse over the rest of the steps suggested here to get an idea of the process and think about how you'll approach each step. Start a journal or notebook and begin jotting notes about not only "what" you plan to do but also "how" you plan to do it.

SET YOUR DEADLINES FOR EACH STEP OF THE ASSIGNMENT. Ideally, you will have at least four weeks from the date it's assigned to complete a research paper of seven or eight pages (2,000 to 2,500 words). Shorter papers requiring fairly simple research (four or five pages—1,500 words) may not require four weeks' "lead time," while a fifteen-page or longer paper might be a semester-long project.

THINK ABOUT POSSIBLE TOPICS: The word "topic" is used variably by many teachers of writing and research to mean anything from the very general "subject matter" to the very specific "thesis statement." Here, the term *topic* is broadly defined, while *focus* means a narrower perspective on the topic, and *thesis* statement is the main point of your paper, which cannot be determined until after research and analysis is complete.

INFO SEARCH—BROWSE, READ, RELAX. Start by thumbing through the textbooks or course pack for the class in which your paper was assigned. Browse the table of contents, chapter headings and subheadings to get an overview of the subject matter. Visit your library and browse in the catalog and reference room to find out what sources are held by the library that may relate to your class. Browse some of the subject-indexed sources on the Internet with the same purpose.

RELATE YOUR PRIOR EXPERIENCE AND LEARNING. The process of successful research and writing involves build-

ing on what you know. You don't need to know a *lot* about a subject to use it as your topic, but choosing one you're totally unfamiliar with could be a mistake. It may take so much time and effort to become informed about the subject that you don't really have time to get into the depth required by your assignment.

JOT DOWN YOUR QUESTIONS AND IDEAS ABOUT POSSIBLE TOPICS. Use your notebook to starting recording questions that interest you or ideas for possible topics.

You'll end up with a list of ideas and musings, some of which are obviously ridiculous and not reasonable topics for your paper, but don't worry about that at this point. Think about things that interest you and that build upon some experience or knowledge you have or build upon things you're presently learning in class.

BRAINSTORM, ALONE AND WITH OTHERS. Toss ideas around in your mind. Bounce ideas off of your classmates, your teacher or your siblings and parents to get their reactions and ideas. Many times another person will have a fresh perspective you might not have thought of, or something they say will trigger an idea for you.

Step 2   Discovering and Choosing a Topic

Goal: Discovering and choosing a topic for your research

INFO SEARCH—READ FOR OVERVIEW OF VARIOUS TOPICS. Use the notes you've made and the thinking you've done so far to select some areas for general reading. Use the library's reference room—encyclopedias, dictionaries, almanacs—to get an overview of possible topics (even if your instructor has told you that you can't use an encyclopedia as a reference—that's not important at this stage).

Explore CD-ROM tools in your library, like newspaper and magazine indexes, searching with key words representing your topic ideas. Explore the Internet by using several of the resources organized by subject.

Remember to keep your concept of topic rather broad at this stage—you can look for a focus later, after you know something about the topic.

CONTINUE THINKING AND JOTTING DOWN QUESTIONS AND IDEAS IN YOUR NOTEBOOK. As you read, ideas and questions may strike you—write them down, or you'll lose track of them. Look for issues that interest you, that arouse your curiosity or your passion. Consider the audience for your research paper: what kinds of things have been discussed in class that seemed to interest the class and the instructor? What kinds of issues were touched upon but could use further study and elaboration?

INFO SURVEY—WHAT PRINT AND ELECTRONIC RESOURCES ARE AVAILABLE? When you've narrowed your choices down, make a quick survey of the research resources that will be available to you on each potential topic. How much information seems to be available in your library's catalog? If it's a current topic, is there information in newspaper and magazine indexes and are those newspapers and magazines held by your library? Is there much authoritative information on your topic on the Internet? Is the available information slanted to one side of an issue versus another? How much work will it take to get the information you need if you choose a particular topic?

TRY DIFFERENT TOPICS ON FOR "SIZE." The topic you choose should "fit" in several important respects: your interests and knowledge, the purpose of the assignment, the type of paper (report, issue, argument), the length of the paper. Don't worry too much about having a broad topic at this point. Look for topic ideas at Researchpaper.com (http://www. researchpaper.com/) or in your library. Ask the reference librarian if the library has books of suggested topics like Kathryn Lamm's *10,000 Ideas for Term Papers, Projects, Reports & Speeches* (New York: Macmillan, 1995).

Step 3   Looking for and Forming a Focus

Goal: Exploring your topic; finding and forming a focus for your research

INFO SEARCH—EXPLORING YOUR TOPIC. Before you can decide on a focus, you need to explore your topic, to become informed about the topic, to build on your knowledge and experience. You'll be locating books, articles, videos, Internet and other resources about your topic and reading to learn! You're looking for an issue, an aspect, a perspective on which to focus your research paper.

This is the first step in which you'll probably be checking books out of the library. Encyclopedias won't be much help here. You're looking for treatments of your topic that are either more comprehensive or more specific than an encyclopedic treatment, with various authors' summaries, analyses and opinions. But, until you've chosen a focus, you're not really on a mission of gathering information. If you gather information on the topic as a whole, you'll waste a lot of time doing it and have way too much to sort through when you are ready to write your paper. Resist the temptation to "gather" until you've chosen a focus. Now you'll be using the library's online catalog, online indexes and the Web search engines along with the reference room and the subject-based Web directories.

INFO SEARCH—PRELIMINARY NOTE TAKING. As you read, start taking notes of what you're learning about your topic—concepts, issues, problems, areas where experts agree or disagree. Keep track of the bibliographic references for the information you're using, and write down a note or two of what's contained in the book, article, Website, etc. There's nothing more frustrating than knowing you read something earlier about a particular point and not being able to locate it again when you decide it's something you need.

Find out what kind of citations are required by your instructor and make sure you're recording what you'll need to do your bibliography.

PURPOSEFUL THINKING ABOUT POSSIBLE FOCUSES. While you're learning about your topic, intentionally look for possible focuses in the material. You could spend enormous amounts of time reading, especially about an interesting topic, without being any closer to a focus unless you purposefully keep that goal in your mind while you read.

CHOOSING A FOCUS OR COMBINING THEMES TO FORM A FOCUS. Try your choices of focus on for "size" as you did your topic. Which ones fit the assignment, the size, scope and type of the paper? Think about which of your possible focuses has the best chance for making a successful paper. If you find several themes within your topic that separately are too small to support the entire paper, can they be combined to form a focus?

Step 4   Gathering Information

Goal: Gathering information that clarifies and supports your focus

INFO SEARCH—FINDING, COLLECTING AND RECORDING. This is the step most people think of when they think of "library research." It's a hunt for information in any available form (book, periodical, CD, video, Internet) which is pertinent to your chosen focus. Once you know the focus of your research, there are lots of tools and strategies to help you find and collect the information you need.

Your information search should be focused and specific, but pay careful attention to serendipity (finding, by chance, valuable things you weren't even looking for). Keep your mind open to continue learning about your focused topic.

Now is the time to carefully record your sources in the bibliographic format required by your instructor. Every piece of information you collect should have bibliographic information written down before you leave the library. You should also pay attention to the quality of the information you find, especially if you're using information you find on the Internet. Now is also the time to learn the details of using search engines. Many of the sources you will want to use are online, whether in the library or on the Internet.

THINK ABOUT CLARIFYING OR REFINING YOUR FOCUS. As you gather information about your focused topic, you may find new information that prompts you to refine, clarify, extend or narrow your focus. Stay flexible and adjust your information search to account for the changes, widening or narrowing your search, or heading down a slightly different path to follow a new lead.

START ORGANIZING YOUR NOTES. Start organizing your notes into logical groups. You may notice a gap in your research, or a more heavy weighting to one aspect of the subject than what you had intended. Starting to organize as you gather information can save an extra trip to the library. It's better to find the gap

now instead of the night before your paper is due.

THINK ABOUT WHAT YOUR THESIS STATEMENT WILL BE. The thesis statement is the main point of your paper. The type of thesis statement you'll be making depends a lot on what type of paper you're writing—a report, an issue analysis, an advocacy paper or another type. As you gather specific information and refine your focus, intentionally look for a main point to your findings. Sometimes, a thesis emerges very obviously from the material, and other times you may struggle to bring together the parts into a sensible whole. The tricky part is knowing when to stop gathering information—when do you have enough, and of the right kind? Seeking a main point as you research will help you know when you're done.

Step 5   Preparing to Write

Goal: Analyzing and organizing your information and forming a thesis statement

ANALYZE AND ORGANIZE YOUR INFORMATION. The word "analyze" means to break something down into its parts. A meaningful analysis identifies the parts and demonstrates how they relate to each other. You may have information from different sources that examines different aspects of your topic. By breaking down the information, you may be able to see relationships between the different sources and form them into a whole concept. When you're trying to make sense of the information coming out of your research process, you often have to look at it from different perspectives and sometimes have to step back and try to get a "big picture" view. Some ways to do this are to try out different organization patterns: compare and contrast, advantages and disadvantages, starting from a narrow premise and building on it,

cause and effect, logical sequence.

CONSTRUCT A THESIS STATEMENT AND TRY IT ON FOR "SIZE." Before beginning to write the paper, write the thesis statement. Boil down the main point of your paper to a single statement. Sharon Williams and Laura Reidy at the Hamilton College site (http://www.hamilton.edu/academic/Resource/WC/Intro_Thesis.html) give this explanation of the thesis statement:

A well-written thesis statement, usually expressed in one sentence, is the most important sentence in your entire paper. It should both summarize for your reader the position you will be arguing and set up the pattern of organization you will use in your discussion. A thesis sentence is not a statement of accepted fact; it is the position that needs the proof you will provide in your argument. Your thesis should reflect the full scope of your argument—no more and no less; beware of writing a thesis statement that is too broad to be defended within the scope of your paper.

Another way to summarize the nature and function of the thesis statement is that it is a single sentence, usually in the first paragraph of the paper, which:

- declares the position you are taking in your paper,
- sets up the way you will organize your discussion, and
- points to the conclusion you will draw.

WEED OUT IRRELEVANT INFORMATION. Now that you have all those wonderful notes and citations from your research, you're going to have to get rid of some of them! No matter how profound and interesting the information is, if it doesn't relate to and support the thesis you've chosen, don't try to cram it into the paper—just set it aside. You'll have an easier time writing if you do this weeding before you start.

Appendix

INFO SEARCH—FILL IN THE GAPS. Once you've identified which of your research notes you'll use, you may see some gaps where you need an additional support for a point you want to make. Leave enough time in your writing plan for an extra trip to the library, just in case.

Step 6   Writing the Paper

Goal: Writing, revising and finalizing the paper

THINK ABOUT THE ASSIGNMENT, THE AUDIENCE AND THE PURPOSE. To prepare for writing, go over once more the requirements of the assignment to make sure you focus your writing efforts on what's expected by your instructor. Consider the purpose of the paper, either as set forth in the assignment, or as stated in your thesis statement—are you trying to persuade, to inform, to evaluate, to summarize?

- Who is your audience and how will that affect your paper?
- What prior knowledge can you assume the audience has about the topic?
- What style and tone of writing are required by the audience and the assignment—informal, scholarly, first-person reporting, dramatized?

PREPARE AN OUTLINE. Try to get a "model" outline for the type of paper you're writing, or look at examples of good papers to see how they were organized. The Roane State Community College Online Writing Lab (Jennifer Jordan-Henley) gives an example of an outline for a paper written to describe a problem. See http://www2.rscc.cc.tn.us/~jordan_jj/OWL/Research.html:

- Introduction
  Statement of the Problem
  Thesis Sentence
- Body: Paragraphs 1 and 2
  History of the Problem (Include,

perhaps, past attempts at solutions. Work in sources.)
- Body: Paragraphs 3 and 4
  Extent of the Problem (Who is affected? How bad is it? Work in sources.)
- Body: Paragraphs 5 and 6
  Repercussions of the Problem (Work in sources.)
- Body: Paragraphs 7 and 8
  Future solutions (not necessarily your own. More sources.)
- Conclusion
  Summarize your findings

WRITE THE ROUGH DRAFT—VISIT THE OWLs. Here's where the Online Writing Labs, or OWLs, excel—there are many dozens of great articles on every aspect of writing your paper. The Links to Online Resources pages (p. 201) have classified these by topic so that you can browse easily and pick out articles you want to read. The entire Links for Writing section will be helpful, and specifically the sections on:

- Title, introduction and conclusion
- Writing style and technique
- Grammar and punctuation

KNOW HOW TO USE YOUR SOURCE MATERIALS AND CITE THEM. See the section Citing Sources on the Links page (p. 201). There's also a nice section on using sources in the middle of the article entitled "Writing a General Research Paper" (http://www2.rscc.cc.tn.us/~jordan_jj/OWL/Research.html) from the Roane State Community College Online Writing Lab (Henley, 1996). The section, "What Happens When the Sources Seem to be Writing My Paper For Me?" describes how to break up long quotations and how to cite an author multiple times without letting the author take over your paper, and it links to both the MLA and the APA style requirements for partial quotations, full quotations, indented quotations, in-text quotations, and paraphrasing.

HAVE OTHERS READ AND CRITIQUE THE PAPER. Read your paper out loud, to yourself. See if the arguments are coherent, logical and conclusive when read aloud. Have several experienced people read and critique your paper. If your school has a writing lab, use the tutors or helpers there as critics.

REVISE AND PROOFREAD. See the "Revision Checklist" section of the article The Research Paper (http://www.chesapeake.edu/Writingcenter/respaper.html) from Chesapeake College. The checklist asks some general questions to help you step back and take a look at the overall content and structure of the paper, then drills down to paragraphs, sentences and words for a closer examination of the writing style. Almost all the OWLs have very large sections on grammar, sentence and paragraph structure, writing style, proofreading, revising and common errors.

Browse some of the larger OWLs like Purdue University and University of Victoria and see the linked articles on Revising and rewriting (p. 201).

Learning to Research in the Library

Get to know your library

Libraries build their collections based on what they think their patrons will need, so the collections of reference materials, fiction and non-fiction will differ between a public and an academic library. Be aware of what kind of collection you're working with, and make arrangements to visit a different library if necessary.

Learn to browse—understand the classification scheme in your library

A library's classification scheme is a system by which books are organized to be placed on the shelves.

Browsing the shelves is an important step when you're trying to get ideas for your research project, so it's worth the effort to become familiar with your library's system.

Most libraries in the U.S. use either the Dewey Decimal system or Library of Congress system, while Britain uses the UDC and other countries use various systems. All of the systems attempt to "co-locate" books with similar subject matter. In a smaller library, many times you can bypass the catalog as a starting point and go directly to the shelves for a first look at your topic, so long as you have a chart of the classification scheme as a guide.

Remember, though, that a book can have only one location in a library. Some books cover more than one subject and the cataloguer has to choose one place to locate the book. Also, non-book materials such as videos and films, will be located in a different section of the building and could be missed by simply shelf-browsing the book collection.

Learn how online library catalogs work

A library catalog is a listing of all the items held by a particular library. A cataloguer examines the item (book, video, map, audio tape, CD, etc.) and decides how it will be described in the library's catalog and under what subject it will be classified. When the item is entered into the library's online catalog database, information is entered into different fields, which are then searchable by users.

Library catalogs usually treat a book as a single "item" and catalog it that way, even if it might be a book of poetry or a book of essays by different authors. You can't find a reference to a particular poem in the library catalog, nor to a particular essay within a book of essays. The same is true of magazines, journals

and newspapers. The library catalog will tell you if the library keeps a particular periodical in its collection, but will not list all the articles within the periodical, nor will it necessarily even list all the issues of the periodical which are kept. There are other publications in the reference room which will help you retrieve these individual items, but usually not the library catalog.

Most catalogs are searchable by author, title, subject and keyword. Some of the important things you need to know about the information in those fields are discussed below.

SEARCHING THE CATALOG BY SUBJECT AND KEYWORD. The subject field of a catalog record contains only the words or phrases used by the cataloguer when assigning a subject heading. If the library is using Library of Congress Subject Headings (LCSH), for example, the subject heading for a book about how playing football affects the players' bodies would probably be assigned the subject heading "Football—physiological aspects." Unless you type in that entire phrase as your search term, you won't find the book by searching the subject field.

Subject field searching can be very helpful, but you must find out how the subject you're looking for is worded by using the subject manuals or getting help from the reference librarian. Once you zero in on an appropriate subject heading, a search in the catalog will give you a list of all the items in the library's collection categorized under that heading, so you can browse the collection online. Note also that most items are classified under one or two *very specific* subject headings, rather than under many subjects. The keyword field of a library catalog generally searches several fields in the database record— the author, title and description fields. The description is any information about the catalogued item which may

have been entered by the cataloguer. *This is not the full text of the book, nor is it an abstract (summary) of the book but rather a short paragraph containing information the cataloguer thought would be helpful to a user.* This is *not* like searching for keywords in an indexed database like Alta Vista on the Internet, where every word in a document has been recorded.

For this reason, keyword searching alone could miss an item pertinent to your research project if the keyword you use was not included in the short paragraph written by the cataloguer. It's best to use a combination of keyword searching and subject-field searching to make a comprehensive search of the library catalog.

SEARCHING OTHER LIBRARIES' CATALOGS. There are lots of library catalogs on the Internet—but so what? You can search the catalog of a library in Timbuktu, but that doesn't get you the book. Remember that library catalogs do not have full text of books and documents but are just a database with descriptions of the library's holdings. There are a few, and will be more, actual online libraries where you can go to read or search full text documents. Just don't confuse these special resources with a library catalog, which is very different.

Find out how to search for journals and newspapers at your library

Most libraries have either print, CD-ROM or online (either in the library or sometimes on the Web) indexes of magazine, journal and newspaper articles (referred to as periodicals) available for users. Some of these are abstracts of the articles, which are short summaries written to describe the article's contents in enough detail so that a reader can decide whether or not to seek out the

Appendix

full text. Some of these sources may be in the form of full text, where the entire articles have been entered into the database.

The databases will include particular periodicals published within a span of time (for example, a popular newspaper index goes back 36 months for certain major newspapers). Know what the database you're searching contains and whether it's represented as abstract or full text.

Note that these resources, whether print or digital, contain information about periodicals which may not be held by your library. If the database does not have full text articles, you may find an article right on point to your topic, but that particular newspaper or journal may not be in your library's collection. Check out your options with the reference desk if you need an article that's not in your library's collection.

Bibliography surfing

Web surfing is finding an interesting Web page and then using the hyperlinks on that page to jump to other pages. If you find the first page interesting, chances are you'll also be interested in the pages the author has chosen to link to. Librarians and researchers have been doing this for a long time, in the print medium. It's a valuable tool for identifying sources on your chosen topic.

What you do is use the bibliography provided at the end of an encyclopedia article, journal article or book that you've found particularly pertinent to your topic and follow the bibliographic references much as you would hyperlinks on the Web. Since you're locating items that influenced the author of the original article and to which he or she referred, they're likely to be "on point" to your topic. Then use the bibliography at the end of *those* cited articles to find even *more* items, and so on.

Consult the reference librarian for advice

Several times above, you've been advised to consult the reference librarian. Reference librarians can help save you a lot of time because they know their library's collection very well—both the reference collection and the nonfiction collection—and can often tell you "off the top of their heads" whether or not the library has a particular item you're looking for. They are also skilled searchers, both of the library's catalog and of online resources such as CD-ROM, online databases and the Internet. In addition, they're trained in teaching others to use these resources and are glad to do so.

Learn about search syntax and professional search techniques

To be successful at any kind of online searching, you need to know something about how computer searching works. At this time, much of the burden is on the user to intelligently construct a search strategy, taking into account the peculiarities of the particular database and search software.

Learning to Research on the Web

Cyberspace is not like your library

When your search term in one of the popular search engines brings back 130,000 hits, you still wonder if the *one* thing you're looking for will be among them. This can be an enormous problem when you're trying to do serious research on the Internet. Too much information is almost worse than too little, because it takes so much time to sort through

it to see if there's anything useful. The rest of this section will give you some pointers to help you become an effective Internet researcher.

Get to know the reference sources on the Internet

Finding reference material on the Web can be a lot more difficult than walking into the Reference Room in your local library.

The subject-classified Web directories described below will provide you with your main source of links to reference materials on the Web. In addition, many public and academic libraries, like the Internet Public Library (http://www.ipl.org), have put together lists of links to Web sites, categorized by subject. The difficulty is finding Web sites that contain the same kind of substantive content you'd find in a library. See the links to *Reference sources on the Web* (p. 201) for a list of some Web-based reference materials.

Understand how search engines work

Search engines are software tools that allow a user to ask for a list of Web pages containing certain words or phrases from an automated search index. The automated search index is a database containing some or all of the words appearing on the Web pages that have been indexed. The search engines send out a software program known as a spider, crawler or robot. The spider follows hyperlinks from page to page around the Web, gathering and bringing information back to the search engine to be indexed.

Most search engines index all the text found on a Web page, except for words too common to index, such as *a, and, in, to, the* and so on. When a user submits a query, the search engine looks for Web pages containing the words, combinations, or phrases asked for by the user. Engines may be programmed to look for an exact match or a close match (for example, the plural of the word submitted by the user). They may rank the hits as to how close the match is to the words submitted by the user.

One important thing to remember about search engines is this: once the engine and the spider have been programmed, the process is totally automated. No human being examines the information returned by the spider to see what subject it might be about or whether the words on the Web page adequately reflect the actual main point of the page.

Another important fact is that all the search engines are different. They each index differently and treat users' queries differently. The burden is on the searcher to learn how to use the features of each search engine.

Know the difference between a search engine and a directory

A search engine lets you seek out specific words and phrases in Web pages. A directory is more like a subject catalog in the library—a human being has determined the main point of a Web page and has categorized it based on a classification scheme of topics and subtopics used by that directory. Many of the search engines have also developed browsable subject catalogues, and most of the directories also have a search engine, so the distinction between them is blurring.

Jack Solock, special librarian at InterNIC Net Scout, classifies Web directories into categories based on the amount of human intervention (see "Searching the Internet Part II: Subject Catalogs, Annotated Directories, and Subject Guides" at http://rs.internic.net/nic-support/nicnews/

oct96/enduser.html). The categories he uses are subject catalogs, annotated directories and subject guides.

A subject catalog classifies Web pages into subject categories and uses excerpts from the Web page as a short description. An annotated directory divides sites by subject but also contains analysis of the site by an editor, librarian or subject specialist, who writes a description to assist the user. A subject guide attempts to provide a selection of sites relating to a particular subject that represent high quality resources, thus representing the highest level of human intervention of the three types because it involves building a collection of sites to represent a subject area.

Mr. Solock categorizes the following resources:

- Yahoo, BUBL and Galaxy as *subject catalogs,*
- Magellan, Lycos Top 5% and InterNIC Directory of Directories as *annotated directories* and
- Argus Clearinghouse and the WWW Virtual Library as *subject guides.*

Learn about search syntax and professional search techniques

To be successful at any kind of online searching, you need to know something about how computer searching works. At this time, much of the burden is on the user to intelligently construct a search strategy, taking into account the peculiarities of the particular database and search software.

Learn some essential browser skills

Know how to use your browser for finding your way around, finding your way back to places you've been before and for "note-taking" as you

gather information for your paper. A large part of effective research on the Web is figuring out how to stay on track and not waste time—the "browsing" and "surfing" metaphors are fine for leisure time spent on the Web, but not when you're under time pressure to finish your research paper.

URLs. UNDERSTAND THE CONSTRUCTION OF A URL. Sometimes a hyperlink will take you to a URL such as http://www.sampleurl.com/files/howto.html. You should know that the page "howto.html" is part of a site called "www.sampleurl.com." If this page turns out to be a "not found" error, or doesn't have a link to the site's home page, you can try typing in the location box "http://www.sampleurl.com/" or "http://www.sampleurl.com/files/" to see if you can find a menu or table of contents. Sometimes a file has been moved or its name has changed, but the site itself still has content useful to you—this is a way to find out.

If there's a tilde (~) in the URL, you're probably looking at someone's personal page on a larger site. For example "http://www.bigsite.com/~jonesj/home.html" refers to a page at www.bigsite.com where J. Jones has some server space in which to post Web pages.

NAVIGATION. Be sure you can use your browser's "Go" list, "History" list, "Back" button and "Location" box where the URL can be typed in. In Web research, you're constantly following links through to other pages then wanting to jump back a few steps to start off in a different direction. If you're using a computer at home rather than sharing one at school, check the settings in your "Cache" or "History list" to see how long the places you've visited will be retained in history. This will determine how long the links will show as having been visited before. Usually, you want to set this period of time to cover the full time frame of your research project so you'll be able to tell which Web sites you've been to before.

BOOKMARKS OR FAVORITES. Before you start a research session, make a new folder in your bookmarks or favorites area and set that folder as the one to receive new bookmark additions. You might name it with the current date, so you later can identify in which research session the bookmarks were made. Remember you can make a bookmark for a page you haven't yet visited by holding the mouse over the link and getting the popup menu (by either pressing the mouse button or right clicking, depending on what flavor computer you have) to "Add bookmark" or "Add to favorites." Before you sign off your research session, go back and weed out any bookmarks that turned out to be uninteresting so you don't have a bunch of irrelevant material to deal with later. Later you can move these bookmarks around into different folders as you organize information for writing your paper—find out how to do that in your browser.

PRINTING FROM THE BROWSER. Sometimes you'll want to print information from a Web site. The main thing to remember is to make sure the Page Setup is set to print out the page title, URL, and the date. You'll be unable to use the material if you can't remember later where it came from.

"SAVING AS" A FILE. Know how to temporarily save the contents of a Web page as a file on your hard drive or a floppy disk and later open it in your browser by using the "file open" feature. You can save the page you're currently viewing or one which is hyperlinked from that page, from the "File" menu or the popup menu accessed by the mouse held over the hyperlink.

COPYING AND PASTING TO A WORD PROCESSOR. You can take quotes from Web pages by opening up a word

processing document and keeping it open while you use your browser. When you find text you want to save, drag the mouse over it and "copy" it, then open up your word processing document and "paste" it. Be sure to also copy and paste the URL and page title, and to record the date, so you know where the information came from.

BE PREPARED TO CITE YOUR WEB REFERENCES. Find out what form of bibliographic references your instructor requires. Both the MLA and APA bibliographic formats have developed rules for citing sources on CD-ROM and the Internet. Instructions for citing electronic sources are available at many libraries, including the Purdue University Online Writing Lab (http://owl.english.purdue.edu/Files/110.html).

Skills for Online Searching

There are many sources on the Web to help you learn search skills. Many of the concepts for using Web search engines also apply to searching online library catalogs and CD-ROMs. This section of the manual will get you started and point you to other online sources where you can learn more.

Learn how search syntax works

Search syntax is a set of rules describing how users can query the database being searched. Sophisticated syntax makes for a better search, one where the items retrieved are mostly relevant to the searcher's need and important items are not missed. It allows a user to look for combinations of terms, exclude other terms, look for various forms of a word, include synonyms, search for phrases rather than single words. The

main tools of search syntax are these:

BOOLEAN LOGIC. Boolean logic allows the use of AND, OR and NOT to search for items containing both terms, either term, or a term only if not accompanied by another term. The links below and all the Web search engines "search help" have a lot of good examples of Boolean logic. Tip: NOT can be dangerous. Let's say you want to search for items about Mexico, but not New Mexico, so you use NOT to exclude the word *New* from your retrieved set. This would prevent you from retrieving an article about *New regulations in Mexico* because it contained the word *New*, though that wasn't what you intended.

WILDCARDS AND TRUNCATION. This involves substituting symbols for certain letters of a word so that the search engine will retrieve items with any letter in that spot in the word. The syntax may allow a symbol in the middle of a word (wildcard) or only at the end of the word (truncation). This feature makes it easier to search for related word groups, like *woman* and *women* by using a wildcard such as *wom*n*. Truncation can be useful to search for a group of words like *invest, investor, investors, investing, investment, investments* by submitting *invest* rather than typing in all those terms separated by OR's. The only problem is that *invest** will also retrieve *investigate, investigated, investigator, investigation, investigating*. The trick, then is to combine terms with an AND such as *invest** AND *stock* or bond* or financ* or money* to try and narrow your retrieved set to the kind of documents you're looking for.

PHRASE SEARCHING. Many concepts are represented by a phrase rather than a single word. In order to successfully search for a term like *library school* it's important that the search engine allow syntax for phrase searching. Otherwise, instead of get-

LINKS TO ONLINE RESOURCES

http://www.ipl.org/teen/aplus/links.htm
Go online to link to over a hundred Web pages that will help you with your research and writing project.

Links for Research

Reference sources on the Web

http://www.ipl.org/teen/aplus/referenceweb.htm
A chart of some of the online reference books available free on the Web

Web directories and subject-classified resources

http://www.ipl.org/teen/aplus/linksdirect.htm
Yahoo, Argus, IPL et al.

Search engines and their "search help" pages

http://www.ipl.org/teen/aplus/linksengines.htm
Alta Vista, Excite, Lycos et al.

Other links for learning to research

http://www.ipl.org/teen/aplus/linksother.htm
Online articles, online library and research instruction

Links for Writing

OWLs on the Web

http://www.ipl.org/teen/aplus/linksowls.htm
Links to Online Writing Labs (OWLs) "handouts"

OWL Handouts by Topic:

Common types of papers

http://www.ipl.org/teen/aplus/linkscommon.htm
Research papers; persuasive essays; narrative essays; cause/effect essays; how to write summaries and more

Papers on special subjects

http://www.ipl.org/teen/aplus/linksspecial.htm
Film, drama and book reviews; writing about poetry; scientific and lab reports; abstracts and others

Planning and starting the writing assignment

http://www.ipl.org/teen/aplus/linksplanning.htm
The writing process; ideas; journal writing; overcoming obstacles

The topic

http://www.ipl.org/teen/aplus/linkstopic.htm
Several articles from the OWLs

Title, introduction and conclusion

http://www.ipl.org/teen/aplus/linkstitle.htm
Several articles from the OWLs

Thesis statement

http://www.ipl.org/teen/aplus/linksthesis.htm
Articles from many points of view

Organizing information

http:///www.ipl.org/teen/aplus/linksorganizing.htm
Taking notes; outlining; organizing by cubing, mapping and more

Writing style and technique

http://www.ipl.org/teen/aplus/linkswritingstyle.htm
Audience and tone; logic and developing arguments; sentences, words and phrases; paragraphs; coherence, clarity, conciseness; transitions; gender-fair writing; writing on the computer other style and technique issues

Citing sources

http://www.ipl.org/teen/aplus/linkciting.htm
Paraphrasing, summarizing and plagiarism; using quotations; styles of citation

Grammar and punctuation

http://www.ipl.org/teen/aplus/linksgrammar.htm
Links to grammar handbooks

Revising and rewriting

http://www.ipl.org/teen/aplus/linksrevising.htm
How to proofread, edit and revise; short proofreading and editing checklists; critiques and peer review

ting documents about library schools you could be getting documents about school libraries or documents where the word *library* and *school* both appear but have nothing to do with a library school.

PROXIMITY. This allows the user to find documents only if the search terms appear near each other, within so many words or paragraphs, or adjacent to each other. It's a pretty sophisticated tool and can be tricky to use skillfully. Many times you can accomplish about the same result using phrase searching.

CAPITALIZATION. When searching for proper names, search syntax that will distinguish capital from lower case letters will help narrow the search. In other cases, you would want to make sure the search engine isn't looking for a particular pattern of capitalization, and many search engines let you choose which of these options to use.

FIELD SEARCHING. All database records are divided up into fields. Almost all search engines in CD-ROM or online library products and the more sophisticated Web search engines allow users to search for terms appearing in a particular field. This can help immensely when you're looking for a very specific item. Say that you're looking for a psychology paper by a professor from the University of Michigan and all you remember about the paper is that it had something about Freud and Jung in its title. If you think it may be on the

Web, you can do a search in Alta Vista, searching for *Freud* AND *Jung* and limit your search to the *umich.edu* domain, which gives you a pretty good chance of finding it, if it's there.

Make sure you know what content you're searching

The content of the database will affect your search strategy and the search syntax you use to retrieve documents. Some of the different databases you'll encounter in your library and online research are:

REPRESENTATION OR SUMMARY OF A DOCUMENT. If a document has been summarized, like a library catalog entry where certain features like title and author have been recorded along with a sentence or two of description, don't expect to retrieve the document by looking for keywords in the text. A search is only searching what's in the database—the representation, not the document itself.

INDEX AND ABSTRACT OF A DOCUMENT. When a document like a journal article has been indexed and an abstract written, a human indexer has helped organize the document for easy retrieval. He or she has chosen some words, phrases and concepts that represent the subject matter of the document and has attached those to the database record as "descriptors." The specific terms usually come from a book of terms used by that

database producer, to promote consistency between indexers.

The indexer, or possibly the author of the article, has written an abstract or summary of the article's content that is included in the database. Again, it's important to realize that you're not searching the entire text of the document but someone's representation of the document. If you can zero in on some of the database's descriptors that accurately describe the topic you're looking for, you can easily retrieve all the articles with the same descriptors. If you do a keyword search in this type of database without checking the permissible descriptors, you're hoping that the indexer will have used your keyword in the summary or that the author will have used it in the title of the article.

FULL TEXT OF A DOCUMENT. Searching full text documents gives you a good chance of retrieving the document you want, provided you can think of some key words and phrases that would have been included in the text. The problem is retrieving too many documents when you're looking for something particular, because common words and concepts can appear in documents irrelevant to your topic. This is one of the problems with Internet search engines that index the full text of Web pages. The more skilled you can become in your use of search syntax, the greater will be your success in finding relevant information in a full text database.

Index

Abortion rights, 141
Abramovitz, Janet N., 181. *See also*
    Worldwatch Institute
Acela Express, 123, 128–129
Acetochlor, 83
Achard, Frederic, 175
Acid rain, 8, 59
Acid Rain Program, 66, 67
Addington, Bill, 35
Agent Orange, 31
Agribusiness, 81
Agriculture
    crop rotation, 86, 89
    erosion, 138–139, 146
    intensive, 138, 148
    irrigation, 138
    organic, 86, 89
    pesticide regulation, 79–80, 81, 84,
        85–86, 93
    productivity increase effects, 138–139
    sustainable, 84, 139, 182, 184
Agriculture, U.S. Department of, 81, 83, 89,
    94
Air conditioning, 74
Air pollution, 118–120, 148–149
Air quality, 8–9, 59
Alar, 87
Alaska National Interest Lands Conservation
    Act, 168
Alaska Native Claims Settlement Act, 168
Albright, Horace M., 166
Albright, Madeleine K., 16
Aldrin, 88
Alternative fuels, 72
Aluminum recycling, 101, 102, 103, 111
Amazon Conservation Team, 174, 176
America Recycles Day, 101
American Automobile Association, 120
American Automobile Association of
    Southern California, 131
American Crop Protection Association, 82,
    91, 95, 96
American Enterprise Institute for Public
    Policy Research, 139
American Farm Bureau Federation, 79, 81,
    85, 92, 93, 94, 96
American Farmland Trust, 41, 45, 50, 56.
    See also Grossi, Ralph
American Highway Users Alliance, 117,
    119, 120, 125, 133
American Land Rights Association, 41, 42
American Petroleum Institute, 73
American Public Transit Association, 121,
    122
American Rivers, 12
American Road and Transportation Builders
    Association, 117
Amtrak, 123, 128–129
Amtrak Reform and Accountability Act, 129
Anheuser-Busch, 6
Anniston, Alabama, 31
Antiquities Act, 164, 165

Army Corps of Engineers, 12, 167, 171
Ashcroft, John, 13
Asthma, 68
Atlanta, Georgia, 119, 123, 126–130
Atoms for Peace, 61
Auto emission standards, 60, 64, 67, 68,
    70–72, 125
Azinophosmethyl, 79, 92

Babbitt, Bruce, 12, 42, 162, 168, 170
Baca Ranch, 41, 47
Bandelier National Monument, 165, 170
Bangladesh population program, 146
Bardeen, Norm, 49
Barna, David, 158, 161
Barnes, Roy, 52, 129
Barry, Dave, 125
Bartosiewicz, John, 121
Basso, Peter "Jack," 119
Batmanian, Garo, 175
Baucus, Max, 44
Beal, Dan, 132
Becker, Daniel, 119
Beckstoffer, Andy, 84
Beller, Dennis, 62
Ben & Jerry's, 180–181
Benbrook, Charles, 86, 95
Bethlehem Steel, 6
BHC (benzene-hexachloride), 88
Bicentennial Malthusian Essay, A (Rohe),
    149, 151
Bicycle commuting, 127
Biodiversity, 176, 177, 182–184
Bioengineering, 151
Bioprospecting, 177, 179, 187
Birth control, 143
Bliley, Thomas J., Jr., 14
Bond, Christopher S., 128
Borné, Dan S., 24, 34, 36
Bowlden, Taylor, 131
BP Amoco Corp., 70, 71
Bradley, Bill, 41, 75
Brenner, Robert, 68
Bresnihan, Terry, 70
Brimmer, Kenneth, 182
Brookings Institution, 23, 117
Brown, Lester R., 137, 151
Browner, Carol M.
    environmental justice, 21, 28, 29
    environmental racism, 33
    federal-state partnerships, 7
    global warming, 3, 4, 6
    long-distance ozone, 63–64, 67
    pesticide regulation, 79, 81, 94
    polluted runoff, 1
Brownfields, 7, 14, 34
Brunswick, Georgia, 30
Brunswick Initiative, 30
Bryant, Dirk, 176
Bryce, James, 169
Bullard, Robert D., 21, 23, 25, 26, 27–28,
    30–31, 36

Bumpers, Dale, 168
Bureau of Indian Affairs, 24
Burnett, H. Sterling, 1
Burns, Conrad, 162
Bush, George
    environmental crime prosecutions, 75
    environmental policy, 16
    environmental racism, 24, 28, 29
    National Park funding, 168
    pesticide bans, 83
Bush, George W.
    air quality standards, 75
    property rights, 41
    Texas industrial emissions, 1–2
Bush, Jeb, 129, 167

California Association of Winegrape
    Growers, 84
California Desert Lands Act, 158
Cancer, 79, 85, 87, 88, 90–91
Car culture, 122–124
Carbamates, 79, 81, 85
Carbarle, Bruce J., 173, 178, 188. *See also*
    World Wildlife Fund
Carbon dioxide emissions, 6, 60, 68, 125
Carbon monoxide, 66, 68
Carbon sequestration, 177, 178
Cardoso, Fernando Henrique, 175, 183, 186
Carrying Capacity Network, 135, 139, 152
Carson, Rachel, 80, 87, 88–90, 107, 109
Carter, Jimmy, 168, 183
Cato Institute, 100–101, 103, 113, 159
Center for Energy and Climate Solutions,
    66, 69, 71
Center for Health, Environment and Justice,
    36
Center for Risk Management, 3, 17
Centers for Disease Control and Prevention,
    30
Chaco Canyon National Park, 166
Chafee, John H., 11, 16, 124
Chamber of Commerce, U.S., 1, 6, 7, 14,
    32
Chavez, Benjamin, Jr., 28
Chenoweth-Hage, Helen, 157
Chernobyl nuclear accident, 61
Chester, Pennsylvania, 32
*Chester Residents Concerned for Quality
    Living v. Seif*, 32
Chevron, 30
Chicago Board of Trade, 107, 114
Child subsidies, 144
Children's health risks
    lead poisoning, 32, 59, 66
    pesticide poisoning, 79, 82, 83–85, 87,
        90
China
    air pollution, 150
    grain crops, 151
    one-child policy, 139, 143, 146
Chlorinated hydrocarbons, 80, 87, 89
Chlorofluorocarbons (CFCs), 13

Index

Citizens' Advisory Commission on Federal Areas in Alaska, 42
Citizens Against Nuclear Trash, 30
Citizens Against Toxic Exposure, 30–31
Civil Rights Act, 21, 25, 29, 32
Civilian Conservation Corps (CCC), 166
Clapp, Philip E., 5, 7–8, 14, 17
Clean Air Act
   amendments, 1990, 8, 9, 66–68, 70
   EPA lawsuits, 60, 128
   MTBE ban, 73
   of 1963, 66
   of 1970, 8, 9, 27, 29, 59, 66–68
   proposed amendments, 119
Clean Beach and Coastal Protection Act, 11
Clean Development Mechanism, 4
Clean Washington Center, 114
Clean Water Act, 9, 10, 27, 29
Clean-fuel technologies, 70
Climate change, global, 173
Clinton, Bill
   air quality standards, 8–10, 67, 70
   environmental justice, 21, 24–26, 28
   environmentalists' view of, 1, 5
   fishing limits, 12
   funding proposals, 7
   global population programs, 139, 143
   GOP-controlled Congress, 75, 170–171
   immigration, 141
   Kyoto Protocol, 3–4, 60, 69–70, 71, 150–151
   National Parks and Monuments, 157, 158, 165, 167, 168, 170–171
   open space protection, 39–40, 41–42, 48–50, 53
   pesticide regulation, 79, 81, 83–85, 90, 92
   rain forest preservation, 178–180, 183, 185–186
   recycled paper, 104, 107
   transportation, 123, 126
Clusen, Chuck, 159, 162, 167
Coalition to Save Evans Farm, 51
Coates, Anthony, 174
Coeur d'Alene Indian tribe, 22, 24–25, 31
Cogeneration technology, 71
Coggin, Amy, 122
Collins, Ken, 167
Colorado Fuel and Iron Co., 49
Colvin, Joe, 61, 62, 65, 74, 75
Commercial recycling, 102, 105
Competitive Enterprise Institute, 45, 56
Compost, 112
Comprehensive Electricity Competition Act, 4
Comprehensive Environmental Response, Compensation and Liability Act (CERCLA), 9, 12, 27, 29
Computer technology, 69
Condorcet, Marquis de, 135, 142, 143
Congestion pricing, 130
Congress, U.S.
   environmental proposals, 2–3
   Kyoto Protocol, 14–16, 17
   highway systems, 122, 123, 124

   land-use initiatives, 14, 40–41, 47, 50–52, 55
   mass transit, 117
   National Parks funding, 155, 157–159, 164–166, 168
   pesticide regulation, 80, 88–92, 94–95
   public land acquisition, 46–48
   rain forest preservation, 183
   Republican-controlled, 2–3, 159, 168, 170–171
   transportation spending, 117, 119, 124–126
Conrad, Joseph, 182
Conservation and Reinvestment Act (CARA), 50, 157
Conservation International, 174, 176, 180, 181, 186, 189, 190
Conservation organizations, 159, 161, 176, 185, 186
Consultative Group on International Agricultural Research (CGIAR), 143, 145, 151
Consumer activism, 11
Consumer demand, 95
Consumers Union, 79, 80, 82, 83, 84, 86, 92, 95, 96
Controlled burn, 165, 170
Convention on Biological Diversity, 13
Convention on Nature Protection and Wildlife Preservation in the Western Hemisphere, 13
Convention to Combat Desertification, 13
Cook, Kenneth, 95
Cook, Rick, 167
Cool Schools, 74
Corley, David G., 179
Corporations
   partnerships with National Parks, 161
   pollution reduction pledge, 71
Council of Economic Advisers, 4
Council on Environmental Quality, 27, 29
Craig, Larry E., 14
Crested Butte Land Trust, 49
Crop rotation, 86, 89
Cumberland Island National Seashore, 162
Curbside recycling programs, 99, 103, 105, 107, 109
Curtis, Jennifer, 89, 96
Curtis, Randy, 173
Cushman, Chuck, 41, 42, 45, 54

Dallas Area Rapid Transit system, 121
Dalzell, Stewart, 32
Dam removal, 12
Damkroger, Courtney, 163
D'Arcy, Diane, 51
Darwin, Charles, 142
Davies, Terry, 3, 17
DDT, 80, 87, 88–90, 91
Debt-for-nature swap, 185
Defenders of Wildlife, 159
Deforestation, 173–190
   chronology, 183
   climate changes, 173
   government initiatives, 185–186
   market-based solutions, 186–189

   outlook, 189–190
   role of developing nations, 174–175
   role of wealthy nations, 178–182
Deinking technology, 110–111
Delaney, James J., 87, 88
Delaney clause, 87, 88, 91, 92
Delaware Water Gap National Recreation Area, 161
Denison, Richard, 100, 103, 113
Denver light-rail system, 121
Desertification, 139, 148
Developing countries, 174–175, 189–190
Devils Tower National Park, 166
Diamond Alkali plant, 31
Dieldrin, 88
Diesel fuel, 59
Dingell, John D., 50, 92
Dioxin, 30, 31
Diversity of Life, The (Wilson), 177
Djekoule, Sep, 174
Donovan, Richard, 186–189
Doolittle, John T., 12
Dow Chemical Co., 70
Downs, Anthony, 117
Drinking water contamination, 2, 83, 177
Duales System Deutschland (DSD), 108
DuPont Corp., 71

Earth Day, 8, 9, 27, 29, 66, 67
Earth Day 2000, 61
Earth in the Balance (Gore), 90
Earth Summit, 67, 68
Earthjustice Legal Defense Fund, 28, 36
East Coast Greenway Alliance, 54
Easter Island, 135
Ebell, Myron, 45
Eberstadt, Nicholas, 139, 151
Echeverria, John, 158
E-commerce, 69
Economic development, 15, 34–36
Ecotourism, 178, 180–181
Ecotourism Society, 180–181
Ehrlich, Anne, 149
Ehrlich, Paul, 143, 149
Eisenhower, Dwight D., 61, 166
El Triunfo Biosphere Reserve, 186
Electric cars, 72
Electric-utility deregulation, 4, 65–66
Emission credits, 66, 67
Emissions trading, 4
Endangered Species Act, 9, 12, 25, 27
Endocrine disruptors, 85, 87, 91
Energy
   environmental issues, 59–75
   safety issues, 65–66
Energy, U.S. Department of
   alternative fuels, 72
   Energy Information Administration, 15
   nuclear waste management, 9, 12–14, 62, 67
   Y-12 nuclear weapons plant, 30
Energy conservation, 69
Energy Information Administration, 15, 76
Energy Policy Act, 67, 70, 72
Energy sources
   alternative fuels, 72

geothermal, 72
natural gas, 60, 72
nuclear power, 60, 61–62
petroleum, 60
renewable, 60
Engelman, Robert, 137, 138, 145
Environmental Council of the States
    (ECOS), 22–23, 33–34, 36
Environmental Defense Fund (EDF)
    rain forest preservation, 178–180
    recycling issues, 100, 103, 113, 115
    transportation, 118, 119, 129, 130, 132
Environmental Equity, Office of, 24, 28, 29
Environmental Equity Workgroup, 28
Environmental justice, 21–36
    brownfield sites, 34
    chronology, 29
    Clinton's policies, 28
    as a distraction, 26
    EPA and, 32–34
    impact on industry, 34–36
    1994 executive order, 24–26, 28
    recent cases, 28–32
    toxic exposure and poverty, 23–24, 27
Environmental Justice, Office of, 1, 22, 23,
    29, 32–33, 34, 36
Environmental Justice Resource Center, 21,
    23, 36
Environmental movement, 1, 166
Environmental policy, 1–2, 118–120
Environmental Policy Project, 158
Environmental priorities, 1–17
    air quality, 8–10
    background, 8–14
    chronology, 9
    costs, 7–8
    consumer choices, 11
    cost-benefit approach, 17
    endangered species, 12
    global warming, 3–5, 14–16
    outlook, 17
    program costs, 7–8
    population concerns, 135–152
    public concerns, 2
    public land, 14
    sprawl, 16–17
    toxic waste, 12–14
    water projects, 12
    water quality, 10–12
Environmental Protection Agency (EPA), 9,
    87
    Acid Rain Program, 66, 67
    air quality standards, 2, 8, 9, 17, 66–68
    auto emissions, 125
    authority, 5–7
    environmental justice, 21, 24, 32–33, 34
    pesticide advisory group, 81
    pesticide regulation, 79, 80, 81, 83, 87,
        88, 90–91, 92–94
    recycling, 99, 103, 107
    regional boards, 8
    Web site, 95
    Worker Protection Standard, 90
Environmental quality, 1, 15
Environmental racism, 21, 22, 24–25, 26,
    29, 30, 36

Environmental refugees, 148
Environmental science, 156
Environmental Working Group, 79, 82, 83,
    84, 92, 95, 96
Erwin, Terry, 184
Escambia Treating Co., 30
Ethanol, 73
European Union, 144
Evans, Ralph, 51
Evans Farm (McLean), 51
Evans Ranch (Denver), 44
Everglades National Park, 9, 10, 155, 167

Famine, 142, 143, 146, 151
Fay, William D., 117, 119, 120, 121, 125,
    128, 130
Federal Aid Road Act, 122, 123
Federal Energy Regulatory Commission, 65
Federal government
    environmental policy role, 5–7
    land acquisitions, 41–42, 46–48, 157–159
    recycling role, 103–105, 109
    spending priorities, 157
Federal Highway Administration, 21, 123,
    127, 131, 133
Federal Insecticide, Fungicide and
    Rodenticide Act (FIFRA), 87, 88, 90
Federal Lands to Parks program, 46, 47
Federal Transit Administration, 123
Feinstein, Dianne, 14, 52, 71
Fertility rate, 140, 144–145
Fertilizers, 146, 148
Fish and Wildlife Service, U.S., 9
Fishing limits, 9
Flannery, David M., 60, 64, 65–66
Flint, Michigan, 31–32
Florida Department of Agriculture and
    Consumer Services, 90
Fogarty International Center, 179, 187
Food and Drug Administration (FDA), 80, 83
Food, Drug and Cosmetic Act, 87, 88
Food production, 137, 145
Food Quality Protection Act (FQPA), 79,
    87, 90, 92
Ford Motor Co., 70, 125
Foreman, Christopher H., Jr., 23, 26
Forest fires, 173, 183
Forest Legacy program, 50
Forest Service, U.S., 14
Forest Stewardship Council, 183, 186, 189
Fort Worth (Texas) Transportation
    Authority, 121
Fossil fuels, 59
Franklin, Bill, 102, 106, 114
Franklin Associates Inc., 102
Freedom to Farm law, 86
French, Hilary, 5–6, 13
Fresh Fields–Whole Foods, 115
Fretwell, Holly L., 161, 168, 169
Friends of the Earth, 181
Frontiers of Freedom, 53
Fuel-cell vehicles, 72
Fungicides, 81

Gaffney, Neil, 39, 44–45
Gateway Coordinating Council, 121

Georgia Regional Transportation Authority,
    129
Geothermal energy, 72
Gephardt, Richard A., 52
German recycling system, 108
Geyer, Georgie Ann, 147
Giant Sequoia National Monument, 170
Gibson Musical Instruments, 186
Gingrich, Newt, 124
Glacier National Park, 161, 162, 164
Glass recycling, 30, 103, 111
Glendening, Parris N., 16–17, 39, 40, 52
Global climate change, 173
Global Climate Coalition, 70, 71, 75, 76
Global Environment facility, 183, 186
Global population, 138, 147–148
Global 2000 report, 183
Global warming, 1
    deforestation, 174
    nuclear power and, 61–62, 65
    scientific evidence, 61
    U.S. role, 3–5, 14–16
Godwin, William, 135, 142, 143, 149
Golden Gate National Recreation Area, 163
Goldman, Lynn R., 83
Gore, Al
    environmental justice, 25
    land conservation proposals, 40, 41, 47,
        121
    Malthusian theory, 149
    nuclear energy, 75
    pesticide regulation, 81, 87, 94
    pesticide resistance, 90
    smart growth proposal, 1, 2, 7, 16, 17
Gorton, Slade, 3, 12
Grand Canyon National Park, 166, 168,
    180
Grand Staircase–Escalante National
    Monument, 41, 47
Grand Teton National Park, 162, 164
Grant, Ulysses S., 165
Gray, Michael E., 89
Great Outdoors Colorado, 54
Great Smoky Mountains National Park, 162,
    166, 168–170
Greater Washington Board of Trade, 131
Green Revolution, 88, 135, 138, 139, 143,
    145–146, 148, 151
Greenberg, Russell, 182
Greenhouse gases
    global treaty reductions, 15, 60, 68–70
    global warming role, 3–5
    1998 emissions, 64
    sources, 64
    voluntary emission reductions, 70
Greenpeace, 21, 28, 36
Greve, Frank, 159
Gridlock, 118
Grossi, Ralph, 41, 45, 50
Groth, Edward (Ned), III, 82, 83, 84
Ground-level ozone standards, 8, 9, 62–65,
    66, 68
Groundwater, 177–178
Group of Seven (G-7), 183, 186
Guide, Lisa A., 169
Gulf Oil, 30

Index

Hagel, Chuck, 14
Haiti, 173
Hakes, Jay, 15
Halprin, Lisa, 127
Halweil, Brian, 137, 141, 148, 151–152
Hambrecht Co., 163
Hamilton, Jacqueline, 93
Hanlon, Gerald, 175
Harding, Russell J., 23, 32, 34
Haub, Carl, 139, 140, 141, 146, 148
Hauter, Wenonah, 65
Hayman, Archie, 32
Hazardous waste facilities, 23–24
Hazel, John T., 40, 55
Headwaters Forest, 50
Heart of Darkness (Conrad), 182
Helbing, Dick, 132
Herbicides, 81
Hercules Inc., 30
Hettenbach, Todd, 92
High-density polyethylene (HDPE), 111–112
High-occupancy vehicle (HOV) lanes, 131
High-speed rail system, 128–129
Highway building, 119–120, 131
Highway Trust Fund, 73, 122, 123, 124
Highway usage, 117
Hildreth, John, 162
Hillel, Oliver, 180, 181
Historic American Buildings Survey, 162
Historic American Engineering Record, 162
Hoeffel, Joseph M., 43–44
Hollowell, Thomas, 125
Home Builders Association, 44
Home Depot, 186
Homestead Act, 46
Honda Motor Co., 72
Hooper, Helen, 41, 45
Huberman, Bernardo, 132
Huntington Park, California, 30
Huse, Brian, 155, 163
Hutchins, James Mason, 164
Hybrid cars, 72, 151–152
Hydrogen fuel-cell cars, 72

Illinois Environmental Protection Agency, 73
Immigration issues, 141, 145, 148
India population program, 146
Indian Point nuclear accident, 65
Indigenous peoples
    Native Americans, 22, 24–25, 27
    rain forest, 174, 181, 182, 184, 185
Indonesia, 181–182, 183
Infrastructure crisis, 124
Inhofe, James M., 10, 71
Inholdings, 42, 46
Insect resistance, 89–90
Insecticides, 30, 81
Institute for Energy and the Environment, 62
Integrated pest management (IPM), 81, 85
Intelligent Transportation System Program, 132
Intensive agriculture, 138, 148
Interior Appropriations Subcommittee, 42
Interior Department, U.S., 12, 169

Intermarriage, 145
Intermodal Surface Transportation Efficiency Act (ISTEA), 123, 124–126
International Conference on Population and Development, 146
International Convention for the Regulation of Whaling, 13
International environmental issues, 17
International environmental treaties, 13
International Monetary Fund (IMF), 178, 181
International Rice Research Institute (IRRI), 143, 145
International Snowmobile Manufacturers' Association, 170
International Tropical Timber Agreement, 13
Internet commerce, 69
Interstate Highway System, 122, 123
Iran population program, 147

Jackson, Shirley Ann, 65
Japan, 144–145
Jefferson, Thomas, 46, 47
Jeffords, James M., 63, 65
Johnson, Ernest L., 22, 25–26
Johnson, Lady Bird, 109
Johnson, Nancy L., 44
Joshua Tree National Monument, 54
Justice Department, U.S., 83

Kahn, Gene, 85, 86
Kakum National Park, 180
Kaplan, Robert, 137
Kasich, John R., 185
Kawada, Kim, 130
Keller, Richard, 101, 104, 105, 110, 114, 115
Kelly, Glenn, 70, 75
Kennedy, Roger, 170
Kenya population program, 147
Kienitz, Roy, 120, 131, 132
Kiernan, Thomas C., 158, 159
Kingston, Jack, 157
Kleckner, Dean, 92, 94
Klim, Edward, 170
Knox, Robert, 22, 23–24, 25, 32–33, 34, 36
Kolankiewicz, Leon, 135, 139, 141
Kovacs, William L., 1, 14
Krakatoa, 188
Kramer, Randall, 189
Krenning, Bruce, 86, 95
Kyoto Protocol
    Clinton support, 9, 67, 150–151
    opposition to, 60–61, 70, 71, 75, 150–151
    ratification, 15, 60
    U.S. compliance, 69–70

La Paz Agreement, 35
LaHood, Ray, 94–95
Land and Water Conservation Fund Act, 14, 40–41, 42, 46–48, 50–52, 54, 55, 157
Land Trust Alliance, 39, 45, 51, 54–55, 56
Land trusts, 39, 43, 45, 48, 54–55
Land use, 39–55

Landfills, 102–103, 107, 109–110
Landrieu, Mary L., 14, 50
Landrigan, Philip J., 79, 82
Lands Legacy Initiative, 39, 42, 47, 50, 53, 55, 157
Lashof, Dan, 59
Law of the Sea convention, 13
LCP Chemicals-Georgia Inc., 39
Le Pen, Jean-Marie, 145
Lead, 8, 32, 59, 66, 68
Leal, Donald R., 161, 169
Leapheart, Stan, 42
Ledbetter, John, 84
Leopold, A. Starker, 168
Leopold, Aldo, 168
Leopold Commission, 165
Levin, Carl, 17
Lieberman, Joseph I., 16, 63
Light-rail systems, 121
Light trucks, 9, 59, 67, 70, 125
Lincoln, Abraham, 164
Lipkis, Andy, 74
Livability Agenda, 40
Livable Communities Initiative, 50, 53
Lodi-Woodbridge Winegrape Commission, 84
Log Cabin Syrup, 161
Lomax, Timothy J., 132
Los Alamos National Laboratory, 62
Louisiana Chemical Association, 24, 34
Louisiana Department of Environmental Quality, 33
Louisiana Energy Services, 30
Louisiana Purchase, 46, 47
Louisiana State Conference, NAACP, 22, 26
Love Canal, 27, 29
Lucas, George, 163

Mack, Connie, 16
Makhijani, Arjun, 62
Making of the Atomic Bomb, The (Rhodes), 62
Malthus, Daniel, 142
Malthus, Thomas Robert, 135, 142, 143, 149
Many Glaciers Hotel, 162
Mao Zedong, 146
Marcel Paper Mills Inc., 110
Marx, Karl, 142
Maryland Environmental Service, 101
Mason, Richard, 22, 26, 34–35
Mass extinction, 148, 173
Mass transit systems, 117, 121–122, 123, 128
Massey, Rheba, 164
Material-recovery facilities, 110
Mather, Stephen T., 166
McCain, John, 75
McGraw Ranch, 164
Mendelsohn, Robert, 177
Mendes, Chico, 183
Merck & Co., 179
Mesa Verde National Park, 164, 165
Metal recycling, 30
Methyl parathion, 79, 80, 92
Methyl tertiary butyl ether (MTBE), 70–72, 73

Metro Chamber of Commerce, 130
Metropolitan Atlanta Rapid Transit
    Authority, 126
Mexico City policy, 139, 143
Michigan Department of Environmental
    Quality, 23
Midwest Ozone Group, 60, 66
Millar, William W., 122
Miller, Frank, 50–51
Mills, Mark P., 69
Mine tailings, 24–25, 27, 31
Mining Law of 1872, 14
Mission 66 program, 165, 166
Mobil Oil Corp., 176
Mobro 4000, 107, 109–110
Moe, Richard, 39
Mojave National Preserve, 158
Monsanto Corp., 31, 179
Montague, Chris, 44
Montana Land Reliance, 44
Montreal Protocol, 13
Moses, Marion, 90, 91
Mosher, Steven W., 137, 138, 139–140, 144,
    150
Mount Rainier National Park, 164
Moynihan, Daniel Patrick, 124
Mueller, Paul, 87, 88
Mulkey, Marcia, 84–85, 94
Municipal Waste Management Association,
    115
Murkowski, Frank, H., 4, 14, 50
Murphy, Edward H., 73
Myers, Norman, 148, 189

National Academy of Sciences, 62, 91
National Association for the Advancement
    of Colored People (NAACP), 22, 23,
    32
National Association of Home Builders, 39
National Audubon Society, 159, 182
National Cancer Institute, 80
National Center for Bicycling and Walking,
    118, 127
National Center for Policy Analysis, 1,
    161
National Environmental Justice Advisory
    Council (NEJAC), 28
National Environmental Policy Act of 1969,
    25, 29, 31
National Environmental Policy Act of 1970,
    165, 168
National Environmental Trust, 5, 7, 14
National Highway Traffic Safety
    Administration, 125
National Institutes of Health, 179, 187
National Monuments, 155, 158, 166,
    170–171
National Park Foundation, 171
National Park Service (NPS)
    chronology, 165
    commercial use fees, 160
    concessionaire use, 160–161, 168
    corporate partnerships, 161
    created by Congress, 165, 166
    funding, 157, 159–162
    goals, 156

land acquisitions, 157–159
legislative initiatives, 168, 170
most-visited, 156
postwar expansion, 166
privatization debate, 158–159, 171
resource-first management, 170–171
self-sufficiency debate, 161, 169
visitor demand, 160
National Park Service Act, 165
National Park Trust, 42, 45, 46, 56
National Parks, 155–171
    background, 164–168
    current situation, 168–170
    expanding mandate, 164–166
    outlook, 170–171
National Parks Conservation Association,
    155, 158, 159, 163, 166, 167, 171
National Parks Omnibus Management Act,
    161, 165
National Parks Pass, 160
National Petroleum Refiners Association, 60,
    76
National Preservation Conference, 162
National recreation sites, 156
National Register of Historic Places, 162
National Research Council, 12, 60, 73, 79,
    87, 93, 168
National Road, 122
National Trust for Historic Preservation
    (NTHP), 39, 158, 161–162, 163, 171
Native Americans, 22, 24–25, 27
Natural gas, 50, 60
Natural Resources Defense Council (NRDC)
    environmental priorities, 1, 16
    park preservation and funding, 158,
        159, 161–162, 163, 167
    pesticides, 81, 83, 85, 87, 89, 91, 92,
        93, 96
    transportation, 59, 120
Nature Conservancy, 37, 39, 41, 45, 54, 56,
    173, 185
Nematicides, 81
New England forestry Foundation, 54
Newark, New Jersey, 31
Newspaper recycling, 101, 102, 107, 109,
    110
Nitrogen oxide emissions
    blown across state borders, 8, 9, 63
    New York caps, 64
    state standards, 2
Nix, Gene, 186
Noel Kempff Mercado National Park, 177
Non-governmental organizations (NGOs),
    139
Non-point pollution sources, 10
Northern Pacific Railroad, 164
Nuclear accidents, 61, 65, 67
Nuclear energy
    global decline, 61–62
    safety standards, 65–66
    utility deregulation, 65
Nuclear Energy Institute, 61, 65, 74, 76
Nuclear Regulatory Commission (NRC), 30,
    65
Nuclear waste management, 12–14, 30, 35,
    62, 67, 72–75

Oak Ridge, Tennessee, 30
Obey, David R., 55
Occupational Safety and Health
    Administration (OSHA), 90
Omnibus Appropriations bill of 1996, 160
Open Lands trust, 44
Open space protection, 39–55
    background, 45–48
    chronology, 47
    Clinton initiatives, 39, 48–50
    congressional proposals, 40–41, 50–52,
        55
    current situation, 48–55
    development patterns, 45–46
    effectiveness, 40
    federal land acquisition, 41–42, 46–48
    federal tax incentives, 42–45
    outlook, 55
    private land trusts, 45, 54–55
    state and local initiatives, 52–54
Operation Amazonia, 184
Organic Act, 166, 170
Organic farming, 86, 89, 96
Organization of Petroleum Exporting
    Countries (OPEC), 59, 67
Organophosphates, 79, 81, 85, 88
Orski, Kenneth, 119, 121, 127, 132
O'Toole, Randal, 159
Outer Continental Shelf (OCS), 157
Overfishing, 11, 148
Ozone, 8, 9, 17, 59, 68, 73
Ozone Transport Assessment Group, 63,
    67
Ozone Transport Commission, 63

Pacific Lumber Co., 50
Pacific Research Institute for Public Policy,
    46
Pahl, Barbara, 162, 166
Paiva, Paula, 180
Pakistan population program, 146
Paper recycling, 102, 110–111
Parathion, 88
Particulate matter, 8, 9, 17, 60, 66, 68
Partisan politics, 3
Pataki, George E., 64
Paul VI (Pope), 142, 143
Pavy, Jean-Michel, 173
Pensacola, Florida, 30
Permanent Protection for America's
    Resources 2000, 50
Peru population control, 147
Pesticide(s)
    agricultural use, 79–80, 85–86, 139, 146
    alternatives, 84, 85–86
    classes of, 79
    consumer education, 95–96
    grape grower use, 84
    health disorder–related, 79, 85
    health effects, 82–83, 90–91
    ingestion, 82–83
    pest resistance, 89–90, 146
    product toxicity levels, 80
    spills, 79
    weed control expenditures, 81
Pesticide Education Center, 90

Pesticide industry, 81, 83
Pesticide Programs, Office of, 91
Pesticide regulation, 79–96
    background, 86–92
    chronology, 87
    current situation, 92–95
    EPA role, 90–91, 92–94
    farmer concerns, 79–80, 81, 84, 85–86,
        90–91, 93
    government role, 83–85, 88–92, 94–95
    manufacturer concerns, 81–82
    outlook, 95–96
    water contamination, 10
Peterson, John E., 55
Petroleum products, 59, 60, 119
Pharmaceutical companies, 179, 187
Pheromones, 86
Phosdrin, 83
Piaguahe, Humberto, 182
Pikrallidas, Susan, 120
Pimentel, David, 138–139, 146
Pimentel, Marcia, 146
Pinkerton, James P., 149
Plant growth regulators, 81
Plastic recycling, 111–112
Plotkin, Mark, 174, 176, 178
Polluter-pays principle, 108
Polonoroeste project, 183
Polychlorinated biphenyls (PCBs), 27, 29,
    31
Polyethylene terephthalate (PET), 111
Pombo, Richard W., 94
Pope, Carl, 141
Population
    agricultural productivity, 138–139
    background, 142–147
    chronology, 143
    concerns, 142–145
    economic development and, 149
    environmental impact, 148–151
    fertility rates, 136, 140, 144–145
    immigration issues, 141
    increase, 135–137, 147–148
    Malthusian warning, 135, 137, 142,
        149
    replacement level, 137
    resource consumption, 150, 151–152,
        189
    traffic congestion, 117
    U.S.-supported population planning,
        139–141
Population Action International, 137, 138,
    145, 152
Population Bomb, The (Ehrlich), 149
Population Explosion, The (Ehrlich and
    Ehrlich), 149
Population programs, 139–141, 146–147
Population Reference Bureau, 139, 146,
    148, 152
Population Research Institute, 137, 138,
    144, 150, 152
Porter, J. Winston, 99, 103, 106
Portman, Rob, 185
Portney, Paul, 1, 5, 8, 10, 17, 71
Poverty
    industry and, 27, 34–36

rain forest preservation and, 189
toxic exposure and, 23–24, 26, 27
Prescribed burn, 170
Presidio Trust, 163
Prickett, Glenn, 176
Pritchard, Paul C., 42, 45, 46, 50, 54
Property-rights advocates, 41, 42, 45, 54
Public Citizen's Critical Mass Energy
    Project, 62, 65, 72, 76
Public land, 14, 46–48
Public Land and Recreation Investment Act,
    52
Public Utilities Regulatory Policies Act
    (PURPA), 107, 109

R.W. Beck Inc., 110, 111, 112
Racism, environmental, 21, 22, 24–25, 26,
    29, 30, 36
Radioactive waste management, 12–14, 30,
    35, 62, 67, 72–75
Railroads, 164–190
    biodiversity, 170, 177, 182–184
    bioprospecting, 177, 179, 187
    canopy, 184
    ecological role, 173
    economic value, 176–179
    ecotourism, 178, 180–181
    indigenous peoples, 174, 181, 182, 184,
        185
    medicinal discoveries, 178, 187
    preservation, 175–176
    reforestation, 188
    remaining, 178
    South America, 175
Rainforest Action Network, 186
Rainforest Alliance, 186
Rainforest Café, 182
Rawlins, Scott, 79, 85, 93
Raymond, Michele, 99, 104, 105, 106, 108,
    112, 114–115
Raymond Communications Inc., 99
Reagan, Ronald
    anti-conservationist policies, 165
    landfill crisis, 109
    Mexico City policy, 139, 143
    pesticide bans, 83
Reason Foundation, 101, 115
Recreation Fee Demonstration Program,
    159–160
Recycling
    background, 106–110
    chronology, 107
    disposal versus, 101
    economics, 102–103, 113
    facilities, 30
    government role, 103–105, 109
    markets, 103–105
    municipal, 112–114
    outlook, 114–115
    polluter-pays, 108
    by states, 100, 110
    variable rate, 105–106
Recycling industry, 110–112, 113
Recycling movement, 106–109
Reference dose, 83
Reforestation, 188

Reformulated gasoline requirement, 70–72,
    73
Regula, Ralph, 42, 159
Regulatory Improvement Act, 17
Reilly, William K., 28
Replogle, Michael, 118, 119, 129, 130, 132
Resource Conservation and Recovery Act,
    107, 109
Resource consumption, 150
Resource Recovery Act, 107, 109
Resources for the Future, 1, 8, 10, 17, 71,
    76, 177, 181, 187, 190
Rettie, Dwight, 168
Rhodes, Richard, 62
Richardson, Bill, 72
Ridenour, James, 159
Road-building, 122, 123, 131
Roberts, Cecil E., 15
Roberts, Robert E., 33
Rocky Mountain National Park, 162–164
Rohe, John F., 149, 151
Romm, Joseph, 66, 69, 71
Roosevelt, Franklin D., 122, 165, 166
Roosevelt, Theodore, 41, 50, 53, 164
Rosenthal, Joshua, 179, 187
Ross, Karen, 84
Royal Dutch/Shell Group, 70, 71
Ruane, T. Peter, 117, 126–128
Ruston, John, 100, 103, 113
Rwanda, 146–147

Safe Drinking Water Act, 7, 9, 11–12
Salinization, 138
San Diego
    Association of Governments, 130
    mass transportation system, 121
    toll lanes, 130–132
Save the People, 30
Sawhill, John C., 185
Scarlett, Lynn, 101, 103
Scheinberg, Phyllis F., 129
Schwartzman, Stephan, 178–180
Scrubbers, 8, 59, 68, 74
Segregation, 26
Sellars, Richard, 156–157, 164
Sequoia National Park, 164
Shaman Pharmaceuticals, 179
Shay, Russ, 39, 45, 51, 54–55
Sherman, William Tecumseh, 126
Shintech Inc., 21–22, 26, 29, 33, 34–35
Shollenberger, Amy, 62, 72
Shuster, Bud, 118, 124, 126, 128–129
Sierra Blanca, Texas, 30, 35
Sierra Club, 28, 119, 120, 125, 141
SiJohn, Henry, 24–25
Silent Spring (Carson), 80, 87, 88–90, 107,
    109
Simon, Julian, 143, 149
Simpson, David, 177, 181, 187, 190
Skerker, Susan, 125
Skinner, Tom, 73
Skumatz, Lisa A., 106
Skumatz Economic Research Association,
    106
Slash-and-burn farming, 174, 189
Slater, Rodney, 132

Small Planet Foods, 85
Smart growth programs, 1, 2, 16, 51, 52
SmartWood, 186
Smith, Orin, 186
Smith, Robert C., 71
Smithsonian Institution
    Migratory Bird Center, 182
    Tropical Research Institute, 174
Smog, 59, 68, 74
Smokestack scrubbers, 8, 59, 68, 74
Snowe, Olympia J., 35
Society for the Protection of New
    Hampshire Forests, 54
Soil degradation, 138–139
Soil Remediation Services Inc., 32
Solid Waste and Emergency Response, 115
Solid Waste Association of America, 115
Solid waste management
    incineration, 109
    landfill space, 102–103
    recovery of products, 104
    throwaway statistics, 102
    variable-rate system, 105–106
Sorantino, Douglas, 59
Southgate, Douglas, 177, 179, 189
Southwest Network for Environmental and
    Economic Justice, 32
Species extinction, 12, 148, 173, 176, 184
Spencer, Bill, 81, 86
Sport and commercial fishing limits, 9, 11,
    12
Sport utility vehicles (SUVs), 9, 59, 67, 70,
    125
Sprawl, 16–17, 45–46, 47, 120–121
Stanton, Robert G., 162, 170
Starbucks, 186
Starr, Jim, 49
State Department, U.S., 141
States
    environmental policy role, 5–7
    land conservation, 40, 52–54
    long-distance air pollution, 62–65
    nitrogen oxide emission reductions, 2,
        63
    recycling requirements, 100, 104, 110
    water quality standards, 11
Steel scrap, 101, 111
Stenholm, Charles W., 95
Stephens, Jack L., Jr., 126, 129
Sterman, Les, 121
Sternfels, Urvan, 60–61
Strategic Petroleum Reserve, 59
Suburban sprawl, 39, 124
Sulfur dioxide emissions, 8, 59, 64, 66, 68
Superfund, 9, 12, 27, 29
Supreme Court, U.S.
    Delaney clause, 87
    environmental racism, 22, 29, 32
Surface Transportation Policy Project, 120,
    132, 133
Sustainable agriculture, 84, 139, 182, 184

Tailpipe emission standards, 68
Target Stores, 161
Tax credits
    child subsidy, 144

conservation easements, 42–45
land conservation, 40
Taxol, 179
Taxpayer Relief Act, 44, 47
Taylor, Jerry, 100–101, 103, 104, 106, 113,
    114
Telecommunications technology, 132
Telecommuting, 132
Terborgh, John, 176
Texaco Inc., 182
Texas, 1–2, 35
Texas Compact, 35
Texas Transportation Institute, 118, 119,
    121, 132, 133
Thailand population program, 146
Thomas, Craig, 168
Thompson, Fred, 17
Thompson, Tommy G., 128
Thoreau Institute, 159
Three Mile Island nuclear accident, 61,
    67
Tierney, John, 99
Timber companies, 14
Tipton, Ron, 167
Tollbooths, 132
Tongass National Forest, 14
Torfs, Marijke, 181
Torricelli, Robert G., 59
Tourism, 155, 164, 178, 180–181
Toxaphene, 30, 88
Toxic waste management, 12–14, 30, 35,
    62, 67, 72–75
Toyota Motor Corp., 72
Traffic computers, 132
Traffic congestion, 117–132
    Albuquerque, 117
    alternate transportation, 127
    Atlanta, 126–130
    background, 122–126
    chronology, 123
    current situation, 126–132
    federal legislation, 124–126
    Hartford, 117
    high-tech solutions, 132
    highway building, 119–120, 131
    increase, 117–118, 121, 124
    mass transit solutions, 121–122, 128
    most-congested urban areas, 118
    SUV emissions, 125
    toll lanes, 130–132
    urban sprawl, 120–121
    Washington, D.C., 117, 119, 131
Transportation
    alternatives, 127
    Atlanta, 119, 123, 126–130
    car culture, 122–124
    environmentally harmful, 11
    traffic congestion, 117–132
    trends, 70–72
Transportation, U.S. Department of (DOT),
    118, 119, 130, 133
Transportation Equity Act for the 21st
    Century (TEA 21), 118, 120, 122, 123,
    127
Tree planting, 74
TreePeople, 74

Tropical Ecosystem Environment
    Observations by Satellites (TREES),
    176
Tropical Forestry Action Plan, 183
Tucurui Dam, 183
Tulane University Environmental Law Clinic,
    21
Tunisia population program, 147

Udall, Stuart, 168
U.N. Environment Program, 67, 68
U.N. Food and Agriculture Organization
    (FAO), 138, 139–140, 145, 175
U.N. Framework Convention on Climate
    Change, 67, 68
U.N. Population Division, 137, 143
U.N. Population Fund, 139
Underground Railroad Network to Freedom
    Act, 158
Union of Concerned Scientists (UCS), 11
United Church of Christ Commission for
    Racial Justice, 23, 27, 29
United Mine Workers of America, 15
Urban congestion, 118
Urban Mass Transportation Assistance Act,
    123, 124
Urban Mobility Corp., 119
Urban sprawl, 16–17, 120–121
U.S. Agency for International Development
    (AID), 139, 174, 185
U.S. Conference of Mayors, 115
U.S. National Intelligence Council, 151
Utility deregulation, 4, 65–66

Van Schaik, Carel, 189
Variable-rate waste management, 105
Volatile organic compounds, 66
Voorhees, Philip H., 160, 161
Vroom, Jay, 82, 83, 91, 95

Wald, Johanna, 163
Wallinga, David, 83, 85
Wallop, Malcolm, 53
Washington, D.C., 117, 119, 131
Washington Monument, 161
Waste Policy Center, 99, 115
Waste production, 150
Waste-to-energy facilities, 107, 109
Water pollution, 1, 10, 71, 148–149
Water quality, 10–12
Water Resources Development Act, 12, 167
Watt, James, 165, 168
Wattenberg, Ben, 144
Welshons, Wade, 85
West Group, 51
Westinghouse Scientific Ecology Group, 35
Wetland protection, 10–11
Wetstone, Greg, 1, 2, 4–5, 16
White, John, 171
Whitman, Christine Todd, 39, 64
Wilderness Act, 165, 166–168
Wildlands Conservancy, 54
Wilkinson, Bill, 118, 127
Williams, John A., 130
Wilson, Edward O., 177, 178, 184, 185,
    188

Index

Wilson, Woodrow, 165
Wine industry, 84
Wirth, Conrad L., 165, 166
Wolf, John, 129
Wolf, Terry, 89
Wood, Megan Epler, 180, 181
Worker Protection Standard (WPS), 90
World Bank, 152, 173, 174, 175, 183, 185
World Food Summit, 143, 151
World Meteorological Organization, 67, 68
World population, 138, 147–148
World Resources Institute, 117, 176, 190

World Wildlife Fund, 79, 173, 175, 178, 188, 190. *See also* Carbarle, Bruce J.
Worldwatch Institute, 6, 13, 137, 141, 151, 190. *See also* Abramovitz, Janet N.
Wright, George, 166
Wyoming State Historic Preservation Office, 164

Xerox Alto Research Center, 132

Yard, Robert Sterling, 166

Yellen, Janet, 4
Yellowstone National Park, 46, 47, 53, 155, 159, 164, 165
Yellowstone Park Act, 165
Yosemite National Park, 155, 164
Young, Don, 50
Yucca Mountain nuclear waste repository, 62, 72

Zahm, Sheila, 80
Zero Population Growth, 152
Zero-emission vehicles, 10